RUSSIA'S REVOLUTION

RUSSIA'S REVOLUTION

Essays 1989–2006

Leon Aron

The AEI Press

Publisher for the American Enterprise Institute

WASHINGTON, D.C.

The characters of nature are legible, it is true; but they are not plain enough to enable those who run to read them. We must make use of a cautious, I had almost said a timorous, method of proceeding. We must not attempt to fly, when we can scarcely pretend to creep. In considering any complex matter, we ought to examine every distinct ingredient in the composition, one by one.

—Edmund Burke, *On Taste*

To a considerable degree, these arguments are flawed by presentism, by a tendency to read history backwards, measuring change over time from the point of arrival rather than the point of departure. . . . But this is the wrong way to measure change. It is like looking through the wrong end of a telescope—everything appears smaller than it really is.

—James McPherson, *Abraham Lincoln and the Second American Revolution*

For Mother and Father

Distributed to the Trade by National Book Network, 15200 NBN Way, Blue Ridge Summit, PA 17214. To order call toll free 1-800-462-6420 or 1-717-794-3800. For all other inquiries please contact the AEI Press, 1150 Seventeenth Street, N.W., Washington, D.C. 20036 or call 1-800-862-5801.

Library of Congress Cataloging-in-Publication Data
Aron, Leon Rabinovich.
  Russia's revolution : essays 1989-2006 / Leon Aron.
    p. cm.
  Includes bibliographical references and index.
  ISBN-13: 978-0-8447-4242-7
  ISBN-10: 0-8447-4242-2
  1. Russia (Federation)—Politics and government—1991- I. Title.

    DK510.763.A76 2007
    947.086--dc22

                                                          2006103252

11 10 09 08 07   1 2 3 4 5

Printed in the United States of America

Contents

Acknowledgments

I am very grateful to Igor Khrestin for his hard work, patience, and perseverance in seeing this book through the many stages on the way to publication. Lisa Ferraro Parmelee has done a superb job editing the manuscript. Her passion for excellence became an inspiration. Sam Thernstrom oversaw all aspects of these notes' evolution from an untidy manuscript to a handsome volume. Karlyn Bowman's advice was very helpful.

Alanna Balaban, Molly McKew, Vance Serchuk, Igor Khrestin, and Jadwiga Rogoża have assisted in researching many of the topics in this collection, Ann Petty ably edited the original drafts, and Milana Vayner helped greatly with the preparation of the chapters for publication.

My boss, the vice president of foreign and defense policy studies, Danielle Pletka, was supportive of this long project. As usual, David Gerson, the American Enterprise Institute's executive vice president, made sure I had all the resources and conveniences a scholar and a writer can dream of. My largest debt, as always, is to AEI's president, Christopher DeMuth, on whose payroll most of the research and thinking that went into this book have been done. Without his constant interest, encouragement, and wise counsel, it hardly would have seen the light of day.

Preface

The still unfolding Russian revolution—an epic experiment in democracy and modern capitalism in a country which has seen little of either in its thousand-year history—is not unlike the movement of a long and disorderly caravan on a vast swampy plain: stopping, stumbling, occasionally all but drowning in muck, yet stubbornly creaking forward. Following closely behind this caravan is a crowd of journalists and experts. Their heads are hung. They look neither back to measure the road already traversed nor to the sides to compare the caravan's progress with that of neighboring nomads, nor yet forward to where the road might lead. Their eyes seem forever to be on the dirt covering the wheels, the ruts in the road, and the ugly swamp creatures feasting on the piles of refuse in the wagons' wake.

Correcting this narrow focus on things of passing significance was very much on my mind as the essays in this book were being written. As a result, the chapters deal only with seminal events and trends in the Soviet Union, and then Russia for the fifteen years from the cleansing firestorm of *glasnost* in 1989 to Vladimir Putin's increasingly risky post-2003 "restoration." Of course, no author could hope to capture every fateful twist and turn of the last great revolution of the twentieth century. Like every historian, I had to choose what seemed to me most important *at the time.*

It might be useful to think of the outcome as a diary kept by a fairly well-informed and analytically inclined spectator at a great historic drama—descriptions of grandiose occurrences and meditations on their meaning. A pointillist portrait, to be sure, but one on a very large canvas and seeking to capture grand themes: demilitarization and de-Bolshevization as the core elements of the revolution; a fierce national debate over capitalism and the extent and nature of the state's control over the economy; the new value system forged in the destruction of Soviet legitimacy and the official mythology; and the post-Soviet middle class as the embodiment of the post-Soviet ethos. With one or two exceptions made for thematical unity, the essays appear in the chronological order of their writing; and, except on technical matters, no attempt has been made to correct the substance of the texts with the benefit of hindsight. I wanted to convey the complexity and enormity of the transition that has changed the lives of millions of ordinary Russians—people who are neither Kremlin bosses and super-rich "oligarchs" nor voiceless victims, but voters who (in turnouts that put Americans to shame) have, by their voices and votes, shaped the course of the country's present and future.

Dr. Johnson's dictum about literary criticism is just as applicable to the writing of political and social history: The result should be neither a "dull collection of theorems nor a rude detection of faults . . . but a gay and vigorous dissertation, where delight is mingled with instruction."[1] With all the usual caveats about reaches and grasps, this is what I wished for these essays to be.

Having had the incredibly good fortune to make a living by watching for almost twenty years the collapse of a huge repressive state and the creation, step by painful step, of a new country, the least I could do to repay my luck was to try to convey the fascination of history on the move, or, in Hugh Trevor-Roper's words, "the sense of wonder, the unpredictability, and therefore the freshness it ought to have."[2] Clio, as another great British historian, G. M. Trevelyan, liked to point out, is a muse.

Therefore this volume is intended to "show" as well as "tell," to give the reader taste and texture along with analysis. Thus, the vagaries of privatization are traced, among other instances, in the battle over Russia's land and in the saga of the Russian middle class (which, despite having been buried by experts and journalists many times since 1998, is very much alive) and the "testimonials" of some of its members. The new business ethic, pride in one's work, and passion for excellence are recorded in a chapter on the recovery of Russia's glorious gastronomic tradition. The signs of a post-Soviet ethos are traced in some of the finest works of fiction and in the new "positive hero."

"History of events, is ephemeral and for the scholars," Trevelyan wrote, "the poetry of events is eternal, and for the multitude."[3] This book is an attempt to impart the "poetry" of the latest Russian revolution while recording its events.

Part I

The Storm

1

What *Glasnost* Has Destroyed
1989

Moscow newspapers and magazines in 1989 must have been the world's most fas-
cinating, even thrilling, read. There was almost a physical sense of relief as the
deadly weight of propaganda lies was removed, and an entire people was unbent
and began to walk upright. Once started, the daily drilling into and the chipping
and chiseling of the layers of official lies could not be stopped until the iconoclasts
of glasnost reached the foundation: the legitimizing mythology of the Soviet regime,
its ideological heart.

Soviet society is in a state of spiritual turmoil for which there is no precedent
in its entire history. A comparison with the Khrushchev years is valid but
insufficient: The passion, the bluntness, the consistency, and, most importantly, the depth and the scope of the upheaval under Mikhail Gorbachev go
far beyond anything that happened between 1956 and 1964. The diagnoses
being made today no longer center on "individual distortions" and "shortcomings" (no matter how repugnant) but are directed instead at virtually the
entire moral universe in which Soviet society functions and from which it
derives its legitimacy. Indeed, this assault far exceeds anything said or even
thought by those who for decades have been branded by Soviet propaganda
as "mad anti-Communists." It is a mood strikingly similar to the one that
swept the Russian intelligentsia at the turn of the twentieth century: bitter
disillusion, anger, radical nihilism, and dense fire aimed at the twin pillars of
the *ancien régime*—orthodoxy and absolutism—and it could well have a
revolutionary outcome of its own.

What is "Soviet humanism"? asks one of the most popular Soviet film
directors, Eldar Ryazanov, and he answers: "Soviet humanism" inspired

Pavlik Morozov to inform on his father; "Soviet humanism" sent Soviet prisoners of war from Nazi camps directly to the gulag; "Soviet humanism" locked artists in lunatic asylums or threw them out of the country for "dissidence."[1]

The historian Yuri Afanasiev goes still further. In the pages of the Communist Party paper *Pravda* itself, he declares: "I do not consider our society socialist, even 'deformed' socialist, [because] these 'deformations' touch upon the very foundations, the political system, the system of the relations of production, and most certainly everything else."[†] His vision of Soviet history is of "millions of *zeks*" (political prisoners); "enslaved, robbed, hapless peasants"; the long-suffering Soviet people who undertook a "great revolution" only to be "deceived" and "humiliated," only to be drowned in "sixty years of nihilism, spiritual void, and decay," only to get a "socialism without freedom and without bread and butter."[2]

✑

Yet it is not just the utterly unprecedented scope of these no-holds-barred philippics that sets the current muckraking apart from any similar campaign in the past. Its most original and most dangerous feature is the precision with which the heavy artillery is targeted, and the depth of shell penetration. In Gorbachev's Soviet Union, almost every major legitimizing myth is being shattered.

Take, to begin with, the myth of "social protection" (*sotzialnaya zashshennost*). According to this idea, the Soviet state, while occasionally inferior to the capitalist West in the quantity and quality of consumer goods, shields its citizens from the ills of capitalism: hunger, poverty, disease, unemployment, crime, prostitution, and, following the latest Western trends, drugs and homelessness.

The debunking of this myth began early in the *glasnost* era with the simple acknowledgment that all these evils plague Soviet society as well. Then the formerly classified data started to pour forth—even as Soviet spokesmen, including Gorbachev himself, continued to tout "social

---

† All translations from Russian here and throughout the book are by the author.

protection" in front of Western audiences. (He did so with passion, for example, in his interview with NBC before the 1987 Washington summit and repeatedly during the summit.)

Of these formerly "capitalist" evils, the newly disclosed scale and depth of Soviet poverty, food shortages, inadequate medical care, and the housing crisis have been especially shocking. With the official poverty level set at seventy-five rubles per person per month ($1,413 a year by the official rate of exchange and $90 by the market rate), the Soviet people have been told that forty-three million of their compatriots are under the poverty level of seventy-five rubles a month, and that fully 40 percent of them (about one hundred million people) live on less than one hundred rubles a month.[3] Pensioners are especially hard-pressed; every third urban senior citizen and eight out of ten villagers—over fifteen million people altogether—receive less than sixty rubles a month.[4] (In case the Soviet reader needed help in understanding what living on sixty rubles a month means, the central government newspaper *Izvestiya* published a letter from an unusually affluent pensioner who complained that she and her husband were unable to spend less than one hundred fifty rubles a month on food: There was little in the state stores, and they had to buy almost all their staples at farmers' markets.)[5] The handicapped are worse off still; an invalid woman with a child was reported to be living on thirty-one rubles and forty-eight kopecks a month.[6] Contrary to the widespread belief that "in the Soviet Union no one goes hungry," the consumption of meat and dairy products by the Soviet poor has declined by between 30 and 35 percent since 1970.[7]

But hunger in the Soviet Union does not result from poverty alone. Another, peculiarly Soviet, cause of it is rationing, a detailed description of which has also been supplied. In the Kirov region of the Russian Northwest, the ration cards allot five hundred grams (slightly over a pound) of cooked sausage per person per month and four hundred grams (less than a pound) of butter.[8]

Perhaps the greatest damage to the myth of "social protection" has been done by the gradually revealed enormity of the health care disaster. A total of 1,200,000 beds are in hospitals with no hot water; every sixth bed is in a hospital with no running water at all; 30 percent of Soviet hospitals do not have indoor toilets.[9] According to Soviet experts, the USSR spends on medical care five times less than the United States—22 billion rubles as compared with $174.8 billion.[10] (Undoubtedly, the perspicacious Soviet reader was quick to make a calculation based on the real market—ten rubles for a dollar—and not the ridiculous official rate—one ruble for a dollar and fifty-seven cents—and found that the Soviet Union spends nineteen times less on public health care than that great capitalist demon, the United States.)[11]

The health care broadside ricocheted into another constituent myth of the "social protection" cluster—the "golden childhood" of Soviet children.[12] The very same children whom millions of posters all over the Soviet Union proudly declare to be "our future" turn out to be attending schools half of which have no central heating, running water, or sewage systems.[13] Children as young as ten work twelve-hour days harvesting potatoes and cotton on collective farms.[14] In 1986 there were thirty-five thousand labor accidents among working children under fourteen; "hundreds" of school-children die in such accidents every year, and "thousands" are crippled.[15]

Not waiting for the Soviet public to recuperate from the disclosure of the infant mortality rates—five times higher than Japan's, two and a half times higher than in the United States, fiftieth place in the world after Barbados, Mauritius, and the United Arab Emirates[16]—the muckrakers provided supporting details: "poverty" in funding for obstetrics; a total absence of ultrasound diagnostic equipment ("Not a single Soviet-made machine in thirty years," wrote the leading Soviet authority on obstetrics and pediatrics, "in the entire era of space exploration!"[17]); or unavailability of single-use paper gowns.

The last nail in the coffin of the myth of "golden childhood" was a short poem called "In the Maternity Ward," by the leading Soviet poet, Andrei Voznesensky. Grim even by the decidedly cheerless standards of mythocide, it is about a rat attacking an infant:

> We ourselves are rats, blubbering
> About things lofty,
> . . . We save people on drifting icebergs
> Send projects to Mars
> A rat in a maternity ward
> Ate through a baby's cheek.[18]

Prostitution and organized crime—which together with unemployment have for seventy years been identified with capitalism in the official mythology—succumbed to the revisionist onslaught. Fifteen-year-old prostitutes in apartment-bordellos, extortion, hired guns (it costs from thirty thousand to one hundred thousand rubles in today's Soviet Union to have somebody killed[19]), street battles between rival gangs—a *Pravda* article went so far as to call organized crime "a state within a state."[20] Lacking, after decades of enforced silence, a vocabulary in Russian to describe the newly acknowledged vices, Soviet reporters have adapted words from the American scene like *kidnapping* and *raket*, and such concepts as money-laundering (*otmyvanie deneg*) and godfather (*krestniy otetz*).

₰

Nothing binds the rulers and the ruled, Communists and non-Communists alike, so tightly as the tragic, heroic myths of World War II, the Great Patriotic War. For over forty years, the official catechism has been simple and dependable: The Soviet Union, confronted with the prospect of an imminent Nazi invasion and betrayed by the West, which was conniving to deflect Hitler eastward, artfully bought time in 1939 by concluding a nonaggression pact with Germany. The Soviet scheme worked: The Nazi onslaught was postponed by two years, during which time the Soviet state strengthened its defenses, trained the army, and stockpiled materiel. Then, after initial setbacks caused by the surprise timing of the German invasion, the Soviet army vanquished the Nazi barbarians and liberated the world from the "brown plague." What is more, the Soviet Union did it all alone, essentially with no assistance from its allies; it succeeded because of the military genius of its marshals and the skill of its rank-and-file soldiers. (As Yevgeni Yevtushenko declared in his famous poem, "Do the Russians Want War?": "Yes, we know how to fight!") Every element of this myth is under attack today in mainstream Soviet periodicals. The nonaggression pact has been labeled "one of the most tragic and shameful pages in our history"[21]— no clever maneuver but, as far as the Soviet Union was concerned, a genuine and inexcusable treaty of friendship. A military historian reveals how, in the spirit of this friendship, the Soviets turned over German Communist refugees to the Gestapo. And, for the first time in almost fifty years, the Soviet people have been reminded of the statement made by Stalin's foreign minister, Vyacheslav Molotov, a week after the signing of the pact: "It is not only senseless but even criminal to wage a war to 'destroy Hitlerism' under the false banner of a struggle for 'democracy.'"[22]

While the very existence of secret protocols contained in the nonaggression pact was officially denied by the Soviet Union until this past August [1989], for over a year the mythslayers had been pointing to actions taken in the wake of the pact which confirmed Western accounts of those protocols, most notably the division of Poland between the Soviet and Nazi occupation forces. As for the adroitness of the "maneuver" itself, it is now said to have allowed Germany to concentrate all its forces in the West, to defeat France, and then to throw against the Soviet Union not only its entire military might but also the newly acquired resources of a conquered Europe.[23] Furthermore, the Soviet press has now disclosed that Soviet deliveries of "military-strategic" materials to Germany in accordance with the terms of the nonaggression pact played "a not insignificant role" in strengthening the Nazi military-industrial potential.[24]

Soviet military strategy in World War II is undergoing a thorough critique as well. As if in answer to Yevtushenko, another popular Soviet writer, Viktor Astafiev, who, unlike Yevtushenko, is a World War II veteran, has said: "We did not know how to fight. We ended the war not knowing how to fight. We drowned the enemy in our blood, we buried him under our corpses."[25] Finally, in perhaps the single most dramatic achievement of *glasnost* to date, the publication of Vasily Grossman's great novel, *Life and Fate*, has struck at the very foundations of the war mythology by explicitly, and repeatedly, bringing up the parallels between the two savage tyrannies, Hitler's and Stalin's, and by depicting the heroic, betrayed, and martyred Soviet people ground between these two giant, bloodstained millstones. Said a shell-shocked participant in a readers' discussion of Grossman's book:

> We used to portray the war [as] "there are Nazis and here are we. Darkness is there, goodness is here." Grossman changed the proportion, portraying the two systems not only in their collision but also in their eerie historical similarity.[26]

But more than anything else, *glasnost* is set apart from all previous Soviet "thaws" by the willingness, and the ability, of the new bomb-throwers to tackle the cluster of myths surrounding the Founding Fathers of the Soviet Union. Within two years, the wave of iconoclasm reached and passed the highest points of Khrushchev's de-Stalinization, to engulf even the previously sacrosanct Lenin himself.

Unlike their counterparts in Khrushchev's time, the issue for the current generation of myth-hunters, brought up on *samizdat* (that is, clandestinely typed and disseminated) copies of Solzhenitsyn's *The Gulag Archipelago*, is not the "rehabilitation" of the Bolshevik leaders killed by Stalin—Kamenev, Zinoviev, Radek, Bukharin. While welcoming such "rehabilitation," the crusading Soviet scholars and journalists of today are in no hurry to make these old Bolsheviks into new icons. They are asking, instead, "How was Stalinism born, on what soil, and why?" And they are finding complicity in Stalinism on the part of the Founding Fathers, including those who opposed Stalin on this or that point. Thus, Soviet readers are already being reminded that Nikolai Bukharin, perhaps the most celebrated "oppositionist," was not just, in Lenin's famous characterization, the "darling of the party." In the 1920s, Bukharin was also one of the most influential members of the dreaded Collegium of the OGPU (the KGB's predecessor); he called executions by firing squads "a method of making Communist humankind out of human material of the capitalist epoch"; and he demanded that the *kulaks* (the well-to-do peasants) be talked to in the "language of lead"—a demand that Stalin later fulfilled by murdering millions of them.[27]

In general, as one of the most daring of the myth-slayers has written:

> It is precisely the old guard that created the political mechanism, the tool for absolute power which Stalin subsequently used for his egotistical purposes. . . . In the final account, it was precisely the old guard . . . that voluntarily and by itself surrendered into Stalin's hands the infinite power created by the revolution. Later, after 1924, it was precisely the old guard with its leftist impatience that urged the country to take leaps which turned into national tragedy.[28]

Like Khrushchev before him, Gorbachev has discovered his own Lenin—this time, a "late," post–civil-war and post-Kronstadt Lenin, a "democratic" Lenin, a Lenin of the New Economic Policy (NEP), the foe of the bloated state bureaucracy, the defender of the private entrepreneur and peasant. But unlike Khrushchev, Gorbachev is unable (unwilling?) to prevent public exploration of alternative images of the erstwhile idol. The water is swirling perilously close to Lenin's pedestal and is rising higher and higher every day.

Significantly, neither Gorbachev nor Aleksandr Yakovlev, the Politburo member closest to Gorbachev, has been publicly committed to Lenin's defense—most likely because neither wants to fight a losing battle. Instead they have let Vadim Medvedev, the Politburo member in charge of ideology, to hold the fort. Yet the myth-hunters, seeing Medvedev for what he is—a hack with no real power—have proceeded to ignore his injunction against breaking the Lenin taboo.

The attack on the shrine commenced with Vasiliy Selunin's master-piece "*Istoki*" ("The Sources"), an essay portraying Lenin as the creator of concentration camps, a doctrinaire fanatic whose "education" before 1921 cost millions of lives and untold suffering, and brought the country to the verge of an economic abyss.[29] Four months after the publication of this work, Medvedev reacted by condemning attempts to "trace to Lenin the beginning of the command-and-administer system."[30] But the icono-clasts, having crossed the threshold of the temple, had begun moving inexorably toward the sanctum sanctorum—the October Revolution and Leninist morality.

Replacing the glorious "Great October Socialist Revolution" is now a gang of conspirators, "taken seriously by very few people," who "did not know how to solve the complicated problems of society but offered instead a set of very simple, primitive, understandable quasi-solutions."[31]

The myth of the October Revolution was dealt another blow by the reprinting, for the first time since 1918, of Maxim Gorky's *Untimely Thoughts*, a classic denunciation of the horrors the revolution had already then visited upon Russia. Although the passages directly attacking Lenin were censored out, the picture that emerges is one of "thousands, yes, thousands of people—workers and peasants—starving in prisons" and of "violence which is unworthy of democracy."[32]

As the veil of lies is lifted from the crushing of the nascent Russian democratic state by the Bolsheviks, the Constituent Assembly of 1918 is beginning to receive sympathetic coverage as Russia's last hope for a parliamentary democracy. With increasing frequency, the dissolution of the assembly after one session on January 18, 1918, is cited today as a precedent for a crackdown that could end the current "thaw" as well.

But what is potentially most damaging to the mythology of the Founding Fathers is the attack on the old moral justification of the Bolshevik terror. This justification was supplied by Lenin himself in a passage that generations of Soviet schoolchildren have had to memorize: "Our morality is completely subordinate to the interests of the class struggle of the proletariat. . . . In the foundation of Communist morality lies the struggle for the strengthening and completion of Communism."[33]

An oblique yet unambiguous repudiation of this doctrine was published recently by the party's main theoretical journal, *Kommunist*, which compared Lenin's "class morality" to the murderous "Catechism of the Revolutionary" of the nineteenth-century Russian terrorist Nechaev ("Everything is moral that expedites the triumph of the revolution"). Going even further, *Kommunist* also declared: "Once everything is evaluated from the point of view of some class, then there is no moral trial and no personal ethical responsibility."[34]

To be sure, there are still limits. When, this past April, in a now-famous TV interview, the theater director Mark Zakharov suggested that Lenin's embalmed body be removed from the mausoleum in Red Square and buried, the director of the State Committee for Television and Radio was fired and the late-night program which aired the interview was "temporarily" taken off the air for "renovation of the sets." Yet despite this rearguard action, the debunking of the Lenin myth will soon reach a double crescendo. First has come the publication in the monthly literary journal *Oktyabr'* of Vasily Grossman's *Forever Flowing*, a loosely jointed narrative from which Lenin emerges both as a theoretician of totalitarianism and as its first practitioner. Lenin is now the "murderer of Russian liberty"; it was he who had laid the foundation of the "state without liberty," which Stalin built.[35] Then there is *Novy Myr's* serialization of Solzhenitsyn's *The Gulag Archipelago*, the first chapter of whose second volume lays the creation of concentration camps squarely at Lenin's door.

The vengeful filling-in of the "blank spaces" in Soviet history, combined with the loss of moral justification for what is now revealed to have happened, has produced a predictable result: people now question the legitimacy not just of parts of the Soviet record but of the Soviet regime itself. Incredibly, the rector of the Moscow State Institute of History and Archives now feels safe in stating that the Soviet regime "was brought into being through bloodshed, with the aid of mass murder and crimes against humanity" and that "one must admit Soviet history as a whole is not fit to serve as a legal basis for Soviet power."[36] The fall of the Founding Fathers may mark the final destination of the Soviet crusaders, beyond which lies a gaping void. Of course, the destroyers themselves are trying to fill the void with new icons, including genuinely religious ones. Thus, in a meeting with Lithuanian intellectuals last August, Aleksandr Yakovlev, the godfather of *glasnost*, several times invoked the term "repentance," while Maya Ganina, a columnist for *Literaturnaya Gazeta*, has called for "kindness and charity for Christ's sake," and the playwright Edvard Rodzinskiy has bemoaned the loss of the Bible, "the greatest book in the world," as a weapon to combat "the deficit of morality and culture."[37] Among political models, the czarist prime minister Petr Stolypin (1862–1911) is currently much in vogue for his attempt to free the Russian peasant from the shackles of the commune and make him into a private farmer; the cult of Stolypin is likely to be given a powerful boost when Solzhenitsyn's *August 1914*, of which he is a hero, is published in the Soviet Union. And following Stolypin, it is safe to predict, will be Alexander II, the czar (1855–81) who abolished serfdom and introduced political reforms that set Russia on the road to capitalism and constitutional monarchy.

As for the orthodox, they are fighting desperate rearguard battles to salvage whatever is left of the legitimizing mythology. Their spokesman, the Politburo member Yegor Ligachev, declares that "the facts of unjustified [sic] repressions" must not "overshadow the feat of the people who created the powerful socialist state." After all, Ligachev points out, in the 1930s the country became second in the world in overall industrial output, while in the much-maligned 1970s "national income" increased four times and "military-strategic parity" was achieved with the United States.[38]

Yet all such attempts to restock the Soviet pantheon with old gods are likely to fail: Once declared naked, idols are even less usable than kings. Of all the much-commented-upon contradictions embedded in Gorbachev's reforms, this is without doubt the deadliest: Having set out to create a reformed one-party state socialism "with a human face," Gorbachev has unleashed forces that are methodically destroying the legitimacy of any such future arrangement. No economic reform, no amount of Western good will, even if concretized with massive transfusions of capital and technology, and no brilliant foreign policy stratagems can hope to fill this spiritual vacuum.

And so the question is: What rough beast, its hour come round at last, slouches toward Moscow to be born?

2

Moscow Diary
January 12–17, 1991

And blessed is he who visited this world
In time to see its fate decided,
Whom, like an equal, gods invited
To their feast before it's cold.

—Fyodor Tyutchev, Цицерон (Cicero)

Apart from the attempted coup of August 19–21, 1991, the closest the Russian rev-
olution came to being stifled and reversed was winter 1991. Moscow was full of
fear and anger, but also of defiance and hope. In the end, the revolution survived—
saved by Boris Yeltsin's courage, Mikhail Gorbachev's aversion to Stalinist repres-
sion, the intelligentsia's wholehearted and vocal opposition to reaction, but most of
all by the Russian people's unwillingness to pay with liberty for the preservation of
the Soviet empire.

January 12

Met at the Sheremetievo airport by our hosts from the Committee on the
Economy of the Supreme Soviet of Russia and told that the timing of our
seminar was auspicious for two reasons. First, it was scheduled to begin on
the first day of the old Russian New Year, January 14. A new year—and a
new era in Russian history, an era of private property and entrepreneurship!
In the second place, Russia and Estonia just signed a treaty recognizing each
other's sovereignty and pledging political and economic cooperation.

We leave for a *dom otdykha*, a rest home, outside Moscow, where the
seminar on privatization will be held. It is eight o'clock on a Saturday night.

A dimly lit highway with but one of the three lanes cleared of snow; only the rare car; dilapidated wooden huts on both sides of the road. The capital of the world's other "superpower."

January 13

At breakfast one member of our delegation who had a shortwave radio told us that the BBC reported an assault by OMON (special anti-riot police) troops on the television station in Vilnius. At least a dozen Lithuanians had been killed. The Soviet TV and radio mentioned the "tragic events" in Vilnius but gave no details. It was Sunday, and our hosts from the Russian parliament were not with us. No one to ask.

A "cultural program" prepared by our hosts called for a matinee at the Bolshoi. Like the telephone numbers and addresses of Moscow friends, the Bolshoi never changes. Stately decay on the outside; its four inner circles still glow with the gold and the red of the plush chairs.

The theater was full of precocious Moscow children, boys in bow ties and girls with huge white ribbons in meticulously braided hair. Chaperoned by their stern but supremely indulgent grandmothers, they were solemn and serious, and ready for one of the most sacred of Moscow rituals: a show at the Bolshoi.

It was a lovely little ballet dressed in festive colors, overflowing with elegance and humor. Western devices of escapism—sports and movies—are powerless against Russian winter and Russian politics. The Russians need the Bolshoi to divert. We did.

January 14

As we prepared to leave the building of the Russian Supreme Soviet (the Russian democrats lovingly, if wishfully, call it the "White House"), we were told by our hosts that Boris Yeltsin, fresh off the plane, was having an emergency press conference at three. Do we wish to attend? *Wish to attend?!* I had been thinking, writing, and speaking about the man for almost two years, yet whenever I was in Moscow, he was out. (Last time, in October, he was recuperating from a car accident in the Desna, the same *dom otdykha* where we are staying now.)

With Gorbachev's turn to the hard-line "right," Yeltsin's importance is bound to increase; he is the only political figure in the Soviet Union around whom a resistance to the reaction can crystallize. If Yeltsin were not around, Gorbachev could have opted for a creeping recentralization, a gentler but ultimately deadly salami technique of repression—cutting up *glasnost* and democratic structures slice by slice, arresting someone here, closing down a paper there. Yeltsin—big, brave, stubborn, unwieldy, and enormously popular—dramatically narrows Gorbachev's options: The president–general secretary and those behind him must further undertake an all-out bloody pacification campaign—or retreat and resign. Only one man is standing between Russian democracy and an all-union Tiananmen: Yeltsin. (A few days later in Frankfurt I saw a headline in *Le Figaro*: "Le seul espoir: Boris Eltsin" . . .)[1]

Arresting Yeltsin would not do; within hours millions would be in the streets. The only way to remove him is by murder. Yeltsin's aides understand that and apparently have persuaded their notoriously reckless boss to stop speaking in public and to move around in sudden and unpredictable ways.

It turned out that Yeltsin had just returned from Tallinn (via Leningrad) where he flew early on Sunday, a few hours after the news of the massacre at the television center reached Moscow. He spent all day in the Estonian capital, and drove at night to Leningrad.

Minutes before Yeltsin appeared in the Hall of Nationalities for the press conference, an aide handed out his appeal to the Russian soldiers in Lithuania:

> Soldiers, sergeants, and officers—our compatriots, who were drafted on the territory of the Russian Federation and who are currently in the Baltic republics! Today, when the country is in economic and political crisis, and when the healthy forces of our society seek ways out of the complicated situation using legal, constitutional forms [of action], you may be given orders to move against the legally created state organs, against the peaceful civilian population who are defending their democratic achievements.
>
> You may be told that your help is needed to restore order in the society. But can violation of constitution and laws be

considered restoration of order? And yet it is precisely in this direction that you are being pushed by those who seek to solve political problems by the force of armed detachments.

Before you storm nonmilitary installations on Baltic land, remember your own hearth, the present and future of your own Republic, your own people. Violence against legality, against the peoples of the Baltics, will engender new crises in Russia herself and in the position of Russians living in other Republics, including those in the Baltics.

The aims of the reaction [are]:

• to undermine the process of democratization in the country and the transition to the forms of economy that would guarantee well-being of all the people, and not just of the privileged groups of the ruling class—the *nomenklatura*;

• to annul the declarations of sovereignty, for which the peoples of the Republics fought and suffered, and thus wreck the establishment of a new union of sovereign states.

Could you possibly agree to the role they assigned you?

I would like to draw your attention to the fact that those drafted in the Russian Federation may not be used for assignments not specified by Article 29 of the Russian Federation's Constitution. Such assignments violate the December 11, 1990, decree by the Extraordinary Congress of the RSFSR [Russian Soviet Federated Socialist Republic] and are, therefore, illegal.

. . . We categorically reject the view of the army as a reactionary, antipopular force. Because we know that the army is first and foremost citizens of our nation, its children, who care about its fate no less than all of us. And we are sure that the healthy forces in the army will not let it start on the antinational road of support for the reaction.

We believe in you, the officers and soldiers of Russia, for whom, as for the previous generations of Russia's warriors, the highest moral values live: honor, valor, courage, allegiance to the people and the Fatherland.

Let us remember the historic experience which postulates: A wrong step today will tell not only on those who make it, but on the generations to follow.

I wish you success in your service, happiness to your families.

Boris Yeltsin, January 13, 1991

How I wish that some of my colleagues—Sovietologists and their media sources and allies, all those responsible for presenting Yeltsin to the American public as a drunken buffoon, a Siberian "rogue populist," and a "maverick"—were here with me today! Although visibly tired and hoarse, his face creased by deep lines, Yeltsin moved and spoke with the confidence and authority of a big and strong leader. As he began answering questions—straightaway, without any introduction—the words were carefully measured and weighty with thought and feeling.

Yeltsin commanded the audience's undivided attention, even its adoration. This was true not only of the deputies but also of the Soviet journalists—who can easily teach their Western colleagues lessons in cynicism. The lines of festive tension and excitement extended from the audience to the podium, enveloped Yeltsin and, reinforced tenfold, returned back to the hall, closing the circuit. His rare smile lit up faces all around him, his jokes invariably caused laughter. He was not addressed by his last name or title but by his first name and patronymic, "Boris Nikolayevich," a Russian way to show respect and affection. (By contrast, the Soviet journalists around me invariably referred to Gorbachev as Gorbatiy, the Hunchback.)

Here are major excerpts, tape recorded by me, in my own translation:

Yeltsin: I spoke to [Lithuanian president] Landsbergis a few times the night before last [the night of the Vilnius massacre]. We agreed to meet so that the Russian republic could express its attitude to the events in Vilnius, support the sovereignty of the republics, and not allow an escalation of the assault on democracy.

. . . Perhaps I should read you the statement?[2] It is short, only two pages. [Reads]

The recent actions of the Soviet leadership with regard to the Baltic states have created a real danger to their sovereignty, have resulted in the escalation of violence and in deaths. Expressing the clear wish of the peoples to preserve and strengthen their sovereignty, declared by the highest legislative bodies; understanding the magnitude of the danger of the violation of human rights of all citizens of the Baltics, regardless of nationality; proceeding from the conviction that further development of our states is possible only on the road of radical reforms founded on liberty and democracy, Latvia, Estonia, Lithuania, and Russia declare:

First: The signatories recognize each other's sovereignty;

Second: All power over the territories of the signatories belongs solely to the legally elected bodies;

Third: The signatories consider it inadmissible to employ armed force to resolve internal problems, except at the official request of the legally elected executive bodies;

Fourth: The signatories consider illegal participation of their citizens in actions that damage the signatories' sovereignty;

Fifth: The signatories pledge to aid each other whenever a threat to their sovereignty arises;

Sixth: The signatories consider unlawful and resolutely condemn attempts to provoke national animosity for the achievement of political aims;

Seventh: Latvia, Lithuania, Estonia, and Russia confirm their determination to continue to develop relations between them based on the principles of *international* [Yeltsin stressed the word] law and negotiated agreements;

Eighth: The signatories call upon both the states that are part of the Soviet Union and those outside of it to condemn resolutely the acts of armed violence against the independence of the Baltic states and their peaceful population—the acts which threaten stability and democracy in the USSR and the entire international community.

This statement is being made available to international organizations, parliaments, governments, states of the world. [Signed] Gorbunovs, Ruutel, Landsbergis, Yeltsin. [Applause]

Question: What is your attitude toward calls for protest strikes?

Yeltsin: I have the impression that [what happened in Vilnius] is the beginning of a vigorous assault on democracy. The Baltic republics are only the first of many victims. Therefore, the appeals to the working collectives to express their attitude toward these events seem logical to me and I support them. [Applause]

Question: I know from competent sources that a Committee for the Salvation of Russia has been created. On the 16th of January they plan to repeat what happened on January 13 in Vilnius. What steps are you ready to undertake to protect the sovereignty of Russia and the Russian parliament?

Yeltsin: First, to be vigilant. Second, to begin implementing the resolution of the Extraordinary Congress of People's Deputies of Russia to subordinate to the Russian parliament the organs of state security, located on the territory of Russia, and to create a Russian Committee on State Security. This should be done immediately. Finally, we are more and more convinced that it is impossible to protect Russia's sovereignty without a Russian army. [Long applause]

Question: Do you consider President Gorbachev personally responsible for the events in Vilnius?

Yeltsin: [after a pause] As diplomats say, thank you for a good question. [Laughter] Our position is well known. We are for moving the [political and economic] center of gravity to the republics, including the Russian Federation. We need a center [of the union] with very limited functions, specified by the first Congress of People's Deputies of Russia. [The union government was to have] only six ministries, and we have already decided to take over the KGB, aviation, and communications. Thus only three ministries are left [for the center].[3]

. . . The Soviet Council of Ministers has already stopped functioning—and a new structure has not yet appeared. If the president rules, I don't know through whom or what. When I asked the president, why are you so sharply moving to the right [that is, toward the reactionary "hard line"], the answer was: because the society is moving to the right. Where did you find this information? You, then, simply do not know what is happening in the society. By no means is the society slipping to the right. To the contrary, the society is consolidating and is moving toward democracy. At the same time, I know that the president is subject to very serious pressure from the right.

Question: In the last two or three months, the conservative press has been suggesting that you are betraying the Russian-speaking population of the republics. I would like you to advance a few arguments in your defense.

Yeltsin: I do not feel I need to defend myself. We are witnessing the struggle for the survival of democracy, and that struggle concerns the Russian-speaking population everywhere, including the Russian Federation itself. A few days ago we signed an agreement with Estonia, and last night an agreement was signed with Latvia. . . . By concluding such agreements we acquire at least some legal basis to influence the events there and react to whatever illegal decisions may be taken by the governments with respect to the Russian-speaking population. Without such agreements we completely lack any channels of influence. Now we have at our disposal plenty of legal, political, and diplomatic means immediately to engage in negotiations. Moreover, in our agreements there are special clauses pertaining to the social defense of the Russian-speaking population of the Russian republics—and, of course, of the Latvians and Estonians in our Russia.

Question: Deciding to act in Vilnius, what objectives, in your view, did the leadership [of the Soviet Union] try to achieve?

Yeltsin: I myself have been racking my brain over this question . . . It seems to me that the leadership of the country, under the influence of certain forces, has decided that it would be difficult to solve our problems democratically, that the time has come to turn decisively to the "iron hand."

Question: Does it seem to you that the events in the Baltics have changed attitudes toward a new union treaty? Secondly, for the second day the [official] mass media have distorted or have been silent about what happened in Vilnius. What can be done in that regard by the leadership of the Russian republic?

Yeltsin: It seems to me that these actions [of the Gorbachev leadership] have struck a serious blow to the possibility of concluding a union treaty. I doubt that very many would be willing to sign a treaty with a noose around their necks. Moreover, the center is trying to push this treaty on us from above, as adopted by the Central Committee's Plenum and by the Congress of People's Deputies: Here is your treaty, go ahead and sign it! Wait a minute. Who is concluding a treaty with whom here? Should not those who are asked to sign also be the ones to work on the text of the treaty, discuss it—and only then sign? Thus the process is proceeding not from the bottom up, as we proposed, but from the top down. . . . As a result of this acting from above by force, today already five republics are practically torn away from a union treaty.[4] And we, in the Russian republic, too, will think hard whether we need a union in which, at every moment, somebody from above will be dictating to us what to do. The events in Lithuania have crossed out even those modest first steps that had been made on the road to a new treaty of the union.

With regard to the mass media: I have spoken at a meeting of the Federation Council . . . about the totally one-sided information [about the Baltic events]. Again, we are witnessing deception of our people. And those independent newspapers and television programs [that are trying to give truthful coverage] are being closed down.

Question: What do you think of the world reaction [to the Vilnius events]?

Yeltsin: . . . I told the president: We are going to be shamed in front of the entire world because this is nothing but the end of democracy. You traveled around the world and asked for help in this difficult period. It is obvious that those countries [that pledged assistance] are going to refuse us the aid. It is simply impossible not to have foreseen this. But if such elementary things are not foreseen, then one gets depressed at the kind of leadership that we have!

Question: The presidents of practically all the republics have assured their electorates that force would not be used in the Baltics. What is their position now in view of what has happened?

Yeltsin: We, the presidents of Kazakhstan, Belorussia, Ukraine, and Russia, have decided to conclude a quadripartite treaty. These republics represent almost 85 percent of Soviet GNP. We decided to meet rather soon. I think I may now say where: in Minsk. But I will not tell you when. [Laughter] I think this [treaty] will prove a stabilizing faction, stabilizing because these four powerful republics are concluding a real, strong treaty concerning all, I emphasize, all aspects of their relations. And then others can join in. Even Moscow can join in! [Laughter, applause]

Question: Could you expand on your trip to Leningrad [on the way back to Moscow from Tallinn]? We hear rumors about an assassination attempt.

Yeltsin: You know, I seem to be getting into many "accidents," four in the last year alone. So when we got word from Moscow that a certain action was being planned, we changed our route.

Question: Are you trying to remove President Gorbachev? Do you think that he is the main problem and that his removal would improve the situation overnight?

Yeltsin: Of course, Gorbachev is not the only problem we have in our country. There are hundreds of problems that have been accumulating for decades. Add to that the economic crisis, the paralysis of power, and the drop in the standard of living to the point where the people every day now get out in the streets to protest. Gorbachev may not be the sole reason for this, and it would be naïve to think that his dismissal would suddenly change the situation. But you must also consider the people's attitude, the [president's] approval rating.[5] It is so low that some press agencies would not even publish it. And what is power? Power is the strength of administration but also people's trust! And if the two are not combined, no renewal in our country is possible, no forward movement.

In front of me was the text of the appeal of Russia, Latvia, Lithuania, and Estonia to the secretary general of the United Nations. The leaders of the four republics called for an immediate conference on the Baltics and for an extension of the UN deadline for Iraq's withdrawal from Kuwait—the deadline that would expire in less than ten hours.

Hearing that the next question to Yeltsin would be the last, I raised my hand:

LA: Given the enormous political capital that the [George H. W.] Bush administration has invested in Gorbachev, don't you think that your request [to extend the deadline] will be used as an excuse for the administration not to support your appeal?

Yeltsin: I share your concern. Especially because this is an appeal by republics that are not members of the United Nations.[6] So the appeal has very little legal force. Rather, it is a moral act. And we hope that this voice will be heard. The next morning after the Vilnius events, I received, at his request, U.S. Ambassador [Jack] Matlock. I told him that I had the impression that the leaders of the United States did not have a clear idea of what was happening in our country. They did not! They only have one political figure [in mind]. And that figure is surrounded by euphoria. And all other events—the increased sovereignty of the republics, the move of the political center of gravity from the center [Moscow] to the republics—are being ignored. This is a *strategic* [Yeltsin stressed the word] error committed by the U.S. leaders![7]

Yeltsin's blitz trip to the Baltics was a brilliant political move: By placing his enormous prestige and that of the Russian parliament between the submachine guns of the Soviet "black berets" and the Baltic peoples, Yeltsin made it clear to the Soviet Union and the world that he is the key to Russian democracy and peaceful decolonization of the Soviet empire.[8]

The trip to Tallinn, the press conference, and the appeals may not reverse the situation, but they are bound to arrest the reaction's momentum. After Yeltsin has spoken, the mood of the country will change, and others will begin to speak out.

Only one event in Yeltsin's political life was equally fateful—his protest against the slow pace of the reforms at a meeting of the Central Committee on October 21, 1987. That speech launched Yeltsin's political star and eventually resulted in his election to the post of chairman of the Russian Supreme Soviet. Today, his political instincts and sense of timing have proved as unerring.

January 15

The propaganda blast in the wake of the Vilnius crackdown leaves one numb, scared, and feeling caught in a time warp. It is as if somebody dusted off Mikhail Suslov's 1968 propaganda guidelines for justifying the Soviet invasion of Czechoslovakia. Again, unnamed "extremists" threaten peaceful citizens, and Moscow is being forced to intervene.

The evening news program, *Vremya*, solemnly reveals the contents of the "Order 031" of some mysterious agency of the Lithuanian government directing internal troops of Lithuania (do they exist?!) to track down and, if necessary, kill the Communists. Yet, as it was with Czechoslovakia, the very volume and comprehensiveness of the propaganda effort make hash of the official, "spur-of-the-moment" version of Moscow's decision to intervene.

Alexandr Nevzorov's documentary is especially revolting. The anchor of a very popular program, *600 Seconds*, Nevzorov is considered a "liberal" (that is, a democrat). The film shows the heroic pro-Moscow defenders of the police station in Vilnius, as they busily, and very photogenically, prepare themselves for martyrdom at the hands of the savage Lithuanian hordes. The last rites are very impressively done, complete with headbands and the word *nashi*, "ours," painted on the magazines of their AK-47 submachine guns, and farewells—on camera, naturally—to their families. For some mysterious reason the bloodthirsty Lithuanian attackers fail to materialize. Instead, the Soviet tanks rumble upon the scene, saving our heroes.

Today Gorbachev responded to Yeltsin by a speech in the Supreme Soviet. The speech was truly hysterical. (I watched it on the television.) Red in the face, the Soviet president ranted and raved, shook his fist, beat his chest, stomped his feet.

Gorbachev's version of the "Vilnius crisis" was even more inept than that of the mainstream propaganda: People had protested against price increases; a civil war was looming; Moscow was forced to intervene to save the lives of the innocent civilians. (In the meantime, the polls taken immediately after the massacre show that close to 100 percent of Lithuanians and over 75 percent of the Russians in Lithuania support the Landsbergis government.)

January 16

Yeltsin's stance has revitalized, if not resuscitated, the democratic resistance. The flagship of *glasnost Moskovskie Novosti* (*Moscow News*) came out today with black borders of mourning on the front page and the banner headline "*KROVAVOYE VOSKRESENIE*" ("BLOODY SUNDAY"), recalling the January 9, 1905, massacre of the demonstrators in St. Petersburg, which precipitated the first Russian revolution.

The front page carried a statement in which the *crème de la crème* of the Russian intelligentsia deplored Moscow's actions. Entitled, "The Crime of the Regime which Refuses to Leave the Stage," it said, in part,

> On the bloody Sunday of January 13, it was democracy that was being shot at. Now that the final hour of the regime is near, it

has joined a decisive battle: Economic reform is blocked, press and television censorship is resuscitated, and a stream of insolent propaganda demaguery has been unleashed. . . . Everything happening in Lithuania cannot be described other than unequivocally—it is a CRIME. A crime against one's own people, which is being pushed toward civil war. . . .

On Monday, from the podium of the Supreme Soviet of the USSR, the president–general secretary, in essence, justified the tactics of his actions in Lithuania. If we had not heard this speech, we could have demanded the resignation of the minister of the interior [Boris] Pugo, of the chairman of the State Committee on Radio and Television [Leonid] Kravchenko, who is misinforming the country, of [the minister of defense] Marshal [Dmitry] Yazov. We could have insisted on an objective investigation of the crime. . . .

But from whom should we demand all this?

After the bloody Sunday in Vilnius, how much is left of what we have heard so often from our president in the last few years: "humane socialism," "new thinking," "the common European home"? Almost nothing. . . .

The Lithuanian tragedy should not leave us despairing. In the opposition to the onslaught of totalitarianism and dictatorship our hopes are with the leaders of the Republics, their alliance, and joint effort. . . .

We count on a mass protest against the antidemocratic wave which moves on the Baltic states and threatens to engulf the whole country. If we are still capable of compassion and charity, let us declare January 20 a day of mourning for the Vilnius victims and all demonstrate on that day.

I met several authors of this appeal today in the Institute of the Economy of the World Socialist System. Despite its name, the outfit, known as the Bogomolov Institute after its longtime director, academician Oleg Bogomolov, has been in the forefront of "new thinking," and its staff is a collection of the most innovative and honest in the Soviet intellectual establishment. I was there to talk to Dr. Igor Kliamkin, by far the most insightful, original, and objective observer of the Soviet political scene today, who has been a friend at a distance since we met in Washington a year ago.

But before my chat with Igor, I was to attend the protest meeting of the staff. The theme of the Soviet invasion of Czechoslovakia—taking place twenty-two and a half years before—permeated the angry speeches. There was something cathartic about it: Seeking to expiate what they consider the cowardice of their silence in August 1968, the intellectuals were telling Gorbachev what they had been afraid to tell Brezhnev. "Today the honor of each person is defined by his attitude toward the Vilnius events," said the draft resolution of the meeting read by Dr. Bogomolov. "No one today can hide from expressing his attitude toward the aspirations of the Baltic people for liberty."

Expressing what I thought was a common feeling of betrayal, one of the staffers said, "I have crossed out Gorbachev in my heart. Listening to the president I felt not even anger but disgust at the depth of the fall of this man."

Igor Kliamkin rose to speak and, as always, was calm, objective—and effective: "In Vilnius the [Gorbachev] regime has proved its genetically anti-democratic nature. What we have is a democracy that failed, a defeat of the democratic forces. In six years, we have failed to form an all-union democratic front. This is not just the fault of those in this hall but also of those who live in Lithuania. The latter oriented themselves on the West and wanted to have nothing to do with democracy in Russia. The main lesson is that the democracy has lost—lost because of its disunity, lack of organization and, let's face it, slovenliness. And the only positive impact of such resolutions as ours is: to unite somehow, in the aftermath of this lesson."

Charged with inserting the staff's editorial comments into the final resolution of the meeting was Dr. Alexandr Tsipko, who two years ago published the celebrated long article, which traced Stalinism directly to Marxism. After the meeting I told Tsipko about the stir his piece had created in the West and mentioned that Ambassador Jeane Kirkpatrick was among his admirers. The affinity, it turned out, was mutual. After meeting Dr. Kirkpatrick in Washington, Tsipko told me, his opinion of her had changed: "A hawk, we were told, a conservative hardliner! What an intelligent, soft, and thoughtful woman!"

The talk with Kliamkin was, as always, stimulating. I begin to understand why Igor is so inspiring. He embodies an indomitable intellectual curiosity, a delight in peeking into nature's design, in the prefiguring and postfiguring of His mysterious ways. This is a part of a divine spark that cannot be extinguished by stupidity and the brutality of dictators, by cold and hunger, by long lines for every scrap of food and piece of clothing— by anything short of killing the body that feeds the brain. Igor is a direct heir of those Russian intellectuals, like the brilliant academician Nikolai Vavilov, who conducted their lectures and seminars in Stalin's Gulag until they died of starvation, exhaustion, or disease. As long as the Igors of the world are among us, we all can hope for the best.

Back at the Desna, I picked up a copy of today's *Komsomol'skaya Pravda*. Page 2 carried a long article by academician Stanislav Shatalin, one of the key authors of the "500 Days" program, Gorbachev's former top economic advisor, and a member of the now defunct Presidential Council. A born member of the Communist nobility (his father and uncle were high in the party leadership), Shatalin titled his piece, "I Would Like to Justify Myself before the People." The article was startling even after the two and a half years of *glasnost's* self-flagellation.

On Soviet society: "The philosophy of robbery, social parasitism, parvenu, and crassitude has become the alpha and omega of our existence. We live in a society of decayed individuality, unbridled passions, disdain for each other, ignorance of the most fundamental problems of the development of culture and civilization, in fact, we live outside culture. We have trampled the faith, we are blaspheming, naïvely hoping that history could be deceived and rewritten as we wish. It is of us that Christ spoke his harrowing words from the cross: 'Father, forgive them, for they know not what they do.'"

On the October Revolution of 1917: "This event has led us to our historic cul-de-sac. . . . Lenin saw the historic mission of the revolution in 'pushing' a world revolution. [But] the world proletariat was not ready for the revolution. . . . Moreover, the Russian proletariat was not ready for the revolution."

On the Soviet political and economic system: "Let us admit honestly: The CPSU [Communist Party of the Soviet Union] has never been a party of workers, it has never embodied 'the dictatorship of the proletariat,' it has always been a 'party of a special kind,' that is, a party of the apparatus, which directed the party masses, myself included. In the name of the workers we have enslaved workers and have made labor forced and the whole system a slave-feudal empire of the 'ruling' class. We have 'abolished' exploitation of man by man, but derive a great deal of pleasure from watching the state of the workers, peasants, and people's intelligentsia exploit all three."

On economic *perestroika*: The 1985 assessment of the [economic] situation was wrong, superficial, and still operating within the 'deformed' socialism paradigm. Then [came] the 'acceleration' course, which glossed over the reality; then the call for a humane, democratic socialism without private property, exploitation, alienation, [which was] another glossing over—and then the edge of the precipice."

January 17

The bombing of Iraq began early this morning. Compared with October, when I was in Moscow last, the official media's coverage has a somewhat pro-Iraqi and pacifist spin. At the very least, the zeal of support for the United States is gone. This is hardly surprising; the political reaction is moving on a broad front, and Shevardnadze's most ambitious projects—the CFE and START conventional and nuclear arms reductions, the diplomatic recognition of Israel, and support for the U.S.-led coalition in the Gulf—appear to be on the verge of abandonment.

Yet even the hardest of the hardliners, witnessing the prodigious display of U.S. technological wizardry, may now be persuaded of the prudence of the Gorbachev-Shevardnadze bailout from the high-tech arms race. To Shevardnadze, who resigned last month, this, alas, does not matter any longer. To Gorbachev, the vindication may mean a somewhat greater acceptance by the military.

Prodemocracy Soviet journalists, shellshocked by the official propaganda blast that followed the Vilnius massacre, are beginning to fight back. The Leningrad television channel, which can be seen in Moscow, has responded by showing the horrific footage of the "black beret" goons' attack on the television center in Vilnius: the thugs swinging the butts of their rifles at unarmed defenders of the Telecenter, shooting at random, and ramming their tanks into the crowd. A Russian orthodox priest in Vilnius was shown saying, "We Russians will pay [for Moscow's savagery]. I used to trust Gorbachev. Now I understand: he does not care about the Soviet Union or Russia. He wants only one thing—the preservation of Communist power."

January 18–19
(on the plane to Frankfurt)

What has happened since January 13 seems nothing short of the change of a political regime, even though the leader remains the same—a rare thing, but not unheard of in history. There is little surprise at the demise of *perestroika*, Gorbachev's variant of one-party socialism "with a human face." Gorbachev was sentenced by history to be a transitional figure. His was the role of throwing the stones, not gathering them. It is Gorbachev's personal tragedy, and his country's political one, that he would not recognize, much less accept, history's sentence.

What is surprising is how long he has lasted. Long gone and forgotten are the oh-so-bold reformist Communists of Eastern Europe: the Petar Mladenovs, the Imre Pozgays and Karoly Groszes, the Egon Krenzes and Hans Modrows, the Karel Urbaneks and Ladislav Adamecs. (Wojciech Jaruzelski was forgotten even before he was gone.) Yet Gorbachev's "Moscow Spring" endured until January 13.

But whatever effect Vilnius may have on the preservation of the union and the suppression of private property, it is not likely to help Gorbachev stay in power. In fact, it will probably expedite his exit; having burned his bridges to the "left" (that is, to the free-market right), Gorbachev after Vilnius may not be of much help to the "right," either. In the eyes of the Soviet hardliners, who will never forgive Gorbachev for *glasnost* and Eastern Europe, Vilnius compromised the two major uses they have for the Soviet president: that of a fig leaf for repression and that of a charmer of the West. In both departments Gorbachev's stock has plummeted.

Most important, Gorbachev's handling of Vilnius has proved to the hardliners that, should things get seriously bloody, the president will not be of much help. In Vilnius, Gorbachev acted like an inept third-world authoritarian and not like the resolute guardian of a totalitarian state. The operation was worthy of Somoza, Batista, or Marcos—not of Deng. It went far enough to infuriate domestic and world public opinion—but not far enough to intimidate the opposition.

Why did Gorbachev balk at wider and bloodier repression? Why did he clearly lose nerve in the aftermath of Vilnius and, instead of moving the tanks forward, over more bodies, attempt both to justify the massacre and to apologize for it? Again, only history will tell. Perhaps politicians do have such a thing as soul, and think of it every now and then. Perhaps, too, killing one's own political children (*glasnost, perestroika*) is not easy even for a protégé of Andropov and Suslov.

Whatever accounts for the incompetence of the repression, Gorbachev's political months, if not indeed days, are numbered: having betrayed the "Left" and disappointed the "Right," he is suspended in a political vacuum.

The Moscow Spring is over. R.I.P. A transitional regime that lingers is bound to become nasty—and nastier, the longer it lingers. We hoped for a miracle—the peaceful self-destruction of one of the most repressive ruling class in mankind's history, a gentle sunrise instead of a long and cold night. We were wrong—Westerners and Soviets alike.

I look again at the resolution adopted at the meeting in the Bogomolov Institute:

> That night [in Vilnius] democracy was shot to death, and buried were our hopes for a bloodless transformation of the regime that has outlived itself. All our illusions about *perestroika* and its creators have perished. The reforms revealed themselves as false; they have brought upon us only death and universal impoverishment. The CPSU is not reformable. It cannot defend its principles other than by blood and death.

3

Two Requiems for *Perestroika*
1992

What was the initial impulse for perestroika, *a set of political and economic reforms which turned out to be a revolution from above? Who were those few at the top of the Soviet hierarchy that started it, and what can they tell us about its course, its achievements and its setbacks?*

Self-administered postmortems of their own careers by retired politicians usually are of little use to historians. These cases are different: The memoirs of Gorbachev's first prime minister, Nikolai Ryzhkov, and the "godfather of glasnost," Aleksandr Yakovlev, fill many gaps in our understanding of the twentieth century's last great revolution while telling absorbing tales.

At 7:20 p.m. on Sunday, March 10, 1985, in the exclusive "Kremlin hospital" in the Moscow suburb of Kuntsevo, died Konstantin Ustinovich Chernenko—the last leader of the Soviet Union, it turned out, to die in office. An emergency Politboro session was scheduled for the same evening. When Nikolai Ryzhkov, a secretary of the Central Committee of the Communist Party of the Soviet Union and the head of its Economic Department, arrived in the Kremlin, he found the candidate members of the Politburo and the secretaries gathered around a long table in front of the massive oak door that led into the sanctum sanctorum of the Communist world, the office of the general secretary.

At exactly 10:00 p.m., the door opened and, striding briskly, in came the "second secretary" of the Communist Party, Mikhail Gorbachev, followed by the Politburo members. Like soccer teams before a match, each of the Politburo members shook hands with each of the lesser Soviet gods. The ritual completed, Gorbachev declared the meeting open. Less than an hour later, the party had a new general secretary and the country a new supreme leader. *Perestroika*, which would "shake the world" as much as the famous "ten days" did in 1917,[1] had begun.

While we wait for scholarly histories of those years, few personal testaments are likely to be as interesting as those of Nikolai Ryzhkov, Gorbachev's first prime minister, and Aleksandr Yakovlev, Gorbachev's key advisor and confidant, who came to be known as the "godfather of *glasnost.*" Their books[†] have added weight and credibility because the authors may have been the only two among Gorbachev's key aides—the others being Eduard Shevardnadze, Yegor Ligachev, Anatoly Lukianov, and, until October 1987, Boris Yeltsin—who were, and remain, utterly void of any political ambition of their own. Both left Gorbachev's side in late 1990. Both accepted the loss of power with Cincinnatus-like equanimity, and neither, as far as we know, strives to get close to the greasy pole again. Ryzhkov, in retirement, wrote his memoirs for his "grandchildren." Yakovlev, although still active in the Movement for Democratic Reform, brought out a collection of articles, the most recent of which was published in 1990—hardly a most effective vehicle for a political comeback.

What good are self-administered postmortems by defeated politicians? Usually very little. But when they are defeated by history, rather than people, as these two certainly were, the profit is obvious: Knowing more about why and how it all began, we may be better positioned to guess why and how it will all end—or continue; for most of the problems facing the Russian revolution today are similar to those encountered in 1985.

In large measure, political movements are informed by the personalities of those who stood at its inception. If so, *perestroika* clearly gained by having had Ryzhkov and Yakovlev for midwives; they were, undoubtedly, among the best of what the highest party *nomenklatura* had to offer in 1985.

Ryzhkov's way to the top was simple and straightforward, typical in many respects of the party's "cadre policy" in the 1970s and early 1980s, when talented professional managers, rather than ideologues, were actively sought out, recruited, and promoted. (Yeltsin, who began as a civil

---

† Nikolai Ryzhkov, *Perestroika: Istoriya Predate'lstv* [*Perestroika*: The History of Betrayals] (Moscow: Novosti, 1992); Aleksandr Yakovlev, *Muki Prochtenia Bytia* [The Torments of Reading Life] (Moscow: Novosti, 1991).

engineer, is another example of the same trend.) A mechanical engineer by education, Ryzhkov started as a deputy foreman at a giant Uralmash plant in Yeltsin's hometown of Sverdlovsk (now Ekaterinburg) and rose to be the plant's director. After twenty-five years there, he was called to Moscow and appointed deputy minister of heavy and transport machine-building, then deputy chairman of Gosplan, the all-powerful State Planning Committee.

Yakovlev's story is considerably more complicated. A son of a poor peasant from a tiny village near Yaroslavl in Central Russia, he was the only World War II veteran among Gorbachev's political advisors. He joined the party at the front and was badly wounded and discharged in 1942, an invalid at nineteen. Yakovlev graduated from a teacher's college, taught school, worked as a journalist, and then began a rapid ascent up the rungs of various party committees, winding up, at twenty-nine, the youngest *instruktor* in the Central Committee apparatus. He graduated from the Academy of Social Sciences, eventually earning a PhD in "Marxist-Leninist philosophy." Along the way, in 1959, he attended the Columbia School of Journalism in New York with Oleg Kalugin. There they were, the epitome of the U.S.-Soviet student "exchanges" in the "social sciences"—a veteran party propagandist from the Department of Higher Education of the Central Committee's secretariat, and a professional spy, the future chief of Soviet counterintelligence.

Although he eventually rose to be head of the Sector of Radio and Television in the Propaganda Department of the Central Committee, Yakovlev felt increasingly uncomfortable on Staraya Square. He was, clearly, a man of Khrushchev's "thaw" and had a reputation of a "liberal," to which he lived up by balking at especially nauseating "greetings" to Leonid Brezhnev, championing the cause of the polluted Lake Baikal, defending heretical articles in the media, and even writing some of his own.

He survived in the apparatus until 1972. After the last vestiges of the "thaw" had been erased and the regime turned to unabashed reaction, there was no longer a place for Aleksandr Yakovlev in the Central Committee. In Brezhnev's softer tyranny, that meant either a retirement, for which Yakovlev was too young, or a sinecure. He was offered the deanship of a college and refused. The only other choice was an ambassadorship. His appointment to Canada was decided in one day, and the ambassador then in the post was taken off the plane as he was boarding for Ottawa after a vacation.

Ten years later, Yakovlev, still in Ottawa, hosted an up-and-coming Politburo member by the name of Mikhail Gorbachev. They liked each other instantly and "talked frankly about everything." Yakovlev, an experienced apparatchik, was "struck" by the "candor and the clarity of positions" of his interlocutor. Shortly afterward, Yakovlev was returned to Moscow and installed as director of the prestigious Institute of World Economy and International Relations.

Under Gorbachev, in addition to his "*glasnost*" portfolio, Yakovlev managed the Committee on International Affairs of the Central Committee, supervising the disengagement from Eastern Europe. He was also in charge of the Commission on Rehabilitation of the Victims of Political Repressions.[2] He was rightly considered Gorbachev's mentor of sorts and the brain behind many of Gorbachev's initiatives. (His book leaves no doubt that it was Yakovlev's style that permeated so many of Gorbachev's speeches—refreshingly intelligent, sometimes even rich, but often maddeningly verbose.)

The Politburo's liberal-in-chief, Yakovlev became the favorite bugbear of reactionaries of all kinds. The anti-Semitic *Pamyat'* movement sent a fact-finding mission to Yakovlev's village to investigate his roots and prove that he was a Jew. Eventually, the Central Committee drummed Yakovlev out of the party, a week before the August 1991 attempted coup and revolution buried the party itself.

The authors testify that the sentiment for fairly radical reforms had been shared by the progressive wing of the party and the government for several years prior to Gorbachev's election. Those around Gorbachev were convinced that something very fundamental must change: "We cannot exist like this any longer" ("*Tak dalshe zhit nelzia*") was, apparently, the motto of these few. By the time Chernenko died, Yakovlev felt "in the air something like a gathering storm." By 1985, recalls Ryzhkov,

> The "stuffiness" in the country had reached maximum; after that, only death. . . . Nothing was done with any care . . . [We] stole from ourselves, took and gave bribes, lied in the reports, in newspapers, from high podiums, wallowed in our lies, hung medals on one another. And all of this—from top to bottom and from bottom to top. . . . The country was drinking itself into the

ground. [People] drank everywhere. Before work. After work. In the *obkoms* (regional party committees) and in the *raikoms* (district party committees). At the construction sites and on the shop floor. In offices and in the apartments. Everywhere.[3]

Yakovlev defined the Soviet political system as "bureaucratic feudalism"—quite a distance from "institutional pluralism," the rage, at the time, of revisionist Sovietology. Yakovlev adds:

In seventy years a system has been built [that is] a priori indifferent to the real, live human being, hostile to him. [This is true] not only with respect to mass repression, which has touched millions. [This is true] also of everyday life, in which a human being means nothing, has nothing, cannot get the most elementary things without humiliation.[4]

The Soviet economy was not just in recession. It operated within an extraordinary, perhaps unique, structural imbalance, which might be called "self-colonization" of an immensely rich and seemingly industrialized nation. "[We were] importing everything," Ryzhkov wrote,

from grain and pantyhose to industrial machinery and equipment. Half of the chemical industry worked on imported equipment, eighty percent of light industry and food production. Of the total imports, the share of machinery and equipment was forty percent![5]

Judging by these books, Ryzhkov and Yakovlev were unanimous in their anger and sadness over their country's manmade plight and in seeing the necessity of and urgency for change. For Soviet apparatchiks, both were also remarkably astute in their perception of economic democracy as the necessary condition for viable political pluralism. Yakovlev, as usual, advanced the same thesis more elaborately:

Totalitarianism, Stalinism became possible here because all the sources of man's subsistence, all the means for his daily survival,

were in the hands of the state. . . . Democracy itself is a market,
a market of interests, wills, ideas, concepts.[6]

The two diverged, however, in their prescriptions for coping with the
crisis, and, in the public realm, these differences have outlasted the protagonists' time at the helm. Ryzhkov was a spokesman for Soviet industrial
managers, who had long and deeply resented the tyranny of "Her Majesty
Ideology" in the economy. He was sick and tired of the party's primitive
policies—but not of planned economy, as such. Behind Yakovlev, on the
other hand, were the intelligentsia, impatient to be rid not just of the party's
command of the economy but of the very principle of centralized planning,
and the party's monopoly on political power as well.

Tellingly, Ryzhkov and Yakovlev differed in their views on *perestroika's*
antecedents. The former credited Yuri Andropov, who during his fifteen-
month reign (1982–84) tried to combine tough "law and order" policies
with mild reformist tinkering in the economic realm. To the democrat
Yakovlev, Andropov, although "clever," was not much different from Chernenko or Brezhnev. He traced *perestroika* to Khrushchev's famous "secret
speech" in 1956, which started de-Stalinization.

Behind this divergence loomed a much larger debate sweeping Russia at the end of the 1980s: the "Chinese variant" of the "gradual and
managed transition" to the market, guided by a strong, even authoritarian, central power, or a rapid "leap" into privatization under a full-fledged
democracy, as advocated by acting prime minister Yegor Gaidar and his
coterie of young radical economists in 1991–92. As early as 1987,
Ryzhkov and Yakovlev sparred at Politburo meetings on precisely the
same subject, Yakovlev insisting that the state should abandon planning
altogether and let the "producers sort things out themselves."[7]

At the time, of course, Yakovlev's prescription could not be implemented for political reasons. Gorbachev, ever the politician, understood
this very well and sided with Ryzhkov. And so, while keeping the reins of
the economy firmly in the hands of the "Center," the prime minister
slowly but steadily let them out by supervising the introduction of the
Law on State Enterprises, which allowed plants and factories to retain
a share of what they manufactured and to set salaries and even, within
limits, prices; the Law on Joint Enterprises, which allowed foreign

investment; the end of the state monopoly on foreign trade; and modest banking decentralization.

Could *perestroika* have avoided the near chaos that followed? Could it, relying on the Soviet Union's still formidable industrial potential and social stability, have navigated the huge country to a "soft landing" into, if not a capitalist democracy, then a one-party socialism with "a human face" and enough to eat? Both books made this a dubious proposition.

True, a few disasters were caused by mistaken policies. Chief among them was granting autonomy to enterprises without demonopolizing the economy as a whole. As a result, instead of "working better," producers simply raised prices on the same shoddy goods. Salaries jumped, productivity remained low, and the country was instantly flooded with money for which there was no equivalent in goods. "We have engendered a monster which is capable of devouring everything," wrote Yakovlev. It was not until 1995 that the genie of hyperinflation was finally back in the bottle.

Yet from the very beginning, *perestroika* was plagued by misfortunes outside of anyone's control. First, it had awful luck: Chernobyl in April of 1986; the Armenian earthquake in December of 1988; plummeting oil prices, which dramatically reduced Soviet hard-currency earnings; the continuing war in Afghanistan, which, despite a unanimous repudiation in the new Politburo, took three years and untold lives and gold to end.

More importantly, there were immense structural problems. First, by 1985, the country had entered a downward economic spiral. According to Ryzhkov, already in 1982 there was no relative increase in incomes—for the first time since the end of World War II. *Perestroika*, Yakovlev insisted, was started "in the situation of a most acute socioeconomic crisis." Second, in any system frozen for decades in so tight a vertical subordination, any action would inevitably generate unintended consequences of major proportions. Yakovlev, rightly I think, rejected the most common charge against the Founding Fathers of *perestroika*: that they had not "thought through" the "theory" of the reforms. "I think this is nonsense. Viable theories are not born in offices."[8]

And then, of course, all the social bills accumulated in the previous decades came due. First, newly liberated labor claimed its rights, with nation-wide miners' strikes in 1989 and 1991 taking a huge bite out of already shrinking national income. There followed a tsunami of ethnic strife—

Alma-Ata, Nagornyi Karabakh, Sumgait, Tbilsi, Fergana—and secessionist movements, first in the Baltic states, later in the Ukraine and the Caucasus. Gorbachev called the ethnic turmoil "the knife in the back of *perestroika*." It was with this knife that *perestroika*'s coup de grâce was eventually delivered.

And so, in the end, *perestroika* proved to be a flight *from* something, rather than toward something; a time to throw stones rather than collect them; a doomed attempt to reanimate "socialism with a human face" twenty years after the Prague Spring. Still, its legacy is enormous and priceless. Yakovlev's brilliant tactical invention, *glasnost*, which was the insurance against Khrushchev's fate, proved not only effective (*perestroika* was finished not by a palace coup but by the quickening pace of history) but lasting as well, destroying Communist mythology and paving the way for proto-democracy.

Other achievements of *perestroika* are less tangible but equally vital. It bequeathed Russia an entirely different ethos of political discourse, in which the traditional penchant for absolute and perennial solutions and messianic millennialism has been significantly, if not, alas, fatally, weakened; and tolerance, gradualism, patience, and responsibility for oneself and one's country have been given a new life. Yakovlev saw *perestroika*'s major achievement as "the end of the monopoly on the truth." And if today in Russia even the secret admirers of the "strong arm" are forced to qualify their public utterances by an insistence on the "temporary nature" of their solutions and protestations of their undying love of democracy, *perestroika* should take credit.

For *perestroika*, for himself, and for his comrades-in-arms, Yakovlev had the following epitaph:

[The] revolution "from above" has exhausted itself, having accomplished everything or almost everything it could have done. Its resources are emptied. It has done a great deal to enable the peoples of our country to begin building the only life befitting man: free, intelligent, moral. What has been achieved is in history forever.[9]

Perestroika is dead. Long live *perestroika*!

Part II

A New Russia:
The Laying of the Foundation

4

The Strange Case of Russian Capitalism
1998

The circumstances of the birth of Russian capitalism are central both to our assessing Russia's failures and progress and to predicting her future. Like post-Soviet Russia in general, newly born Russian capitalism was profoundly influenced by the Soviet and Russian legacy of an institutional, legal, and spiritual void and patrimonialism. In addition, the economic revolution was launched in the middle of a severe crisis, while the former industrial nomenklatura *(the Ministries bureaucrats "red directors") kept their control of the enterprises and enjoyed enormous political influence to shape the reforms to their advantage.*

Russian capitalism is a subject of heated debate in academic and business circles. Some see nothing but robber barons, a giant mafia in place of government, universal theft, economic stagnation, ostentatious luxury for a few, and impoverishment for millions.

This is a grossly oversimplified and distorted picture. Russian capitalism is real and increasingly robust. It has already begun benefiting Russian society in small but critical ways. Yet the severe deficiencies pointed up by the critics are just as real. The emergent economic system is full of incongruities and contradictions. The best way to put them in perspective and arrive at a more or less coherent picture is to recall the beginning.

No matter how much and how long a system develops, from the Big Bang to the conception of a baby, the first billionth of the first second, hour, day, and month define much of the result. So it is with economic and political revolutions. A great deal in the present character and the future course of Russia's nascent capitalism may be explained and forecast by recalling the circumstances that attended its birth.

Four powerful antecedents combined to shape the character of the Russian post-Communist economy. First, there was the legacy of Russian and Soviet economic and political arrangements, profoundly antithetical to modern market economy. Second, a dire economic and political crisis, from the depths of which the economic revolution was launched, resulted in an abruptness and speed of change that left practically no time for laying down the institutional, legal, and social foundations of "civilized" capitalism. The third factor was democracy, which in the West came centuries after private property and capitalism had been firmly established, but which in Russia overlapped with it. Finally, as in most other post-Communist societies, the new Russian revolution was "velvet"; it left the economic ruling class (the industrial *nomenklatura*) in charge of the nation's wealth.

⎯⎯⎯

The transition from traditional societies to modern capitalist democracies took centuries of gradually expanding islands of societal autonomy and self-rule, of corporate and individual sovereignty wrested from kings, first by the church and the nobility and later by towns, guilds, corporations, and universities. Strengthened at the same time were the institution of private property and its legal underpinnings: commercial law, the contract, and an impartial court. The two processes were parallel and mutually reinforcing.

By comparison, the soil in which the seeds of Russian capitalism were planted on January 2, 1992, was not just hard or barren; in key elements its composition was the direct opposite of the one from which Western capitalism had sprung. Apart from the monumental economic distortions, waste, and militarization, which were the legacy of the Soviet state, post-Communist Russia inherited four centuries of patrimonialism—a system of rule in which political authority presupposed substantial (often nearly complete) control not only of the nation's economy, but of the individual property of the state's subjects as well. Property rights (which in the West contributed so greatly to the political autonomy of civil society and eventually to the emergence of democracy) had been weak in Russia even before the Bolsheviks established a near-perfect patrimonial state that owned the livelihoods of the entire population.

Russian patrimonialism and Soviet state socialism had thwarted the development of the interlocking networks of laws, institutions, and what de Tocqueville called "habits of the heart" which undergirded capitalism over the past two centuries and endowed it with its "civilized" character. Nearly to the very day of its sudden collapse, the totalitarian *ancien régime* relentlessly sought to extirpate, suppress, subvert, or co-opt voluntary associations in which habits of self-governance, personal responsibility, and peaceful reconciliation of interests could have been instilled and reproduced: neighborhoods, religious associations, charitable organizations, clubs.

After depriving generations of political liberty and economic and social autonomy, the Communist regime delivered to its successor not citizens but wards of the state. In the absence of an even rudimentary social contract between the Russian state and Russian society, the former was viewed by the latter as the absolute master and provider but never as a partner. The people's compliance with laws was a product of terror and fear rather than of freely assumed obligation. Decades of contesting with unjust and often irrational rules turned Russians into a nation of lawbreakers. Ferocious individualists, jealously protective of their private space, resourceful and wily fighters for personal amenities, they were at once dependent on the state for everything and deeply resentful, cynical, and hostile to it—or, for that matter, to any organized political power. In the words of a leading Russian political sociologist, the forced "Communist collectivism" had been replaced by "nonliberal individualism."[1]

The signs of the unprecedented normative and institutional void from which Russian capitalism emerged were ubiquitous, vivid, and deep. What Marx called "primary accumulation" was everywhere and at all times attended with crass inequality, fraud, indignities, and cruelty toward the weak (all of which had long ago and happily faded from the collective memory of the West). The Russian case was made even less attractive by the absence of even minimally restraining mitigation by the church, by professional associations or corporations, or by the habit of charity or personal responsibility.

This moral vacuum exacerbated another common feature of societies undergoing a rapid capitalist expansion, or "de-etatization," of the economy. Like beached whales, the state possessions—huge but no longer shielded by fear—are waiting for the vultures to tear them apart. The newly empowered and hungry private entrepreneur meets a weakened but still omnipresent and rich state represented by a venal bureaucracy that controls access to the beach with licenses, quotas, and credits. Repeated in thousands of daily transactions, this encounter is the key source of corruption and organized crime in transitional societies (post-Communist and post-etatist), from Estonia to China and from the Czech Republic to Mexico and Argentina. And nowhere is the whale bigger, and in few, if any, places is the habit of honesty and self-restraint more eroded, than in Russia.

✑

In the short run, the most detrimental bequest of the omniscient patrimonial state and of the atrophied personal responsibility it spawned is the mammoth budget deficit. It is a result of the state's enormous social and economic presence and commitments, on the one hand, and rampant tax evasion, on the other. At around 7.5 percent of the gross domestic product, the deficit is uncomfortably close to the Mexican case, where the government also financed a shortfall of around 8 percent of the GDP by short-term government bonds and was eventually forced to devalue the peso in 1994–95 at the cost of severe economic dislocation and political destabilization.

In addition to the military-industrial complex[2] with its payroll of tens of millions, among the heaviest burdens inherited from the Soviet state are the subsidies for housing and utilities. Today, the average Russian family pays no more than 3 percent of the real service costs. Even in Moscow, Russia's most expensive city, the average tenant pays only 17.6 percent of the actual cost of electricity, heating, and telephone.[3] The housing subsidies now cost the Russian state more than the entire defense budget.

Another stark and debilitating legacy is communal ownership of land. Except for a brief interlude at the beginning of the twentieth century, when Prime Minister Petr Stolypin (1906–11) attempted to create a class of independent farmers by granting them titles to individual plots, the land in Russia was owned by the crown, feudal lords, the *mir* (the village commune), or, after Stalin's "collectivization" (1929–33), the state.

Since 1993, the Communist-led plurality in the Duma (the lower house of the Russian legislature, the Federal Assembly) has resisted the privatization of land to further the agenda of its most important constituency: the rural *nomenklatura* of chairmen of *kolkhozy* and *sovkhozy*, who effectively continue to rule most of the Russian countryside. In July 1997, President Boris Yeltsin vetoed the land code passed by the Duma because it banned citizens from selling, giving away, or mortgaging farmland. (Yeltsin called the legislation "the most reactionary of documents ever passed by the Russian parliament.")[4]

The character of Russian capitalism was further shaped by the deep economic crisis in which the market revolution was launched. Five years of Mikhail Gorbachev's half-hearted on-again, off-again tinkering with the "socialist market," as well as his well-meaning but incompetent policy of increasing salaries and subsidies in the absence of growth in productivity or budget revenues, had left Russia in the worst of two worlds: between the fatally undermined command economy and a still suppressed market.

The result, by the fall of 1991, was a contraction of the economy by 13 percent of GDP; a budget deficit of 30 percent of GDP; inflation of 138 percent; an empty state treasury; the collapse of the ruble, which had lost 86 percent of its value against the dollar; and barter trade.[5] In October 1991 the Vnesheconombank, which handled foreign trade of the Soviet Union, declared that it could no longer service foreign debt and defaulted on domestic hard currency accounts.

No one who visited Moscow in the fall and winter of 1991 will forget the shortages, on a scale unknown in Russia since the end of World War II. Sugar, salt, matches, potatoes—all were rationed, if they could be found at all. With famine, civil war, and the country's disintegration not only possible but probable (and widely predicted by many Russian and Western experts), the price liberalization of January 2, 1992, and the beginning of privatization half a year later were undertaken in haste and with an urgency that left neither time nor energy to engineer, test, and deploy even rudimentary structures and institutions of liberal democratic capitalism. The country, state, and democracy were saved, but at a considerable cost.

Another fundamental characteristic that marked the emergence of Russian capitalism was its coincidence with electoral democracy. As mentioned earlier, this concurrence was absent in the West, where capitalism was centuries older than the universal franchise, and in most Southeast Asian and South American nations, where capitalist modernization preceded democracy by at least several decades.[6] When Macaulay described what we today call liberal capitalism as a system in which "the authority of law and the security of property were found to be compatible with a liberty of discussion and individual action,"[7] the implied order—first, private property protected by law; second, democracy—corresponded to the historical record of the classic evolution.

In Russia (as in other post-Communist nations), the sequence was reversed: Democracy came first and commanded an incomparably greater popular allegiance than the free market. Capitalism was a consequence (and not always an intended one) of a revolt against the totalitarian Communist state.

This coincidence matters a great deal because of the fundamental heterogeneity of capitalism and democracy. In older capitalist democracies, equality and subjugation to the will of the majority, which are at the heart of democracy, coexist in relative harmony with inequality and liberty of individual action, which are the essence of capitalism, although not without occasional tension. In Russia, as in other post-Communist societies, the conflict is raw and constant.

In macroeconomic policy, this uneasy partnership, in which democracy is the much stronger partner, has produced what might be called "capitalism-by-majority." It accounts for much of the inconsistency and contradiction of the market reforms and the glacial speed with which economically urgent but politically unpopular policies are implemented. (One need only look at today's France and Italy, where the state is perceived as the guarantor of "economic rights," or New York City, with its "rent-controlled" housing, to appreciate the political constraints that democracy imposes on the market even in far more mature capitalist societies.)

Finally, perhaps in no other instance has democracy's impact on the course of the Russian market revolution been more immediate and pronounced than in the repercussions of another common feature of anti-Communist revolutions: the historically unprecedented preservation and subsequent return of political and economic elites of the *ancien régime*. One of the most celebrated features of the anti-Communist revolutions of 1989–91 was their "velvet," nonviolent character. Other revolutions killed off, arrested, exiled, or at least dismissed the old ruling classes; these bought theirs out. The post-Communist "velvet" was the largest political bribe in history. The Communist *nomenklatura* handed over political power practically without a shot (Romania was the only exception) in exchange for effective ownership of the state assets they had administered on the Communist Party's behalf. When the music of Communism stopped, they kept the chairs.

The defeat in the Cold War did not wipe the Russian political slate clean—as had, in the case of Germany, Italy, and Japan, defeat in World War II. On the contrary, granted complete freedom of political participation, the former Communist *nomenklatura* successfully deployed its unmatched organizational resources, skills, and solidarity to thwart and dilute the capitalist transition.[8]

✑

The first and second phases of privatization (1992–95) determined a great deal for years, perhaps decades. Quite apart from the errors, malfeasance, and simple ignorance that invariably accompany such mammoth undertakings, the result was in many ways preordained by two "genetic" factors.

First, the patrimonialism of the Soviet state was replicated on the local level, where enterprises owned and operated the kindergartens, hospitals, schools, and housing of their workers and, in many cases, entire towns, cities, and "workers' settlements." As the party's grip relaxed toward the end of Gorbachev's rule, the managers of these enterprises (soon to be known as "red directors") emerged as the most powerful and coherent interest group in Russian politics. The second factor was the velvet revolution, which left "red directors" in possession of all the economic assets and privileges they had enjoyed in Soviet times.

How, under these circumstances, does one go about privatization? One could, in a Bolshevik fashion, send armed detachments to tens of thousands of state-owned enterprises, forcibly eject old managers from their offices, and severely restrict the rights of the employees to buy shares in order to ensure the fair treatment of outside buyers and a subsequent enterprise-restructuring (which, in almost every case, would have meant massive layoffs). This scenario, in the case of Russia in 1992, may have led to civil war.

A hectic search for a formula that would satisfy the "red directors" and the increasingly recalcitrant, nationalist, and left-populist Supreme Soviet, inherited from the Soviet era, resulted in an arrangement that left two-thirds of the stock in the hands of managers and employees. Subsequently, 144 million privatization "vouchers" were distributed (one to every Russian man, woman, and child), to be exchanged for shares in any privatized enterprise. Yet the novelty of the procedure, the passivity of the Russian workers and their trade unions, management's near-complete mastery over them, and the absence of a legal and accounting infrastructure to protect the rights of outside investors have combined to produce a corporate governance that was hardly conducive to transparency and accountability. Worst of all, the first phase of privatization (1992–94) did little to effect the desperately needed radical restructuring of the Russian economy, which was a key objective of the entire exercise. Only one-fifth of all the Russian firms were majority-owned by outsiders in 1996, 6 percent by one block-holder and 5 percent by several blockholders.[9]

Still, next to the perpetuation of state ownership of the economy, this insider "*nomenklatura* privatization" was viewed by Russian reformers as a lesser evil. As the testimony of those in charge made quite clear, the objective during the first phase was not so much to secure immediately the best management of the assets for a particular enterprise, but to depoliticize the Russian economy—to remove as many economic assets as possible from the state's control as quickly as possible. "Controlling managers is not nearly as important as controlling politicians," wrote associates of Russia's privatization czar, Anatoly Chubais, "since managers' interests are generally much closer to economic efficiency than those of the politicians."[10]

The reality proved far grimmer than the theory. After seventy-five years of a state-owned economy, "red directors" behaved more like corrupt civil servants than entrepreneurs. Control was preeminent, productivity and workers' well-being secondary and tertiary. Indicative of this mentality were the results of a survey of Russian managers conducted in 1995 and 1996. Two-thirds of those polled said that they "and their workers" would oppose selling a majority of the shares of their enterprises to outside investors even if an outsider would bring all the capital necessary to modernize and restructure the firm.[11]

Forced on their own, most managers sought "rent" from assets and political connections, not profit from production and innovation. The response to the gradual diminution of subsidies and the cancellation of state orders was not restructuring, the development of new products, or a search for new markets. It was lowered production, the sale of inventory, profligate and reckless borrowing, withholding of taxes, and the accrual of enormous interenterprise debts. In these strategies, the "red directors" were encouraged by their ability to secure a flow of state subsidies in the form of "loans" at a negative (that is, below inflation) interest rate. In 1993 and 1994 the subsidies to the enterprises amounted to, respectively, 9 percent and 5 percent of the Russian GDP.[12] The regime's timidity in forcing bankruptcies of failed enterprises[13] further strengthened managers' belief in their political invincibility and in the eventual demise of market reforms. All they had to do was to wait—and live well while doing so.

❦

Many features of Russian capitalism hardened after the second stage of privatization (1995–96), when the Kremlin moved from giving away state property to selling off some of Russia's blue-chip companies. This operation, in which twenty-nine of the country's most profitable and largest enterprises were auctioned, became known as the loan-for-shares deal. The state, desperate to plug huge gaps in the budget and to tame inflation (both resulting largely from the industrial subsidies and inflationary budgets adopted by the Supreme Soviet, which lasted until September 1993), received loans from the private banks in exchange for the "management" of the state's shares in the enterprises offered as collateral. In reality, this was a sale (or, at best, a long-term lease) of choice assets, for there was little hope that the Russian state would ever repay the loans.

It quickly became apparent that there were few domestic buyers; even fewer were those whose wealth had been obtained entirely by legal methods and who were not in one way or another connected to organized crime. And none could afford to pay anywhere near the book value for the shares. As foreign investors stayed away, frightened by political instability and high inflation, the shares were "sold" at insider auctions, at bargain-basement prices and to politically better-connected (and more "generous") banks, many of which acted as the organizers of those same auctions.

The economic system that thus emerged in Russia sharply diverged from the traditional capitalism of what might be called the Northern European or Anglo-Saxon variety, inherited and refined by the United States. Instead, the Russian variation incorporated some of the worst characteristics of the French, Italian, and Asian versions of capitalism, in a considerably cruder edition featuring secretive, tightly closed, bank-led corporate "families" or "financial-industrial groups" (FIGs) with intimate political connections. Most vivid in the South Korean *chaebols* and Japanese *keiretsus*, this capitalism is marked by incestuously overlapping and interchangeable political, corporate, and bureaucratic elites; bureaucratic sway over the economy stemming from either the state's direct ownership or *dirigisme* (intervention, direction, or control); the corruption that such arrangements inevitably breed; economies driven by banks and exports, instead of by the stock market and domestic demand; "authorized" (*upolnomochennye*) banks in which, in the absence of a state treasury system, the Russian government deposits its revenues; subsidized credits, "informal" lending practices, and loose (or nonexistent) disclosure rules, which result in mountains of bad loans; the absence of independent institutions of banking and stock market oversight; crushing taxes and nigh-universal tax evasion; protectionism for select industries and restrictions on foreign participation in the economy, especially in banking; a giant underground economy; and organized crime.

Much like the *chaebols* and the *keiretsus*, Russian FIGs owe their wealth (and often their origins) to political connections and the state's regulation and "guidance" of the economy. They obtained the export licenses and arbitraged between the world market prices on oil and raw materials and the controlled domestic prices (which, for political reasons, Yeltsin could not bring himself to free and which were, at times, up to one hundred times lower). Another source of wealth was duty-free imports, especially food, hard liquor, and cigarettes. In 1992 and 1993, the FIGs profited hugely from credits at the below-inflation interest rate, issued by the Central Bank then controlled by the Supreme Soviet. Finally, most banks at the heart of the largest FIGs were designated as "authorized" holders of government revenues (pensions, custom duties, taxes, salaries) and, in effect, used these enormous resources as short-term, interest-free loans.

This is a far from stellar report card. Yet, if history is a guide, neither does this record augur a uniformly cloudy future. First, several decades of the *keiretsus* and the *chaebols* coincided with political stabilization and the transition from authoritarianism to democracy (in the case of South Korea). And, of course, that was also the time of huge profits for domestic and foreign investors, of industrial expansion, of a remarkably fast growth of national wealth, and of a dramatic rise in the standard of living—some of the characteristics already evident in the revival that the "urban corporatism" of Moscow's mayor Yuri Luzhkov brought to the Russian capital.

✎

Despite its glaring flaws, the Russian version of oligarchic capitalism can already point to several real achievements. The seemingly doomed cohabitation between the reformist, right-of-center executive and the leftist legislature brought to Russia the first nonauthoritarian political stabilization in its history. Inflation in 1998 is down to 11 percent (compared to 160 percent in 1995 and 24 percent in 1996)—lower than in Poland or Hungary. In 1997 the Russian economy ended a free fall: industrial production, which accounted for a third of Russian GDP, grew 1.8 percent, and, for the first time since 1990, the country's GDP registered a minuscule positive growth of 0.4 percent. Adjusted for inflation, the average wage in 1997 grew at an annual rate of 3.3 percent. In September 1997, the dollar equivalent of the average monthly wage was $175, compared with $75 in September 1993.[14] Domestic automobile production is 13 percent higher than in 1996, and an estimated thirty-one of one hundred Russian families now own a car (compared with eighteen families in 1990). Russian tax collection agencies estimate that 20 million Russians traveled abroad in 1997 (of the total population of 144 million).[15]

Even in the absence of large-scale privatization of land, market prices, a stable currency, and efficient distribution contributed to a surplus of grain. For the first time since the early 1960s Russia could feed itself. It did not import grain and, in fact, had ten million tons to export after the 1997 harvest.

In the long run, a number of factors might help mitigate the more dangerous excesses of the Russian version of capitalism. First, the Russian transition coincides with economic globalization, when a dependence on foreign capital imposes greater discipline on the Russian government and the country's financial institutions. More important, unlike the modernizing authoritarian Asian regimes of thirty years ago (and unlike China and Indonesia today), Russia is an imperfect but functioning democracy, with freedom of speech and the press, a political process open to the opposition, and regular, free elections. Along with making the transition much more tortuous, contradictory, and lengthy, democracy also made it more consensual and thus politically stable. Popular sentiment for a less corrupt, more open, and more equitable economic system eventually translates into pressures that force change.

Friedrich Hayek wrote that should such a strange society be found in which there were no rich people, it would be better off selecting them by lots and endowing them with wealth at the state's expense. Russia's undeniable advantage over the currently more successful post-Communist nations and China is that it has, in fact, undertaken a privatization of the economy that is both decisive and unprecedented in scope.[16] This move sharply distinguishes Russia from Poland and the Czech Republic, both of which postponed industrial privatization, continued state ownership of inefficient and corrupt banks and subsidies to inefficient industrial enterprises (in the Czech case, despite the uncompromising free market rhetoric of its ex–prime minister, V. Klaus), and relied on retail trade, services, agriculture, and foreign investment to revitalize the economy and provide political stability. Following Deng Xioaping's decision not to privatize state-owned industry, China spends today a third of the entire state budget to keep afloat profitless plants and factories.

Just as important, at least some of President Boris Yeltsin's most trusted aides have a clear understanding (much strengthened by the emergent markets crisis of 1997–98) of the perils associated with the model of capitalism that Russia seems to have adopted. They see an urgent need for another cycle of economic liberalization that would, in the words of former acting prime minister Yegor Gaidar, further "separate power and property."[17]

Such seemed to have been the goal of the second economic revolution that Yeltsin heralded in his March 7, 1997, state of Russia address to the Federal Assembly. Among the measures announced by the president were an overhaul of the tax code, a crackdown on tax dodgers and corrupt officials, a smaller and more competent government, welfare reform, and the end of the use of authorized banks.

A new tax code, which the leftist plurality in the Duma has held up for over a half-year, fixed the levy on business profit at 30 percent and reduced the general tax burden on the economy from the current 33.0 percent of GDP to 30.7 percent. It is a vast improvement over the convoluted and constantly shifting maze of over three hundred federal and local taxes, with punitive wage taxes of 60 percent and levies on profit, which, if paid in full, often add up to much more than 100 percent of earnings.

A concerted attack was commenced on the unlimited power of FIGs and the "authorized" banks. They could no longer acquire the choicest pieces of Russian industry at bargain-basement prices in rigged auctions. (In August 1997, Yeltsin signed a new privatization law prohibiting loans-for-shares deals.) Instead, a 25 percent stake in the national telecommunication giant *Sviazinvest* went to the highest bidder, who had to pay the market price of $1.875 billion, half of it in cash. The position of the "authorized banks" is likely to be significantly undermined by the creation of the Federal Treasury in 1998. In the meantime, Yeltsin ordered the government to hold open competitive bidding among the banks for government deposits, beginning January 1, 1998. Following yet another presidential decree, the Ministry of Finance was banned from guaranteeing bank loans to enterprises. Finally, even such a politically well-connected corporation as the natural gas monopoly, Gazprom (Prime Minister Victor Chernomyrdin's industrial alma mater), has been forced to pay billions of dollars in back taxes.

The shrinking of the bloated state budget continued apace. In May 1997, the government imposed sequestering (an across-the-board spending cut) on the state budget, reducing it by 20 percent. Agricultural subsidies were cut by half, compared with 1996. The largest demilitarization effort in history was given an impetus by Boris Yeltsin's promise to reduce the share of GDP consumed by the military from 5 percent to 3 percent by the year 2000.

Radical welfare and housing reform, spearheaded by Boris Nemtsov, was designed to reduce expenditures by tightening eligibility, instituting a means-tested system for social benefits, gradually diminishing the rent and utility subsidies, and creating private pension and medical insurance funds.

The Russian economy was opened further to foreign participation by presidential decrees that allowed direct foreign bidding in privatization auctions, permitted foreign exploration of natural resources (oil, gas, iron ore, and gold) on a product-sharing basis (that is, in exchange for a percentage of resources extracted in the future), and lifted restrictions on foreign ownership in Russian oil companies, which had been limited to 15 percent of the shares.

"So what do we have after five years of reform?" Chubais was asked in 1997. "What kind of capitalism has been built, Anatoly Borisovich: 'state,' 'nomenklatura,' 'criminal'?"

"It is too early to sum up," Chubais answered,

> The process is not complete. There are giant holes in the edifice. Many weight-bearing parts of the structure are not strong enough. Several segments are simply wrong and even harmful. Yes, there is a danger of a *nomenklatura* capitalism. There is a danger that the half-constructed building will be frozen in its current version: with all the holes and rusty armature. No matter where you look, you see how much has been done—and how much more still needs to be accomplished. Still, there is a real chance for us to finish the construction of at least the main areas of both the state and the economy by the year 2000.[18]

This is a fairly objective analysis, but its timetable is overly optimistic. Given the crisis in which it was born and the crushing burden of its genetic defects, it is unrealistic to expect Russian capitalism to become liberal and democratic within the next decade. In the meantime, oligarchic capitalism, with the growth, prosperity, and stability that this model brought to Southeast Asia, is the best result one can hope for in the Russian case. In the longer run, Russian development will depend on the outcome of the clash between two fundamental and competing tendencies, both very much in evidence today: statist, oligarchic, authoritarian, closed, and left-populist, on the one hand, and liberal (in the European sense of the term), democratic, open, and centrist, on the other. A great deal will also depend on the caliber of Russian political leadership, continuing democratic institutionalization, and the state of the world economy. The battle for the soul of

Russian capitalism is likely to be tough and long. Its outcome is uncertain. Yet, given the adversity in which the market revolution began and what has been accomplished since January 2, 1992, the chances for success are real.

5

Russia's New Foreign Policy
1998

In September 1995, the last Russian soldiers left the Paldiski submarine train-
ing base in Estonia. Russian military presence in East-Central Europe was over,
and with it over two centuries of imperial conquests, from Peter the Great at the
beginning of the eighteenth century to Joseph Stalin in the 1940s. Compared to the
Soviet Union only a few years before, Yeltsin's Russia spent at least six times less
on defense in relation to the GDP.

What was behind this revolution in foreign and defense policy—"economic
weakness," which has become an explain-all cliché, or a genuine transformation
in the priorities brought about by democratization and privatization inside the
country? What policies followed and how sustainable are they? What do they
augur for Russia's relations with the United States?

Few propositions about the world can be stated with greater certainty:
Never in the four and a half centuries of the modern Russian state has there
been a Russia less imperialist, less militarized, less threatening to its neighbors and the world, and more susceptible to the Western ideals and practices than the Russia we see today.

Although obvious even to a person with only a cursory acquaintance
with Russian history, this state of affairs results from a long series of complex, often painful, and always fateful choices made by Russia's voters and
its first post-Communist regime. Some of the most critical decisions were
made between 1991 and 1996, when Russia was reeling from economic
depression, hyperinflation, and postimperial trauma. Many a nation, even
in incomparably milder circumstances, succumbed to the temptation of
making nationalism the linchpin of national unity and cohesion at a time of

dislocation and disarray. From Argentina to China, Malaysia, and Indonesia, in various degrees of crudeness and militancy, countries resorted to the palliative of nationalism to dull the pain of structural reforms or reversals of economic fortune.

In Russia, too, retrenchment and truculence were urged by leftist nationalists inside and outside the Supreme Soviet and, since 1995, by the "national patriotic" plurality in the Duma, which early in 1996 "annulled" the 1991 Belavezhskie agreements that legalized the de facto unraveling of the Soviet Union. This deafening chorus is led daily by the flagships of Communist and nationalist media—*Pravda*, *Sovetskaya Rossia*, and *Zavtra*, with a combined daily press run of more than half a million—and by the nearly three hundred local pro-Communist newspapers.

Yet even when the chance to propitiate the national patriots and to reap a political windfall by adopting a rigid and hostile stance was handed to President Boris Yeltsin on a silver platter, the Kremlin passed—as in the case of NATO's expansion, which included East-Central European countries that used to be members of the Soviet-led Warsaw Pact. After much blustering, Yeltsin chose to sign the NATO-Russia Founding Act and to accommodate the United States and its partners rather than to repeat (even if rhetorically) the Cold War. "It already happened more than once that we, the East and the West, failed to find a chance to reconcile," Yeltsin said in February 1997, when the final negotiations with NATO began. "This chance must not be missed." The leader of the national-patriotic opposition and the chairman of the Communist Party of the Russian Federation, Gennady Zyuganov, called the founding act "unconditional surrender" and a "betrayal of Russia's interests."

This instance was emblematic of a broader strategy of post-Communist Russia. Between 1992 and 1995, Moscow implemented all Gorbachev's commitments and completed the contraction of the empire inherited from the Soviet Union—a contraction remarkable for being undertaken in peacetime and voluntarily. On September 1, 1994, when the last Russian units left Germany, most troops had already been removed from Poland, Hungary, and the Czech Republic. In four years, Russia repatriated (frequently without homes for officers or jobs for their spouses) 800,000 troops, 400,000 civilian personnel, and 500,000 family members.

Even as Moscow publicly and loudly linked its retreat from Estonia to the granting of full civil and political rights to the ethnic Russians there, it quietly continued to withdraw. In two years, between the end of 1991 and the last months of 1993, the number of Russian troops in Estonia diminished from between 35,000 and 50,000 to 3,000. The departure of the last Russian soldier from the Paldiski submarine training base in Estonia in September 1995 marked the end of the Russian presence in East-Central Europe. The lands acquired and held during two and a half centuries of Russian and Soviet imperial conquests were restored to the former captive nations. Russia returned to its seventeenth-century borders.

Unfolding in parallel was demilitarization, historically unprecedented in speed and scope. "Reduction" is too mild a euphemism for the methodical starvation, depredation, and strangulation to which Yeltsin subjected the Soviet armed forces and the military-industrial complex. In a few years, the Russian defense sector—the country's omnipotent overlord, the source of national pride, the master of the country's choicest resources and of the livelihoods of one-third of the Russian population—was reduced to a neglected and humiliated beggar.

Beginning with a 90 percent decrease in defense procurement ordered by Yegor Gaidar in 1992, the share of the Russian gross domestic product spent on the military declined, from at least 20 percent to 5–7 percent today, and is very likely to go on diminishing. According to Sergei Rogov, a leading Russian expert and the director of the USA and Canada Institute, the 1996 expenditures for organization and maintenance of Russian armed forces were at least two and a half times lower than in 1990, for procurement and military construction nine times lower, and for research and development ten times lower. In the May 1997 "sequestering" of the budget (mentioned in the previous chapter), no exception was granted the defense expenditures, which were cut by 20 percent.

Along the way, the Russian army shrank from 2.7 million in January 1992 to about 1.7 million by late 1996. In July 1997, Yeltsin signed several decrees mandating a further reduction of the armed forces by 500,000 men, to 1.2 million. A week later, the minister of defense, General Igor Rodionov, referred to himself as the "minister of a disintegrating army and a dying fleet."

At the same time, Yeltsin promised what surely will be the coup de grâce of Russian militarism: the ending of the draft and the institution of an all-volunteer armed force of 600,000 by the year 2000. Even though this plan almost certainly will take longer than three years to implement, mere talk by the Russian leader about ending almost two centuries of conscription epitomized the distance that the new country put between herself and the traditional Russian (let alone Soviet) militarized state. In the meantime, following the Supreme Court's October 1995 decision that allowed local judges to rule on constitutional matters, Russian judges have thrown out dozens of cases brought by the army against the "deserters" who exercised their constitutional right to alternative civil service.[1]

The extent of the rout of the formerly invincible defense sector became evident in the twelve months following the 1996 presidential election. An often sick president Yeltsin fired two defense ministers, the head of the general staff, and the commanders of the paratroop and space forces, and he ordered the retirement of five hundred generals from the immensely bloated Russian field officers corps. With the 40 million votes that he received on July 3, 1996, Yeltsin apparently felt no fear. Dictatorships and autocracies depend on the army's good graces; democracies (even young and imperfect) can afford to be far less solicitous.

✑

Russia's historic disarmament results from democratization and privatization, not from a weak economy, as is often suggested—as if national priorities were determined by accountants and economists and as if, throughout human history, economic rationale had not been invariably and completely overridden by fear, hatred, wounded national honor, messianic fervor, or a dictator's will. In our lifetime, one is hard-pressed to attribute to a "strong economy" and excess wealth the policies of the Soviet Union in the 1930s and after World War II; Vietnam between the 1950s and the 1980s; Castro's Cuba; Ethiopia under Comrade Mengistu; an Armenia fighting for Nagorny-Karabakh; a Pakistan developing a nuclear arsenal; or an Iraq starving its people to produce the "mother of all weapons."

No, the shrinking of the Russian military is due to the weakening of the Russian state's grip on the economy and to the constraints imposed on imperialism, aggressiveness, and brutality by public opinion, the free mass media, and competitive politics, which forced the Kremlin in 1996 to end the war in Chechnya.[2] Tardy in bestowing on Russia its other blessings,

Russian democracy has already made high defense expenditures and violent imperial projects quite difficult to sustain.

Most fundamentally, Russian demilitarization is a consequence of rearranged national priorities, of a change in the criteria of greatness, and of the society's gradual liberation from the state. Russia has abandoned the tradition of the unchallenged preeminence of the state's well-being and concerns, particularly in matters of foreign policy and national security, over domestic economic and social progress. Vigilance against foreign aggression, the strength of the fortress-state, and allegiance and sacrifice to it have been replaced in a new national consensus by the goals of societal and individual welfare, new civil and political liberties, and stabilization within a democratic framework.

In June 1997, in a television address to the nation on the seventh anniversary of the Declaration of State Sovereignty of Russia, Yeltsin said,

> A great power is not mountains of weapons and subjects with no rights. A great power is a self-reliant and talented people with initiative. . . . In the foundation of our approach to the building of the Russian state . . . is the understanding that the country begins with each of us. And the sole measure of the greatness of our Motherland is the extent to which each citizen of Russia is free, healthy, educated, and happy.[3]

Unless this new consensus is extinguished by economic catastrophe and a return to dictatorship, Russian militarism is not likely to recur. For that reason, as stated in one of Ronald Reagan's magnificently vindicated theorems—nations mistrust one another not because they are armed; they are armed because they mistrust one another—Russia, while far from a model of openness and consistency, is easier to trust today than at any other time in its history.

This connection between democratization and national security policies makes the Russian case very different from the Chinese. For the same reason, one should not expect any time soon a reversal in the enormous Chinese military buildup and modernization, helped by a burgeoning economy and fueled by resurgent nationalism, with which China, unlike Russia, chose to anchor and unite the nation during its dizzying economic transformation.

Historically, the key feature of a transition from a traditional to a modern society and from a village to an urban-based economy was the "disposal" of surplus peasantry. Everywhere this process was attended with enormous societal convulsions, revolutions, violence, and cruelty (with England showing the way). For Russia, the problem was "resolved" by the terror of Stalin's "collectivization" of agriculture, which starved to death millions of peasants, and industrialization. For China, with its eight hundred million peasants, the resolution is still ahead. The justified fear of instability felt by the Chinese political class, already anxious about the migration of millions of destitute peasants into the cities, is the single biggest impediment to Chinese democratization—and to the prospects of a Chinese demilitarization.

China is relevant in another respect, as well. Of all the morbid fantasies about the innumerable facets of the alleged Russian menace, the prophecy of a coming Sino-Russian alliance directed against the United States is intellectually the most embarrassing one. What historical precedent is there to support such a forecast in the case of two giant nations that vie for regional superpowership, that share over two thousand miles of border (much of it in dispute), and that have for centuries competed for the huge, underpopulated land mass to the east of the Urals? As with history's other pair of perennial combatants, Germany and France, such an accord will have to wait until both countries are stable and prosperous democracies—not in our lifetime and, alas, perhaps not in our children's, either. In any case, should it ever come to pass, an alliance of two democracies is unlikely to be anti-American.

To be sure, there will be periods of rapprochements when, as today, Russia will sell its submarines and MIGs, and Chinese migrant workers and entrepreneurs will flood the Far East and Siberia, setting up Chinese language schools for their children and opening the best restaurants in Ekaterinburg, Irkutsk, and Khabarovsk. Russia will attempt to play the Chinese card in its dealings with Washington—just as China, at the same time, will be using a Russian card in its relations with the United States, which will remain far more important to both than they will be to each other. Just as certainly, a Sino-Russian truce will be followed by acrimonious and perhaps violent ruptures.

Along with finding its place and role in the post–Cold War world, Russia also had to make some critical choices about the "post-Soviet political space," as the territory of the former Soviet Union has been referred to in Moscow since 1992. At that time, everyone—from the national patriots on the left to the radical free-marketeers on the right—agreed on four things. First, a stable and prosperous Russia was impossible without a modicum of stability in the "post-Soviet space," which from Moldova to Tajikistan erupted in a dozen violent civil and ethnic wars. Second, some sort of mending of millions of ruptured economic, political, and human ties ("reintegration") was imperative if the entire area were to survive the transition. Third, with the "new world order" buried in the hills around Sarajevo, Russia could count on no one but herself in securing peace and stability in the area. Finally, Russia's preeminence as the regional superpower was not negotiable.

Beyond this agenda, the consensus dissolved into two sharply divergent objectives and strategies. One was aimed at making the post-Soviet space resemble the USSR as closely as possible and as quickly as possible. The cost—in money, world opinion, or even blood—was no object. All means were acceptable, including the stirring of nationalist and irredentist tendencies among the twenty-five-million-strong ethnic Russian diaspora in the newly independent states—just as Serbia did among the ethnic Serbs in the newly independent Bosnia and Croatia after the disintegration of Yugoslavia. In this scenario, the regime in Moscow was urged at least to threaten recalcitrant states with the politicization of the ethnic Russian community and the "massive redrawing of borders" to join to the metropolis the areas heavily populated by ethnic Russians, especially northern Kazakhstan and eastern Ukraine. Advocated largely, but not exclusively, by the nationalist left, this was an imperial, revanchist, and ideological agenda.

In the other model, which might be called postcolonial, reintegration was given a far less ambitious content. Its advocates relied on the incremental pull of a privatized Russian economy and its democratic stabilization to do the job. Its timeframe stretched over decades.

Haltingly and inconsistently, Russia opted for the latter game plan. Even the April 1997 "union" with Belarus—which some American observers hastened to declare the beginning of Russia's inexorable march to the West—was quietly but substantially diluted and slowed to a crawl, despite the Kremlin's rhetorical fanfare, the conjugal ardor of Belarussian President Alyaksandr Lukashenka, and the exuberance in the Duma. Already, five months later, in September, First Deputy Prime Minister Boris Nemtsov declared that "unity" between Russia and Belarus, with its Soviet-style economy and Lukashenka's dictatorship, would be just as impossible as a union between North and South Korea. A week later, ostensibly in retaliation for the jailing of a Russian journalist in Belarus, Yeltsin refused to grant permission for Lukashenka's plane to enter Russian airspace.

Regarding the maintenance of regional dominance, however, there ought to be no illusions: Russia is likely to deploy much the same combination of roguery, bribery, and diplomatic pressure that great land powers have used for millennia to assert control over a self-declared sphere of influence. Heading the list are economic and military assistance to friendly regimes and the denial of aid to neighbors deemed insufficiently accommodating. In the case of especially recalcitrant countries, support for all manner of internal rebellions is always an option. Given the economic and political fragility of most post-Soviet states, their dependence on Russian resources (especially energy), and their susceptibility to ethnic and civil strife, Moscow's stance could sometime make a difference between a young state's life and death.

While relentlessly probing for weaknesses, exploiting neighbors' troubles, and taking advantage of openings to further regional superiority, the postcolonial policy is constrained by a cost-benefit analysis. There is a wariness of open-ended, long-term, and expensive commitments in the "near abroad." Such considerations were anathema both to the Russian "messianic" (the Third Rome) and, especially, to the Soviet "ideological" (world socialism) varieties of imperialism.

More critically, Moscow has chosen not to cross the thickest lines in the sand: the independence and sovereignty of the CIS nations. While "near," the Confederation of Independent States is still "abroad." In the end, this is the critical distinction between the imperial and the postcolonial modes of behavior in the region.

This difference is akin to the one between twisting someone's arms and cutting them off. Much as observers may (and do) find both activities equally reprehensible, to the owner of the arms the actual choice makes a great deal of difference. Unlike some American journalists and columnists, whom they quickly learned to overwhelm with complaints about Russia, the leaders of neighboring nations from "near" and even "middle-range" know this very well.

Hence their wholehearted support for Yeltsin in his September–October 1993 confrontation with the left-nationalist radical supporters of the Supreme Soviet. Czech President Václav Havel said October 4 that the clashes in Moscow were not simply "a power struggle, but rather a fight between democracy and totalitarianism."[4] In a joint statement, presidents Lennart Meri of Estonia, Guntis Ulmanis of Latvia, and Algirdas Brazauskas of Lithuania called the struggle in Moscow "a contest between a democratically elected president and antidemocratic power structures."[5] Their Moldovan counterpart, Mircea Snegur, called the Supreme Soviet supporters "Communist, imperialist forces who want to turn Russia into a concentration camp."[6] "In my thoughts I am on the barricades with the defenders of Russian democracy, as I was next to them in August 1991," Eduard Shevardnadze said in a message to the Kremlin on the late afternoon of October 3, 1993, when the outcome looked quite grim for Yeltsin. "Deeply concerned about the events in Moscow, I am again expressing my resolute support for President Yeltsin and his allies."[7] Hence, also, the almost audible sigh of relief with which the neighboring countries welcomed Yeltsin's victory over Zyuganov in 1996. The tone of the greetings sent to the victor by the leaders of the new states far exceeded protocol requirements. "The future development of Ukraine depended on the results of the Russian election," president of Ukraine Leonid Kuchma said on July 4, 1996. Yeltsin's victory, he continued, was "a signal that Ukraine should press ahead with economic reform."

☙

For the proponents of the postcolonial choice, to which demilitarization of conflicts in the near abroad had always been central, 1997 was, by far, the most productive year. Following Yeltsin's near-miraculous resurgence after heart bypass surgery, Moscow moved to settle all hostilities in the region. Only in Nagorny-Karabakh, over which Armenia and Azerbaijan had fought to a standstill, did Russia fail to make some progress.

On May 12, Russia signed a peace accord with Chechnya, granting it all but an official recognition of independence. Within days, after two months of shuttle diplomacy by the Foreign Minister Evgeny Primakov, Moldova's President Petru Lucinschi and Igor Smirnov, the leader of the self-proclaimed Transdniester Republic (a Russo-Ukrainian secessionist enclave on Moldova's border with Ukraine), signed in the Kremlin a memorandum that effectively affirmed Moldova's sovereignty over the area. The signing was attended by presidents Yeltsin and Kuchma as "coguarantors" of the agreement.

In June, the Tajikistan regime, supported by Russia, and the Tajik Islamic opposition ended five years of a bloody civil war by signing in Moscow a Peace and National Reconciliation Accord. Primakov and his first deputy, Boris Pastukhov, reportedly continued mediation until the final agreement emerged two hours before the signing ceremony.

The same month, Abkhaz President Vladislav Ardzinba spent two weeks in Moscow with top mediators (Yeltsin's chief of staff Valentin Yumashev, security council secretary Ivan Rybkin, and Defense Minister Igor Sergeev) to discuss an interim protocol, drafted by the Russian Foreign Ministry, for a settlement between Georgia and secessionist Abkhazia. In August, Ardzinba traveled to the Georgian capital, Tbilisi, for the first face-to-face meeting with Shevardnadze since the war began in 1992. In his weekly radio address at the end of August, Shevardnadze "expressed his appreciation" of Primakov's effort in arranging Ardzinba's visit.

On September 4, in the presence of Prime Minister Victor Chernomyrdin, the presidents of North Ossetia and Ingushetia (autonomous republics inside Russia) signed in Moscow an agreement settling a conflict over North Ossetia's Prigorodnyi Raion, which had festered since fighting broke out in November 1992. During the next two days, in Vilnius, the capital of Lithuania, Chernomyrdin held bilateral meetings with the presidents of Estonia, Latvia, and Lithuania. At the end of the sessions, each of the presidents announced that his country would "soon" be able to sign border agreements with Moscow.

But by far the most momentous diplomatic coup of that busy year was the "Treaty of Friendship, Cooperation, and Partnership" between Russia and Ukraine, signed by Yeltsin and Kuchma in Kiev on May 31. By the terms of the treaty, the two nations undertook to "respect each other's territorial integrity" and "confirm the inviolability of the existing borders, mutual respect, sovereign equality, a peaceful settlement of disputes, non-use of force or its threat."[8]

The success of this settlement after five years of turbulent negotiations is all the more stunning because so much augured failure. First, the technical complexity of some issues bordered on intractability. One was the fate of the Soviet Black Sea Fleet, on which both countries had legitimate claims. Another contentious point was the sovereignty over the beautiful and fecund island of Crimea, where ethnic Russians outnumbered Ukrainians by more than two to one. For almost two centuries a staple of Russian poetry and the most popular Russian resort, teeming with czars' summer palaces and dachas of the best Russian painters, musicians, and writers, Crimea was "given" to the Ukrainian Soviet Socialist Republic by Nikita Khrushchev in 1954, when the end of the Soviet Union and an independent Ukraine seemed beyond the realm of the possible. Yet another political and emotional hurricane was touched off by the status of the port and naval base of Sevastopol, a symbol of Russian military valor. The defense of the city in the 1854–55 Crimean War against the British and the French and in World War II against the Germans had earned Sevastopol an honorary designation of City-Hero.

And then there were precedents of similar postimperial divorces, all attended by horrific bloodshed: England and Ireland, India and Pakistan, Bosnia and Serbia. In 1992, many a Western expert confidently predicted a war between Russia and Ukraine, some even an exchange of nuclear strikes.

Perhaps the greatest obstacle to the recognition of Ukraine as a separate state was her unique place in Russia's historic memory and national conscience. Kiev was the birthplace of the first Russian state and its first baptized city, from which Christianity spread throughout Russia. No other part of the non-Russian Soviet Union was so pivotal to Russian national identity as Ukraine. In no other instance was the tempering of Russia's imperial tradition and instinct put to a harsher, more painful test than by an independent Ukraine.

In the end, Russia gave up Crimea and Sevastopol and ceded to Ukraine the entire Black Sea Fleet. Some of Sevastopol's naval bays were to be leased and half of the fleet rented by Russia from Ukraine, with the payments subtracted from Ukraine's enormous debt to Russia for gas and oil deliveries, estimated at the time of the treaty signing at three to three and a half billion dollars—perhaps the most generous, and least publicized, bilateral foreign assistance program in the world today.

∽

The most fundamental choice that Russia had to resolve both on the world scene and in the post-Soviet space was the one between nonrevisionist and revisionist policies. The former seek advantage within the constraints of an existing framework accepted by the majority of the international community. The latter are aimed at undermining and changing the framework itself. Russia has chosen nonrevisionism. She may bemoan the unfairness of the score (and does so often and loudly), but she does not try to change the rules of the game.

To be sure, the imperatives of history, geography, and domestic politics will cause Russia to be less than happy about much U.S. behavior in the world and to challenge it often. In poll after poll, a majority of Russians have agreed that the United States was "using Russia's current weakness to reduce it to a second-rate power." As de Gaulle said to Harry Hopkins, "America's policy, whether it was right or not, could not but alienate the French." Wherever the United States provides an opening by seeming either not to care much about an issue or, as in Iraq in the late 1990s, to hesitate, Russia is likely to seize the opportunity to further its claim on being reckoned with as a major international player.

Yet, as with France, the tweaking, the shouting, and the occasional painful kick in the shins must not be confused with anti-Americanism of the kind professed by the Soviet Union, Iran in the 1980s, or Iraq, Cuba, and Libya today. Russian truculence is not informed by ideology. It is not dedicated to a consistent pursuit of strategic objectives inimical to the truly vital interests of the United States, and it is not part of a relentless, antagonistic struggle to the end. Rather, it is pragmatic and selective. And when America's wishes are communicated at the highest level, forcefully, directly, and unambiguously, Moscow is likely to moderate opposition and even extend cooperation, as it did in ending the civil war in Bosnia

But just as Francis Fukuyama's much misunderstood "end of history" was never meant to suggest the absence of lapses, reversals, lacunae, or lengthy and furious rearguard battles, neither does the end of seventy-five years of relentless Soviet revisionism spell the end of our Russian problem. Indeed, it may become worse before it becomes better. The reason is the "underinstitutionalization" of Yeltsin's foreign policy—the lack of organizational and personnel structures that could carry on the present policy in the absence of the impulse from the top. The new foreign and security policies of Russia have stemmed mostly from Yeltsin's domestic political and economic revolution, not from implementation of some long-term strategy or a conscious effort at restructuring the policymaking process.

Like every great and successful modern political leader, with the notable exception of de Gaulle, Yeltsin is a domestic leader. His interests, his instincts, and his passions, like Ronald Reagan's (and unlike Nixon's, Carter's, or Gorbachev's), are engaged mostly (and most profitably) by his country's domestic politics. For that reason, Yeltsin never cared to establish a foreign policy alter ego (a Kissinger, Brzezinski, or Shevardnadze), a strategic thinker and confidant endowed with a great deal of power and independence.

There have been only two exceptions, two areas of international relations that Yeltsin has firmly arrogated for himself. One is the relationship with the United States, which Yeltsin single-handedly salvaged by signing—against the advice and dire warnings of almost the entire political class—the NATO-Russia Founding Act.

The other *domaine réservé* is the settlement with Ukraine, into which Yeltsin put enormous personal effort and which he pushed along, ignoring or evading dozens of stern resolutions by the Supreme Soviet, the Duma, and the Council of Federation (the upper house of the Russian legislature) and pretending not to hear fiery statements of the country's top political leaders, from his own ex–vice president, Aleksandr Rutskoy, to the perennial chairman of the Duma's Committee on Foreign Relations, Vladimir Lukin, to the mayor of Moscow, Yuri Luzhkov. After the treaty was signed, Ukrainian officials told reporters that "only Yeltsin had the political will and strength to drop Russia's residual claims on Ukraine," and that the Ukrainian leadership "prayed that Mr. Yeltsin would not die before doing so."

Outside these two areas, Yeltsin considers foreign policy a distant second to his domestic agenda and is content to use it to accommodate the opposition rather than to expend his political capital. The choice of Primakov as foreign minister is characteristic: The man's announced objective of a multipolar world—without American hegemony but also without a challenge to the key postulates of the established order or a slide into a new cold war—made him the only key minister in Yeltsin's cabinet acceptable to all major political forces in the country.

In the next two years, the pitfalls of such a modus operandi will become especially apparent. Until now, Yeltsin's unique place in Russian politics, his political weight, and the confidence that came from a landslide victory in 1996 kept the vector of Russian foreign policy pointed in the right direction. The president's inevitable physical decline and lame-duck status change a great deal. Like an old bulldozer—once mighty and responsive but now more and more awkward, slow, hard to handle, and with the motor nearly worn out—Yeltsin today clears the boulders deposited by the receded Soviet glaciers one at a time, with much screeching, creaking, and even retreats.

Any worsening of Yeltsin's physical condition would further increase the policymaking impact of the Ministry of Foreign Affairs and the Russian diplomatic corps—perhaps the most authentic and recalcitrant relic of the Soviet past among Russian institutions, a class whose fall from the pinnacle of Soviet society in terms of material stature and prestige can be compared only with that of the military. Predictably, the zeal of Russian diplomats in defending the reformist regime often seems less than overwhelming.

An additional toughness and shrillness in the tone of Russian foreign policy rhetoric in the next two years will come about because of domestic politics, as the Foreign Ministry will more and more look to please the undeclared contenders in the 2000 presidential election, all of whom seem far less impervious to nationalist temptation than Yeltsin. Russian behavior in the worsening of the crisis between Iraq and the West, with Yeltsin, clearly disengaged, mouthing a bizarre line about World War III, is a foretaste of things to come.

⚮

This should not take us by surprise. Seven years ago, an enormous and evil empire, which had deformed and poisoned everything and everyone it touched, broke into pieces. Yet its harmful rays, like light from a long-dead star, will continue to reach us for some time. The current Russian leaders came of political age and advanced under the empire. They cannot be counted on fully to fashion a world of which they know little. At best, in domestic politics, economy, and behavior in the world, they will forge a hybrid. If we are lucky (as we have been with Yeltsin), more than half the product will be new and benign, while the rest will be instilled with various degrees of malignancy. It is up to the next generation of leaders (with lots of good fortune) to turn the hybrid into a purebred.

U.S. policymakers must be prepared to encounter the Soviet legacy in Russian foreign policy—such as relentless and often senseless spying or the sale of technology and weapons to nations hostile to the United States—and to counter them with unflinching resolve. What will never serve American interests, however, is the wholesale imposition of old stereotypes on a different new reality, remarkably auspicious in some of its key ingredients.

6

Land Privatization:
The End of the Beginning
2001

The Bolsheviks abolished private ownership of land on their first day in power,
October 26, 1917. Seventy-three years later, a Russia in the throes of another
revolution resolved to end the state's monopoly on 637 million acres of urban and
agricultural land. Yet eleven more years had to pass before the bitterly divided
country and the split political class forged the legal foundation for the private
ownership of land. A tale of both hope and caution, the chronicle of the battle over
the land epitomizes Russia's painful and uneven search for economic arrange-
ments best suited to its national tradition.

Between the route to capitalism taken by most post-Communist nations
and the West European and American experience, two distinctions stand
out. First, the former attempted a leap to modern liberal capitalism without key normative, legal, and economic attributes of its foundation in the
West. These included the separation of economic possession from political power, the sanctity of the contract, the impartiality of the courts, and
self-policing professional associations. Absent also were such elements of
the Western economic system—taken for granted in the West—as the
private ownership of large industrial enterprises and the right to hire and
fire workers, to charge market prices for rent and utilities, and to buy and
sell land.

Second, the attempt to implement such practices occurred within a
barebones and flawed, but real, democracy, often against well-organized
popular opposition. Few issues illustrate this predicament more vividly
than the privatization of Russian urban and agricultural land. Although the

story is far from over, the events of the first half of 2001 have probably given this revolutionary transformation a decisive momentum.

Before the 1917 Bolshevik Revolution, private ownership of land was well established in Russian cities. But no more than 10 percent of agricultural land was in private hands (those of the landed gentry, merchants, and farmers).[1] The rest belonged to the *mir*, the village commune, from which a male head of household received a land allotment and to which the plot reverted after his death.

On October 26, 1917, one of the first decrees of the Bolsheviks' first day in power abolished private ownership of land. The 1922 land code nationalized all land and prohibited its purchase, sale, bequest, and mortgage. Land in cities became state property, together with all buildings. In the countryside land was divided among the peasant families. The use of hired labor was banned. Leasing, however, was permitted, and allowed the more productive and ambitious peasants to increase their holdings. Even with severe limitations, between 1920 and 1928 these family farms produced an abundance of food, the like of which Soviet Russia would not know for the rest of the twentieth century.

In the next four years (1929–33), Stalin's murderous collectivization destroyed family farms. More than five million hardworking peasant families, each averaging five to seven members,[2] were labeled *kulaks* (literally "fist," a pejorative for a well-to-do peasant), stripped of all their possessions, and exiled to the swamps and forests of the north, where many died of disease, starvation, and exhaustion from punitive labor. Those remaining in the villages were robbed even of seed grain by state requisitions, and an additional seven to eight million starved to death in 1932–33 alone. Almost six decades of de facto serfdom followed, as peasants were denied internal passports, prohibited from leaving their villages, and forced to work in collective farms for meager—and irregular—payments in kind.

Productivity plunged. Soviet agriculture was never to reach the level of the 1920s. Shortages of most staples—meat, milk, butter, flour—tormented the country. Except for a handful of the largest cities, meat was rationed. Beginning in the mid-1960s, the country that encompassed millions of acres of the world's most fertile black soil, and which before 1917 had been known as the breadbasket of Europe, imported millions of tons of grain annually. By the 1980s every third loaf of bread sold in the USSR was made from foreign grain.[3]

From the collapsing Soviet Union, Russia inherited almost 89 million acres of state-owned land in urban and industrial areas and 27,000 collective farms on 548 million acres of agricultural land—the latter territory four times the size of France. Forty million people, or one-fourth of the Russian population, derived their livelihood from agriculture. At least 80 percent of the collective farms were de facto bankrupt and survived with state subsidies that amounted to 10 percent of the Soviet gross domestic product.

⁂

In November and December 1990, under Boris Yeltsin's chairmanship, the Congress of People's Deputies of Russia, then part of the Soviet Union, adopted three laws that were to form the legal foundation for the first stage of land reform. The laws "On Land Reform," "On The Peasant Farm," and "On Private Property" repudiated the state monopoly on land, transferred—free of charge—the ownership of agricultural land from the state to private individuals and collective farms, and required farms to reorganize as joint-stock companies. The legislative package established procedures for dividing land and assets among collective farm members and employees and affirmed the unconditional right of peasants to leave a state farm with their fair share of land and assets and to set up individual farms.

In addition to peasants, land was to be distributed to any other qualified individuals who requested it and intended to use it for agricultural purposes. The laws acknowledged the existence of private property and permitted the buying and selling of land. (The latter right was promptly nullified by the leftist plurality in the legislature, which pushed through a ten-year moratorium on the sale of land.) The next year, an amendment to the constitution of the Russian Soviet Federated Socialist Republic recorded the right to land ownership by legal entities other than the state.

In December 1991, a few days before the demise of the Soviet Union, Yeltsin's presidential decree ordered collective farms to expedite the transfer of land to their members, who were to hold a number of shares commensurate with the duration of their work on the farm. The decree also allowed the sale and lease of land shares to other collective farm members (though not to outsiders).

Over the next five years, twelve presidential decrees and government resolutions confirmed the right of and outlined procedures for former collective farm employees to obtain their shares of land and property, to exchange those shares for physical assets, and to leave collective farms (kolkhozy and sovkhozy) for private farms. Adopted in a national referendum on December 12, 1993, the constitution of the Russian Federation declared that land could be private property (article 9) and affirmed the right of citizens and their organizations to "to have land in private ownership" (article 36).

In this gradual but steady legislative advance toward private land, two documents may be considered radical breakthroughs. Signed seventy-six years plus one day after the Bolshevik decree that abolished private ownership of land, the October 27, 1993, presidential decree, "On the Regulation of Land Relations and Development of Agrarian Reform," annulled the moratorium on the sale of land and specified procedures for the registration of private ownership of land and the issuance of land deeds. The decree gave collective farmers the right to use their land shares however they chose without the approval of their fellow-shareholders.

The March 7, 1996, decree, "On Realization of the Constitutional Rights of Citizens Concerning Land," gave the peasants complete freedom to dispose of their land shares. Their shares could be sold, exchanged, bequeathed, leased, or given away. The procedures for leaving the collective farm were simplified, and local authorities and collective farm chairmen were ordered to complete the issuance of deeds. A year later, a May 16, 1997, presidential decree allowed industrial enterprises to privatize the land on which they were located.[4]

By 1998, three-quarters of the Russian population owned a piece of land, no matter how small. Twenty-two million urban families became legal owners of garden and dacha (country house) plots.[5] In the countryside 90 percent of the former collective farms became joint-stock companies or cooperatives. Some 345 million acres of state-owned agricultural land (63 percent of the total) became the property of individuals or the joint-stock companies, in which 12 million members of former collective farms held shares.[6] In addition, 16 million rural families held the deeds for household (priusadebnye) plots, on which they grew food for personal consumption and produced most of Russia's vegetables and fruit for sale. Private farms numbered 270,000. Relative to the size of the land owned by the state before 1990, Russia redistributed much more land than did Mexico or Venezuela—the countries whose land reforms had been considered among the most successful.[7]

∽

The 1990–97 reforms denationalized most of Russia's urban and arable land. In the cities the presidential decrees gave privatized industrial enterprises the right to own the land under their plants and factories and endowed millions of city residents with deeds to their beloved dacha plots. In the countryside, as mentioned, collective farms were transformed into joint-stock companies from which the peasants could leave with their share of land and property.

Yet without detailed federal laws approved by the national parliament, the land, though denationalized, had not become bona fide private and thus an integral part of the fledgling market economy. Many Soviet laws remained on the books. Absent was even the memory of private ownership of land, which was so instrumental in the successful privatization of land in most post-Communist nations of Central and Eastern Europe. (Land there had been privatized not by equal distribution, but by restitution to former owners or their heirs.)

As usual, the gray legal area was filled with local interpretation and implementation of Yeltsin's decrees on ownership for commercial and residential purposes. Thus, the privatization of land belonging to industrial enterprises and firms in the cities proceeded apace in St. Petersburg, Novgorod, Nizhniy Novgorod, and Tver. At the same time, the politically well-connected Moscow city authorities succeeded in exempting the capital from the privatization decrees and in making the city itself the owner of all the land within its boundaries. That land could be leased (for up to forty-nine years) but not owned by private businesses. In most other Russian cities, myriad bureaucratic regulations entangled land privatization. In the end, only 3 percent of Russian private industrial enterprises owned the land under their plants.[8]

The situation with arable land was similar. As mentioned, some 12 million former collective farmers nominally held shares of land and equipment in the abolished *kolkhozy* and *sovkhozy*, and any private individual or commercial enterprise could receive land from local authorities (provided the buyer pledged to use it for agricultural purposes). But after the initial rush, when 270,000 private farms had been set up (most by migrants from cities or city commercial firms), the private farm movement came to a virtual stand-still. There were serious economic obstacles: a weak banking sector, difficul-ties in obtaining loans, and the peasants' de facto inability to use land as collateral (a presidential decree notwithstanding). But, most important, family farming had been dead for four generations, while the memory of the *kulaks'* fate was very much alive. Few Russians were willing to risk their families' futures without strong legal guarantees in the form of federal laws.

Federal legislation was urgently needed to provide the legal where-withal for making denationalized land fully private and for making privati-zation irreversible. Not surprisingly, the most ferocious and intractable political battle over the privatization of land was joined over compendiums of laws collected in the civil and land codes.

Affirming the right to private ownership of land, article 36 of the con-stitution stipulates that rules and regulations governing the use of land are to be further elaborated by federal laws. Submitted to the Duma by the government in June 1994, chapter 17 of the civil code was to provide such laws. Yet the very title of the chapter, "The Right of Land Ownership and Other Real Estate Rights," all but doomed the section of the civil code in a parliament where the left had plurality. The leftist deputies succeeded in deleting the words *private property* from all but one article of the code, where the mention survived only as a quote from the constitution. Because of chapter 17 the code was about to be voted down. Confronted with a choice of no post-Soviet civil code at all or a civil code without the land chapter, the Kremlin retreated and agreed to suspend the enactment of chapter 17 indefinitely.

The stakes were higher still in the fight over the land code, without which the reform's legal framework remained "fragile and ambiguous," and private property rights had little protection.[9] In June 1997, the Duma passed a code that prohibited the purchase and sale of agricultural land and banned foreign ownership. Yeltsin quickly vetoed the bill and added, "I have said and I will never get tired of repeating: Land in Russia should be bought and sold. This is how it is in the entire civilized world. It should be the property of the peasantry, and they themselves should decide what to do with it."[10]

Two months later the Duma overrode the veto. Citing "flagrant procedural violations," especially absentee voting, and calling the code "the most reactionary measure ever passed by the Russian parliament,"[11] Yeltsin refused to sign it into law and appealed to the Constitutional Court. A reconciliation commission was established to work out a compromise version of the code. Yet in February 1998, after the Federation Council upheld the presidential veto, Yeltsin again declared that he would not sign a code that did not permit private ownership of land or land sales. The Kremlin forwarded two dozen corrections to the compromise version. The Duma rejected most of them and passed yet another version of the bill that banned the sales.

Having battled each other to a standstill, and with the financial crisis unfolding in the summer and fall of 1998, both sides abandoned the land code fight for the remaining year and a half of the Yeltsin presidency.

In the middle of the national political stalemate, history was made in the small town of Balakovo in Saratov province. In the first week of March 1998, amid heckling by Communist protesters, Russia's first land auction in eighty years was held in a local cinema. In two hours twenty plots of state-owned urban and farm land were sold for what was then a huge sum of money—486,000 rubles, or $80,000. The haul was five times larger than the amount organizers had anticipated.[12]

The auction took place five months after the regional legislature, spurred by Governor Dmitry Ayatskov, passed a law allowing the selling and buying of land. The Duma passed a resolution condemning Ayatskov. Yeltsin awarded him the Order for Services to the Fatherland. Since then, seventeen regions have followed Saratov in allowing the sale of agricultural land.

◁∾▷

Although failing in the ultimate goal of privatizing Russia's land, the panoply of laws created in the 1990s laid a foundation for a final legislative breakthrough, which had to await a change in the balance of political power. As with other key liberal reforms, the moment arrived after the December 1999 parliamentary election, which shifted the legislative plurality to the center-right after eight years of dominance by the left. The momentum became stronger still after the election of Yeltsin's handpicked successor, Vladimir Putin, three months later.

The Communists continued to command the allegiance of one-fourth to one-third of the Russian electorate, and their faction was still the largest; but they no longer had a plurality in the third Duma. Together with its rural allies, the Agro-Industrial group, or the Agrarians, the opposition Communist Party of the Russian Federation (KPRF) had 131 seats in the 450-strong lower house (Federal Assembly), compared with 140 for the progovernment Unity, allied with the People's Deputy faction. This alliance plus four liberal or propresidential parties—Fatherland-All Russia (OVR) with 37 seats; the Union of Right Forces (SPS), with 32; the Liberal Democratic Party of Russia (LDPR), 21; and Yabloko, 16—held a majority of 246 seats. For the first time in post-Communist Russia's nine-year history, the parliament had a stable pro-Kremlin and proreform majority.

In January 2001, the government brought to the Duma floor an updated version of chapter 17 of the civil code. Its opening article declared that "individuals having in their possession a plot of land have the right to sell, gift, mortgage, and lease it or dispose of it in any way they wish."[13] Many experts saw the code's main achievement as precisely this "absolute and unconditional acceptance of the right of individuals and private entities to own land."[14]

But unlike the 1991–97 presidential decrees, the code went well beyond declarations. Its purpose, amply fulfilled, was to provide a detailed and practical guide to commercial land transactions.[15] With agricultural land excluded to facilitate passage in the Duma, the code's twenty-eight articles described ownership rights of private citizens, corporations, municipalities, and the federal state. The document set forth norms and rules for relations between landowners on the one hand and all other legal entities, including the state, on the other.[16]

The code clarified a number of previously ambiguous areas of the real estate law, including the property rights to the land under purchased buildings. Article 273 stated that the transfer of property rights to such structures automatically presupposed the transfer of land ownership. Other articles established mechanisms for the purchase of land by city authorities and the norms governing the relationship between cities as landowners and private owners of buildings. In all such transactions the code granted private citizens the same rights as it did municipal governments.

In the words of Pavel Krasheninnikov, one of the code's authors and legislative sponsors and the chairman of the Duma's Legislative Committee, an updated chapter 17 provided a "legal foundation for and defense of the right to own land both for private citizens and legal entities."[17] The law's enactment would "stimulate not only the economy of Russia but also the emergence of a civilized, lawful state in our country."[18]

Although agricultural land was excluded, the left opposition was every bit as determined as in 1994. In the first reading, on January 25, the legislation cleared the Federal Assembly by three votes and the upper chamber (the Council of the Federation) by one vote. After the passage of the bill, the Communist-Agrarian faction walked out of the chamber in protest.[19]

Stating that it was "time for Russia to review a blanket ban on land sales,"[20] President Putin gave strong support to land reform in his first annual state of Russia address to the Duma on April 3, 2001. He endorsed a new land code and called for "not impeding the development of the land market" and for "formalizing the most modern forms and methods of regulation of land relations."[21]

Public opinion was sharply divided: At the end of March 2001, 48 percent of Russians supported buying and selling agricultural land with or without restrictions, and 45 percent thought that such transactions ought to be banned. (As with other liberal reforms, age and education were the variables most responsible for the difference in attitudes.)[22] As is his wont, Putin proceeded cautiously. At a Kremlin meeting, he promised the Communist and Agrarian leaders to exclude agricultural land from the code. The promise was given, in the words of an unnamed Kremlin official, so as "not to stir up public opinion."[23]

At the same time, Putin instructed the government to draft a federal law on the sale of agricultural land and to submit it to the Duma in the summer of 2001. The president also suggested letting the regions "decide for themselves when they can start selling and buying agricultural land."[24] Putin's chief economic adviser Andrei Illarionov dismissed the exemption of agricultural land from sale as a mere "temporary compromise."[25]

Describing the essence of the land code, Krasheninnikov said in Moscow in May 2001 that the document "develops chapter 17."[26] Indeed, in the code's nineteen chapters and 106 articles, land is a commodity. The document defines different categories of nonagricultural land—for instance, forest, water-covered, industrial, transportation-zoned, environmentally protected, reserved for state purposes, or withdrawn from market (museums, national parks, endangered species habitats, or access to coastal strips)—and provides rules for their custody or sale.

The code greatly simplifies the privatization of land. Deadlines are established for the examination of privatization applications by local authorities. The latter cannot refuse to sell land to private individuals or corporations unless it was specifically designated by federal law as withdrawn from the market or reserved for municipal needs.[27] The code provides safeguards for private owners at all stages of a transaction—acquisition, use, or buyback by the authorities for public needs.

There are no limits on the amount of land that individuals or corporations can own and no restrictions on foreign ownership. Reinforcing the civil code, the land code views a building and the land on which it stands as a single real estate entity. Industrial enterprises, which, together with roads, occupy almost 43 million acres, can choose whether to buy the land on which they are located or to continue to rent it from local municipalities. In accordance with Putin's plan, the code omits agricultural land, yet the document contains no ban on buying or selling such real estate.

Given potential state and local revenues from taxation or direct sales, the economic stakes are huge. Last year the Saratov region received over 300 million rubles, or $11.5 million,[28] from land sales and taxes. "We are paupers," wrote Russian experts, "largely because our main wealth, land, is not appraised, and normal land taxes are not being paid."[29]

According to Krasheninnikov, in the year 2000 more than one million land transactions took place in Russia.[30] The absence of legislation had forced those sales into the shadow economy, where the land market existed for years and included some of the most fertile arable land.[31] A report prepared by the Moscow State Legal Academy pointed to the existence of "an illegal, criminal turnover of land" and the "enormous criminalization" of the real estate market.[32] In all, the new code covers industrial and municipal land worth an estimated $1 trillion—the sum more than three times larger than the country's officially recorded GDP.[33] (At least 40 percent of the Russian economy is in the "gray" and "black" areas.)

⟨✐⟩

What mattered to the left was the principle: For the first time the constitutional right to private ownership of land was to be backed by the Russian parliament and endowed with enabling legislation. Once private ownership and residential and industrial real estate became the object of commercial transactions, in time—perhaps a short time—agricultural land would follow suit. As the leader of the Agrarians, Nikolai Kharitonov, put it, "The problem is that the draft opens a door, gives a loophole that could be widened later."[34]

In the left's opposition to the bill, ideology blended with powerful political imperatives. The Communists' lobbying and political blackmail had extracted trillions of rubles—amounting to 2–3 percent of the Russian GDP annually over the past ten years—in "loans" and outright grants to bankrupt collective agriculture. As with industrial subsidies, most of the money never reached the peasants but was stolen along the way by local authorities and collective farm management.

In turn, the collective farms' chairmen—who lorded over their villages because of their complete control of the meager but vital resources on which the daily subsistence of the villagers depends (tractors, granaries, schools, fuel, wood for heating and cooking, pastures for cows and sheep)—spared no effort to ensure that the peasants voted the "right," that is, left, way. Next to the rapidly dwindling cohort of World War II veterans, no other segment provided as reliable a political base for the Communists as the villages, many of them impoverished, mired in alcoholism, and populated largely by older men and women.

In the words of a leader of the centrist Fatherland-All Russia faction in the Duma, unprivatized land is the Communist Party's "last ideological bastion: if it falls, [the party] simply will have nothing to say to the people."[35] The leader of the liberal Yabloko faction, Grigory Yavlinsky, attributed the Communists' resistance to the "fear of losing the votes of the downtrodden peasants" and predicted that after the code's implementation the Agrarian faction in the next Duma would no longer be Communist in its orientation.[36]

For the first time since Putin's election in March 2000, the Communists began attacking the government and even the popular president. In the months leading to the Duma vote, the left loosed a rhetorical barrage unequalled in hysteria and crudity since the castigation of Yeltsin during the

1996 presidential campaign. Adopting the land code would be "a crime against the nation," the Communist Party (KPRF) chairman, Gennady Zyuganov, charged after the debate on the code began in the Duma. "It would be war."[37]

After Putin endorsed land reform in his state of Russia address, the Communists accused the president of pushing Russia further into poverty and demanded the resignation of Prime Minister Mikhail Kasyanov. In early May the KPRF led a protest march in Moscow and called for a "struggle against the antipeople regime of President Putin."[38] Three weeks later, with the Duma vote looming, Zyuganov said in a radio interview that

> [the former acting prime minister Egor] Gaidar's people were there [writing the code] and I suspect there were some CIA people, and they built into the code some articles whereby the whole country can be sold out. If this code is adopted the country will go under.[39]

A week later Zyuganov called on his party to "wage an all-out offensive" against the Kremlin, which had "camouflaged" its "devastating liberal approach" and "antipeople essence."[40] On the same day the leader of the Agrarian faction of the Duma, Nikolai Kharitonov, announced that the faction's deputies might resign from the parliament if the code passed.[41] At a press conference on the eve of the vote, Zyuganov warned of a civil war the moment a foreign owner stepped onto Russia's black-earth soil.[42]

On June 15, the day of the vote, leftist demonstrators surrounded the Duma and temporarily blocked traffic along Okhotny Ryad Street, a few hundred yards from Red Square. The protestors held a streetwide banner reading "We won't allow trading in Russian land" and signs declaring "No to private property." Red flags were waved and cries of "Putin traitor!" and "Shame! Shame!" were heard. Addressing the crowd, Zyuganov called for civil disobedience, including the blocking of the country's roads, if the bill passed.[43]

Inside, the Communist and Agrarian deputies—clenched fists in the air and a banner reading "Selling land means selling Russia" aloft—blocked access to the rostrum to prevent the minister of trade and economic development, German Gref, from introducing the legislation. Unable to restore order, speaker Gennady Seleznyov, a Communist, called for a break in the proceedings.

After the session was resumed, Gref, shielded by proreform deputies who formed a protective circle around him, spoke from the floor through a handheld microphone while the chanting Communists and Agrarians attempted to drown out his speech. In the end the leftists marched out of the chamber. The code passed by a vote of 251 to 222. The legislation's passage in the third and final reading in July was assured.

Following the June 15 vote, a statement by Zyuganov charged that

> all Russia is being put up for shameful bargaining, in which foreigners, stateless people [the code words for Jews], and anyone with a fat purse can take part. We will not allow mercenaries and unscrupulous oligarchs to be the proprietors of our land.[44]

An ardent supporter of the reform and chairman of the Peasant Party of Russia, Yuri Chernichenko—who began advocating land privatization at the dawn of Mikhail Gorbachev's *glasnost* in 1987—described the fight over the code as the Communists' "last real battle in Russia. Today they felt quite vividly for the first time that land is literally slipping from under their feet."[45]

In April 2001, as Mikhail Kasyanov urged the Duma to pass a package of reform bills—judicial, land, pension, tax, labor relations—he promised that their adoption and implementation would make Russia "a different country—more advanced, free-market and democratic."[46] Thanking the parliament the day after the land code passed, Kasyanov called the vote "one more serious brick in the economic foundation" of a new Russia.[47]

⁂

Between 1992 and 2001, post-Communist Russia was engaged in an epic struggle to turn 89 million acres of urban and industrial land and 548 million acres of agricultural land into market commodities capable of enriching millions of Russians, boosting state and local revenues, securing urban renewal and new housing, and providing the country with an abundance of food. The road has been rocky and will still be lengthy.

The adoption of chapter 17 of the civil code and of the land code—to recall Churchill's famous phrase—is not the end. It is not even the beginning of the end. Yet it may well prove to be the end of a long and painful beginning.[48]

7

From State-Owned Justice
to a Law-Based State
2002

Post-Soviet Russia inherited justice owned by the state, all-powerful prosecutors, timid and demoralized judges, decrepit courts, no trials by jury, and a conviction rate of over 99 percent. Within less than a decade after the 1991 revolution the courts—from district courts to constitutional—had vigorously challenged authorities, including the regional governors and the president; hundreds of thousands of Russians had sued the government, and many had won; and a Russian environmentalist had been acquitted of charges of espionage brought against him by the heir to the KGB—the first such acquittal ever in Russian history. Epitomizing these achievements, the first post-Soviet criminal procedural code has brought to Russia some of the key elements of a modern system of justice.

Democracy and liberal capitalism require powerful, respected, and independent institutions to mediate the interests of the state and the citizen and to dispense justice fairly and efficiently. The most important such institution is the judiciary.

In the West, the rule of law emerged from centuries of political conflict and institutional and intellectual growth. Russia has now had one decade to begin to recapitulate those developments. In the 1990s, following seven decades of totalitarian terror, secrecy, arbitrariness, and corruption, Russian courts began to acquire the authority, resources, and will to stand up to the Russian state. Now, with the passage of a new criminal procedural code and related statutory reforms in December 2001, the long trek toward a true Russian *Rechtsstaat*—a lawful state—has achieved another milestone.

In the Soviet Union, justice, like everything else, was owned by the state. The Decree on Courts, signed by Lenin a month after the Bolsheviks seized power in 1917, pronounced the existing court system "bourgeois," "unwieldy," and "expensive" and abolished jury trials, introduced in Russia in 1864. The courts became another cog in the elaborate machine serving the political needs of the Soviet regime.

Membership in the Communist Party was a requirement for judgeship. Like any other Communist, a judge was subject to party discipline and followed orders. In many court cases, orders from local authorities (the so-called "telephone law") supplemented the party's policy line, laid down by the Central Committee and enforced by local party organizations. The local party apparatus controlled a judge's tenure in office and his or her promotion by "recommending" or "not recommending" the judge for single-candidate "elections." At times the infamous "troika" tribunals entirely bypassed even such caricatures of courts. Those tribunals meted out, often in absentia, hundreds of thousands of death sentences during the purges of the 1930s.

In salaries and, even more important, in nonmonetary perks, judges were among the lowest white-collar employees. Their salaries were "barely adequate."[1] Most judges in the 1970s and 1980s did not have individual apartments but lived in single rooms in communal apartments or dorms, or rented meager space in private homes.[2] Courthouses were among the "worst maintained" of all public buildings.[3]

The institution of procuracy epitomized the state ownership of justice. In name, the Soviet procurators bore a resemblance to Scottish procurators fiscal, district prosecutors appointed by the lord advocate. In the Soviet version, however, procurators had the authority not only to investigate and prosecute crimes but also to monitor "legality" in their districts, including judges' conduct in courts. Invariably party members in excellent standing, they were at the pinnacle of the local power elite, together with the first secretary of the party committee, the head of the local branch of the secret police, and the head of the military district.

Procurators wielded unchecked power of search and seizure, arrest, and unlimited pretrial detention, which was often used to force a confession. If dissatisfied with a verdict (in most cases, an acquittal), a procurator could seek a retrial. The acquittal rate in the Soviet Union was a fraction of 1 percent of all verdicts.[4]

Judges and courts rarely provided more than a background to the all-powerful procurators' efforts to convict. After assigning a case file to a judge, a prosecutor often did not even appear at trial; he fully trusted the judge to do his work for the prosecution. When evidence was flimsy even for a Soviet judge, the trial was discontinued, and the case file returned to the prosecution for supplementary investigation (*dosledovanie*). Since the criminal code did not permit adjournment of a trial for longer than three days, once the prosecution amended its case the defendant stood for another trial (sometimes a third) for the same crime.

Unable to interpret laws, serving as props in scripted political trials (including the pillorying of those involved in underground economic activities), and beholden to prosecutors in criminal cases, Soviet judges were relatively independent only in civil matters, such as property divorces and disputes between neighbors.

The Rokotov-Faibishenko case of the early 1960s epitomized the status of law, the courts, and justice in the Soviet Union. Several young men and women were charged with providing tourists and Soviet citizens with currency exchanges, which were prohibited, as were all private economic activities. The defendants were tried and duly sentenced to five years in jail, the maximum sentence specified by the criminal code. Infuriated by such leniency, the party's first secretary, Nikita S. Khrushchev, ordered the law changed. The Supreme Soviet quickly adopted a law mandating capital punishment for currency crimes. The defendants were resentenced, and the two leaders of the group were promptly executed.

♱

In the late 1980s, *glasnost* revealed the enormous complicity of impotent courts, shamelessly manipulated by political authorities, in the reign of terror and the lawlessness of the past seven decades. Under Boris Yeltsin's chairmanship, the Supreme Soviet of Russia—then still part of the Soviet Union—began to draft and adopt initial reform measures.

The breakthrough occurred in July 1991, when the legislature passed a law creating the Constitutional Court of the Russian Federation. Appointed to fixed twelve-year terms, the justices were to be independent of the executive and legislative branches, immune from prosecution, and irremovable. Unprecedented in all Russian history, the court was to rule on the constitutionality of international treaties, federal laws, the laws of constituent autonomous republics, and the codes, laws, and regulations governing the legal system. As leading students of post-Soviet legal reform observed, until then "at no time in Russian history . . . were the rulers obliged to obey their own laws."[5]

Three months later the Supreme Soviet of Russia approved a blueprint for a comprehensive and radical legal revolution: *The Concept of Judicial Reform*, a hundred-page manifesto written by nine lawyers and legal scholars. The document spelled out the measures necessary to empower judges and make Russian courts independent of the state and equal in power to the executive and legislative branches. The proposals included life tenure for all judges. The right to discipline and remove judges would rest solely with peer associations. To lessen the chance for manipulation by local authorities, judges' salaries would be paid from the federal budget rather than local budgets; judges would be guaranteed housing and access to health care.

The document struck at the heart of the procuracy's power by suggesting the transfer of all the procurators' key prerogatives to the courts. Judges would be given the power to review administrative acts and the exclusive right to authorize pretrial detention, search and seizure, and wiretapping. Judges, not procurators, would ensure the legality of trials.

The accusatory bias of Soviet proceedings—in which the prosecution and the judge for the most part worked hand in glove to convict and the prosecutor's rights far outweighed the defense counsel's—would be replaced with a more adversarial procedure, with defense and prosecution more or less on an equal footing and judges as impartial arbiters. Most critical, juries would be revived.

The 1993 constitution immensely strengthened the cause of the Russian legal revolution by incorporating many postulates of *The Concept of Judicial Reform*. Proclaiming Russia a "lawful state" with the main duties of "recognition, observance, and defense of rights of the individual and the citizen" (articles 1 and 2), the constitution affirms—in terse, commanding sentences—the features of such a state. Their importance is underscored by each meriting a separate article:

- "Everyone is equal before law and the court."

- "Everyone is guaranteed the right to defend his rights and liberties in court."

- "Judges are independent and follow only the constitution of the Russian Federation and federal law."

- "Judges are irremovable."

- "Judges are immune [from prosecution]" (literally, "inviolable," or "*neprikosnovenny*").

- "Legal proceedings are conducted on the basis of competition between and equality of the sides."

- "The funding of the courts is to be obtained solely from the federal budget and is designed to secure comprehensive and independent dispensation of justice."

The constitution guarantees Russian citizens the right to a defense attorney from the moment of detention, arrest, or notice of charges. A person is considered innocent until guilt is proved in accordance with procedures "specified by federal laws." Only the court may authorize arrest, detention, search of a private residence, or violation of the privacy of correspondence. The constitution also gives those charged with crimes carrying the death penalty the right to a trial by jury. (Even before the constitution was adopted, the first jury trial since 1917 was held in Saratov, on November 15, 1993. The two defendants charged with murder were acquitted.)

❦

Following the initial design, the reforms aimed simultaneously at creating and strengthening the independence of judges and courts (through immunities, self-governance, self-policing, funding, and physical security of judges) on the one hand and at dramatically expanding the courts' jurisdiction on the other.

Beginning with the 1999 "On the Status of Judges," a series of measures signed into laws by President Yeltsin secured life appointment for judges and protected them from disciplinary sanctions by any authority other than the judges' own corporate bodies. The latter, created in the early 1990s, include regional conferences of judges that elect regional or republican councils of judges, establish judicial qualifications collegia (JQCs), and nominate delegates to the national Congress of Judges. The congress, meeting at least once every three years, elects the national governing body, the Council of Judges, as well as the Supreme Judicial Qualification Collegium (SJQC).

The Russian president appoints district and regional court judges only after the nominees have been examined and endorsed by the appropriate JQC and the Supreme Court. (Nominated by the president, the justices of the Constitutional and Supreme Courts must be approved by the upper house of the national parliament, the Council of the Federation.) Before the "appointment without limit" (that is, for life) is conferred, judges must serve a probation—ten years for those appointed in 1992 and 1993 and three years for those appointed after 1995. By 1998, almost one in four judges (in district, regional, and republican supreme courts and the Supreme Court of the Russian Federation) held life tenure. They included 77 of 111 justices of the Supreme Court and 75 percent of the judges on the regional and republican supreme courts.[6]

Judges are immune from recall, dismissal, or prosecution; only a local JQC can remove immunity. The SJQC must then confirm those decisions. Until more restrictive laws were passed in December 2001, a judge could not be arrested even if caught in the act of committing a crime and could not be prosecuted (or summoned) even on such minor charges as driving while intoxicated, speeding, or disturbing the peace.

The transfer of the administration of the courts from the Ministry of Justice to the Judicial Department of the Supreme Court strengthened judicial independence, as well as the separation of the judicial and executive branches of power. The department's regional units were created at that time and attached to regional courts and the supreme courts of the constituent ethnic republics.

Although still meager by Western, and especially U.S., standards, judges' salaries were increased to the equivalent of several hundred dollars a month, becoming comparable to those of government officials of middle rank and putting judges within Russia's new middle class. Their compensation packages included free transportation and priority access to apartments, health care, and child care.[7]

During most of the 1990s, perennial delays and budget cuts diluted the benign effect of funding the court from federal (rather than local) budgets (to make judges less susceptible to pressure and manipulation by local authorities). A 1999 law sought to redress the problem by granting courts the right to draw back-payments directly from government accounts without additional authorization.

The law's passage highlighted the changes both in the status of the Russian courts and in the methods available for successfully addressing their concerns. In 1998, desperate to alleviate the financial crisis brought about by a mounting budget deficit (and following the precedent established in 1997), the government instituted a sequester—that is, an across-the-board slashing of the budget. Citing the provisions of a 1996 law that prohibited reducing the courts' budgets without the consent of the national Congress of Judges, the Supreme Court and the Supreme Arbitrazh Court (the highest court in the network of specialized commercial courts created in 1991) sued the government in the Constitutional Court, which ruled in their favor. Late that year, the financial crisis of 1998 notwithstanding, the government paid some overdue obligations and, early in 1999, passed the law authorizing the courts' direct access to government funds.[8]

Over the past decade Russian courts have steadily expanded their purview and power. Among the most significant advances have been the review of procurators' decisions, challenges to local and federal authorities, and constitutional tests of local and federal laws.

The courts won a significant, though far from complete, victory over the procurators in the battle for control of criminal procedures : Judges acquired the authority to "review procedural legality and grounds for procuratorial decisions" regarding pretrial detention when inmates appealed.[9] (The courts now review around seventy thousand complaints of wrongful arrest every year and rule in favor of one-fifth of them.)[10] Since 1995, police and procurators must obtain court permission for wiretapping and for violating the privacy of personal correspondence. Implementing article 120, section 2, of the constitution—which empowered judges to "rule according to law" when they established "incongruity" between acts of "state bodies" and the law—district and regional courts began to review administrative acts of both local and federal authorities.

≪⁄∞

Nothing delineated the change from Soviet days more starkly than the previously unimaginable ability of citizens to sue the authorities—and win! Russian citizens now sought redress in matters ranging from rescinded hunting licenses and curtailed unemployment benefits to procedural matters in elections to the national parliament, tariffs on interregional commerce, and privatization of state assets.[11] Although implementation of the court rulings was spotty, between 1993 and 1998 the number of such suits increased from 9,701 to 91,300, with the courts ruling for the plaintiffs in more than three out of four cases.[12] Citing cases in which judges ruled against local and federal executives and legislatures, leading students of Russian post-Soviet jurisprudence concluded that "the ordinary courts in Russia now play an active, and apparently independent, role in safeguarding fundamental civil rights."[13]

For the first time in Russian history, the Kremlin was no longer immune from court challenge. Dismissed by presidential decree in December 1994 following a row with the head of the regional administration appointed by the president, the mayor of Vladivostok, Viktor Cherepkov, sued Yeltsin in a Moscow district court. After a lengthy battle, the court found the dismissal unlawful; twelve days later Yeltsin signed a decree restoring Cherepkov to office.

Along the way the courts shaped and encouraged Russia's first class action lawsuit. In 1998 the government introduced a coefficient for calculating monthly pension payments based on wages at retirement and length of service. The law established temporary restrictions on the coefficient's value—in effect lowering pensions for millions of retirees entitled to higher-than-average benefits. A few months later many of Russia's 38 million pensioners went to court. First the Supreme Court, on appeal, sided with a plaintiff and ordered the Ministry of Labor and the pension fund to recalculate benefits.[14] A month later a district court in Novosibirsk ruled in favor of another pensioner, established a different calculation

procedure, and raised the plaintiff's pension.[15] By spring 2000 an estimated 220,000 pensioners' suits were pending. The Supreme Court
instructed the government and the Duma to enact legislation clarifying
disputed provisions of the pension laws. In May 2001 the coefficient
"restrictions" were rescinded.[16]

The courts' jurisdiction dramatically widened in October 1995 when a
Supreme Court "instruction" opened the door to district and regional
courts' review of the constitutionality of the actions of local and federal
authorities. Arming the courts with the constitution has produced landmark decisions for human rights and liberties in Russia.

Constitutional reviews have upheld freedom of religion in the face of a
reactionary and discriminatory law passed in 1997 by a Duma dominated
by leftist "popular patriots." Aimed against foreign denominations that had
become increasingly popular in Russia, the law gave local authorities the
power to deny registration (and thus legal status) to such groups if they did
not satisfy often hard-to-meet criteria.

In invalidating such denials, courts all over Russia drew on the freedom
of religion clause:

> Everyone is guaranteed freedom of conscience, freedom of
> religious beliefs, including the right to practice individually or
> with others any religion or none, freely choose, have, and spread
> religious and other convictions, and act in accordance with
> them (chapter 2, article 28).

In March 1999 a Moscow judge stayed a ban of the Jehovah's Witnesses
by ruling that a panel of experts must decide the validity of alleged violations (the church had been accused of "breaking up families and preaching
intolerance").[17] Two months later the Ministry of Justice reregistered the
church nationwide. In the same month a court in Magadan threw out the
ban of a Pentecostal church.[18]

Among the most encouraging developments in establishing the rule
of law has been the application of the constitution even in seemingly triv-
ial cases. Citing the equal protection clause of the 1993 constitution
("Everyone is equal before the law and the court," chapter 2, article 19), a
judge sided with a foreign plaintiff in Ekaterinburg, who challenged the

habitual overcharging of foreigners in Russian hotels, and awarded damages in the amount of the overpayment.[19]

By 1997 the courts began to challenge the state in its sanctum sanctorum: the armed forces and the three-hundred-year-old draft. Drawing on the constitutional right to a nonmilitary ("civilian") alternative to military service (article 59, section 3), many judges threw out criminal charges of desertion and draft-dodging against those who had claimed that right.[20] Although an estimated 1,500 Russian young men request alternative service annually, there were only two convictions: one of a Jehovah's Witness in the Black Sea resort city of Sochi and the other of an antidraft activist in Obninsk in the Moscow region. Both were overturned on appeal.[21]

The constitution has left it to the Duma to spell out the criteria for granting requests for alternative service and the forms of such service. With leftist pluralities in the pre-2000 Dumas, such legislation would have been dead on arrival. Introduced by the government in February 2002, the law on alternative service now has a good chance of passage in the next few months.[22]

✍

As described in article 125 of the constitution, the Constitutional Court of the Russian Federation is charged with "establishing conformity to the Constitution" of federal laws and administrative acts of the president, the government, and the Duma. A court finding of unconstitutionality invalidates laws and acts. The Constitutional Court has proved the single most effective instrument of the post-Soviet legal revolution.

Until the post-Soviet criminal procedural code was adopted in December 2001, the Constitutional Court, in effect, amended the existing code by reviewing the constitutionality of the code's provisions based on cases before it. In the process, as a prominent Russian lawyer put it, "the existing code [was] gradually being brought into compliance with due process standards."[23]

Among the major victories for human rights was the insistence on trial by jury for crimes that carry the death penalty. Though granted by article 47 of the constitution, jury trials were in place in only nine of eighty-nine "subjects of the Federation" (regions, ethnic republics, Moscow, and St. Petersburg) and available to only 20 percent of Russian citizens. In February 1999 the court noted unequal access to trial by jury and cited the equal protection clause as grounds for suspending the use of the death penalty. (For two years preceding the court's decision, President Yeltsin had effectively abolished the death penalty by regularly pardoning all those sentenced.)

In another attack on the Soviet legal legacy, an April 1999 ruling narrowed the grounds for "supplementary investigation" (when, finding a prosecution's case too weak for conviction, a judge would "return" the case to a prosecutor to amend it). The court allowed such investigation only when procedural laws were violated in pretrial investigation (for instance, if there were a failure to provide a translator for non-Russian speakers, or a conflict of interest for a defense counsel).[24]

Between 1996 and 1998, the court tackled a major remnant of the Soviet police state. The justices declared unconstitutional aspects of local and federal residence registration and residence permits (the infamous *propiskii*) as limiting the constitutional right of "everyone who is lawfully staying on the territory of the Russian Federation . . . to move freely [and] to choose place of residence" (article 27). In 1998 the court ruled that the authorities could not require citizens to produce residence permits as a precondition for issuing passports for foreign travel. (At the time, residence permits were in effect in at least one-third of Russia's eighty-nine regions, with the strictest registration requirements, as in Soviet times, in Moscow and St. Petersburg.)[25]

Among the more significant recent decisions has been the constitutional defense of a key aspect of the economic revolution: private ownership of urban land as set forth in the land code (which became effective October 29, 2001, after a bitter fight in the Duma; see chapter 6). The security of urban real estate was tested in a suit brought by a Moscow citizen against the city authorities who had invoked a city ordinance in claiming almost half her plot because it exceeded the maximum amount allowed by the ordinance.[26] In contesting the constitutionality of the ordinance, the plaintiff cited article 55, section 2, and article 55, section 3, of the constitution, which ban laws "abolishing or diminishing rights and liberties of individual and citizen." Curtailing those (though only by federal law) is allowed solely in the defense of the constitutional system, the defense of the country, and the defense of the health, rights, and "legitimate interests" of other citizens.

In siding with the plaintiff, the court also invoked article 35, section 3, which prohibits "depriving [a citizen] of [private] possession" other than by a court decision. Such "alienation" in the interests of the state is allowed only on condition of "preemptive and fair reimbursement." Citing recent decisions in which the notion of "possession" had been extended to cover privately owned real estate as well as other property, the court found the city ordinance unconstitutional and upheld the land code, which prohibits limiting the amount of legitimately acquired private urban real estate.[27]

❧

Nothing was as emblematic of the bitter contest between the legal revolution and the totalitarian legacy as the handling by Russian courts of treason charges brought by the Federal Security Service (FSB), the KGB's successor.

The most notorious case—and the most important in terms of the legal precedents it established—was the "spy" trial of Alexander Nikitin, a naval captain turned environmental activist. He was arrested by the FSB in late 1995 in St. Petersburg and charged with high treason for espionage and the disclosure of state secrets. The accused had contributed to a report by a Norwegian environmental group on the environmental damage from accidents on nuclear submarines of the Russian Northern Fleet. He argued that he had obtained the information from unclassified and publicly available sources.

The presiding judge ordered Nikitin free on bail after ten months in pretrial detention (bail was then unheard of in a treason case; it remains a rare practice in Russian criminal procedure). In October 1998 the St. Petersburg City Court returned the case to the prosecutors for supplementary investigation. In a year the prosecution returned to court with the same indictment. Within two months, in December 1999, the judge found the accused not guilty. In September 2000, on appeal by the FSB, the Supreme Court upheld the ruling—the first acquittal since October 1917 on charges of treason brought by the Russian secret police.[28]

In addition to the novelty of the acquittal, the Nikitin case was remarkable for the defense based on the constitution, the success of the strategy in the St. Petersburg City Court, and a ruling by the Constitutional Court that dealt a major blow to the secrecy that for eight decades surrounded trials initiated by the secret police.

The first issue was the legal representation of the accused. FSB investigators had initially refused to deal with the defense counsel because he was not cleared for classified information. (Instead, as the KGB did in such cases, the FSB named a lawyer, a former KGB officer, to act for Nikitin.) Responding to Nikitin's petition, in March 1996 the Constitutional Court ruled that the 1993 Law on State Secrets, which required clearance to gain access to classified information, could not be applied to the defense counsel in criminal procedures.[29] The court based its decision on the constitutional right to legal representation (article 48) and the equality of sides and competitiveness of trial procedure (article 123, section 3). The court invalidated as unconstitutional the existing procedure of admitting only FSB-vetted lawyers as counsel in cases involving classified information.

The Nikitin defense team then drew on the constitution to undermine the legality of the state secrets in the case. Though considered secret by government regulation, the information in question was not legally secret because the constitution granted everyone the right to "truthful information" about the environment (article 42) and because the Law on State Secrets excluded accidents and the state of the environment.[30]

The legality of secrecy was further undermined by the constitutional right "freely to seek, receive, pass on, produce, and disseminate information." The same article (29) mandated that federal law define state secrets. Yet such a law did not appear until more than two years after Nikitin allegedly violated state secrecy. Since the constitution bans the application of unpublished laws as well as "any normative acts" (article 15, section 3) and prohibits retroactive application of law (article 54), prosecution based on the Law on State Secrets violated the constitution.[31]

In a post-trial interview, the judge in the case explained that the prosecutors' key error was their "stubbornly ignoring the defense's assertions that one must pay attention not merely to questions of fact but also to questions of law"[32]—a concept that must have struck the KGB's successor as utterly novel and exotic. The judge added: "With this decision, we upheld the principle of judicial neutrality and insulation from outside forces. The decision is an important one, because it shows that, despite the nature of the accusation and the fact that it came from the FSB, the court followed both the letter and the spirit of the law . . . we answer only to the law."[33]

&

Between 1995 and 2000, politics and the economy impeded the legal revolution. Both the passage of new laws and the implementation of those adopted in 1991–95 suffered from the "cold civil war" between the prore-form president and a parliament dominated by the reactionary left, which voted down or stalled laws submitted by the Kremlin. Without clarifying legislation, particularly a post-Soviet criminal code, several key provisions of the constitution—most conspicuously court-sanctioned arrest, search, and seizure—could not be put into effect.

Taking advantage of the infighting in the center and the Kremlin's limited economic powers, many regions violated both the constitution and federal laws. For instance, Moscow's popular and powerful mayor ignored the rulings of the Constitutional Court and continued to restrict the right of residence under the guise of registration.

Implementation and enforcement also suffered from a lack of funding as Russia coped with the legacy of the Soviet economic collapse, an empty treasury, enormous subsidies to money-losing enterprises, and the absence of a modern tax system, which had to be created from scratch. The shortage of means precluded raising meager judicial salaries, appointing thousands of new judges needed to exercise court review of the procuracy's actions, and enforcing the constitutional right to a jury trial or a defense counsel.

To address such deficiencies, in December 2001 the Russian parliament passed, and President Vladimir Putin signed, four laws critical to the legal revolution: two that deal with judges' qualifications, appointment procedures, retirement age, and administrative, civil, and criminal liability; a law on compliance with decisions of the Constitutional Court; and, most important, a law that put into effect the post-Soviet criminal procedural code.[34] The legislative package was the product of almost two years of work by a group of progressive jurists under the leadership of Dmitry Kozak, deputy chief of the presidential administration, and Pavel Krasheninnikov, chairman of the Duma's Legislative Committee.

A number of articles in the new criminal procedural code spell a major victory for the rights of the defendants and human rights. Nearly all key provisions expand the power of the courts and diminish that of the procuracy. After a decade of heated debates, relentless efforts by reformers, and determined opposition of the procuracy, the authorization of arrest, search, seizure, and extension of pretrial detention, as well as access to information about bank accounts and mail interception, has shifted from the procuracy to the courts.[35] Absent a judge's review of arrest or extension of detention within forty-eight hours, the code orders the detained to be released immediately and unconditionally.[36]

Signaling the seriousness of the reformers' commitment to court-sanctioned procedures, an amendment to the code earmarked large sums in the 2003 federal budget[37] for the appointment of hundreds of judges required to deal with the additional duties. Kozak estimated at the time that in the next four years the state would spend an additional 44 billion rubles ($1.4 billion) to finance a "federal program of the development of the judiciary."[38]

The same amendment stipulates that the court authorization of the above measures become effective on January 1, 2004. Until then, authorization was to remain a prerogative of the procuracy (subject to a judicial review following the defendants' complaints). Already on March 14, however, in a ruling on separate complaints from three citizens in pretrial detention, the Constitutional Court struck down that amendment as violating the constitutional right to a court hearing after forty-eight hours of detention (article 22). The court ordered what is known in Russia as judicial arrest (as opposed to arrest ordered by procuracy) to become effective June 2, 2002. Calling the court's decision "extraordinary" and "sensational," the Russian liberal media interpreted the ruling as parting "with yet one more remnant of the Soviet legal practice" and hailed it as "a revolution" in criminal procedure.[39]

Other fundamental changes have been instituted as well. For example, until now, in flagrant violation of the rights of the defendants, the procuracy could easily extend pretrial detention, regardless of the seriousness of a crime, for eighteen months and then an additional six months, ostensibly to give the defense time to read the case file. Because of overcrowding, pretrial detention centers—so-called SIZOs (sledstvennye izolyatory, or investigative isolators)—were much worse than prisons or labor camps. As many Russian and international human rights organizations have testified, confinement in SIZOs, where thousands of prisoners every year contracted tuberculosis as well as other diseases, amounted to torture.

The code limits initial pretrial detention to two months. Extending the term to six months requires another court decision. Continuing incarceration must be requested by the chief procurator of a region only in the cases of "grave" and "especially grave" crimes. Holding a prisoner beyond twelve months is allowed only in "exceptional cases" and at the request of the procurator general of the Russian Federation or his deputy. Pretrial detention beyond eighteen months is forbidden; the accused must be released "immediately."[40]

A lengthy *dosledovanie* was eliminated. The prosecution will no longer have unlimited time and several tries to obtain a guilty verdict. Following the 1999 decision of the Constitutional Court, the code narrowed the grounds for returning a case to a procurator to a judge's discovery of procedural violation in the investigation. Moreover, the procuracy now has only five days to amend a case.[41]

Further, for the first time in Russian history, those indicted on minor crimes with a maximum sentence of five years can avoid trial (and pretrial detention). After the required consultation with defense counsel, an accused may plead guilty and be sentenced. A judge cannot impose a term of incarceration that exceeds two-thirds of the maximum sentence allowable for that crime.[42] Plea bargaining could reduce the number of prisoners in SIZOs by as much as half.

Other innovations include the introduction into Russian jurisprudence of the notion of bond (*zalog*), and the establishment of trial by jury. Bail—determined by the nature of the crime and the personal history of the accused—can be posted by the accused or anyone else.[43] For now, twelve-member juries are limited to cases of "grave" (*tyazhkie*) crimes, such as murder, rape, and terrorism,[44] but by January 1, 2003, jury trials are to take place in all regions.[45]

In a lessening of accusatory bias, the code's first chapter affirms the presumption of innocence. The defendant does not have to prove innocence; the prosecution must prove guilt.[46] Any doubt should be interpreted in the defendant's favor.[47] The same chapter states that the legal process is based on the competition of defense and prosecution, which are "equal."[48] No longer "an organ of criminal prosecution," the court functions to "create conditions for the sides to carry out their duties under the established procedure."[49] In Kozak's words, the revolutionary change in criminal and civil procedure was to ensure that "in acting . . . on behalf of the state, the prosecutor should have the same procedural rights as the other side has."[50]

The requirement of the prosecutor's presence in court at all times delineates the functions of the judge and the prosecutor.[51] Judges are no longer required to do the prosecution's work but will, instead, become objective arbiters of the prosecution-defense contest.

Defendants' lawyers are given the right to conduct pretrial investigation and collect evidence.[52] (Formerly the defense could only "study" the case file presented by the prosecution.) Following the precedent in the Nikitin case, the code sets no special clearance, qualification, or vetting requirements for defense attorneys in cases involving state secrets; they are obligated only to sign a promise not to publicize secrets.[53] For the first time, judges are given the power to rule out evidence obtained in violation of law.[54] Inadmissibility pertains to all evidence provided by the accused when their attorney is not present.[55]

Finally, the amendment to the Law on the Constitutional Court, also included in the reform package, gives the executive branch (from district authorities to the head of the region or republic and the president of Russia) two months to abolish a law or regulation found unconstitutional. Noncompliance could result in the dismissal of the executive; a local legislature's refusal to pass necessary laws could mean its dissolution.[56]

⨋

Russia's ten-year-old legal system continues to suffer from many hereditary defects. Among them are meager salaries, insufficient education and training, and, not infrequently, outright incompetence among judges and prosecutors alike, as well as overcrowded and crumbling prisons. The Russian media are rife with allegations of the bribing of judges to influence their rulings, particularly in provinces and ethnic republics.

Many federal and local laws and ordinances contradict the constitution, most conspicuously Moscow's continuing restriction of residence. In at least some cases, courts continue to do the bidding of local or federal authorities instead of following the law. In a politically motivated lawsuit—encouraged if not instigated by the Kremlin—a judge invoked an obscure (and soon to be repealed) commercial law to force Russia's most popular independent television channel, NTV, off the air.

Despite the Nikitin case, standing up to the FSB is hardly the norm, as evidenced by the prosecution of Moscow arms control expert Igor Sutyagin on charges of espionage.[57] Although Sutyagin has already spent two and a half years in prison, his requests for bail have been repeatedly denied, and his case has recently been returned by the judge to the prosecution for "supplemental investigation" in apparent violation of both the Constitutional Court decisions and the new criminal procedural code.

Perhaps even more debilitating is the deeply cynical view of the legal system held by millions of Russians. The supply of laws, no matter how excellent, must be met with an equally strong demand. In Thomas Jefferson's words, "It is the will of the nation that makes the law obligatory."[58] To resuscitate that "will" after four generations of state terror, lawlessness, and fraud may take decades. Still, those in Russia and outside who rightly see in the emergence of a Russian *Rechtsstaat* the final break with the Soviet past can take solace in the progress in the first of these long decades.

Part III

Reinventing Values and Virtues

8

In Search of a Russian Middle Class
2000

Left for dead time and time again by many experts and journalists (most recently in the wake of the financial crisis of 1998), the Russian middle class stubbornly refuses to disappear. Sketched in this chapter are the first and tentative attributes of the societal segment so vital to the success of a modern liberal capitalist democracy, as that class emerged from the creative chaos of the revolution: its brief history, composition, income, political and cultural preferences, and, most importantly, values.

How does one go about ascertaining the size, income, and demography of a middle class in a country where 40–50 percent of the economy is hidden from the tax collector, where the official—that is, declared and taxed— salary is often only a small fraction of the actual income, and where government statistics have notoriously underreported the size of the national economy and the people's well-being?

In many respects, the Russian middle class today is a black box—a phenomenon whose key attributes cannot be ascertained directly with satisfactory precision and validity. In these circumstances sociologists must try to glean the key attributes of the object by what comes out of the box—in this case, the patterns of self-identification, behavior, and consumption consistent with accepted notions of middle-class values and pursuits.

In such an exploration government data are not the end but, rather, the first step, to be followed up by market research, public opinion polls, journalistic accounts, anecdotal evidence, and, perhaps most important, field research. To be sure, such a mosaic will not yield a photographic image, correct and reliable in every detail. Yet, like a pointillist portrait, it may convey the tones, contours, and the dynamics. As Yogi Berra said, sometimes one can see a lot just by looking.

∽

The birth of the post-Soviet middle class in 1994–96 coincided, unsurprisingly, with the taming of inflation, which had been unleashed by the abolition of state control over most prices. The new social stratum grew swiftly, with abundant signs of strength and depth, until the onset of the August 1998 financial crisis and devaluation of the ruble, brought about by the combination of the worldwide investor panic that swept the emerging markets and the mushrooming domestic debt that resulted from the government's inability to reduce the enormous budget deficit.

Along with the alleged collapse of the Russian experiment in capitalism, many U.S. journalists and experts solemnly announced the end of the Russian middle class. For the foreseeable future, the structure of Russian society was to remain exceedingly simple: a handful of super-rich "oligarchs," the starving masses—and nothing in between. Fortunately for Russia (and the world), the report of the death of the Russian middle class was premature. In less than a year, the dead and buried stratum staged a remarkable comeback. The roots of this resilience lay in the group's professional and demographic characteristics and its relations with the post-Soviet economy.

Two monumental changes in the Russian economy and society have shaped the composition of the post-Soviet middle class since 1992. First, there has been a shift from manufacturing to services. This process began in the West in the 1940s but was delayed in Russia for nearly half a century by the state-owned economy—politically driven, autarchic, heavily militarized, and relentlessly consumer-hostile. Second, income and prestige within the upper crust of the middle class were redistributed away from professions serving the state to those needed by individuals and private businesses.

The results were painful and often tragic for millions of scientists, military officers, university professors, and engineers employed by the enormous military-industrial complex. Defense had consumed as much as half of the country's GDP, funded most fundamental and applied research—and was decimated by Boris Yeltsin's demilitarization. Equally devastated were the ranks of the "fighters on the ideological front": journalist-propagandists, teachers of Marxism-Leninism, and hundreds of thousands of staffers of various "scientific research institutes" in the employ of local and central party authorities. Still harder must have been the fall for the Soviet upper-middle class—regional and federal party and government functionaries, members of official "creative unions" (writers, composers, artists, actors), diplomats, and top military brass.

Replacing them are the formerly humble accountants, physicians now in legal private practice and private clinics, and lawyers. Joining them are freshly minted capitalist professionals in advertising, marketing, and real estate; computer and Internet engineers and programmers; architects; journalists at leading local and national newspapers, magazines, and television stations; translators; teachers at private high schools ("gymnasiums") and at private colleges; home design and remodeling experts; insurance salespeople; and owners of small family businesses: cafes, bakeries, delis, tailor shops, gas stations. (Poorly remunerated in Soviet times, doctors and public school teachers remain woefully underpaid today.)

The upper segment of the post-Soviet upper-middle class includes managers of major Russian and foreign law firms and companies (for example, Gazprom, Lukoil, RJR, Mars, Coca-Cola, Procter & Gamble, and Nestlé); managers and owners of medium to large restaurants, stores, advertising agencies, travel and real estate agencies, and market research, public relations, political consulting, and home design and repair firms; chefs in the best restaurants; and top fashion models. Of hired labor, the single most-numerous group in this category consists of professionals in banking and financial services.[1]

Membership in the Russian middle class is heavily and positively correlated with age, education, and place of residence. Other things being equal, the younger one is in Russia today, the more educated and the closer to a large metropolis, the better one lives. Although not everyone who is young, highly educated, and living in a big city is part of the new middle class, the group consists primarily, perhaps overwhelmingly, of urban college graduates younger than forty.

As in Soviet times, Moscow remains Russia's gateway to the world and the magnet for the country's most energetic and successful citizens, as well as its cultural and social trendsetter. As the headquarters of most foreign and domestic companies, Moscow's share of the middle class is well above the national average.

✑

The entry point to the Russian middle class is significantly lowered by the state's providing free, or heavily subsidizing, services that represent significant expenditures for their Western European and, especially, American counterparts. Most colleges are free to those who score well on the entrance examination. As of this writing, tenants, regardless of income, pay less than half the real cost of rent and utilities of their "privatized" apartments (which they have been given for free or at a nominal charge); and the fares for public transportation in the cities are minuscule.

Relatively low expectations—the legacy of Soviet days—further reduce the income brackets. According to the Soviet press, in 1989 a typical family of young engineers or doctors (starting salary of 140 rubles a month, or around $14 on the black market) could not afford a refrigerator, a color TV, or furniture without help from their parents. Another member of the Soviet middle class, a skilled blue-collar worker, reportedly spent nearly 70 percent of her salary on food and was dependent on parental assistance for a winter coat.[2] As the Russian middle class emerges from four generations of crushing poverty under the Soviet regime, its aspirations (especially those of its lower segment) ought to be compared not with the aspirations of its Western European (let alone American) counterparts today, but with those of the European middle class immediately after World War II: a reasonably comfortable apartment of one's own, a compact car, a tiny country house to own or to rent, and an annual trip abroad.

If the lower boundary of the Russian middle class today is at or above a monthly income at least twice the 1999 national per-capita cost of living for a working-age person as estimated by the federal statistical committee, the Goskomstat,[3] then the entry point is 2,000 rubles ($78 a month) per capita, or $234 for a family of three. Recent surveys have come reasonably close by including in the lower-middle class those with monthly incomes between $300 and $550 for a family of three.[4] The breadwinners are receptionists, security personnel, chauffeurs, bank tellers, and secretarial assistants (especially in foreign-owned firms); bakers, cooks, truck drivers, and waiters in popular restaurants; and skilled construction workers. According to the same estimates, the "middle-middle" class stretched between $550 and $1,500, and the upper-middle extended to $3,500.[5] (Reflecting the cost of living, the sizable presence of Western firms, and the concentration of the nation's best and brightest,[6] these limits are, on the average, two and a half to three times higher in Moscow.)

Income distribution and, hence, the size of the Russian middle class are impossible to certify because of pandemic underreporting of revenues. With both employees and employers trying to hide as much as possible from multiple—and until recently draconian—taxes, remuneration is often given as cash payments and bonuses, private medical insurance, rent subsidies, child care, and even in-kind. Second and third jobs are often paid in unrecorded cash. As a result, for millions of Russians, declared salaries are only a part (in many cases a fraction) of the total income.

Nevertheless, the most recent survey by Goskomstat found that the share of the population with declared and taxed earnings above 2,000 rubles a month almost doubled, from 19 percent in 1999 to more than 35 percent by October 2000.[7]

Taking into account the rapidly growing economy and increased real incomes in 1999–2000,[8] Russia's basic socioeconomic structure looks as follows: 25 percent are destitute with incomes at or below the cost of living (less than $120 a month for a family of three); 35 percent are poor with enough money for food and clothes but not for much else (under $240);[9] 35 percent are lower-to-upper middle class; and the remaining 5 percent are "rich," with more than $3,500 a month for a family of three in the provinces and more than $7,000 in Moscow. (In 1992 Russia inherited from the Soviet Union 50 million destitute citizens, or 34 percent of the population, living below the official "subsistence level." During the next five and a half years, until the August 1998 crisis, the segment declined to 31 million, or 21 percent, and then increased to 23 percent in 1998.)[10]

While declared monetary income alone is hardly a reliable indicator, in capitalist Russia demand generates supply and makes it possible to supplement the official statistics with observations about consumption. After the fall of communism, the post-Soviet middle class had a seemingly insatiable longing for five things: decent food, travel, good books, a car, and a comfortable home. Unlike their grandparents and parents, who lived amid abject poverty and shortages, these men and women have been able to pursue and, in many cases, to realize their dreams as they dramatically change their country's economy.

⚬∕⚬

In a country where, nine years ago, people needed to show ration coupons to buy sugar and butter and stood in bread lines, the purchasing power and tastes of the middle class have created a food cornucopia. Most delicacies formerly available only to the party *nomenklatura* and—in a strict and finely gradated order of quantity and quality—to those whom the party deemed important are now always on sale and entirely within the purchasing power of even the lower-middle class.[11]

According to a summer 2000 marketing survey, 32 percent of the Russian middle class use computers and the Internet at home and at work.[12] In spring 2000 there were over 30,000 Russian websites and 380 Internet service providers.[13] Several leading search engines now have Russian sites—for instance, yahoo.ru and aport.ru. There are 1 million cellular phone subscribers in Moscow.[14] Households with cable packages get most U.S. channels, including CNN. When a fire temporarily disabled the Ostankino television tower in August 2000, a firm that installed satellite dishes was deluged with service requests and added 1,500 customers daily.[15]

A still more telling sign of the growing market presence of the post-Soviet middle class has been a 72 percent increase in the number of cars: from eighteen per one hundred households in 1990 to thirty-one in 1998.[16] In 1997 alone, one million Russians bought new cars at an equivalent of $7,000–$12,000 cash for each vehicle.[17] Despite the 1998 financial crisis, car ownership again has increased by over one-fifth in the two years since then, with forty cars per one hundred households by May 2000.[18]

In the past ten years the number of cars in Moscow tripled to 2.5 million vehicles in a city of 9 million.[19] Despite such an increase, a traveler on a Moscow beltway finds no sign of formerly ubiquitous long lines at gas stations. The latter multiplied in the past three years mostly because of the addition of new Russian oil companies (AstOil, Nefto, Kedr, Lukoil, Proton,

Alpha, and Trans), which are now far more numerous than BP and AGIPP, which had dominated the business in the first post-Soviet years.

Judging by billboards in Moscow and along major highways leading to the capital, the home repair, remodeling, and building boom is in full swing. Ads offer everything for the job: air-conditioning units and windowpanes, parquet and roofing materials, bricks and kitchen appliances, bathtubs and drywall. This past March, forty thousand Muscovites flocking to the opening of a giant Ikea furniture store backed up traffic for two miles.[20]

Along any major highway around Moscow one can see bedroom communities springing up at a furious pace, with trimmed hedges and lawns, barbecues in backyards, and volleyball and tennis courts. As with most middle-class trends, Moscow is leading the way, but new homes are being built around almost all large cities. Conceived by a thirty-two-year-old developer, the Kolomyaga townhouse complex in a St. Petersburg suburb includes twenty-one condominiums, at a cost of $75,000 a unit. The purchasers are primarily couples in their thirties with children.[21]

Those who cannot afford to build a house in the suburbs or are unwilling to part with cheap apartments close to work undertake the so-called "Euro-repair," which costs around $10,000 and includes, at a minimum, the installation of dishwasher, washer, dryer, stove, and microwave. Renting or selling an apartment in Moscow without these amenities is becoming increasingly difficult.

⚘

As early as the summer of 1994, with the first signs of economic stabilization, foreign consulates in Moscow were deluged with visa applications. The French Embassy received 700 applications a day, compared with a total of 2,700 visas granted to Soviet tourists in all of 1988. Talking to those bound for Paris on an Aeroflot flight in August 1994, an American reporter found the group "positively middle class . . . not wealthy or well-connected but simply comfortable, determined and lucky enough to have saved a few hundred dollars"—a policewoman, a high school chemistry teacher, a physical therapist.[22]

A year later, Russian tourists spent $11.6 billion on travel abroad.[23] According to the World Tourism Organization, of twenty-five top country-by-country spenders in 1996, Russian travelers were tenth, behind Americans, Germans, and Japanese, but ahead of South Koreans, Brazilians, Spaniards, and Chinese.[24]

In both 1996 and 1997, 17–20 million Russians (of a total population of 150 million) traveled abroad for business or pleasure, compared with 500,000 in 1991.[25] This past summer (2000) 16,000 travel agencies operated in Russia. The most popular destinations for a middle-class family were Turkey, Cyprus, Egypt, Greece, and Spain. Russian agencies offered two-week packages including food, lodging, and airfare for $500–$800, about two months' salary "of a rank-and-file professional in a private firm."[26]

※

The nascent middle class has boosted book publishing as well. In the last years of the Soviet Union, an average of 1,500 new titles were published in Russia each year. By the end of the 1990s the number increased to 12,000.[27] Last summer a typical middle-size Moscow bookstore, Mir Pechati, offered 11,000 books from 281 publishers.[28] Orders could be faxed or placed at the store's website at www.prestorg.ru. Books in stock were guaranteed for courier delivery within greater Moscow in two days, with the handling and shipping of up to three books costing twelve rubles, or forty-three cents. (Out-of-stock items were delivered from warehouses within ten days.)

For anyone who remembers Soviet bookstores, the change is thrilling. Inviting browsing, with no counters or rude salesclerks between the shoppers and the books, the collections are as delightfully eclectic as in any Western store. Unhampered by censorship the Russian bookselling business eschews ideology, except that of selling the wares to as many customers as possible. Standing side by side are beautiful volumes of Solzhenitsyn and Trotsky, Pasternak and Nabokov, Sakharov and Bukovsky, Hayek and Keynes; biographies of Bill Gates and Monica Lewinsky; the latest translations of Tom Clancy and John le Carre; a children's Bible and manuals for Microsoft Word; Michelin guides to Europe, North America, and Asia; English–Russian and Russian–English dictionaries (legal, banking, environmental, medical); books on the Holocaust and on Russian history; translations of medieval French poetry and of Robert Burns.

The prerevolutionary and Soviet Russian classics from Pushkin and Gogol, Chekhov and Dostoevsky, and Tolstoy and Turgenev to Yuri Olesha, Vasily Shukshin, and Yuri Trifonov are plentiful and accessible. The volume of Isaak Babel's selected prose works costs seventy-two rubles ($2.62); poetry of a wonderful Soviet poet and bard, Bulat Okudzhava, forty-three rubles; a beautifully produced translation of collected works of Francois Villon, twenty-three rubles; and Yuriy Lotman's excellent biography of Russia's great historian Nikolay Karamzin, thirty-two rubles. Karamzin's multivolume classic, *History of the Russian State*, never published under the Soviets, is displayed nearby.

Another item scarce in Soviet days, children's books, now dazzle with beautiful covers and illustrations. Among them are Pushkin's *Tale of the Fisherman and the Fish* and the *Tale of the Golden Rooster* (thirty-five and thirty-four rubles, respectively), coloring books, including one of Pushkin's fairy tales (three to five rubles); and a pop-up version of the folk tale *Teremok* (*Little Castle*, nine rubles).

⁓

Theater is another tradition that lives on. "If you wish to locate a large group of representatives of the Russian middle class," noted a popular Russian weekly news magazine, "don't construct sophisticated samples—just go to the theater." In repeated polls of theatergoers from Moscow to the smoke-stack city of Magnitogorsk in the Urals, at least six of ten identified themselves as middle class.[29]

Because of the continuing and enthusiastic patronage of the middle class, Russian theaters have survived the painful transition from total ownership by the state to a mixture of state and private funding or to entirely self-supporting entrepreneurship. This switch has been accomplished without losing a single major classic theater, while dozens of smaller, modern, and experimental outlets have been launched. An American playwright and theater critic who recently visited Moscow found most theaters "packed" and the audience "engaged, lively and attentive." He added: "One never gets the feeling in this city that classical culture is vestigial or superfluous. Quite the contrary: it remains a central fact of everyday life."[30]

For the week of October 19–26, 2000, a weekly guide to Moscow arts and leisure listed performances in seventy-nine permanent theaters: twelve "musical" (showing ballet, opera, operetta); twenty-four drama houses; thirty-three modern, experimental, and studios; and ten children's.[31] The repertoire included *Eugene Onegin* at the Bolshoi, *Swan Lake* at the Kasatkina-Vaslilev Theater of Classic Ballet, Schiller's *Treachery and Love* at the Maly, *Three Sisters* and *Cyrano de Bergerac* at the MkhAT, Marlowe's *Dr. Faustus* at the Malaya Bronnaya Street Theater, *Diary of Anne Frank* at the Russian Youth Theater, *Jesus Christ Superstar* at the Spesivtsev Studio, and Steinbeck's *Of Mice and Men* at the Factory of Theater Events. The prices ranged from four hundred rubles ($14.50) at the Bolshoi to between ten and one hundred rubles ($0.30–$3.60) in most other theaters, including the Maly and the MkhAT. (For popular plays and first nights, the last-minute theatergoers pay the scalpers as much as $50 a ticket.)

Lovers of classical music patronize thirty-three concert halls in Moscow, starting with the Moscow Conservatory and Tchaikovsky Hall. There are seventy-nine permanent art galleries and museums (admission is either free or costs less than a dollar)—from the venerable Kremlin, Tretiakov, and Pushkin exhibits to smaller private exhibits—and eleven children's museums.

Middle-class moviegoers are gradually transforming decrepit cinemas. Of the sixty-nine movie theaters in Moscow, ten are state-of-the-art, Dolby-sound multiplexes with their own websites and fresh popcorn. Bowling and pool (called American billiards) are all the rage.

✂

Concentrated in Moscow (and comprising at least one-fifth of the capital's population), the Russian middle class is also in evidence in the larger cities, from St. Petersburg and Novgorod in the west to Samara in the southeast, Perm and Ekaterinburg in the Urals, Novosibirsk and Omsk in Siberia, and Vladivostok on the Sea of Japan. Everywhere, however, it exhibits attitudes indicative of a common set of values. Judging by public opinion polls and newspaper interviews, the most common among these is independence—a reliance on one's own hard work and abilities.

According to a national market research survey of the "middle-middle" class (with family incomes from $450 in the provinces to $900 in Moscow), the "representative attitudes" of the respondents included "freedom, the possibility to determine one's own destiny, self-confidence, the desire to work and to progress, preparedness to run risks to achieve success."[32] Asked to assign values from 0 to 5 to various factors responsible for success, students at the elite Higher School of Economics gave an average score of 4.1 to the "betterment of their lives through their efforts" and only 2.0 and 2.8 to local and federal authorities, respectively.[33]

After three generations of compulsory work for the state, to be self-employed or, better yet, to own one's business is the ideal. "Middle class is a small businessman, who has his own business, supports his own family, works for himself, rather than for someone else," said a participant in a middle-class focus-group discussion.[34] "I wanted both freedom and money, and that is how I came around to starting my own store," wrote a former Moscow physicist in a remarkable middle-class manifesto entitled "I, a Small Store Owner."[35] Another new entrepreneur, a thirty-eight-year-old regional distributor of medical supplies in the city of Voronezh (three hundred miles south of Moscow), said to an American reporter in late 1999,

> I don't know who will be leading Russia in a year's time. But in this little piece of Russia, I know what we will do. We will improve services. We will hire new people, we will improve salaries. These are our plans, and most of them are realistic. We will do what we can in our own house.[36]

Such attitudes are behind the steady growth of small and medium businesses all over Russia. Even in the red-belt agricultural province of Voronezh, which primarily sends Communists to the national parliament, 61,000 small businesses were registered at the end of 1999.[37] Altogether, there are 890,000 registered businesses in Russia. Most are owned by the middle class, which is estimated to produce 30 percent of the country's GDP.[38]

Men and women in the new Russian middle class are almost twice as likely to enjoy their work as the rest of the population—70 percent to 38 percent. Asked if they would continue working if they had "a lot of money," 73 percent said yes, as compared with 42 percent in the country at large.[39]

"It gives me pleasure to create new jobs," a thirty-six-year-old Novgorod restaurateur told an interviewer. "I not only sell these products," he added. "I can bake goods myself. It is this part of my business that brings me pleasure."[40] A twenty-seven-year-old Moscow owner of a small mail-order electronics firm saw a similar "moral aspect" to his work: "I have created only four but, still, new jobs—and two of them for my friends."[41] Another entrepreneur stated that his business had given him an opportunity to "participate in the life" of the society.[42]

Both demographic characteristics and political preferences of the Russian middle class came into sharp relief in the watershed 1996 presidential election, in which President Boris Yeltsin's opponent was Communist Party Chairman Gennady Zyuganov. According to exit polls, Yeltsin led Zyuganov 71 percent to 23 percent among those between the ages of eighteen and twenty-nine, and by 57 to 36 percent in the thirty- to forty-four-year-old category.[43]

Yeltsin won in eighty-six of Russia's hundred largest cities (including every regional capital). Among the ten candidates in the first round of the election, he was preferred by 42 percent of professionals to Zyuganov's 18 percent, and by 38 percent of white-collar workers as opposed to Zyuganov's 26 percent.[44] Among college students, 84 percent voted for Yeltsin in the runoff and 7 percent for Zyuganov. Of those who said that they planned to vote for Yeltsin, 75 percent valued equality in "realization of everyone's abilities," and only 22 percent thought equality of income and standard of living were most important.[45]

∽

Much like the middle class in other free societies, the Russians value education and are inclined toward charity. In a recent survey, three of four middle-class respondents had college educations, compared with one in three persons in the country at large. As they seek to ensure good educations for their children, middle-class Russians take advantage of new choices, and no effort is spared to secure good schools early in the game. Between 1991 and 1997, the number of private schools (gymnasiums) in Russia increased from 177 to 1,606.[46]

The number of colleges and universities in Russia grew by 75 percent between 1992 and 2000, and the number of students by 50 percent, primarily because of the emergence of private institutions of higher education.[47] The competition for college education is ferocious all over the country, with as many as twelve applicants for each admission slot. Reflecting the shift in the desirability of employment away from the state and toward the private sector, the most sought-after schools are no longer those of journalism, foreign languages, and diplomacy, but of law, economics, and medicine. Private tutors (known as the professor mafia) charge exorbitant fees, often reaching $50 per session, to prepare boys and girls for four entrance exams, at least two of which are oral.

As the Russian middle class grows, so does charity. Between 1988 and 1998, the number of charities in Russia grew from zero to sixty thousand.[48] The first Rotary Club was founded in Moscow in 1990; nine years later there were fifty-four all over the country, including the ones in Vladivostok, Petropavlovsk-Kamchatskiy, Yakutsk, and Naryan-Mar, beyond the Arctic Circle. Among the Moscow club's projects is the Krug learning center for mentally retarded children.[49]

Because of the perennial fear of tax authorities and also because charitable contributions are not deductible under the current tax code, rich and middle-class donors keep a low profile. One such benefactor was identified by a teacher at a private shelter for abandoned children—a thirty-year-old owner of a potato chip factory who contributed more than $8,000 a month and paid the institution's food bill.[50]

⁂

Still poor by Western standards, barely recovering from the devastating financial crisis of 1998, and accounting for no more than one-third of the Russian population, the country's middle class is a long way from becoming a dominant force for the better. Yet coupled with the country's rapid economic recovery and growth of incomes on the one hand, and the government's economic policy, which includes support for the private sector and the sharp reduction of the tax burden, on the other, the values of the Russian middle class, its demography, and its undeniable early successes warrant optimism.

A great deal remains to be done to lower obstacles to the hard work, energy, and intellect of these resilient and brave men and women. First priorities today are the strengthening of private property rights; a modern banking system that would provide long-term home mortgages and loans for business creation and expansion; and tax laws with deductions for business expenditures and charitable donations. The ability of local and federal bureaucrats to meddle in the business affairs of the middle class, blackmail property owners, and extort bribes must be eliminated.

In the past nine years the Russian middle class has learned to succeed with scant assistance from the state—and a great deal of hindrance. Extending some of the former but mostly reducing the latter will work still more miracles for capitalist, democratic Russia.

9

An Anchor in the Mud: Three Novels as a Guide to Practicing Freedom and Constructing a New Self

2001

For almost two centuries—since Alexander Pushkin's masterpieces laid the foundation—Russian literature has persisted in addressing the core issues and dilemmas of human existence, taking humanity's measure and explaining Russia and Russians to themselves and the world. Fiction was a guide in the relentless national search for honorable and dignified living. After a brief pause during the turbulent decade following the 1991 revolution, the best of post-Soviet Russian literature renewed the search for answers to the "deepest, unanswerable questions," as Dostoevsky wrote of Gogol's work. Among the finest in the post-Soviet oeuvre, the three novels in this chapter continue the masterful practice by recording, in the language and imagery of great art, the quest to practice freedom and construct a new moral code amid the debris of discarded values.

Falling asleep next to a drunk in one of Moscow's ubiquitous "pretrial detention cells" (part sobering-tank, part halfway house for the homeless), a middle-aged Russian writer-turned-night-watchman suddenly feels the moon: "It was not there. But, unseen, it was hanging majestically somewhere above the roof."

Like that moon from Vladimir Makanin's novel *Andegraund, ili Geroy nashego vremini* (*Underground, or the Hero of Our Times*), the luminous presence of talent and the glorious tradition in which it is rooted unite this and two other recent Russian novels[†] and shine through material encrusted with muck and crisscrossed with scabs.

Set in the late 1980s and early 1990s, the three narratives supply some of the first artistic interpretations of the still-unfolding revolution. Much different in style and context, they are united by metathemes: the occasional exhilaration and daily painful responsibilities and choices that freedom (*Svoбoдa*,[1] the title of one of the works) brings; the arduous task of restocking one's moral universe; and, perhaps most of all, art (first and foremost, language and literature) as the ultimate healer, a guide to vital self-knowledge and the most reliable mooring, "an anchor in the mud," as Makanin's protagonist puts it.

The mastery of language and the delightful whimsy of abundant talent made these books Russia's literary events. Butov's *Svoбoдa* received the Russian Booker, the country's highest literary prize. Ger's novel was short-listed. And, although passed over by the Booker committee, *Andegraund* is very much worthy of its author's reputation; Makanin, who won the 1993 Booker, is considered by many critics Russia's finest writer of "serious" fiction.

Makanin and Butov share a decidedly modernist sensibility smothered in Russia (though not in Russian) by "socialist realism" for over half a century. Both *Andegraund* and *Svoбoдa* are narrated by the main characters. The time lines are jumbled, especially in Makanin's novel. The past invades the present. Plot is replaced by a cascade of self-contained stories, scenes, vignettes, observations, and meditations. Sketched with a few masterful, appetite-whetting phrases, friends, relatives, neighbors, and lovers wander into the narrative—and disappear without a trace. With the exception of the narrator's best friend, the twisted and ultimately tragic Andrey, no one in *Svoбoдa*, including the narrator, has a name.

The rhythm is a pulsating, deliberately dissonant staccato, the tone is Dostoevskian—convulsive and sharp. The jagged narrative is constantly subverted, interrupted, and shattered, and then just as abruptly retrieved and reassembled. The searing, frenzied onrush of thoughts, images, and

---

† Vladimir Makanin, *Andegraund, ili Geroy nashego vremini* [Underground, or The Hero of Our Times] (Moscow: Vagrius, 1999); Mikhail Butov, *Svoбoдa* [Freedom] (St. Petersburg: Inapress, 2000); Ergaly Ger, *Skazki po telefonu, ili dar Slova* [Fairy Tales over the Phone, or the Gift of the Word] (St. Petersburg: Limbus Press, 2001).

sensations appears to overwhelm syntax: The boundaries of sentences are widened into paragraphs, and parentheses are spawned like extra limbs with which to contain the torrent. Like the shadows thrown by the sputtering and wavering candle in Boris Pasternak's famous poem,[2] sentences now soar on angels' wings, straining toward some sublime and ultimate truth of the human condition, now fall to earth, often landing in the gutter of a language rough and abrasive, like a smashed vodka bottle.

His novel's kinship with Dostoevsky's *Zapiski iz podpol'ya* (*Notes from Underground*) underscored by the title, Makanin exhibits a seemingly inexhaustible Dostoevskian appetite for filth, awful sights and smells, warped passions, cruelty, and what Dostoevsky called in *Notes* "the poison of unsatisfied desires."[3] Buried deep in this dense and dark narrative are even two murders committed by Petrovich, one in self-defense; the other, premeditated, of a KGB informer. The echoes of *Crime and Punishment* become audible when a cunning police detective engages Petrovich in a grueling mental duel, as Porfiry Petrovich did Raskol'nikov.

The mundane and the exalted do not clash but, as in Auden, Brodsky, or Bellow, forge a symbiosis: precise, penetrating, enjoyable. Despite their mostly cheerless subjects, the novels do not sink into maudlin self-pity. Like his hero, Makanin's sentences are wry, tough, shrewd, and sparse, as if cured by alcohol and the wisdom of age—and then suddenly a vulnerable and rambling—search for truth and love.

The language is replete with *mots*. Thus, seeing another unpublished writer after many years, Petrovich notes that the poor man's face exhibits "extinguished passions but still vigilant vanity." "Ideology," muses the protagonist, "is when complex constructions are invented in order to avoid admitting simple things."

The texts are awash in slang, juicy and often bawdy. Freed from priggish Soviet censorship, the authors successfully overcome the childhood thrill of all postauthoritarian literatures of wallowing in the previously unprintable just for sake of seeing it in print. They plumb the previously *verboten* layers of human passions and the physiology of sexual commerce frankly but also with adult confidence and taste.

In one characteristically earthy instance in *Andegraund*, Leonty, an ethnic Russian engineer from the faraway province of Kostroma, comes to Moscow to immigrate to Israel. Three days before boarding the plane for

Tel Aviv, he undergoes circumcision and legally changes his name to Khaim. His new Moscow friends venture that Leonty is overdoing it a bit. But the man from Kostroma is resolute: "I like to have everything in order. My passport. My ticket. My visa. My member."

Metaphors and similes—sparkling and witty—pour out with naturalness and ease, and the humor is heightened by unexpectedness. The loving descriptions of food and drink served at each gathering are among the best in the books, from plastic-tasting ubiquitous cubes of processed soft cheeses (*syrki*), vile sausages, and cheap port to good vodka from Kuban and wonderful homemade *blini* and *vatrushki* (Danishes). Amidst the universal Soviet penury, filth, and rationing, the Russians remained a nation of frustrated but persistent gourmands and sybarites—just as they remained a nation of terribly earnest talkers in a censored and bugged state. Petrovich offers a historical explanation for the national predilection for long, soul-searching conversations: Over centuries, he says, rare visits across boundless frozen expanses required so much catching up that conversations continued after the goodbyes, after the guests stood in their fur coats in the foyer, and "until the sled's bell began to ring."

✑

The main characters of Butov's and Makanin's books are spiritual self-exiles from late Soviet Russia. Their descent to the *dno*, the bottom, is a deliberate act of defiance in defense of personal and artistic freedom. It is a choice made not out of desperation or by default but, as the protagonist-narrator of *Svoboda* explains, something "sought long and hard," something he had "rushed" toward—a journey that, in the end, he hoped, would "bring [him] to some destination" of dignity and usefulness. The price for challenging the Soviet state—poverty, hunger, and homelessness—is stoically accepted, at least most of time.

Exercising what Isaiah Berlin called "negative freedom"—the freedom to be left alone, to walk away from the state—was a feat in Soviet Russia, where the state owned everything and provided everyone's livelihood. Only work for the state secured *propiska* (a residence permit) and thus an apartment (or, for tens of millions of Russians, a room in a communal flat). Severing ties to the state was an act of moral secession, the affirmation of private sovereignty over one's life, and one of the worst of many punishments for it (which included arrest as a "loafer" and "parasite" and sentencing to a labor camp or exile) was the lack of a place of one's own.

Both Makanin's Petrovich (the patronymic; his given name no one can recall any more) and Butov's principal personage, whose name we never learn, depend on apartment-sitting and rely on a network of friends, friends of friends, and neighbors for a roof over their heads. (Geologists, with their months-long expeditions, are the best.) Butov's character is lucky never to have found himself without a place to stay. Petrovich, whose "home" between apartment-sittings is a cot in the worst section of a workers' dorm, once had to resort to shelters, which in the late 1980s began to complement jail, camp, or exile as the destination for the Soviet homeless.

For the young narrator of *Svoboda*, the condition is relatively short— no more than a year or two, although one is never sure. Toward the end of the book he finds contentment (perhaps even happiness) in a return to what most readers would consider a normal state: a full-time job, a permanent home, even a wife and a child.

The case of Petrovich is much harder. He begins practicing freedom long before *perestroika* makes such pursuits relatively safe from persecution, and the end of the book, somewhere in the early 1990s, finds him still in the *andegraund*. The self-conscious affinity with Dostoevsky's *Notes from Underground* extends well beyond the title; it begins with existential resistance. Like Dostoevsky's Underground Man, who would not surrender his independence and give in to the outside world "just because it is a stone wall and I am lacking in strength,"[4] Petrovich persists in the refusal to play by the Soviet-made rules; by the time we catch up with him he is in his late fifties and has been *agshnik* (a denizen of *andegraund*) for nearly two decades.

Not one of his novels or stories, though read in *samizdat* (literally, "the Self Publishers," as the body of uncensored manuscripts circulated in the underground was known in the Soviet Union) and highly praised by fellow writers, has seen the light of day. After fifteen years of "total rejection," his *oeuvre* is clogging "the bowels" of editorial offices and publishing houses. Petrovich refuses to compromise with censors and "socialist realism": "I am serious; and if you will not give me attention and respect, I am not going to bow to you. I have the underground."

Petrovich has not written for years: "Words piled up, quite a few precise and . . . tender words, but they no longer aimed at the empty sheet of paper." Still, like a character from a Chekhov story, who always recalls his study and his writing desk in times of trouble, at every turn for the worse Petrovich thinks of his old made-in-Yugoslavia typewriter—an existential synecdoche, a stand-in for his art and hope, the one item he has managed to save from a temple of the only god he ever worshipped.

Petrovich is a watchman in a workers' dorm-turned-apartment building. (In the catastrophic Soviet housing shortage, millions of dorm tenants never received apartments of their own and settled in their dorm rooms for life.) Prized for his honesty and helped by the aura of a "writer"—which in Russia always has connoted not only an occupation but also a high moral standing— Petrovich usually has no shortage of apartments to sit, where he can luxuriate with his own phone and books, a normal bed, a refrigerator (sometimes even with bits of chicken and sausage left behind), and a few cans in the cupboard.

Harmless and trusted, Makanin's hero is also a confessor to the dorm tenants, who bring their tales to his silent acceptance. "Oh how they want to be understood! This is why they drink with you and sleep with you," Petrovich notes. "The feeling of being understood is an intoxication of a special kind. A necessity but also a nearly narcotic dependence." Interrupted only by the gurgling of poured vodka, the confessions fill the book with amusing, sad, sometime tragic vignettes of Soviet life.

By far the most powerful segment of *Andegraund* is the protagonist's meticulously and mercilessly recorded three-month descent into the drug-induced hell of a psychiatric ward for criminal suspects. (Petrovich's brother Venedikt, a brilliant artist who had taunted KGB thugs, was reduced to semi-idiocy in the same psychiatric ward twenty years earlier.) The detailed record of the torment is likely to be among the most horrific passages one is likely ever to read: the destruction of individuality ("scraped away with a steel scraper," in Petrovich's words); the brain's inability to concentrate on even the simplest thoughts; and the reduction of otherwise healthy adults to a teary vegetative state, in which they are incapable of holding their own waste. It is the first such detailed, lengthy, and piercing treatment of punitive psychiatry in Russian *belles-lettres*.

A "cocktail of chemicals" dissolves Petrovich's "I" and creates a new life, "or, rather, nonlife, protolife," with feelings turned into "ersatz feelings, tiny feelings" ("*chuvstvishki*"). Drugged relentlessly with huge injections of "restraining substances" and ready to cry at the slightest provocation, Petrovich wanders around like a "stupid ghost," with "stupid thoughts, like birds, flying into my brain"—the brain that is no longer "mine but theirs," his tormentors'. His body becomes "a long piece of meat with tiny bones," nobody's body—"one could hang it on a hook, like a towel." Tormented by diarrhea and starved, he retains vestiges of sanity through the "memory of old words" and "mental exercises in empathy" with other patients. In the end, it is the miraculously preserved ability to empathize that saves him from succumbing to idiocy. He accosts sadistic orderlies who are beating a fellow inmate, is savagely pummeled, and, with two cracked ribs, is transferred to a regular hospital.

❧

For both Petrovich and the narrator-protagonist of *Svoboda*, by the late 1980s, the *dno* becomes a vantage point from which to watch the disintegration of Soviet civilization without being contaminated by its detritus: "Unrushed and a bit sleepy you lie on a sandy bottom in blue water, while on the surface large and small piles are floating by," Petrovich records. "The water is clear, the sun shines, shit floats by."

Yet with the demise of the Communist regime in August 1991, protecting their art and their souls from corruption can no longer serve as the justification for self-exile. There is now a much broader and deeper agenda. The god of communism is dead. The elaborate and omnipresent official ideology has expired together with the way of life it spawned and enforced. The emptiness requires a painful adaptation, even for those—perhaps especially for those—who, like Petrovich and his friends, have defined themselves by moral opposition to the dictatorship. Living honorably is no longer synonymous with a solitary, personal struggle against totalitarian conformity. The old moral compass can guide no longer; it must be reinvented and recalibrated daily.

Values have become a matter of choice rather than a given; men and women must create their own meaning and instill their lives with it. "We are free from the past. We are a clean slate," Petrovich concludes. "The world must be thought through from zero." They are to exercise free will amidst the ruins of state socialism—an existentialist project that would make Sartre turn in his grave. (Makanin's book begins with Petrovich's settling, in the precious safety and warmth of one of his borrowed apartment-havens, into a cozy chair to read Heidegger, whose favorite term was "abandonment"—the abandonment of man by God.)

Among the many echoes of Dostoevskian "underground" in these books, this one is the loudest: man standing alone, naked without the cover of private and official verities and religious and political "isms"; petty, angry, small, insulted and insulting, yet insisting on one's right to be self-conscious, to sort things out, to face ugly and merciless truths about oneself—and then follow one's wishes, however irrational at times, to "rush to find one's own road if only to avoid the designated one . . . and stubbornly blaze another—difficult, ridiculous—searching for it almost in the dark."

Recalling Chekhov's imperative of "squeezing out the slave" from one's soul, drop by painful drop, Petrovich discovers that "our post-slave vacuum is being filled badly." Determining how and with what it is to be filled is the daily task of men and women as they drift in and out of Makanin's and Butov's narratives, sifting through the rotting debris of the *ancien régime*, and examining their own past in search of something that might prove usable in a new universe.

⁂

Distraction from this difficult work is a grave danger. People may "forget," Petrovich worries, "forget, turn on television," with its screen like a "giant magnifying glass over a gnat." The prisoners of "group dependence," they talk too much to one another, but not to heaven. Corrupted by seven decades of censorship and terror, the language itself must be scrubbed from the alluvium of propaganda and self-illusion. "Freedom," Butov writes, "begins when things stop hinting at anything but themselves." (One of *Svoboda*'s characters, an amateur director of a modernist theater company, is convinced that a theater—of gestures, not words—ought to fill the gap while language is being purged and reinvented.) Although wandering in a desert like ancient Hebrews, Petrovich's compatriots—and humanity as a whole—seem incapable of "exploding with the Word. . . ."

The Herculean task of generating and deploying that Word in the daily construction of selves endows the *dno*, its denizens, and their art with a new and vital function. "Their Russian-Soviet world collapsed," Petrovich notes of his neighbors. "They were grateful. Their warped souls, trampled out by daily travails, needed . . . a moment of silence. A pause." Butov's hero, too, "hoped to find a solution in silence, a means to remake life into an existence that would coincide with his innermost self"—a silence that would be "palpable and weighty like a well-chosen word," a silence that would instill "the longing for the unattainable—the yearning which is as sweet and powerful as opium."

Great art's perennial effect of recuperative, restorative silence that transports us from the din of petty, lying thoughts and shallow impressions and into the bliss and pain of self-knowledge becomes doubly crucial. Petrovich's favorite painting is Kazemir Malevich's *Black Square*; its "web of invisible light" is a plea for "a stop, a universal slowing down," a warning for humanity hurtling along toward another sweet and dangerous illusion.

Neither Makanin nor Butov offers solutions to this existential quest: This is a time of analysis, not synthesis. "Scrutiny and interpretation," Joseph Brodsky wrote, "are the gist of any intense human interplay, and of love in particular. . . . They are also the most powerful source of literature."[5] Existence, freedom, love, and art, which are blended in Brodsky's dictum, are precisely the cocktail that Makanin's and, especially, Butov's characters drink straight up as they scrutinize, squeeze, pinch, and even puncture the mundane, the overlooked, the quotidian, the better to extract the juice of meaning.

The main character and narrator of *Svoбoдa* begins quite literally at the bottom, carefully observing the mice, cockroaches, and spiders abundantly represented in an apartment he temporarily occupies. He notes the behavior of cockroaches dying en masse from the effects of a new and powerful poison. He trains a spider to understand gestures serving as a prelude to food offerings. To subvert the ordinary and to keep themselves off-balance in order to awaken and sustain the capacity for daily self-construction, Butov's characters turn their lives into one lengthy happening by engaging in all manner of strange endeavors. Their chronicle gives the novel the texture and tempo of a diary kept by a precocious, wonder-struck child.

The narrator joins a friend in prowling Moscow in search of "peculiar movements" when people "lose control over their bodies," with an intent of photographing them. (They witness an epileptic seizure and a heart attack, administer CPR, and observe an hysterical woman "bellowing accusations to the world.") He agrees to his peripatetic friend's offer to guide him in an expedition inside the Arctic Circle (and nearly freezes to death somewhere between Archangel and Murmansk). In a country where the possession of weapons is a very serious criminal offence, he assists Andrey in transporting old carbines on a Moscow commuter train. He hears a sermon that rids a renovated local Orthodox church of rats.

❧

With Russian literature, at long last, having ceased to be a substitute for political discourse, both novels relegate politics in a narrow sense to the background. Yet, while their art, their thoughts, and their passions extend well beyond the politics of the day, the books' characters are far from oblivious to or ignorant of the revolutionary change around them. Gorbachev, *perestroika*, Yeltsin, and the "tank invasion" of August 1991 are parts of conversations. Toasts are drunk to the freedom of the Baltic nations. A hint of tectonic shift is discerned in the "trembling hands scratching on the walls of the apartment buildings the very first, heart-stopping slogan of *glasnost*: "Misha [Gorbachev], you are wrong." "Is the motherland the same as the state?" asks the narrator of *Svoboda*. "Are the authorities and the people one and the same?" To him these already are rhetorical questions.

Like a majority of Russians, when the chips are down, the novels' main characters choose the "democrats" over the Communists. Petrovich and his friends, the "unofficial artists," participate in the mass pro-Yeltsin demonstrations in Moscow in the winter and spring of 1991 and even attempt to march in their own small column under a banner of a giant brush and palette. From that occasion Petrovich remembers "the air oversaturated with excitement (as if induced by many cups of good coffee, free coffee, drunk in someone's house)" and "hundreds of thousands of people, so merrily, so explosively drunk with freedom." One of their group suddenly cries out "*Svobo-o-oda!*" ("Free-e-edom!") and they all join the chant.

Petrovich is ready to "forgive the democrats their lack of power instinct, their vanity, their real estate games—forgive for the first, clean gulp of freedom."

Half a year later, one of Petrovich's closest friends, the unpublished writer Mikhail, helps to build barricades around Yeltsin's "White House." Watching a Communist demonstration on TV, the mother of Butov's main character spits: "Scum. Zombies."

In the last pages of the novel, a glass of vodka in hand and to an approving chorus of guests at a large party to celebrate an addition of a room to a tenant's apartment, he raises a toast: "Here's to changes, ladies and gentlemen! Changes and a new grandiose wave of successes, luck, and shocks."

And change is everywhere. There are inflation and a sudden abundance of food. The protagonist of *Svoбoдa* works for awhile in a "resurrected" Moscow Orthodox church which begins to publish books on theology, philosophy, and history banned since 1917. The church has a newly painted cupola and newly installed bells, now permitted to ring. After years of underground existence, the narrator's friend finds sponsors for his tiny *avant-garde* theater, can rent a permanent large room, and can even pay small "stipends" to the two actors (the entire troupe). The new openness and the sudden interconnectedness with the world beyond the disappeared Iron Curtain are heralded by the title of Butov's book: the first two letters in *Svoбoдa* are the Latin s and v, instead of the Cyrillic с and в.

Usurped (though never extinguished) by the totalitarian bureaucracy, luck and chance begin to reclaim their role in people's fates: enlivening lives, creating opportunities, opening doors. As is the case with millions of urban, college-educated young Russians, after many a futile attempt at forging an honorable living in a new Russia, *Svoбoдa's* lead finds his harbor in a publishing venture, started by an acquaintance. This one-time impoverished Moscow hermit is confident and happy enough with his newly-constructed self to marry, and a new baby instills in him "a totally different mode of loving."

Petrovich, by contrast, refuses offers to publish his old work, no longer censored. It might be too late, of course: He is tired, broken, ailing, and years out of the practice of creation. Yet in his quiet determination to remain on the margins, one senses an existential mission. Like holy fools and court jesters, the *andegraund* tribe must go on regardless of political regime, a precious escort to vain and bustling humankind; gentle subversives who force a pause and a look from the outside.

༄

Though much in tune with Makanin's and Butov's broader themes, Ergaly Ger's short novel is by comparison subdued and less ambitious in depth and scope. It is also stylistically exquisite and the easiest of the three books to enjoy. The dialogue—gritty, brimming with energy, chockfull of slang but never vulgar, and often hilarious—is delectable. Ger's is one of those rare books to which one is drawn to leaf through the already read pages and find them strewn with previously overlooked gems.

Skazki po telefonu is a story of two young misfits and loners, Seryozha (or Seryoga) and Angelika, who find their "anchor in the mud," a refuge and love in and through the Word. The Word here is of the purest, unadulterated, primeval kind: not only detached from paper, but—spoken exclusively over the phone—stripped of all sensual attributes and contexts other than audile.

Ger's choice of the transforming medium—elemental and preliterary—fits the national mood. In the 1990s the desperate search for roots unsoiled by the Soviet era and thus usable in the foundation of new aesthetic and moral structures has made primitive art—music, painting, sculpture, singing—all the rage among the Moscow intelligentsia. Along with dish-washers and microwaves, renovated apartments are full of souvenirs brought from Altai, Chukotka, India, Africa, and Australia: sitars, tam-tams, didgeridoos, and newly-minted CDs of throat-singers from the Khakass and Tuva provinces on the Mongol border in southern Siberia.

Seryozha is a genius dramaturge, actor, director, and producer of what are, in effect, multi-hour post-modern phone plays, improvised and open-ended. He is the absolute master of his chosen medium: "In conversations with him words bloomed, and played, and sparkled, and changed shades." Touched by his art, his partners (girls and young women all) suddenly "articulated better, thought freer, breathed easier (or forgot to breathe at all)," their "voices became resonant and juicy, and the words burst on their lips like bubble gum."

The eponymous "gift of the Word" is the reference both to Seryozha's talent and to the treasure of self-knowledge that he so generously bestows on his female interlocutors—first suspicious, then enthusiastic, accomplices (and coproducers and stars) in the construction and execution of the phone plays. His last and most successful coactor, and love, is the depressed Angelika, the heiress to her mother's bootleg-liquor business empire.

Seryozha worships his medium. To him, it is far superior to the written word: "Writers work with the cooled-down word, the word without roar, freshness, palpitation—[while the spoken word] wriggles like a newborn, coming out head first, or side first, or any other way." One of the finest English poets of the twentieth century, Robert Graves, declared truth and art "wide apart."[6] Seryozha raises the stakes by claiming for his art a place above truth. The word, as he practices it, is "bigger than the truth, stronger than the truth": "There are many truths, but the precise word is always one and only. . . . Everything begins with it, everything ends with it, and everything is borne by it. I cannot do anything else. For me it is the main business on earth."

Like Petrovich, Seryozha is incapable of compromise and bastardization where his art is concerned. Petrovich refuses to publish censored words. Seryozha cannot force his words into the Procrustean bed of the small talk of ordinary human intercourse (and he remains, until Angelika, dateless, womanless, and, with the exception of his army buddy, friendless):

> Uttered purposelessly, the heartfelt word grates on the ear—but Seryoga had no others; a neutral, varnishing small talk was beyond his ability. A strange, depressing deafness to petty words sealed his lips and his ears: He looked at people and saw that what they lived by was not at all what they talked about; he read their lips, hands, eyes, and wrinkles to tease out the true meaning, falling out of the circle of conversation into loneliness, lagging behind the general merriment, like a child who falls behind the grownups on a walk.

Seryozha too senses the danger in the sudden onrush of freedom and modernity that must be balanced by an effort at self-discovery. Hence, a plea for a pause, a time-out, and a paean to silence where, "if one listens carefully, there is wind, and the rustling of leaves, and words dry up, die, and are born again, like flowers on burial mounds in steppes."

For Seryozha, art's ultimate gift, freedom, is an existential notion. "Love and freedom are given to us in physical sensation," he concludes, "like soaring or the soul's leaving the body and blending with other souls." The two—love and the ultimate liberation of self-discovery—happen to Angelika simultaneously:

> With a thunder-like clap and the burying of the Middle Ages, there burst out the era of geographic discoveries of self. Like a generous Columbus, Angelika gave Seryozha a tour of her past—as if he were a co-ruler of this vast but gone to seed kingdom—and he always managed to snatch a souvenir from her past, to pull out of her stories something important, touching, missed by Angelika because of stupidity or ignorance. In return, she was becoming real. For the first time in her life she felt—so penetratingly, so truly—that she lived, not slept; for the first time in her life, she realized that she was a real, live Angelika.

Freedom bestowed by art is far superior to the new and imperfect economic and political liberties. "Aren't you free?" Angelika asks one of the most powerful wheeler-dealers of *perestroika* Moscow and her one-time lover, Timofey. No, he answers, even though, for the moment, he is on top of Moscow, having "cunningly looped around" his many and ruthless enemies.

After Seryozha's violent death, Angelika carries on his infatuation with the ethereal Word. The book's last line finds her learning the Internet: Seryozha's art, into which she was initiated by the master, is about to find a new medium.

∽

Despite the decidedly modern subject, Ger's is an old-fashioned Russian novel, with a third-person narrator and a dynamic linear plot into which all characters, even secondary and tertiary, fit snugly. The text is smooth and stately, and replete with delightful similes and metaphors. The polished sentences are redolent of Ivan Turgenev, Sergey Aksakov, Mikhail Bulgakov, or the Boris Pasternak of *Doctor Zhivago*.

Here's autumn in the center of Moscow:

September gurgled in the still cold pipes of the apartment radiators, the shaggy green water of the Patriarshiy pond blackened
and rippled, and the limes around the pond turned yellow—
slowly and reluctantly, flooding the room now with warm honey
gold, now with greenish copper. . . . Like stilled faces of watches,
all four windows of the room showed the time of rain.

A town in the Caucasus, where Seryozha wasted two years as a draftee
in the Soviet army, is a

typical Russian backwoods, dusty or muddy depending on the
season, with a forgotten bust of Pushkin in the sickly public garden and monumental fences, above which sunflowers proudly
soared and, higher still, ancient Tupolev bombers roared as they
headed to guard one was not sure what, either the Northern sea
route or the Silk Road. . . . In the summer the crests of foothills
bulked out across the river, and in the fall, after the rain season,
like a bolt from the clear sky, mountains of unimaginable beauty
sprang in the sky, now white in the frosty blue, as if etched
by a diamond, now pink in the rays of the languorous steppe
sunsets.

The lines about the hyperinflation of 1992–94 could be the finest on
this horrific subject anywhere:

The country "swam," like a knocked-down boxer . . . and people lived not by the past or the future but by dollar rate, daily
checking the inexorably ticking meter. Inflation ate away at
people's innards, like an invisible pernicious plant-louse, ren-
dering their souls colorless, devaluing their labor, their lives, and
confining their hopes and thoughts to today's cash value.

And here is a Russian dinner party:

[There was] mad fullness of being, compressed by alcohol, and
the triumph of dialogue, which, like a strong fish snatched by

four hands from the waters of the Lethe, lashed the lips with its prickly and slippery tail.

The masterfully rendered background of *Dar Slova* is Russian primeval capitalism between 1989 and 1994: capitalism growing on and through the slimy sediment of utterly corrupt police socialism and its crime-ridden, underground private economy. The side-story of Angelika's mother's climb up a very greasy, and often bloody, pole, from the manager of a state wine store to a multimillionaire and ruthless boss of the Moscow underworld, is a reminder of a key formative event of Russian capitalism: Gorbachev's 1986–91 "dry law." Just like its namesake in the United States, Russian "prohibition" created nationwide and violent organized crime that for years to come would torment Russia and the world and launder its billions of dollars abroad and at home.

⸎

In one of his most beautiful and profound poems, the 1946 "Hamlet," Boris Pasternak forged an unmatched portrait of the doomed struggle of the artist and the man of honor in a modern police state (and foretold with chilling prescience his own torment by Soviet propagandists and death fourteen years later, following the Nobel Prize for *Doctor Zhivago*). The last stanza reads:

> Но продуман распорядок действий,
> И неотвратим конец пути.
> Я один, всё тонет в фарисействе.
> Жизнь прожить — не поле перейти.

Or, preserving the meter but sacrificing the rhyme to precision in translation:

> But the order of things has been settled,
> And the road will end where ruled.

I'm alone, all's drowned in falseness.
Life is harder than crossing a field.

In the last pages Butov evokes the same Russian proverb—(Жизнь прожить—не поле перейти) ("*Zhizn' prozhit'—ne pole pereyti*," or "Life is not a walk across a field")—but in a more hopeful context:

> I think everyone has one's own space in front of him, one's own time—one's own field, which has to be crossed, sacrificing something but holding fast to something else. But what is to be sacrificed and what is to be preserved—that must be decided anew every time.

That decision is still very hard—yet defeat in the business of honorable living is no longer preordained as it was fifty years earlier, when Pasternak wrote his poem, or even ten years ago. Petrovich calls the cot in the dorm his "anchor in the mud." Yet it soon becomes clear that something else has a considerably stronger claim to that title. He declares great Russian literature his "sole collective judge, the only authority before which he (sometimes) feels the need to confess" because only from there, "from the XIX century" blows "the breeze of true morality," and because, Petrovich is convinced, that literature is "indirectly connected with God."

Neither epigones nor literary nihilists, the best post-Soviet Russian writers appear to consider themselves the rightful heirs to that glorious trove: confident enough to be irreverent and even familiar—but also worshipful and aware of their giant responsibility. Judging by these novels, Russian literature continues to be fully and passionately engaged in this age-long quest and continues relentlessly to "press on the brain with deepest, unanswerable questions, which cause most disturbing thoughts in the Russian mind," as Dostoevsky wrote of Gogol.[7]

The precious craft is alive, mastered, burnished, honed, and built upon. (The second half of the title of Makanin's novel is an exact copy of Mikhail Lermontov's 1840 masterpiece *The Hero of Our Time*. There are also direct references to Gogol's *Overcoat* and Chekhov's *Ward Number* 6.) Unafraid of experimentation, the craftsmen venture in new directions.

"There cannot be Russia without literature!" Petrovich avows. One believes him because he, his creator, and at least two other writers in the emerging Pleiad of post-Soviet Russian authors prove very much worthy of our trust.

10

A Private Hero for a Privatized Nation: Boris Akunin's Mysteries

2002

What is the secret of the phenomenal success of Boris Akunin's novels, the first "quality" murder mystery series to become truly national bestsellers in post-Soviet Russia? To be sure, the plots are intricate and fast-moving, and the language is delectably stylized and wonderfully old-fashioned. Mostly, however, the appeal seems to emanate from the novel's hero-sleuth, Erast Fandorin. Craftily placed by Akunin (the pen name of Grigory Chkhartishvili) in the last third of the nineteenth century—a time in many respects remarkably similar to the late 1990s to early 2000s—Fandorin confronts the same new and difficult dilemmas and choices that the Russian middle class faces today: How does one live decently in times of dazzling change and freedom from the state's tutelage and uncertain values? How does one help one's country when total obedience to the regime or an equally total rejection of it is no longer the definition of good citizenship? Contrary to the age-old intelligentsia tradition, Fandorin chooses "private" virtues of personal honor and betterment—the remaking of oneself—over the overhaul of the "system."

Without doubt the most interesting phenomenon in Russia's contemporary literary marketplace is the popularity of the Erast Fandorin mysteries written by Grigory Chkhartishvili, a professional philologist, literary critic, editor, and translator of classic Japanese literature who writes under the pseudonym Boris Akunin.

Today, Chkhartishvili is Russia's most popular writer. Despite their unusually high price—for Russian books—of the ruble equivalent of almost $3 each, the series sales skyrocketed from 50,000 in 1999 to 3 million in 2001.[1] In July 2000, 200,000 copies of the latest two books sold in one week; by early August, the two volumes were in their third printing.[2] By the end of that year Akunin-Chkhartishvili became "Russia's most widely read contemporary writer."[3]

Chkhartishvili's success in Russia is particularly startling, since none of his books contains the ingredients said to be the sine qua non of popularity in a postauthoritarian, postcensorship literary market: There is little sex (and its brief descriptions are positively Victorian); fights, while brutal and explicitly portrayed, are infrequent; the language is not just clean but pristinely old-fashioned. The texts are crafted carefully and tastefully after the classic nineteenth-century Russian prose of Nikolai Leskov and Ivan Goncharov, with echoes of Nikolai Gogol and Fyodor Dostoevsky. Indeed, every novel in the Fandorin series is dedicated to "the Nineteenth Century, when literature was great, the belief in progress boundless, and crimes were committed and solved with elegance and taste."[4]

❧

In keeping with the genre, the Akunin books owe much of their appeal to their main character, a master sleuth. Orphaned at nineteen when his father, a bankrupt nobleman, died, Fandorin is a descendant of German knights, crusaders, and soldiers of fortune, one of whom, by the name of Von Dorn, came to Russia in the seventeenth century and became the captain of Czar Alexei Mikhailovich's palace guards. (Every one of these details is important, for sooner or later all are put to work by the author.) Fandorin is intelligent, hardworking, and fearless. A fitness enthusiast, he practices Japanese martial arts daily, which gets him out of many tight corners. (Mirroring the lifelong judo hobby of the country's widely popular and youthful President Vladimir Putin apparently does not hurt sales.)

A tall, broad-shouldered, trim brunet with bright blue eyes and a neat moustache, Fandorin dresses impeccably and looks like "a model in the latest Paris fashion magazine," with his perfectly tailored coats and snow-white collars and cuffs. Unless working undercover, he is never without gloves, top hat, and elegant walking stick, which, naturally, conceals a razor-sharp blade. The finishing touch is his gray temples, incongruous because of the youth and vigor that the rest of his body signals, even as we

see him approach and pass the forty-year mark. This incongruence invariably piques women's curiosity and pity—a combination that proves fatal to
many a female heart. The grayness is the result of a personal tragedy at the
end of the first book. Losing his bride to a terrorist bombing makes
Fandorin a confirmed bachelor and thus opens the narratives to all manner
of sidelines and subplots to enliven the mysteries with the hero's intense but
almost always chaste relationships with willful, independent, strong, intelligent, feminist-minded, and beautiful young women.

In the sleuthing pantheon, Fandorin most closely resembles Lord Peter
Wimsey, Dorothy Sayers's athletic, smart, and charming aristocratic playboy
(and, like Fandorin, a car enthusiast)—at least until Lord Peter renounces
bachelorhood by marrying Harriet Vane. Chkhartishvili would want Hugh
Grant to play his Fandorin.

Yet there is far more to Fandorin's appeal than his smarts, courage,
and good looks. In Chkhartishvili's intricate narratives, multilayered and
chockfull of allusions, the protagonist's attractiveness to the Russian reader
is likely to be magnified by the era in which the author places him.

Born on January 8, 1856, Fandorin, in *Azazel'* (brought out as The *Winter Queen* by Random House in 2003), investigates his first case in 1876.
The last Fandorin cycle book, *Almaznaya kolesnitza* (*The Diamond Chariot*),
is set in 1905. If today's Russia can be found in a "distant mirror" (that is,
following Barbara Tuchman, a moment in history that in some key respects
is remarkably similar to the way a country lives now), such a mirror is
almost certainly located in the last three decades of the nineteenth century.

First came the abolition of serfdom in 1861—an event, in its impact on
the national economy and psyche, not unlike the elimination of price controls
and privatization in 1992–95. There followed Russia's first and, until Gorbachev, only liberal revolution from above. In addition to the manumission of
the serfs, the reforms of Alexander II brought radical decentralization and
local self-government by elected representatives; abolition or curtailment of
nobility privileges; courts "in which all the subjects were equal" before the
law; trial by jury in capital cases and a competitive judicial process, in which
the defense (*advokaty*) freely vied with state prosecutors for juries' votes
(which, among other marvels, resulted in the verdict of not guilty for the
female assassin of the head of the Russian secret police); huge increases in the
number of primary schools, funded and run by local authorities and open to

children of all social and ethnic origins; access to higher education for women and Jews; and growing autonomy and self-government for universities.[5]

Enormous gains in personal freedom included the ability to leave the country and to return. Newspaper, magazine, and book publishers were freed from prepublication censorship, making late-nineteenth-century Russian periodicals and books among the most raucously polemical in the world. The number of books printed and sold skyrocketed. Russian culture reached its apogee in the music of Mussorgsky, Rimsky-Korsakov, and Tchaikovsky; the books of Chekhov, Dostoevsky, Tolstoy, and Turgenev; and the theater of Stanislavsky.

After the assassination of the czar-liberator Alexander II in 1881, the boundaries of self-government were tightened and liberties cut back—again, very much like the change that followed the transfer of power from Yeltsin to Putin. What Adam Ulam called the temporary "political stability and normalcy"[6] of Alexander III's reign was achieved, in the words of Sergei Platonov, a leading nineteenth century Russian historian, by "strengthening the supervision and influence of the state over . . . social self-rule and, in general, strengthening and raising the prestige of the top executive authority."[7] Still, major newspapers continued to be exempt from prepublication censorship,[8] the intense political and social debates went on, and civil society would never again be terrorized by the state into complete subjugation until the Bolshevik Revolution of 1917.

Meanwhile, Russian capitalism grew by leaps and bounds. Banks and savings and loan associations mushroomed. Foreign investments poured in. The economy expanded rapidly and became one of the world's fastest growing. Cities burgeoned as former serfs became workers. Thousands of miles of railroads were laid, including the Trans-Siberian railroad, which for the first time connected European Russia to the Far East. Large capitalist farms made Russia Europe's main producer of grain.

The vulgar displays of wealth by the nouveau riches all but replaced the discreet enjoyment of power and privilege of the old nobility—just like the outrageously expensive boutiques, restaurants, and gyms for the "new Russians" supplanted the secret food and clothing depots, drugstores, and "cafeterias" savored by the Soviet *nomenklatura* amid the squalor and poverty of the USSR. Almost every day, thousands became the victims of crooked banking and stock schemes. Part and parcel of the Russian state for centuries, corruption (which everywhere attends a transition from a state-dominated economy to an early capitalist system) became brazen.

As is always the case after a revolution, exhaustion and disillusion set in. The liberals were bitterly disappointed in freedom's inability to deliver wealth quickly and equitably. Liberal ideals were badly damaged, and everyone doubted that Russia could ever become part of what the Russians then called "Europe" (and now, the "civilized world"). The old ethical canon, enforced by state repression, was gone; the new mores were shocking. There commenced a desperate search for something to replace them both. As Chekhov observed, "It is as though we were all in love, fell out of love, and now are looking for something new to enchant us."[9]

It is in relation to this search for "something new," as fateful in the Fandorin-Chekhov time as it is today, that the stunning popularity of Grigoriy Chkhartishvili's hero may have a meaning beyond the literary realm.

❦

Then, as now, national tradition assigned the role of seeker after the "new" to a class that has monopolized such endeavors since the 1830s, and is central to both the best and the worst chapters of Russian history. That class is, of course, the intelligentsia, and the singular significance of the Fandorin series is that it offers an alternative to both the means and, more important still, the ends of the intelligentsia political culture.

Much in that culture can be explained by its origins. The emergence of secular education in Russia coincided with (indeed, was caused by) the expansion of the Russian state under Peter the Great to nearly totalitarian proportions.[10] (Every nobleman was, at least pro forma, the czar's soldier from birth.) Unlike Western Europe, the spawning ground of the intelligentsia—the Russian university—was never independent and private. It was set up not by church or city but by the state. The professors were salaried state employees. Educated by the state, the educated class were overwhelmingly in its employ, in innumerable "committees," "commissions," "archives," or "ministries." (Three of Russia's greatest poets—Griboedov, Pushkin, and Tyutchev—served in the Ministry of Foreign Affairs.) In Soviet times, one had state-owned "research institutes," as well as official "creative unions" of writers, composers, architects, artists, and journalists. What Nabokov wrote of Nicholas I, who volunteered to be Pushkin's personal censor, held true for the general relationship between the Russian (and Soviet) state and the literati: "With striking perseverance he tried to be everything in relation to Russian writers of the time—a father, a godfather, a nurse, a wet nurse, a prison warden, and a literary critic all rolled up in one."[11] (Nabokov added elsewhere that Nicholas I's "entire reign was not worth a single foot of Pushkin's verse.")[12]

Yet where the state was concerned, the intelligentsia's roots manifested themselves in bonds far stronger and deeper than education and employment. Although alienation from and opposition to the state have been that class's defining feature—the very term "intelligentsia" came into use in the reign of Alexander II amidst the withering criticism of the autocracy by the liberal press and the world's first sustained and ideologically motivated suicide-bombing campaign by People's Will—its ire and resistance were directed at a particular political regime, rather than at the state as an instrument of change and the key tool of social, political, and economic engineering. For most of the *intelligenty* most of the time, solutions to Russia's ills were state solutions: total, systemic change directed from above. No national betterment was possible without the state's first becoming—at most in a few years, and by the decrees of an enlightened ruler who listened to his intelligentsia advisers—entirely "European" or "civilized." The appearance and appeal of such a perspective were aided and much enhanced by the absence of a Russian version of the Reformation, which in the West tied daily personal behavior—or, in the case of Calvinists and other Protestant fundamentalists, even business success or failure—directly to salvation.

❧

An unsurpassed record of the intelligentsia's beliefs and modi operandi was produced by leading intellectuals—and Fandorin's contemporaries—in the 1909 collection of essays entitled *Vekhi* (*Landmarks*). Profound and beautifully written from the first page to the last, *Vekhi*'s philosophical, historical, and political discourses are by far the most insightful, comprehensive, and detailed portrait of the radical Russian intelligentsia's *Weltanschauung* ever compiled.[13]

From its publication and to the Bolshevik Revolution, the book was subject to intense debates and continued to influence Russian thinkers outside the Soviet Union, where it remained banned for seventy years until the *glasnost* era.[14] Before 1917, *Vekhi* went through four reprints and generated over two hundred books and articles of comments.[15] All major intelligentsia-led parties—from Constitutional Democrats (Kadets) on the center right to Socialist Revolutionaries, Mensheviks, and Bolsheviks on the radical left—rushed to produce their own volumes in response.[16] Lenin personally weighed in with a characteristically crude and lying polemic. (All but two of *Vekhi's* seven contributors were former Marxists.)

The *Vekhi* prescription was unambiguous and unsparing. The intelligentsia could reclaim moral leadership and guide Russia to "European" ("civilized") laws, liberty, and prosperity only by recognizing the "individual's inner life as the sole creative force" and renouncing the ideology of "unconditional primacy of social forms."[17] The authors beseeched their former comrades to "shift . . . the center of attention to oneself and one's own obligations," and free themselves from "the false state of mind of [being] the unsummoned savior of the world and the inevitable pride associated with it."[18] They must undertake "inner work" for the sake of "renewal"; it must "embrace the absolute value of individual self-improvement."[19] Only such a thorough and painful reexamination of received dogmas would allow the intelligentsia to rid itself of the "desire to be assuaged in all instances with the cheap thought that 'it's the authorities' fault.'"[20]

Only if this "inner slavery" is expunged first and the intelligentsia learns to "take responsibility [for our life] and stop blaming external forces for everything," only then "we shall be free of external repression":

> It is not worthy of thinking people to say: We are corrupted and will continue to be corrupted until the cause of our corruption is eliminated. Every man is obliged to say: I must not be corrupted any longer.[21]

If the cultural elite continued to spurn self-examination and reject personal, quotidian responsibility for themselves, their families, their neighborhoods, and their country, *Vekhi* predicted a disaster. Eight years before the Bolshevik Revolution; more than two decades before Hitler and Stalin consolidated power; four decades before the publication of Orwell's *Nineteen Eighty-Four*; ninety years before a new global totalitarian religion came of age on 9/11; Semyon Frank's *Vekhi* essay, "*Etika Nigilizma*" ("The Ethics of Nihilism") must rank among the most prophetic and piercing Jeremiads ever uttered:

> The great love for mankind of the future gives birth to a great hatred for people; the passion for organizing an earthly paradise becomes a passion for destruction; and the faithful populist-socialist becomes the revolutionary. . . . [The intelligentsia's] political activity has a goal not so much of bringing about some kind of objectively useful, in the worldly sense, reform, as of liquidating the enemies of the faith and forcibly converting the world. . . . Secular affairs and needs are . . . subject to execution according to a universal plan determined by metaphysical dogmas. [22]

✑

Chkhartishvili's Fandorin is an existential refutation of the intelligentsia tradition of thought and action as described by *Vekhi*. There is little doubt about the philosophical framework within which Akunin-Chkhartishvili places his hero. As one searches for a philosophical antithesis to the intelligentsia school, one can hardly do better than a school of thought which *Vekhi* adumbrated so strikingly, both in the description of symptoms and of prescribed cure.

From Nietzsche's "God is dead" to Heidgegger's "abandonment"— including, among others, brilliant hints from Dostoevsky's *Notes from Underground* (with its insistence on man's right to "my own, free wish," even to "the wildest," or "crazy caprice" against the makers of the "crystal palaces" of a future totalitarian paradise[23]) and Kafka's parables of lonely struggle against the modern world's cruel absurdities—to Sartre and Camus, existentialism's widely disparate expounders postulated the absence of universal ethical structures to guide us and man's aloneness in facing the entire world and insisted on grave personal responsibility for his life and for the choices he makes. That burden was not to get lighter; neither History nor Hero, neither Jesus nor Marx could provide relief. (Camus's Sisyphus was a perfect metaphor for this never-ending quest.)

In the *Koronatsiya* (*Coronation*) novel of the Fandorin cycle, the principal's credo, as told to another character, could have come from Sartre or Camus:

> "Do you know, Afanasiy Stepanovich, what your mistake is? You believe that the world rests on some rules, that it contains meaning and order. And I have long understood: Life is nothing more than chaos. It has no order at all, and no rules. Yes, I do have rules. But those are my own rules, which I made for myself, and not for the world. So let the world be on its own, and I will be on my own. To the extent that I can. Personal rules, Afanasiy Stepanovich, are not a desire to rearrange the universe, but an attempt to organize, the best one can, the space closest to you. Not beyond that."[24]

As in today's Russia—warily enjoying a fragile economic and political stabilization after almost a decade of revolutionary turmoil—in Fandorin's times the old rules had been swept away.

Opposition to the regime could no longer serve as the sole moral compass, and millions of men and women were attempting to devise and adhere to their own guides to worthy living. Like a true existentialist (and like millions of his compatriots today) Fandorin could count only on himself in deciding how to live an honorable and virtuous life.

Both in the privacy of his objectives ("organizing the space closest to you") and, even more, in the solitude of daily compliance with self-invented and self-enforced rules of dignified existence, Fandorin's credo is the opposite of the intelligentsia's. As if heeding *Vekhi's* call, Fandorin's first priority is not to change Russia, but to change himself—or, rather, to change Russia by changing himself and helping others around him to change as well. He is not defined—and does not define himself—by his attitude toward the state, but by his attitude toward his countrymen, many of whom he guides and some of whom he saves. He does not look to the state, either with hatred or hope.

Fandorin's virtues are private, not only because they are not advertised, in the intelligentsia's fashion, to all and sundry but, more importantly, because their worth is measured not by the currently fashionable short-term objectives of the Russian state, but by the long-term goals of Russia.

Fandorin's occupation is an ideal venue for a man of his convictions. In the tradition of Sherlock Holmes, Hercule Poirot, and Lord Peter Wimsey, Fandorin is an individualist, fiercely guarding his independence. This being Russia, he is not quite a "private" eye; employed by the Moscow police and, later, as an "official for special assignments" ("*chinovnik po osobym porucheniyam*") by the Moscow governor-general, he is more like Simenon's Commissaire Maigret.

(Because individualism is a sine qua non of the genre, Soviet literature failed—or rather was not allowed—to produce a single great detective in seventy years, despite the immense popularity of translated detective stories. In the mid-1970s a television series, *Sledstvie vedut znatoki*, or *Experts Are Investigating*, gingerly introduced three police detectives. An instant hit, the show was canceled after a few years. One can catch reruns on Russian television today.)

Fandorin attempts to put into practice a radical—for Russia—idea first articulated by Chatskiy, the hero of Alexander Griboedov's classic 1820s play, *Gore ot uma* (*Woe from Intelligence*): "To serve the cause, not the individuals" ("*sluzhit delu, a ne litsam*") and to "serve" ("*sluzhit'*") but not be "subservient" ("*prisluzhivat'*").[25] Often risking his life in carrying out his duties, Fandorin lets everyone know that he has assumed these tasks voluntarily. Occasionally, he threatens to resign and eventually does, walking away from a promotion to the head of the Moscow police. Disliked by a new Moscow governor-general appointed by the increasingly insular and incompetent court in St. Petersburg, Fandorin leaves Russia, works as a detective for hire in Europe and the United States, and returns to his country only to help solve crimes that pique his curiosity or to pursue criminals who had escaped him.

Seizing the opportunities offered by a new, freer Russia, Fandorin thus devises nothing short of an existential breakthrough—an alternative to the silent opposition to the regime and alienation from state produced resignation, dour cynicism, sullen submission, and often shoddy work characteristic of the intelligentsia's way of life. By contrast, Fandorin acts as an honorable and free man, offering the state his conscientious service until and unless his job contradicts his private moral code.

Chkhartishvili seems to have constructed his hero as a living antithesis to every negative stereotype of the Russian *intelligenty*. He is practical, pragmatic, attentive to detail, energetic, competent, physically fit, and disciplined. (His hobby is constructing and testing a new means of transportation, the automobile, and he sets several distance records, including one from Moscow to Paris.)

Chkhartishvili sees Fandorin as an embodiment of something that "a national Russian character—for different political and historic reasons—has always lacked: honorable self-restraint, privacy, and dignity."[26] Fandorin makes clear that he serves neither the chief of the Moscow police nor Moscow's mayor, nor even, as the reader discovers in *Koronatsiya*, the czar himself. He serves his country. "I serve not you but Russia," Fandorin tells the head of the Russian police. "And I will not participate in a war that is useless and even harmful to Russia."[27]

In *Smert' Akhillesa* (*The Death of Achilles*), a beloved general, a hero of the victorious campaign against the Ottoman Turks and a symbol of Russian military valor, is found murdered in highly compromising circumstances. The general's aide-de-camp implores Fandorin, "Promise that you will not use your detective talent to harm the motherland. Russia's honor is at stake!" Fandorin answers, "I promise that I will not do anything against my honor, and, I think, this should be enough." It is not that Russia's honor does not matter to Fandorin, but to him the honor of the motherland equals, and cannot be more than, the sum total of its citizens' individual honors.

His patriotism, while strong, is also intensely personal. In *Lyubovnitsa smerti* (*Death's Mistress*), Fandorin and his woman companion encounter nationalist demonstrators celebrating a minor military victory over the Chinese in the Far East:

> They carried portraits of the czar, icons, church banners (*kho-rugvi*). They chanted "Hurrah, Russia!" They marched, sweaty, red-faced, happy but, at the same time, irritated, as if someone had insulted them.
>
> "Look," said Kolombina. "They are crude, inebriated, and angry, but they are patriots and they love the Motherland. See

how happy they are? And you and I, educated, polite, nicely dressed, don't care at all about Russia."

"These are not patriots." [Fandorin] shrugged his shoulders. "These are just loudmouths. Just a safe way to bawl, nothing more. True patriotism, like true love, never crows about itself."[28]

❦

In assessing Fandorin's challenge to the intelligentsia tradition of political and social change, one cannot wish for a better witness than the writer whose name became an adjective virtually inseparable from the Russian intelligentsia. By coincidence or design, Fandorin's life and career unfold alongside those of Anton Chekhov.

The stereotype, in Russia as well as in the West, is that Chekhov's attitude toward the intelligentsia was vastly sympathetic, like that of a generous family toward a lovable misfit of a relative. Nabokov, for one, felt that in portraying his *intelligenty* as "full of such fervor, fire of abnegation, pureness of spirit, moral elevation" Chekhov was telling the reader: "Blessed be the country that could produce that particular type of man."[29]

Nabokov was wrong. The most private, subtlest, and—because of his detached irony, concealment of authorial preference for characters, and marked distaste for preaching—perhaps the most "modern" and un-Russian of the great Russian writers, Chekhov carefully hid his sympathies and dislikes, allowing for a multiplicity of interpretations. By contrast, time and again in private he pointed out qualities of the intelligentsia that he found most harmful to Russia.

He resented its sloppiness in reasoning, addiction to negation, and even physical flabbiness. He called them "sluggish, apathetic, lazily philosophizing," and "cold"; they "grumble and with gusto decry everything, because it is easier for a lazy mind to decry *everything* than to affirm. Sluggish soul, sluggish muscles, the lack of movement, unsteadiness in thought."[30]

The heart of Chekhov's discord with the intelligentsia was the same as that which animated *Vekhi*: He seemed to believe that the path to a happier life ran not so much (or even primarily) through change of the external (such as socialist revolution), but through the fashioning of one's own way of honorable living in the world and the following of it daily. "When you turn around your life, everything will change," Sasha tells Nadia Shumina in the novella *Nevesta* (*Bride*). "The most important thing is to turn around one's life; everything else is unimportant."[31] Chekhov considered the decent and productive lives of individual men and women immeasurably more important for Russia's progress than the future idyll brought about by state reforms. In a letter he wrote, "I believe in individuals. I see [Russia's] salvation in individual persons."[32]

Like Fandorin, Chekhov, too, was busy "organizing," as best he could, "the space closest" to him. He donated money to build schools and health clinics in and around the village of Melikhovo where he had bought land and a manor, personally supervising "bricklayers, stove-installers, and carpenters";[33] collected books for libraries and sent thousands of them to the remotest parts of the Russian empire, including the easternmost island, Sakhalin; gathered donations to help the peasants of central Russia in the horrific famine of 1891 and rode through starving villages in the worst colds of the Russian January; practiced charity medicine, fought the cholera epidemic in the summer of 1892 by manning a village clinic, and made rounds of twenty-five neighboring villages (treating, in addition to cholera, dysentery, worms, syphilis, and tuberculosis).[34] He organized and funded the Yalta clinic for tubercular patients from all over Russia.

When Chekhov was accused of "indifference toward questions of struggle and protest," "aloofness toward topical events, which agitated the Russian intelligentsia," and lack of interest in "public interests . . . and . . . the burning questions of his time,"[35] he retorted by declaring himself "neither liberal, nor conservative" but "hating lies and violence in all their incarnations"; thinking political labels "prejudice," and worshiping the "human body, health, intellect, inspiration, love and . . . freedom from force and lies, no matter what form they assume."[36]

With modernist self-consciousness suffusing Chkhartishvili's texts, it is hardly a coincidence that Fandorin's personal history, his habits, and even his appearance seem to be modeled on Chekhov. Fandorin, like Chekhov, is sent into the world with no connections and no money and makes himself by an intense and successful deployment of willpower in the daily bettering of oneself. Chekhov, the son of a bankrupt shopkeeper from the sleepy southern Russian town of Taganrog who supported his family by writing stories between studying for medical school exams and attending hospital rounds, knew firsthand the price of such effort: "incessant daily and nightly labor, constant reading . . . [and] willpower." In this work, Chekhov wrote, "every hour was precious" and not to be wasted.

Fandorin's temperament, too, is unmistakably that of an Anton Chekhov—he is neither an optimist nor a pessimist, but a pragmatic skeptic, wary of grandiose social projects and believing in a few self-made and self-policed rules of honorable living. Chkhartishvili's lead character daily practices the four virtues that Chekhov seemed to consider Russia's only hope: decency, dignity, competence, and hard work.

Four years younger than Fandorin, Chekhov is remembered by contemporaries as "rather tall," "lean," and, until TB ruined him, "muscular," broad-shouldered, and "light and graceful in his movements."[37] He was a lover of coffee, of clean and large rooms, and of (many) women, to whom he was just as irresistible. (One of his secret admirers was Tolstoy's youngest daughter Tatiana.) He was never seen "carelessly dressed," did not "approve of lazy habits," such as wearing slippers or dressing gowns during the day, and always sat at his writing desk "impeccably and neatly dressed."[38] Contemporaries remember him as charming, calm and composed, never losing his temper, and combining "tenderness," "delicacy," and "kindness" with "complete candor."[39]

With the competence and fastidiousness of private existence extending into public and professional life, Fandorin, like Chekhov, negates the Russian national stereotype of laziness and incompetence, indifference to those below, and servility to those above. He is a response to Chekhov's complaint to Maxim Gorky:

"In order to live well, to live like a human being, one must work, mustn't one?! Work with love, with faith. But we [in Russia] cannot do it. I have never met a single civil servant who had any idea of the meaning of his work: Usually he sits in the capital or a provincial center, and writes instructions and sends them to [remote fictional provinces of] Zmiev and Smorgon' to be carried out. Yet whom these instructions will deprive of freedom in Zmiev and Smorgon'—about that our official thinks as much as an atheist about the tortures of hell. . . . They all have the same dog psychology: When beaten, they whimper and crawl into the dog houses, when stroked—roll onto their backs, paws in the air, and wag their little tails."[40]

By contrast, Fandorin loves his work, and performs it brilliantly; he treats others according to their abilities and effort, not rank. Amid corruption, Fandorin repeatedly refuses bribes. Where rulers and ruled alike disregard laws, he is scrupulously law-abiding. Surrounded by vulgarity, he shows a refined taste. Above all, Fandorin values individual liberty as much as did Chekhov. "There is nothing I love so much as personal freedom," Chekhov told his close friend and publisher, Alexei Suvorin.[41]

In a letter written in 1889, thus anticipating *Vekhi* by two decades, Chekhov made clear (by his own and his father's life stories) that the freedom he so treasured was the product of a backbreaking and sustained personal effort to rid himself of qualities incompatible with those of a free man. His was a story of

a young man, the son of a serf, a former shopkeeper, a chorister, a schoolboy, and a university student, brought up on reverence for rank, on kissing priests' hands, on veneration of other people's thoughts, thankful for every crust of bread, flogged many times . . . who lied to God and people, lied without need, simply out of the realization of being a nobody . . . this young man is squeezing drop by drop the slave out of himself, and wakes up one fine morning and feels that it is real human blood flowing in his veins, not a slave's.[42]

✌

The finest Russian literature has anticipated and powerfully illuminated discontinuities and transformations in the nation's values and aspirations well ahead of its rulers, officials, social scientists, and even its secret policemen. There are tantalizing hints in the phenomenal success of the Fandorin cycle as well.

Could millions of Russians have spent their hard-earned rubles to buy more than a clever plot, elegant style, and engaging hero? Might not they have also found in the book's existential credo a usable guide to forging their way through the onrush of modernity and freedom of choice, to charting their lives amid the ruins of erstwhile moral, economic, and political certainties?

Fandorin's ideals may be precisely what is required in Russia today, where personal efforts (what used to be called the "small deeds" in Chekhov's days) by the millions are far more important than the feats of a few: Work hard, be honest, do not take bribes, pay taxes, be creative, take risks, abide by laws, and help others to do so. Most important, Fandorin's insistence on serving and assuming personal responsibility for his country is key to the emergence of a civil society, without which Russia will never become a liberal capitalist democracy.

Has Fandorin's goal of organizing the space closest to him been found consonant by the Russians responsible for the explosion of private charity, human rights groups, private funding for the arts, hundreds of new print and cyber media that spring up every year, and thousands of voluntary associations? What might be called the privatization of Russian national goals is well underway. For the first time in Russian history, the very criteria of national greatness appear to be concerned not with the glory and military might of the state but with the welfare of individual citizens.

In his 2002 state of Russia address to the Duma, Putin declared the state's well-being inexorably linked to the individual effort and individual success of Russia's citizens:

> The most important thing today is to create conditions for the citizens of Russia to earn money . . . to earn and invest in the economy of their own country with profit to themselves. We must make Russia a flourishing and rich country [in which people are] comfortable and secure, [where they are] free to work and make money for themselves and their children without limitations and fear.[43]

Might not, then, the success of Chkhartishvili's books signal the beginning of a tectonic and, for Russia, a most benign shift for the intelligentsia—

which for over two centuries was bound to the state by employment and a belief in statist approaches to social change—to a self-supporting middle class?

"Russia never had commercial literature for the middle classes—partly because it never had a middle class," Chkhartishvili told an interviewer. "We either had pulp fiction that intellectuals were embarrassed to read or high-brow literature."[44]

Recalling Chekhov's squeezing-the-slave-out letter, Fandorin's creator pointed out in a 2001 interview that ridding oneself of inner slavery was the most important result of the revolution. "We have squeezed out a lot," Chkhartishvili said. "In the past ten or fifteen years, people living in this country have straightened their backs."[45] For him, the "most precious product of this evolution" is dignity—a quality that had been "in catastrophically short supply" throughout Russian history (he has identified its scarcity as Russia's "main problem") but is inbred in the post-Soviet generation.[46] "These are people," Chkhartishvili says of his readers, "with an absolutely new mentality, who are used to relying on themselves, not on the government. These are people thinking big of themselves."[47]

Suddenly, Fandorins are everywhere in Russia. The nation that for ages has told itself that it is lazy and unlucky and incapable of getting anything done right has become, among many twenty-five- to forty-five-year-olds, a country of perfectionist workaholics and seekers after quality in work and life—the accountant, the software developer, the lawyer, the shop owner, the doctor in private practice, the tailor, the political consultant, the journalist, the clothes designer, the real estate agent, the restaurateur, the owner of the local newspaper or television station.

According to public opinion polls, the "main interests" of the post-Soviet middle class are family and work, while income is third and is looked at not as a main goal but a "consequence" of good work performance. They are *trudogoliki*, literally, "laborholics," and an overwhelming majority believe that the betterment of their life depends on them, not the boss, and not the authorities at all levels.

According to polls conducted every four years since 1990 by the Center for the Study of Social and Cultural Changes, of the Institute of Philosophy of the Russian Academy of Sciences, between 1990 and 2002 the share of Russian citizens who said they relied on themselves and not the state grew from 43 percent to 78 percent. The share of those who preferred to work for privately owned businesses rather than in the state sector increased from 20 percent to 85 percent. Despite the hardships, disappointments, and dislocation of the last twelve years, pluralities or majorities continued to support liberty, independence, and private initiative. Liberty, in particular, was among the most consistently supported values of this period. When asked to choose between "democracy that guarantees freedom and strict state control that guarantees security," 50 percent opted for the former and 30 percent for the latter.[48]

May we, years or decades from now, look back at the popularity of the Fandorin cycle as a signal that, in choosing between the "intelligentsia tradition"—of solemn dreams and sordid reality, of relentless statism, all-or-nothing politics, shoddy work, and sterile castigation of everyone and everything but themselves for everything that is wrong with the country—and the Chekhov-*Vekhi*-Fandorin liberal vision of progress founded on self-improvement, personal responsibility, gradualism, patience, and quotidian hard work, post-Soviet Russia has given the latter at least a sporting chance?

11

Restauration: The Art of Eating Returns to Russia

2002

Few things epitomize the vastness of change from the Soviet days more than the return of Russia's superb gastronomic tradition. Reflecting the national trend, Moscow's rise from poverty and grayness to a vibrant and bright European metropolis (and likely one of the best restaurant values on the continent) is a sign of two very hopeful developments: the private ownership that brings with it creativity, dedication, and perfectionism, and the emergence of the middle class, who can afford these new delights and appreciate their rediscovered art.

O Babel, Isaak Emanuilovich Babel—you gourmand, Jewish cavalryman, admirer of Maupassant and seeker after Flaubertian perfection, rotund little bon vivant in steel-rimmed glasses; you who compared your life to "a meadow in May, the meadow on which women and horses wandered"— where was your soul that night? Your fierce, voracious, and restless soul, which left your body in the basement of the Lubyanka in January 1940 after the customary midnight shot in the back of the head, like hundreds of thousands of other "enemies of the people" swept out in Stalin's Great Purge? We ate cold stuffed fish with horseradish, like the ones your grandmother served on Saturday nights in Odessa—the dish of which you wrote it was "worth converting to Judaism for." We drank a toast to your Aunt Bobka, in whose jam strudel and poppy-seed pie you tasted "the heart of our tribe, the heart so good at struggle"—and our strudel and our pie were just as stirring.

And yours was not the only ghost looking down on us. The fabulous food was a medium for communing with another son of the fat and fecund soil of the Russian empire's southern rim—Russia's strangest genius, a depressive and anti-Semite, who produced some of the funniest pages of the Russian literary canon; a passionate patriot who loved Russia from "the beautiful far-away" of an apartment on Rome's Via Sistina above the Spanish Steps; a gourmand who called the stomach his "noblest inner organ," left unmatched descriptions of Russian and Ukrainian food, and starved himself to death. Gogol was there with Babel, like Jewish tavern owners, shinkari, and their Ukrainian and Russian customers—and occasional pogrom murderers—who lived together for centuries of mutual suspicion, need, and loathing.

We were in the Shinok ("Tavern"), number 2, 1905 Revolution Street, and it was May 2001. Behind the glass wall next to our dark table, two milk-white goats, a red horse, and a spotted pig chewed and slept and walked about attended by a woman of ample proportions in the Ukrainian folk dress of a bright red jacket and a full green skirt with a few inches of linen petticoat showing below the hem, and the customers ate and drank, as they did (minus the glass partition) in Gogol's Evenings near the Village of Dikan'ka.

Here were all the requisite dishes, as if prepared by Gogol Pulkheriya Ivanovna of Old World Landowners for her perennially hungry husband or by lascivious Khavronya Nikiforovna from Sorochinskaya Fair for her cowardly lover: syrniki (cottage-cheese pancakes), pampushki (rolls), galushki, irregularly shaped pieces of dough, white and slippery, served hot with sour cream (known as klyotski in the Russian-Jewish version), and vareniki—ravioli-like large dumplings stuffed with fruit or cheese and served with either sour cream or sweet fruit sauce. Vareniki were served in small earthenware crocks—"little pots," Gogol wrote, "with lids sealed by wax or grease lest some mouth-watering creation of the old tasty cuisine lose its flavor."

Our Shinok waiter put on the table a tall, cold pitcher of kvas beaded with moisture. Recalling, again, Gogol's Evenings, we had asked for an elaborate pear-and-blackthorn-berries version. They had it.

Zakuski—hors d'oeuvres—continued to arrive: the velvety forshmak— a soufflé of herring soaked in milk overnight to take away the salt and baked with eggs, onion, and breadcrumbs—with roast potatoes, followed by pirozhki. Unlike the Moscow variety—oval, flaky, layered, and uniformly browned—these gifts of southern Russia were perfectly round brown cupolas on white bottoms. Faced with a choice of nine different stuffings, I recalled Gogol's Old World Landowners and ordered two with liver and two with buckwheat and cabbage sautéed with onions and dill.

Appearing in solemn silence, the king of Russian soups, steaming borscht, heralded the end of the appetizer prelude. The classic borscht's inimitable bouquet of flavors comes from the harmonious multiplicity of ingredients that are sautéed together in animal fat and sprinkled with lemon juice and a dash of sugar before being ladled into beef bouillon fortified with potatoes, cabbage, carrots, onions, peppers, garlic, tomato paste, tomatoes, and bay leaf. Potatoes, sour cream, and a few pinches of deep-fried flour together produce the thick, almost chewy, but creamy and fluid texture. Our borscht was strong and dark purple, with floating islands of beef and potatoes. It was accompanied by hot *pampushki*, but we asked for black rye bread and garlic cloves to rub against the crust: the gentle rolls were no match for this monster. The ultimate prize of every borsch connoisseur was there as well: "in the fiery thickness something tastier than anything in the world—a marrow bone," as another great Russian writer born in Ukraine, Mikhail Bulgakov, wrote in his phantasmagoric and brilliant *Master and Margarita*.

If borscht is the king and stuffed fish the queen, the prince of the traditional southern Russian (and Jewish) table is undoubtedly *kislo-sladkoe zharkoye*, a sweet-and-sour beef stew. A species of *tzimmes* (generic Yiddish for sweetened meat-and-vegetable stews), the beef is dressed with tomato paste, carrots, and onions. The key to the dish is the elusive and precarious balance between sugar (or honey) and lemon juice. (The sweet side also may be fortified with prunes and apricots, and the sour, with vinegar.) Here, too, the Shinok passed with flying colors: served piping hot, under a thick, dark orange sauce, the cubed brisket was tender but fully textured.

The tea came with an apple strudel of cinnamon, nuts, and raisins; *pirog s makom* (poppy-seed pie); and *smetannik* (a sour cream and jam pie). All were freshly baked, their slightly moist interiors harboring the intense sweetness and spice that over the centuries have fortified the Russian-Jewish heart against disasters.

The dessert was accompanied by the homemade digestive *nalivka*, in its most popular—cherry—version. The juiciest fruits are mixed with the best vodka and plenty of sugar and allowed to stand for at least a month before straining. I found the Shinok's concoction stronger and not as sweet as my Grandpa Abram's homemade version but just as flavorful. "We do not drink vodka," Grandpa Abram used to declare to the bitterly disappointed Russian porters, painters, or plumbers claiming the customary glass of vodka upon the completion of a job. "*Vot nalivka, pozhaluysta!*" ("But, by all means, please help yourself to the *nalivka!*")

I silently dedicated the few last drops of vodka to the memory of my grandmothers, Sima Shvartz and Roza Atlas, who had forged delectable masterpieces out of the poverty and strain of Soviet existence.

✑✑

When I left Moscow for the United States in 1978, the humorists in the city of my birth were fond of circulating a reportedly true story about a Politburo member's daughter who, having come down with food poisoning, was greeted at the exclusive Kremlin hospital by her mother's reprimand: "*Ty s'ela shto-to v gorode?!*" "You've eaten something in the city, haven't you?!" Supplied weekly with enormous food parcels from secret depots, the top party bosses, their children, their servants, and, in the finely calibrated order of seniority, the rest of the *nomenklatura*—from the military brass and Central Committee staffers to propagandists, writers, journalists, and movie directors—considered suspect anything sold in stores.

At the time, however, Moscow was still better off than the rest of the country, where meat appeared in stores twice a year: around the anniversary of the "Great October Socialist Revolution," on November 7, and "Labor Solidarity Day," May 1. During the rest of the year, one could purchase (with a valid ration coupon) a monthly allotment of "meat products," which in 1988 amounted to to 500 grams (about a pound) of "cooked sausage" and 300 grams (11 ounces) of "smoked sausage."[1] In the late 1980s, along with milk and cheese, meat was available at semiprivatized "farmers' markets," but to buy it required monthly food outlays of at least 150 rubles—an astronomical sum in a country where one-third of the citizens lived on less than 100 rubles a month (then about $10).

By that time Moscow's relative prosperity, sustained by robbing the rest of the country, had collapsed under the assault of hundreds of thousands of hungry visitors from the provinces, where, as a Russian newspaper columnist put it, children had to be told "what was meat and what, in theory, could be done with it." Every day the commuter trains, called *kolbasnye elektrichki,* or "sausage trains," disgorged the foragers at the capital's seven train stations. In the 1970s an underground joke circulated about a Moscow Jew, who, when asked why he was emigrating, said: "I am tired of holidays: bought sausage—a holiday; found toilet paper—a holiday; got to buy shoes—holiday again. I long for a dreary, nonfestive existence." Writing about those days, a young woman who is a columnist for the leading Russian daily *Izvestiya* recalled how, on a visit to the apartment of a classmate whose father worked at the Council of Ministers, she was stunned to discover that there was such a thing as a wafer with raspberry jam inside, and that *escalope* actually existed and meant "pork steak." Both of the writer's parents were professionals with advanced degrees.

In December 1989, by way of a farewell gift, my Moscow friends gave me a small, pink square stamped *Сахар/Декабрь*—the sugar coupon for the month of December. By the fall of 1991, the collapsed state-owned economy had left behind absolutely bare shelves of grocery stores, bread lines around the block, and sacks of potatoes on the balconies of Moscow residents preparing for famine.

Today, the would-be émigré is likely not to find the excuse to celebrate. The streets are brightly lit; the shop windows, inviting. The sidewalks, no longer littered with cigarette butts, are scrubbed clean. At every major metro station there are gorgeous roses for sale, reportedly trucked in from Holland or flown in from Honduras. The flow of cars is thick and furious, and Audis, BMWs, and Toyota Land Cruisers no longer turn heads. Moscow women, who used to beg their male bosses to bring back a pair of panty-hose from a trip abroad, now sport European fashions and haircuts. Metro riders are no longer morose and rude; smiles and jokes are suddenly common. It seems that everyone has a cell phone.

The shift to a more open economy has given rise to a post-Communist middle class, which consists largely of the young, the college-educated, and the residents of large cities. The tastes and preferences of this modest but energetic and increasingly self-confident population account for all manner of new trends sweeping Russia in the past decade.[2]

The stifling ownership of everyone's livelihood and tastes by an impoverished, corrupt, and autarkic state has gone the way of *Pravda*, the jamming of foreign broadcasts, compulsory classes of political education, and awful clothes. Nowhere is the metamorphosis as vivid and as easily discernible, even to a casual tourist, as in the national gastronomic renaissance. That gastronomy has been ahead of many other areas of life in the speed and robustness of recovery is due to the fact that the Russian table was always one place where the state receded. The kitchen was a substitute for the public square, the table-talk a surrogate for free political discourse. In the long run, liberty creates wealth everywhere, but in Russia it has repaid the debt to the table a hundredfold.

The Politburo mama would have no cause to worry. An amazing abundance and variety of edibles are now available in Moscow. Snack bars and kiosks dispensing not only Russian but Mexican, Japanese, Chinese, Greek, and Middle Eastern fare dot the same sidewalks where crowds of shabbily dressed people, weighed down by enormous bags and bundles, used to shuffle silently and sullenly, like a herd of foraging beasts of burden, from store to store in search of food.

Menus, cookbooks, lunch counters, and home pantries brim with items rediscovered after an eighty-year hiatus: pineapple and kiwi, asparagus, squid and baby-octopus salad, frogs' legs, or pizza. People everywhere in the city walk around munching on *shawarma*, which every New Yorker will instantly recognize as a species of gyro—chicken or lamb sliced off a hot rotating cone, wrapped, falafel-like, in either pita or flat Georgian *lavash*, and dipped in spicy yogurt.

In Moscow's new gastronomic universe everything has to be fresh and hot. Between appointments on my last visit I found myself, a ten-ruble bill in hand, in front of a kiosk selling *chebureki*, the large Crimean meat pasty. "And heat it up, will you?" an older woman in a white kerchief ordered the vendor. The latter complied by putting the pie in a microwave oven. Inspired by the intrepid babushka, I overcame the inbred fear of Russian salesclerks and requested that my order be warmed as well. Quite apart from being its own virtue, the courage paid off handsomely in gastronomic terms when the first bite through the thick, chewy skin revealed a hot and smooth meatball of lamb and beef with garlic and parsley in an aromatic gravy.

Resistance collapses at the sight of *vypechka*—freshly baked goods sold for a few rubles on street corners, outside all major metro stations, and, of course, in the bakeries that seem to grace every other block: puff pastry (*sloyki*) and Danishes (*vatrushki*) with fillings of cheese or prunes or poppy seeds; buns with raisins; tarts with apricots, apples, or blueberries; meringue cookies, eclairs, almond rings (my favorite), napoleons (vanilla-flavored cream between four or five layers of very thin and flaky puff pastry), rum babas, large muffins (*keksy*), or *sochniki*: hefty little bricks of sweet cottage cheese surrounded by a crumbly dough shell.

All of the former *nomenklatura* delights now are to be found in ordinary grocery stores (*gastronomy*)—like the Razumovskiy *gastronom* near a friend's apartment in a quiet residential neighborhood on Leningradskoye Highway, close to the Airport Metro. There were the precious holiday treats of my childhood: the delicate, smooth, and aromatic *doktorskaya* and the hard, peppery, fat-speckled salami *servelat* at the equivalent of $1.60 and $2.50 a pound, respectively. *Servelat* used to be available either in snack bars set up at polling places on "election" days to attract "voters" or during the week before New Year's Eve (officially, there was no Christmas in Soviet times), and, along with oranges, bananas, or apples, was among the best gifts one could bring to a friend's house. Among the sixteen kinds of cheeses the *gastronom* displays are the hard, piquant, light-yellow *poshekhonskiy*; the round and softer *gollandskiy* wrapped in red wax; the slightly salty and viscous Georgian *sulguni*; and feta-like *brynza*. The breads vary from the fat, white, all-wheat ellipses of *bulki* (which, with soft butter, are the best pedestal for caviar), to darker hues of rye, to the dense, crusty, and round *orlovskiy* and the black, pungent *borodinskiy* studded with caraway seeds.[3]

The Razumovskiy carries, among former rarities, smoked or cured sturgeon (*osetr, beluga*, and *sevryuga*) and salmon (*syomga, gorbusha, keta*, and *nerka*) for between 31 and 75 rubles for 100 grams (or $1.00–$2.50 for three and a half ounces). Caviar in small tins and glass jars with metal lids range from salmon's red (ripe and briny) at 99 rubles for a 113-gram can ($3.20 for 4 ounces) through *osetr*'s small and firm kernels (300 rubles, or $10) to the luscious, silvery-gray *beluga* at 500 rubles ($16). Except for holidays, these fish were virtually absent from the Russian diet in Soviet times.

For those in need of a serious dessert—for an evening tea at home or, following the tradition, a gift to bring to a dinner party—there are torte kiosks. Chocolate, cream, or soufflé, or filled with nuts, layered with waffles, or any combination thereof, these round, square, or loglike concoctions with names like *adagio, polyot* ("flight"), *ptich'e moloko* ("birds' milk"), *shchelkunchik* ("nutcracker"), *stratosfera, kapriz* ("caprice"), and *nezhnost'* ("tenderness") weigh between one and four pounds each and cost between 32 and 280 rubles ($1–$9). One of the kiosks near the Airport Metro sells fifty-seven varieties.

Nearby, Azeri vendors sell homegrown tomatoes, cucumbers, honeydew melons, apples, watermelons, and large southern cherries (*chereshni*), as well as imported pineapples, oranges, and bananas. Bananas were the impossible dream of every Moscow child of my generation (most Soviet children outside the city didn't know what a banana was), the ultimate prize our mothers captured once or twice a year after queuing for hours. They were often green and small, and turned black with rot within a few days. No matter: We loved their exotic shape and sweet mushy flesh, which was like nothing else we had ever had. Now they sell for less than fifty cents a pound, and children do not yell and drag their mothers toward the stalls, and no one is surprised or even especially pleased at their availability. People buy one or two at a time and, children and grownups alike, eat them casually while walking and irreverently throw the beautiful yellow skins into sidewalk trash cans.

Another national craving is also now amply supplied by the market: Between August and October no Moscow grocery store is complete without mushrooms. There are tall and firm *podberyozoviki* ("the ones under a birch tree") in dark-brown bonnets; all-white *gruzdi* ("the heavy ones"); saffron milk caps, or *ryzhiki* ("little red ones"); yellow *maslyata* ("little buttery ones"); chanterelles (*lisichki*, or "little foxes"); and, of course, the noblest fungi of the Russian forest and a dream of every mushroom-picker: the squat, fleshy, tawny-brimmed *belyie* ("the white ones") on chubby white stems.

Some mushrooms are used in soups; others are fried in butter with scallions and potatoes, or stewed in sour cream, flour, and parsley, and then baked in pies, or salted and marinated to form one of the three best accompaniments to vodka. (The other two are herring and pickles. To make the latter, sprinkle cucumbers with grated horseradish and sliced garlic, layer with dill and currant leaves, and cover with hot saltwater.) The mushroom season having begun early last summer because of unusually heavy rains and cool weather, the Razumovskiy offered half a dozen ready-to-eat mushroom salads—in sour cream or olive oil, and with beets, carrots, and potatoes.

Like the sudden abundance of food, the transformation in the way it is consumed has been nothing short of dramatic. Dull and heavy, like Russians' lives, food used to be gorged on—after months of relentless foraging and hoarding—on birthdays, the November 7 anniversary of the revolution, and New Year's Eve, and drowned in vodka. The rest of the year, the food was meager but the vodka still plentiful. It was the shortage of food and the cheapness of vodka, which contributed up to one-fifth of the state budget both in czarist and Soviet times, that were responsible for the stereotype of Russia as a nation of depressed drunks.

More and better food and the appearance of colorful beer bars, especially the ubiquitous Zolotaya Bochka ("Golden Barrel") chain, are likely to change this stereotype. Whetted by the opening of the market to imports, Russia's thirst for beer has increased by leaps and bounds since 1991. After 1998, when most Russians could not afford the imports because of the ruble devaluation, 1,500 private breweries filled the market with domestic brands, with the Zolotaya Bochka brand among the most popular. For the first time in history, Russians started to drink more beer than vodka—a development immensely beneficial for the national health, the public order, and the life expectancy for Russian men, for whom alcoholism was among the leading causes of death.

✑

The new casualness in acquiring food and the appreciation of taste and freshness are Russian gastronomic trends that were merely interrupted in 1917, as was the country's rapid progress toward advanced capitalism and democracy. Classic Russian literature and classic Russian cuisine were born and reached their golden age at about the same time—between, approximately, 1830 and 1890—and the former has compiled a marvelous record of the latter. Here, for instance, is the "gentleman of average means" from Gogol's *Dead Souls*, who ordered ham at the first tavern on the road; suckling pig at the next stop; a "chunk of sturgeon or sausage with onions" farther down the road; and finished on sterlet soup with *rasstegai*—round, open, literally "unbuttoned" fish pies with filling exposed in the center—and *kulebyaki*—multilayered puff-pastry pies, stuffed with rice, mushrooms, onions, or baked salmon and dripping with melted butter.

Chekhov gave Russian literature its first gastronomic martyr. The mid-level bureaucrat Semyon Petrovich Podtykin is ambushed by cruel fate after what seems to him an interminable wait for his first post-Lent Easter meal. At last the housekeeper-cook carries into the dining room a tall stack of *blini*. The hot, thin pancakes are beautiful: crisp on the bottom, white, porous, and soft, "like the shoulder of a merchant's daughter." Semyon Petrovich tears off the top two round sheets, douses them in hot melted butter, and slowly spreads caviar. Spots devoid of caviar are covered with sour cream. He looks with an artist's pride on his succulent canvas, pauses yet again to survey the table covered with *zakuski* (hors d'oeuvres), adds a slice of *syomga*, then a sardine and a sprat; rolls the *blini* into a tight tube, drinks a shot of vodka, sighs in anticipation, and then—in an object lesson to all perfectionists—dies of apoplexy.

The flowering of classic Russian cuisine coincided with the rapid economic expansion and explosive growth of the middle class in the aftermath of Alexander II's liberal reforms. Moscow offered culinary delights to suit every taste and almost every wallet. For a few kopecks street vendors sold pies and *blini, kalachi* (white rolls), fried buckwheat *kasha*, or smoked sturgeon with horseradish and vinegar, to be washed down with hot *sbiten'* (a mead drink spiced with cardamom and nutmeg) in the winter and *kvas* (Russia's national nonalcoholic drink, made from rye bread fermented with sugar) in the summer.

Filippov's bakery produced kopeck buns, loaves, and warm little pies, *pirozhki* (the word deriving from the Russian *pir*, or "feast"), with meat, rice, mushrooms, cottage cheese, or raisins. For five kopecks one could buy pies big enough to provide, with a cup of tea, a hearty Russian breakfast. The official purveyor to the St. Petersburg court, Filippov, bought only the best rye grain from Tambov Province and sent inspectors to watch over the milling. Frozen by a secret method, his *kalachi* were shipped all over Russia, thawed in wet towels, warmed, and served, according to witnesses, "hot and aromatic."

Muscovites were notorious *traktir*-goers, and in the capital there were thousands of these tavernlike forerunners of restaurants. The poor would pay kopecks for a bowl of *shchi* (cabbage soup) with meat and porridge. In the frigid winter, the ubiquitous coachmen (*izvozchiki*) would warm themselves at roadside *traktiry* with a pot of tea, fried pork, giblets with pickled cucumber, smoked catfish, and a loaf of bran bread.

The Gurin's and the Egorov's, the best in a long line of great Moscow *traktiry*, fed the city gourmands between 1850 and 1890. The Gurin's was renowned, along with its food, for the largest organ in Moscow, and people flocked there to listen to the music. Located at the end of present-day Okhotny Ryad street, the Egorov's sets the national standard of excellence for *blini*, which were served right off a huge wooden spatula all day long, plain or with caviar, smoked fish, or a score of other fillings, and for *rasstegai* adorned, in the center of the top layer, with the crown jewel of a glistening slice of roast sturgeon or baked turbot's liver. In the seafood restaurant on the second floor, wealthier customers drank their *sterlet ukha* (fish broth) next to a giant tank of live fish.

Some of Europe's leading chefs worked in Moscow in the second half of the nineteenth century. One of them, the Frenchman Olivier, who owned the expensive and fashionable Hermitage, gave his name to the hearty salad of meat, potatoes, eggs, pickles, peas, scallions, and mayonnaise without which to this day no festive Russian table, no matter how exalted or poor, is complete.

Waiting on tables in the best Moscow *traktiry* was a much sought-after profession. According to Vladimir Gilyarovskiy's *Moskva i Moskvichi* (*Moscow and Muscovites*), an apprenticeship began with dishwashing and was followed by six months in the kitchen (to remember "all the sauces") and four years as a busboy. A successful graduate was required to purchase the uniforms, consisting of six shirts and trousers of expensive Dutch linen, to be kept "white as fresh snow" and free of wrinkles.

All was lost when the last vestiges of private enterprise disappeared in the early 1930s. Taken over by the state, a few good restaurants lingered for years, most conspicuously the one at the Union of Soviet Writers on Povarskaya, or Cook's, Street. Yet by the mid-1930s, in *The Master and Margarita*, Mikhail Bulgakov mourned the restaurant's decline: "Do you remember sterlet in a silver saucepan, cut into pieces and interlaced with lobster tails and fresh caviar?" he asked wistfully. "Or eggs filled with pureed mushrooms and served in tiny cups? And how about blackbird filets—with truffles? Or quail a la Genoa?"

No major Soviet Russian author wrote in praise of fine food after that.

✍

A decade after the end of the relentless Soviet deprivation, incompetence, universal thievery, and daily indignities—the world Nabokov called "so shoddy, so crabbed and gray"—the Russian capital seems to have been remade into one of Europe's best (and best-hidden) gastronomic destinations. The change in taste, decor, and service is even more startling than the availability of food. Outside of the *stolovye* ("dining rooms") of the high *nomenklatura* (closed to ordinary mortals), meals were equally awful in the glitzy Metropol or Natsional (which catered to foreigners, their KGB minders, and "official Russians") and in the "cafes" and "restaurants" for the "masses"—except that in the former the execrable food was dispensed with servility in kitschy chic, while in the latter it was ladled out in rudeness and squalor. All this has been replaced by cleanliness, politeness, good training, competence, and, in many cases, polish and even panache.

Of course, far from all of Moscow's more than four thousand restaurants are within the middle-class range. For those who, following Dr. Johnson, wish to smile with the wise but feed with the rich (that is, the 5 percent with monthly incomes of over $3,500), there are several dozen superb establishments. Among them are Tsarskaya Okhota ("Czar's Hunt") in Zhukovka, near Stalin's favorite dacha, where in 1997 Boris Yeltsin entertained French President Jacques Chirac; the CDL, in the former headquarters of the Union of Soviet Writers; the Sirena, Moscow's best seafood restaurant, which serves lobsters, oysters, crabs, and giant shrimp in a hushed, wood-paneled décor, as enormous sturgeon swim under the glass floor and sea creatures frolic behind the glass walls; and the Savoy, the Grand Imperial, Le Romanoff, the Metropol, and the Grand Opera—with their cavernous dining rooms, crystal chandeliers, silver cutlery, and floor-to-ceiling mirrors.

A step below this grandeur are restaurants that middle-class Muscovites enjoy on special occasions. Across Tverskaya Street from Pushkin Square is Cafe Pushkin, an example of an intense but tasteful quest for authenticity that characterizes Moscow dining today. The restaurant is housed in a typical early-nineteenth-century Moscow building, quite a few of which miraculously survived Soviet decay and demolition. The inside looks very much like a Moscow museum: parquet floors, mirrors fogged with age in heavy bronze frames, a patina of fine cracks on the marble stairs and the walls, a medium-size dining room under a thirty-foot ceiling, and a wide staircase with cast-iron banisters leading to the second-floor library. But all is an illusion: the restaurant is barely four years old and was built from scratch on an empty lot within five months.

The Pushkin offers the mainstays of Russian cooking: *kvas* and *sbiten'*; suckling pig with apple gravy (as a cold appetizer); *blini* with *osetr* and salmon caviar; mutton Hussar, "stewed in beer for more swagger," as the menu describes it, and baked with mushrooms into a pie; beef stroganoff; chicken giblets with mushrooms in rye bread "pots"; salmon and sturgeon (grilled, stewed, or jerked), *pel'meni* (dumplings) with beef, pork, veal, salmon, or mushrooms; and catfish "baked into a potato puree under a spinach sauce." Appetizers and soups are between $6 and $9, and most entrees are between $10 and $23, with the most expensive—saddle of lamb accompanied by vegetables—at $29.50.

It being July, my hosts (up-and-coming lawyers in their early forties) and I ordered the summer classic of chilled *kvas*-based soup, *okroshka*. Thinly sliced scallions, radishes, beef, potatoes, boiled eggs, and cucumbers, dill, a dollop of sour cream, and a touch of horseradish blended harmoniously, each ingredient true to its character and texture. Marinated Baltic sprats were delicate, their sharp briny taste balanced by an accompanying vinaigrette of potatoes, beets, onions, dill pickles, eggs, and mayonnaise. The entrées were faultless: golden-brown veal cutlet a la Pozharsky (a famous nineteenth-century Russian chef, who made the dish from wild game) and crisp grilled sturgeon.

Both in the fare and the setting, Beloye Solntze Pustyni, or BSP ("White Sun of the Desert"), on Neglinnaya Street is as far from the lean elegance of the Pushkin as St. Petersburg is from Bukhara or Samarkand. It dazzles with brilliant colors and pampers shamelessly. The restaurant is a festive blend of a Central Asian *chai-khana* (teahouse) and a movie set. The film that gave the restaurant its name is an irreverent tragicomedy about the Russian civil war, set on a barge marooned on Turkestan's Caspian shore. The movie miraculously made it past the censors in the late 1960s and became a cult hit. The dining room is wrapped in red, gold, and black Persian carpets: on the floor, over the whitewashed clay walls, and on the seats. Female servers wear gold, red, and mauve paisley silk tunics over silk *sharavari* (baggy trousers) and matching embroidered skullcaps. Life-size papier-mâché soldiers crouch behind a Maxim machine gun. A few feet away, swarthy, white-bearded elders smoke hookahs on wooden boxes inscribed "*ОПАСНО: ДИНАМИТ!*" ("DANGER: DYNAMITE!").

In the center of the room, circling an enormous tree trunk, is a *dastarkhan:* a *prix-fixe* collection of at least two dozen hot and cold Central Asian dishes, including such standards as *lagman* (noodles-and-lamb stew); *manty* (large lamb dumplings); *shashlyki* of sturgeon, lamb, and chicken; tender and pungent sausage *kazy*, and baked eggplant stuffed with nuts. The patrons' tables are constantly resupplied with clear, cool, tart pomegranate juice and hot, flat white bread extracted with long-handled wooden spatulas from the ovens through openings in the walls. *Plov* (pilaf), which is the heart and the obligatory dish in every meal, never stops cooking in the iron cauldrons hung over a low fire, where the rice is steamed with chunks of lamb shoulder or leg, carrots, onions, hot red pepper, and saffron. Although sautéed in lamb fat instead of olive oil and considerably more pungent than risotto, the classic *plov* is as much a product of constant stirring. Solemnly borne by two sous-chefs, the giant clay pot of *plov* was placed on a wooden pedestal next to our table and ladled onto the plates by the chef himself, a strapping Uzbek in a monumental starched toque.

In post-Soviet Russia, however, as in any other country, the backbone of the national cuisine is to be found not in the almost theatrical elaborateness of the Pushkin or the BSP, but in places that are "neither chic nor sordid," in A. J. Liebling's immortal classification—the restaurants where a meal is not an event, but an uncomplicated and affordable pleasure. An entrée in scores of such places in Moscow rarely exceeds the equivalent of $12. Muscovites stop by after work for a bit of smoked salmon or pickled Baltic Sea herring, marinated mushrooms, fresh *kholodetz* (pork or veal in aspic), a plate of *pel'meni*, *pirozhki* with chicken or beef bouillon, a bowl of borscht or fish broth, a cup of tea—and, often, listen to live jazz or romantic Russian ballads.

The Bochka ("Barrel") serves pigs roasted on a spit, veal brains with mushrooms in a pot, and grilled salmon. The Oblomov, named after the hero Ivan Goncharov's great nineteenth-century eponymous novel, features waitresses and waiters in crinolines and tails and a giant of a maitre d' in luxurious muttonchops and a morning coat, who converses with customers in Fyodor Chaliapin's deep bass. Those tormented by nostalgia for their Soviet youth may avail themselves of the New Vasyuki (the name is from the hilarious 1928 satire, *The Twelve Chairs*, by Il'ya Il'f and Evgeniy Petrov), on whose menu one finds "the union of the sword and the plough": two plump pieces of sturgeon with black and red caviar inside and a side of fried potato shavings under cream sauce.

A more elaborate retro gastronomic experience is offered by Club Petrovich, named after the main character of a popular cartoon strip: a plumber who is an incorrigible *sovok* (Homo sovieticus)—petty, cunning, thoroughly corrupt, and fiercely competitive for meager Soviet amenities. The theme appealed to Russian P.R.-niks—a hardboiled and cynical lot—and the place became the hangout (*tusovka*) of admen and adwomen, imagemakers, and political-campaign managers. Its walls covered with original black-and-white photographs of Soviet movie stars and hanging toilet plungers, the restaurant is a combination of a crummy communal apartment and a *kontora* (office)— the Soviet shrine and the citadel of sadistic petty bureaucrats on whose bribe-induced mercy untold millions of hapless tenants threw themselves with their tales of leaking roofs, burst sewer pipes, cold radiators, and rusty drinking water. The menu is delivered in the Soviet bureaucrat's indispensable carrying case: a thick, cardboard folder with tassels (*papka*) stained with imitation grease. Served by generous platefuls, the retro food—*sosiski* (fat frankfurters), *bitochki* (small steaks), *grechnevaya kasha* (boiled buckwheat groats), *lapsha* (noodles), *kupaty* (crisp fried sausages stuffed with spicy mincemeat)— is incomparably fresher and better-tasting than the Soviet originals but perfectly recognizable.

$$\backsim\!\!\!\!\sim$$

Walking with an old friend and his nine-year-old son along Pyatnitskaya Street in Zamoskvorech'e—Moscow's sedate residential district, populated before 1917 by well-to-do merchants and today home to less important embassies—we saw four tables on the sidewalk. The small restaurant inside, with white curtains on the windows and cheerful Gobelins on the walls, looked like a Moscow apartment.

After a short July shower, the air was fresh and cool. In the soft bluish dusk, a sudden burst of light from the sidewalk signaled a small but safe harbor of friendship and intimacy. What I thought was possible only on the edge of a sleepy piazza in Rome's Trastevere or on a narrow street on Paris's Left Bank was suddenly part of Moscow.

The marquee read Soosy Poosy—the cooing of a Russian parent over a baby. A children's cafe? No, no, laughed a beautiful young woman. "It's just that we are trying to be like your family's apartment. Also we are a family restaurant: I wait on tables, my parents cook. Are you coming in?"

Full of beer, jambalaya, fried shrimp, and oysters from the Louisiana American Steak House up the street, where waiters wore tight jeans and toy silver guns in holsters, we had to decline.

"*Prikhodite k nam koga-nibud.*" "Come see us sometime," the woman called out. "*Pridyom. Pridyom, ob'yazatel'no pridyom.*" "We will be back. We certainly will," I promised.

Part IV

Making Sense of the 1990s

12

Is Russia Really "Lost"?
1999

In the United States, Russia is "lost" at least once every four years, as the contenders for the White House seek to burnish their foreign policy credentials by raking the incumbent over the coals for the many ruts, bumps, and detours on Russia's road to liberal capitalism and democracy. Some of the alleged failures stem from errors of fact. Most are real, but, distorted by hyperbole and the absence of a larger context in which Russia's progress could be compared to that of other transitional states and economies, they provide less than stellar guidance for U.S. policymakers, as the period leading up to the 2000 presidential election in the United States illustrated.

"Who lost Russia?" has suddenly become part of the daily disquisition of America's political and writing classes. Featured by the *New York Times* on the cover of its Sunday magazine in August of this year, the question has since been the subject of long articles in the *Times* and the *Washington Post*, as well as innumerable columns and op-ed pieces in almost all major U.S. newspapers. The *New York Times* and the *Wall Street Journal* have been mostly indistinguishable in their relentless anti-Russian animus—a coincidence that surely ought to give pause to editors of both papers. With the Republicans in the House of Representatives threatening hearings on the subject, and with George W. Bush's presidential election campaign quickly turning the issue into a major attack on the Clinton-Gore record, "lost Russia" is likely to remain a prominent fixture of the national political discourse over the coming months.

Unfortunately, this important debate is being conducted like a kangaroo trial. Not only have the accused—Americans and, especially, Russians—

been tried and found guilty in absentia, but, contrary to the Anglo-Saxon legal tradition, the stage of discovery, which establishes underlying facts and allows both sides to present their version of events, has been skipped almost entirely. Before the sentence is carried out, ought we not at least try to determine whether there was a crime? Has Russia indeed been "lost"?

A hodgepodge of undeniable facts, half-truths presented as a complete account, outdated clichés, grotesque exaggerations, and outright distortions, the evidence for prosecution comes down to a few simple, monochromic, and well-integrated postulates concerning post-Communist Russia's economic performance, politics, and foreign policy, and the future of capitalism and democracy in Russia.

First, regarding the *economy*, free-market reforms have failed to produce a prosperous country with a growing gross domestic product. A typical *New York Times* op-ed piece defines the Russian "reforms" (rarely used without quotation marks these days) as "entrenchment of a kleptocracy in which corrupt officials ally with a very few business magnates to send wealth out of the country."[1] The "reform" never enjoyed even a modicum of popular support and was, instead, forced on the defenseless country by "reformers around Yeltsin" and their Western advisers, especially from the International Monetary Fund (IMF), and with the connivance of the White House. Eight years after the fall of communism, Russia still does not have even an approximation of a market economy. Instead, the "reform" has brought poverty, alcoholism, and health care disaster. Russia today is a handful of thieving "oligarchs" feasting amidst general near-starvation.

In *politics*, democratic institutions have failed to take root. This "Weimar Russia" is an unstable, "failing state," in the words of Dr. Condoleezza Rice, Governor Bush's top foreign policy adviser, who mentioned Russia in the same breath as the "failed states" of North Korea and Iraq.[2] As House Majority Leader Dick Armey put it ever so elegantly, "Russia has become a looted and bankrupt zone of nuclearized anarchy."[3]

In *foreign policy*, Boris Yeltsin has not "delivered" where America's core national interests were concerned, and the "investment" in him by the Clinton administration was wrong and wasteful. These combined failures have soured the Russians on capitalism, democracy, the West in general, and the United States in particular, and have made them ripe for Communist

revanche, an anti-Western nationalist dictatorship, or an even scarier combination of the two.

❧

One of the most puzzling features of the "lost Russia" argument is its ahis-
toricism. Post-Communist Russia has no past—not even one that is a decade
old. The entire discourse is enveloped in a near-total amnesia about the country's prior conditions, which were so memorably revealed by *glasnost* (and
noted in the opening chapter of this book). For instance, in 1989, the last year
of relative stability before the crisis in the Soviet Union became uncontrol-
lable, the average salary was two hundred rubles a month: $33 officially and
$13 on a still illegal free-currency exchange market. (The average salary in
Russia today is $75.) Forty-three million Soviet citizens (or 17 percent) lived
on less than the "official" poverty level, set at seventy-five rubles per person
per month ($5).[4] Another 100 million (or 40 percent) lived perilously close
to penury on less than one hundred rubles ($6.50) a month. One-third of the
58 million pensioners in the cities and eight out of ten in the villages received
less than sixty rubles a month.[5] The Soviet Union was seventy-seventh in the
world in personal consumption.[6] Of 211 "essential" food products, only 23
were regularly available in state stores.[7] Russians spent, on average, forty to
sixty-eight hours a month in queues.

When Kuzbass miners walked off the job in July 1989 and precipitated
Russia's first national strike since 1918, their demands included a towel and
800 grams of soap a month for after-shift wash-up, and padded cotton jack-
ets. As part of the settlement, the government agreed to deliver to Kuzbass
10,000 tons of sugar, 3,000 tons of detergent, 3,000 tons of soap, more than
6,000 tons of meat, 5 million cans of dairy products, and 1,000 tons of tea.[8]

The Soviet Union consumed an estimated eight liters of " hard" (forty- to
eighty-proof) alcoholic beverages per capita—more than any other country in
the world.[9] Production of vodka doubled between 1958 and 1984.[10] Each
year, on the average 15 million drunks were arrested and put in sobering-up
stations. Premature deaths directly or indirectly caused by alcohol accounted
for about one-fifth of all deaths in the USSR. Fifty-one thousand people died
of acute alcohol poisoning in the late 1970s—19.5 deaths per 100,000 (as

compared with the 0.3 average for the nineteen countries that compiled and published such data). Between 1964 and the end of the 1970s, male life expectancy fell by five years, from sixty-seven to sixty-two years.[11] The State Statistical Committee disclosed that just 19 percent of the hospitals had central heat, 45 percent lacked bathrooms or showers, and 49 percent had no hot water.[12] The Soviet Union, behind Barbados and the United Arab Emirates, had a higher rate of infant mortality than forty-nine nations.[13]

By the time Boris Yeltsin took over in the fall of 1991, the country's economy was collapsing. Domestic production declined 13 percent compared with the previous year, the budget deficit soared to 30 percent of GDP, the annual inflation rate was 93 percent, hard currency and gold reserves were nearly exhausted, and the USSR defaulted on its international loans. No one who was in Moscow that autumn will ever forget the grocery stores empty of anything for sale, or the ration coupons for sugar, tobacco, and soap.

✑

Even such a thumbnail sketch belies the postulate of a Russia "ruined" by reform. The queues—a national shame and curse of four generations—have disappeared, and Russian shops, for the first time since the mid-1920s, offer a plethora of high-quality food and other goods. In 1997, for the first time in forty years, Russia produced enough grain so that it did not need imports. In fact, it exported millions of tons in 1998, even as agro-bureaucrats in the Kremlin and the U.S. Department of Agriculture arranged for emergency shipments from the United States to ward off a nonexistent famine.[14]

While millions—especially pensioners, collective farmers, and workers in the mammoth military-industrial complex—were impoverished by galloping inflation and budget cuts, millions of others—the urban, younger, and better-educated (who voted for Yeltsin in overwhelming numbers in the 1996 presidential election)—saw a dramatic improvement in their daily professional and personal lives. For the first time in Russian history, there is a sizable middle class and intelligentsia outside state employ. Before the August 1998 crash, Russian experts estimated the size of the middle class (those making $300–$1,000 a month, depending on the region) at one-fifth to one-third of the country's population. It included, for instance, skilled workers in successful industrial and commercial enterprises, small and medium entrepreneurs, mid-level managers, lawyers, accountants, teachers, journalists, programmers, drivers, and tailors.[15] In the polls before the crash, almost one-fifth (18 percent) of those responding stated that the economic "situation" of their own family was improving.[16]

After market economy became a taboo term in Washington (when applied to Russia) and "virtual economy" all the rage, after the very word "reform" was impossible to mention at congressional hearings without provoking much clucking and snickering, we are discovering that the Russian market economy does, after all, exist and, despite many and deep distortions, responds to economic stimuli much as any economy would. In full accordance with the tenets of supply-side theory, the continuing absence of price controls, a cheaper but stable national currency, and a drastic reduction of imports unleashed domestic production. Russian-made food and goods filled the stores. Industrial production (or, rather, its registered and taxable part) grew by 4.5 percent in the first six months of 1999, compared with the same period in 1998, and jumped, month-on-month, by 13 percent in July. Contrary to many an augury in the fall of 1998, there is no famine.

With the collapse of astronomically high interest rates and of the fantastically lucrative domestic bond market in 1998, money is becoming available to industry. Barter is down. The stock exchange index of top Russian companies (RTS) grew 300 percent since October 1998. Exports declined by 5 percent in the first eight months of 1999, and imports fell by 45 percent; the resulting large trade surplus is likely to stabilize the ruble. A cheaper ruble and a sharp increase in oil prices have greatly helped to reduce the budget deficit. In August of this year, Russia collected the largest monthly tax in its eight-year post-Communist history: 30.8 billion rubles ($1.25 billion). In September, the state fully paid the pension backlog, which amounted to 26 billion rubles ($1 billion) in January 1999. Contrary to many a confident prediction of hyperinflation, the 1999 inflation is not likely to exceed 40 percent, or the exchange rate to dip below 32 rubles for a dollar.[17]

Breaking with the "state capitalism" of the "oligarchs," thousands of entrepreneurs—many of whom began their careers in the financial empires of the "oligarchs" and became rich in Treasury bills, currency speculations, and arbitrage—start up new businesses by investing their own money in pharmaceuticals, paper, dozens of new brands of beer, packaged snacks, and clothing. Bypassing the largely insolvent Moscow-based banks, which have been little more than bond-recycling stations, successful Russian firms are acting as small banks, often investing their profits outside their immediate sectors and making loans to other businesses.

⁓

Far from evincing a national "rejection of capitalism" (another mainstay of the "lost Russia" thesis), after three generations in total state employ, Russians continue to be sharply divided on the issue of private or state ownership of the economy. In a national poll commissioned by the U.S. Information Agency (USIA) in the beginning of 1999, 41 percent favored a "mostly" or "completely" state-owned economy, while 50 percent felt either that the economy should be "mostly" or "completely" privately owned (16 percent) or a "mix" of private and state ownership (34 percent).[18] The most reliable polls of all, national elections and referendums, confirm a conflicted but hardly universally anticapitalist electorate. In a national referendum of April 1993, with inflation at 19 percent *monthly*, a narrow majority voted to support "the social and economic policy" of Yeltsin. Two and a half years later, in the 1995 Duma elections, 21 million votes (or 30 percent of the total) were cast for proreform and progovernment right-of-center parties and blocs, while the Communists and their allies received 22 million votes (32 percent). (Because of the splintering of the right-of-center parties and blocs, 9.6 million votes cast for right-of-center, proreform, and progovernment parties and blocs were wasted, and only "Yabloko" and "Our Home Is Russia" managed to achieve the 5 percent minimum required for Duma membership; the hard left ended up with 35 percent more deputies—187, compared with 121 seats.)

Contrary to another myth of the "lost Russia" canon, in which Yeltsin, somehow, "bought" 40 million votes with the money of the "oligarchs," Russians made a monumental and informed choice in the presidential election worthy of a great people: a choice between two cardinally different visions of Russia. Yeltsin ran on the platform of a continuing but "modified" and "socially oriented reform." Gennady Zyuganov, the Communist candidate, called for a return to state control (if not outright ownership) of the economy. The Communist alternative was daily presented by more than 150 pro-Communist local and national newspapers (the latter alone with daily circulation exceeding 10 million), by tens of thousands of door-to-door Communist organizers, and by millions of leaflets; the position was reiterated at hundreds of rallies along the route of Zyuganov's vigorous national campaign and during his three and a half hours of free prime time on the national television. In the end, Yeltsin won, 54 percent to 40 percent.

The older and less-educated—most of those in the countryside and in many depressed industrial regions—voted for Zyuganov, while Yeltsin enjoyed astronomical leads among those under forty, as well as professionals and white-collar workers. He carried eighty-six of Russia's hundred largest cities. Even in the heavily Communist agricultural "red belt" south and southwest of Moscow, the president won every regional capital by at least 15 percent. In Moscow and St. Petersburg (with a combined total population of 14 million), Yeltsin trounced Zyuganov 77 percent to 18 percent and 74 percent to 21 percent, respectively.

Regarding the alleged "anti-Americanism," another USIA-commissioned national poll established that most Russians blame their own government for their economic problems. Unless "prompted" by pollsters, "few" think of the "foreign connection."[19] Instead, the "cooling" toward the United States is the price of specific American foreign policy actions: the NATO expansion, the bombing of Iraq, and, especially, the air war against Serbia. Still, in a national poll commissioned by the USIA in the beginning of this year, 54 percent of Russians held a favorable opinion of America and 30 percent unfavorable,[20] a sharp loss of popularity compared with the revolutionary euphoria of the early 1990s, but still considerably better than the United States fares in, say, Mexico, France, or Italy.

✐

Although most Russians are dissatisfied with the "way democracy works" in their country, in national polls solid majorities reject the restoration of "order" if it comes at the price of forgoing key civil and political liberties, such as habeas corpus limits on police, meetings and demonstrations, free elections, travel abroad, and no censorship. In 1994, essentially the same proportion of respondents (35 percent) supported a dictatorship to "restore order in Russia" as opposed it (33 percent).[21] In 1997, the opposition to a dictatorship grew to 55 percent, while support stagnated at the same 35 percent.[22]

In the past six years this allegedly "failing state" and "zone of nuclear-ized anarchy" has held three free national elections (two parliamentary and one presidential), two national referendums, and at least one local election (in some regions two) for the regional legislatures and governors in each of Russia's eighty-nine regions. Thirteen electoral blocs or parties and 1,567 candidates outside the party lists competed in the 1993 legislative elections. In 1995, there were forty-three blocs and 2,688 candidates. There were 10 candidates on the 1996 presidential ballot, and 236 contenders for fifty governorships at stake in 1996 alone. Opposition was free to campaign and to win. The opposition candidate, Zyuganov, defeated Yeltsin in thirty of eighty-nine regions. Candidates supported by the leftist "People's Patriotic Union of Russia" won a third of the contested governorships. Only half of the incumbent governors appointed by Yeltsin were reelected. Only on one occasion—the Duma elections and the simultaneous constitutional referendum in December 1993, two months after the leftist-nationalist rebellion and the bloodshed in Moscow in late September–early October 1993—did the turnout fall below 64 percent of all eligible voters. Nearly 70 million Russians (just under 70 percent of all eligible adults) voted in the presidential election in 1996. There were 50 human rights groups in Russia in 1996. Today, there are 1,200.[23]

Despite many real and gross flaws, Yeltsin's is the most open and liberal regime in the country's history. The press is free from government censorship. Opposition, no matter how radical, is free to publish and campaign for elected offices. Free and fiercely competitive multicandidate elections are the norm at both the local and national levels. After a thousand years of authoritarianism and totalitarianism, Russia is both radically decentralized and whole, with the Kremlin's power dispersed both geographically among the regions and their elected governors and among diverse political centers of power on the national level. No party (much less person, even the president) can dominate and mold Russian national politics at will.

Following the Constitutional Court at the national level, local judges routinely rule against local authorities (when, for example, the latter tried to restrict the activities of "foreign" religious denominations), the Kremlin, the army (when it sought to punish conscientious objectors), and the secret police (as in the cases of Captain Grigoriy Pas'ko in the Far East and Captain Alexandr Nikitin in St. Petersburg, both charged with espionage).[24] In a typical case, last July an Internet provider in the southern Russian city of Volgograd rejected the demand of the Federal Security Service (FSB) to monitor customers' use of the Web. The security agency retaliated by cutting off the firm from the satellite channel that provided access to the Web. The firm brought a suit against the FSB.

Although woefully inadequate by the standards of older democracies, Russia is the freest, most democratic nation of all the post-Soviet states, save the three Baltic countries. Even as severe a test as last year's financial crisis with the ruble's devaluation and the default on the government domestic debt did not result in riots and the disintegration of authority, as in Indonesia, or in show trials of high-level scapegoats or the jailing of journalists, as in Malaysia. There was not the slightest infringement of human or political liberties or restrictions on the freedom of the press or the political opposition. The Communists' attempt to capitalize on the crisis failed miserably when the much ballyhooed "Red October" turned out at best 200,000 people on the streets—in a country of 150 million.

In the December 1999 Duma elections, the All-Russia-Fatherland alliance (VRO) is likely to occupy the crucial left-of-center political space, which has remained unclaimed since the August 1991 revolution. Together, the VRO, the Yabloko party, the center-right Union of Rightist Forces and "right liberal" deputies, and reform-minded "independents" are almost certain to receive more than half the Duma seats and to end the Communist plurality in the Duma. With the Communists' deadly grip on the legislature removed, as early as next spring the Duma might begin passing crucial reform measures held up for years by the reactionaries of the left: private ownership of land; the end of monopolies in housing utilities (gas, electricity, and water) and gradual reduction of budget-busting housing and utility subsidies; bankruptcy implementation and restructuring for failed enterprises; and changes in corporate governance, including, first and foremost, the rights of outside shareholders.[25]

⁓

Of all the charges in the "lost Russia" brief, Yeltsin's alleged failure to "deliver" in foreign and security policies is the most astonishing because the evidence to the contrary is so unambiguous. Never before have the foreign and security policies of a Russian regime been (and probably not again for a long time will they be) as beneficial for the United States and its allies.

First, of course, came the demilitarization of the state and society, the scope of which is likely without precedent in modern history for an undefeated country. Last year the then foreign minister, Evgeny Primakov, declared Soviet defense-related expenditures to be 70 percent of the country's GDP.[26] (Now, there's the "looting of Russia," about which some columnists have been so exercised lately—the looting that hourly, daily, and annually reduced to poverty one of the world's richest countries!) By 1996, the expenditures for procurement and military construction were nine times lower than in 1990 and, for research and development, ten times lower. In 1999, spending on defense is 2.3 percent of the country's GDP. Between January 1992 and January 1998, the Russian armed forces were cut by more than half, from 2.7 million to 1.2 million.[27]

In 1991, Russia had 10,000 deployable strategic nuclear weapons. That number was reduced to 6,000 after START I went into effect in December 1994. Even though the Duma never ratified START II, Russia unilaterally cut its arsenal by 25 percent below the START I limit of 4,500 warheads. Instead of adhering to the START II schedule of 3,000–3,500 warheads by the year 2007, Moscow proposed to the United States to reduce the totals to a maximum of 1,500 weapons.

Another boon to the West—the peaceful dissolution of the Soviet domestic empire—exceeded practically everyone's expectations and defied myriad gloomy scenarios. Signed by Yeltsin in Kiev on May 31, 1997, after painful territorial concessions to Ukraine made in the face of almost uniform opposition by the leading Russian politicians across the political spectrum, the Treaty of Friendship, Cooperation, and Partnership between Russia and Ukraine[28] is as critical to the stability of post–Cold War Europe as the French-German rapprochement, engineered by Charles de Gaulle and Konrad Adenauer in 1958, was to the post–World War II order.

Time and again, Yeltsin took foreign policy positions distinct not just from those of the "popular patriotic" left but, at the time, most of the Russian political class as well. He was repeatedly served opportunities on a silver platter to bolster his popularity by whipping up nationalism and anti-American hysteria, and every time he declined, patching up frayed relations with Washington by accommodation and cooperation. Such was the case with NATO expansion; with sanctions against Iraq; with Bosnia; and, despite hollers of protest from the left and the resistance of his own foreign ministry, with Kosovo. (He fired the darling of the Moscow political class, Primakov, in large measure because of his stubborn opposition to NATO-Russian cooperation over Kosovo.)

ᶜᵒ⁄ᵒ

Of all the components of the "lost Russia" canon, the corruption charge is by far the most solid. Corruption is a real and pervasive scourge that saps the legitimacy of the Russian state, distorts the market, impedes foreign investment, and, ultimately, costs Russian consumers and taxpayers trillions of rubles every year. Before the subject was suddenly "discovered" by the "lost Russia" crew, scholars had discussed it for years. The challenge here is not the facts themselves (although they, too, are affected by hyperbole), but the failure to locate this evil in a historic and geographic context. Much as it might displease American columnists and members of the U.S. Congress, the truth is that the northwestern European version of capitalism, which began as Protestant, Anglo-Saxon, and Scandinavian, is more of an exception than the rule today and will require decades, perhaps centuries, for other economies to attain. The going is likely to be especially tough in Russia's geographic "neighborhood": Europe and Asia east and south of Poland and Hungary. Without exception, these countries—from Romania and Bulgaria to Turkey, Iran, Pakistan, Afghanistan, Iraq, and China, are (and for centuries have been) notoriously corrupt.

Like its neighbors, Russia has been corrupt for centuries. By extirpating, suppressing, or subverting civil institutions that promote self-restraint and personal responsibility (churches, charities, professional associations, independent courts), by censoring everything that was published, and by making the Communist *nomenklatura* immune to criminal laws, Soviet totalitarianism created the most venal Russia that ever existed.

Thievery and bribery were universal. "Tell me where you work, and I will tell you what you are carrying in your bag coming home," went a Soviet underground joke in the 1970s. In a superb primer on Soviet corruption (*USSR: The Corrupt Society*, written in the 1970s and published in the United States in 1982), a former leading Soviet legal scholar and lawyer, Konstantin Simis, called the Soviet Union "the land of kleptocracy."[29] Gorbachev's first prime minister, Nikolay Ryzhkov (now a leading member of the Communist faction in the Duma), wrote of the Soviet Union's "horrible moral state" in the 1980s: "We stole from ourselves, we took bribes, we wallowed in lies."[30] (Still, Russia is the *least* corrupt of all the countries of the former USSR, with the exception of the Baltics.)

Corruption was the central issue in "transitional" economies (that is, economies moving from state ownership or control of major assets to their privatization)—Carlos Menem's Argentina, Fernando Cordoso's Brazil, Carlos Salinas's Mexico, Kim Dae Jung's South Korea, Turgut Ozal's Turkey, and Nelson Mandela's South Africa—as it is in all post-Communist nations, without exception.

A combination of authoritarian politics and limited free market, China epitomizes the phenomenon. In his book on China's "unfinished economic revolution," Nicholas R. Lardy of the Brookings Institution quotes the Communist Party's own newspaper, *People's Daily*: "Criminal activities in banking and finance are rampant." In an article entitled, "Will China Become Another Indonesia?" Minxin Pei of the Carnegie Endowment reports in this fall's issue of *Foreign Policy* magazine that "corruption has reached epidemic proportions and resulted in the theft and waste of huge amounts of national wealth." He estimates that corruption costs China 4 percent of GDP annually.

Of course, neither history nor political economy may absolve the guilty. However, there are clear policy implications. The roots of Russian corruption extend much deeper than mistakes or the alleged personal frailties of Yeltsin and the "reformers." In such hereditary corrupt societies, the problem can be alleviated only by decades of democratic politics, a free press—and several post-Communist generations. In the meantime, we ought to be realistic, patient, and firm in sanctions against corrupt practices and officials.

Fortunately, dealing with corrupt regimes in pursuit of national interests or world economic stability is nothing new, either for the United States or for world financial institutions. There is, for instance, Italy, our steadfast NATO ally, a leading trading partner, a favorite vacation spot of millions of Americans—and a country of systemic and ubiquitous corruption, where an estimated 25 percent of all taxes go uncollected every year and where, in 1992–93, nearly the entire leadership of the Christian Democratic Party, which had ruled the country for fifty years since the end of World War II, was indicted, including the seven-times prime minister Giulio Andreotti.

Farther east, Ukraine—by all accounts a considerably more corrupt country than Russia—is the fourth-largest recipient of direct U.S. assistance: It received $195 million last year, compared with $130 million for Russia. ("Over the six years of your premiership and presidency, Ukraine has lost [to corruption] more than during the Nazi occupation," the leading Ukrainian opposition leaders wrote in an open letter to Ukrainian president Leonid Kuchma this August.) In 1998, the authoritarian and utterly corrupt Egypt received $2.5 billion of U.S. taxpayers' money.

To date, the IMF has extended almost $18 billion to a very corrupt Mexico, almost $17 billion to South Korea, and more than $8 billion to Indonesia, the most corrupt of all. (As of this writing, Russia received a total of $15.6 billion from the IMF.) Nor, contrary to much sanctimony and pious hand-wringing, is corruption an insurmountable impediment to foreign investment, as Indonesia, Mexico, and, especially, China have amply demonstrated.

It would be a terrible blunder to make Russian corruption synonymous with the failure of Russia's grandiose experiment with a free-market economy. There is a critical distinction between the countries in which the level of corruption overwhelms the state and the economy, makes "normal" politics and economy impossible to sustain, and leads to a breakdown or permanent crisis (as, for example, in Albania, Colombia, Indonesia, Sicily until the mid-1990s, and Venezuela), and those where corruption, no matter how ugly or ubiquitous, still allows for democratic order, economic progress (Brazil, South Korea, continental Italy, or Turkey), and integration in the world economy. Today Russia appears to be evolving along the latter path.

෴

Refuting revisionist historians' claim that the American Civil War and Reconstruction accomplished little, in *Abraham Lincoln and the Second American Revolution*, James M. McPherson charged his opponents with "presentism"—a tendency to "read history backwards, measuring change over time from the point of arrival rather than the point of departure." McPherson compared this mode of observation with "looking through the wrong end of a telescope—everything appears smaller than it really is."[31] (These words are reprised in an epigraph to this book.)

Apart from the political and ideological motives of its perpetrators, much of the confusion that is responsible for the "lost Russia" myth is attributable to a similarly distorted view.

A longer and broader view yields different observations. To the citizen of a mature, liberal capitalist democracy, much in today's Russia appears flawed, ugly, and outright revolting. Yet measured from the point of departure, the progress is as undeniable as it is immense.

The Civil War and Reconstruction are relevant in another respect as well. Lincoln liberated 4 million slaves. Yeltsin (following in Mikhail Gorbachev's footsteps), liberated 150 million Russians from Communist totalitarianism. Lincoln left his successors a country that, at the time, could easily have been pronounced "lost"; exhausted and cynical, it was in the throes of a vigorous, hungry, and crude early capitalism, complete with crass inequalities, fraud, cruelty toward the weak and the vanquished, robber barons, ubiquitous and vast corruption, unemployment, and the economic depression of 1873.

The promise of Lincoln's liberating revolution took more than a hundred years to implement fully. Although overcoming three-quarters of a century as a Communist state is not likely to prove much easier than eradicating two centuries of slavery, it seems safe to predict that Yeltsin's revolution will take less than a century to answer the hopes of most Russians.

13

In Search of a Historic Yeltsin
2000

What are we to make of the man who led post-Soviet Russia in its first nine years? Was he the "crude populist," and "erratic" and hard-drinking "quasi-autocrat" of the lore of many an expert and contemporary report in U.S. newspapers, magazines, and television? Or was he indispensable to a profound and vital transformation of Russia? The answers should start with an examination of the choices Yeltsin made in the context of the Soviet legacy and Russian history.

I wrote *Yeltsin*[1] because of a most rare concurrence of subjects: a fascinating and complicated man, who in his prime could touch, sway, and lead millions; a great nation at one of the most fateful moments in its history; and the twentieth century's last great revolution. This was a chance to write history while telling an absorbing tale.

Few protagonists are better suited for the man-and-his-times genre than Boris Yeltsin. The great Russian poet Marina Tsvetaeva used to say that her dear friend Boris Pasternak looked at once like an Arabian thoroughbred and its rider, the driven and the driver. Yeltsin was both a bellwether of the gathering Russian storm and part of the storm itself. As the pace of the revolution quickened, Boris Yeltsin's personal story and his country's history became tightly intertwined and, in several shining instances, welded together. The revolution was the wind, he the sail. Together they began to turn Russia around.

But what was that Russia? Without recalling, however briefly, the country, the state, and the nation that Yeltsin inherited from the Soviet Union in fall 1991, both his achievements and his failures, and thus his place in history, are impossible to judge.

༄

> The legal insecurity that has hung over our people from time immemorial has been a kind of school for them. The scandalous injustice of one-half of the law has taught them to hate the other half; they submit only to force. Complete inequality before the law has killed any respect they may have had for legality. Whatever his station, the Russian evades or violates the law wherever he can do so with impunity; the government does exactly the same thing.[2]

Alexander Herzen, one of Russia's greatest liberal thinkers, wrote that in the early 1850s.

The legacy of authoritarianism was compounded with that of seven decades and four generations of the Soviet Union: a system that deployed mass murder, fear, and lies to extirpate the very concepts of private morality, truth, charity, and justice. The result, sketched in 1989 by two of *glasnost's* leading essayists, was the Homo Soveticus (as the type was referred to in the Soviet press at the time), who had been

> raised in an atmosphere of lies, treachery, servile loyalty to the leader, brought up in a society in which the meaning of many concepts was shifted and took an opposite meaning (white became black, honor and nobility were faults, and informing on neighbors a civic duty). . . .
>
> Fear was instilled in our brains forever, and so was treachery in our blood and mistrust in our eyes.[3]

Summarizing the effects of the reign of Ivan the Terrible on the subsequent history of Russia, the great nineteenth-century Ukrainian-Russian historian Nikolai Ivanovich Kostomarov warned that "serious illnesses of human societies, like physical illnesses, cannot be cured quickly. . . . Those spoiled juices which had built up during the frightful epoch of Ivan's atrocities finally rose to the surface."[4]

As the weight of the police state was lightened, the same "spoiled juices" began rising to the surface. The decades of terror and lies, lawlessness, crushing poverty; the Soviet state's countless atrocities against other peoples, and, most of all, against its own, had bred servility, callousness, and coarseness of mind and soul. In such a normative wasteland, those who had been brutalized for generations were almost certain to become brutalizers—and did, as the savagery of Russian troops in both Chechen wars has demonstrated so graphically.

Revealed by *glasnost*, official corruption, along with inequality ("social justice"), became the most powerful mobilizing theme of *perestroika*. A leading Russian journalist recently described the Russia Yeltsin took over in fall 1991 as "a country depraved to the core, a state rotten from top to bottom, a great power of fast thieves and bribe-takers."[5]

Each year, fifteen million drunks were arrested and put in sobering-up stations (*vytrezviteli*). Premature deaths directly or indirectly caused by alcohol accounted for about one-fifth of all deaths in the USSR. At least 14 percent of state revenue (and perhaps as much as 25 percent) came from the sale of vodka.[6]

The Russia that was passed on to Yeltsin was also desperately poor. "Upper Volta with nuclear missiles," the Social Democratic German Chancellor Helmut Schmidt called the Soviet Union, and he was not far from the truth. Military expenditures were bleeding the country dry. Counting family members, every third Russian—that is, fifty million people—lived off defense expenditures.

Apart from its tanks, planes, and missiles, Russia was, in effect, a colonial, third- or even fourth-rate economy, which exported raw materials and imported almost everything of quality. Almost all hard currency sales abroad came from four commodities: oil, gas, gold, and weapons.

The country's machinery and technology were years, often decades, behind Western equipment. It was commonplace, especially in heavy industry, to find equipment imported from the West during the first two five-year plans half a century earlier. There were fewer miles of paved roads in the entire Soviet Union than in the state of Ohio.[7] One hundred million Soviet citizens (a third of the country's population) had less living space than was prescribed by the minuscule Soviet "sanitary norm" of nine square meters per person.[8]

Half of Soviet schools had no central heating, running water, or indoor toilets.[9] Everywhere except Moscow there was a shortage of milk, which could be purchased occasionally and only after queuing for hours. Millions of Russian children grew up without ever seeing an orange.

When under *glasnost* such things could be reported, we learned of people taken to hospitals with frostbite after queuing for hours in winter and of policemen crushed and seriously injured trying to restrain crowds that stormed stores after shipments arrived (as happened, in 1990, outside a Khabarovsk store that had just received, of all things, pencils for sale). In the ancient Russian city of Kostroma, one could purchase children's soap (no more than three bars per customer) only after showing one's domestic passport with the children's names stamped in it, to prove that there were children under three years of age in the household.[10]

By 1990, virtually every major staple, including sugar, was rationed and could be obtained, when stores had it, only with a ration coupon. On my first day in the Sverdlovsk archives in July 1991, I inquired casually where I could buy something for lunch. There was silence and much embarrassment among the staffers of the Museum of Youth Movements. A few minutes later a young woman archivist gently put in front of me her gift: a small package tightly wrapped in white paper. On the package, in blue ink, was stamped a number and a month. It was her monthly allotment of sausage. In 1991, production dropped to 79 percent of the 1990 level.

⁓

Like Lincoln or de Gaulle, Yeltsin took over a great nation at the time of a mortal crisis and held it together. In Yeltsin's case, there were three crises at once—political, economic, and imperial. Not only did the country's political and economic systems lie in ruins, the country itself had to be reinvented. Against impossible odds, he succeeded, forging, for the first time in a thousand years, a sustainable Russian state that was neither a monarchy nor a dictatorship. In the process, Yeltsin did enough to make half a dozen lives memorable. He dissolved the Soviet domestic empire—a stark departure from the national pattern in which state-building (from Ivan the Terrible and Peter, through Catherine the Great, Lenin, Stalin, and Brezhnev) had invariably included imperial expansion and strengthening of the empire as key components.

The territorial and economic concessions that Yeltsin made to Ukraine, whose independence he recognized ahead of all other world leaders on December 3, 1991, after it had been part of the Russian empire for almost three and a half centuries, may be without precedent in the relations between metropoles and their former territories. The very special and tragic case of Chechnya aside, one needs only to recall the massive and systemic violence that accompanied the breakup of other colonies—India and Pakistan, Britain and Ireland, Ethiopia and Eritrea, and, of course, Yugoslavia—to appreciate the magnitude of Yeltsin's accomplishment.[11]

Yeltsin also decimated the garrison state by slashing the defense budget to under 5 percent of the GDP. He reduced Russia's nuclear arsenal by almost one-half.

Until Yeltsin, the unity of Russia had been achieved only by rigid and ruthless control from Moscow. Whenever the control loosened and the iron hand grew rusty or shaky, the country swiftly fell apart, descended into fratricide and anarchy, and then was reconstituted by a new tyrant. At Yeltsin's departure, Russia was, for the first time, both radically decentralized and whole.

The first Russian president oversaw the birth of a new Russian politics as well. He institutionalized the vital liberties that Gorbachev had granted only provisionally and often by default. *Glasnost* became freedom from government censorship of speech and of the press. Gorbachev's "political pluralism" evolved into freedom of political organization for all, including the regime's most radical and implacable opponents; free, multicandidate elections, both legislative and presidential; and a parliament, which was dominated by a radical opposition during Yeltsin's entire tenure, save half a year between his inauguration in July 1991 and the beginning of economic reforms in January 1992. His eight and a half years were by far the freest, most tolerant, and open period Russia had ever known, except for the eight months between February and November 1917.

Rid of its traditional cruelty and revenge, the new Russian political system, started by Gorbachev and decisively shaped by Yeltsin, granted losers not only their physical lives but their political lives as well. Not a hair fell from the heads of the leaders of the August 1991 putsch. They were never even brought to trial. In February 1994, Yeltsin signed into law the amnesty voted by the Duma for them and for the leaders of the armed rebellion in Moscow of October 3–4, 1993. Remarkable in any revolution, in the bloodstained Russian history this act was nothing short of astounding—the victorious head of state releasing, unmolested, his violent and unrepentant foes, who would almost certainly have killed him had they prevailed.

Although woefully underfunded and plagued by corruption, Russian courts under Yeltsin were nevertheless home to a judiciary that was immeasurably more powerful and independent than in Soviet times. Russian citizens by the thousands sued federal and local authorities and won.[12] The courts also repeatedly overruled local authorities who banned "nonnative" religious groups following the restrictive 1997 law initiated by the Duma. Even the traditionally most sacrosanct Russian institutions—the military and the secret police—were no longer entirely immune from due process.[13] Even before the Constitutional Court in effect declared capital punishment unconstitutional, Yeltsin (acting against the dominant sentiment in the Duma and in the country's public opinion) had commuted all death sentences—this in a country that traditionally executed prisoners savagely and, until a few years before, together with China and the United States had led the world in number of executions.[14]

✑

And yet, and yet, if amid all these epochal leaps and breakthroughs, notoriously parsimonious History were to settle on one theme, the leitmotif of Yeltsin's political life—what Yeats called the "great melody" (and Conor Cruise O'Brien made the title of his fine political biography of Burke)—what would it be? What is the place where a search for a historic Yeltsin should begin? I think that theme and that place, that "great melody," is likely to be the furtherance of liberty.

Such a verdict does not necessarily bode Yeltsin well.

On the pediment of the portico of the Paris Panthéon, where, among others, Voltaire, Rousseau, and Zola are buried, there is a bas-relief of France between Liberty and History, bestowing laurels on famous men. If the two—Liberty and History—agree, then good and well. But do they, invariably?

I think rather no than yes. Of all heroes, liberators fare the worst. Among the components of progress, liberty, like greatness, is perhaps the most suspect to social scientists (at least those of my generation), who were taught in graduate school that that which cannot be quantified is not worth dealing with. The elusiveness and misperception of the criteria by which liberators are judged bear much of the blame as well. In keeping with his central conviction of the multiplicity and occasional incompatibility of even the most noble of human wishes and values, Sir Isaiah Berlin greatly clarified the matter when he wrote, "Liberty is liberty, not equality or fairness or justice or culture, or human happiness or a quiet conscience."[15] In the Russian case, one can easily add to what liberty is not honest and competent bureaucracy, universal sobriety, enlightened and generous captains of industry, pensioners paid on time, peace in Chechnya, a 5 percent annual growth of GDP, foreign investments, improvement in corporate governance, and decreasing male mortality.

Yet Berlin's injunction remains largely ignored. Sublime though it is, liberty can, of course, also be terrifying and often cruel. Economic freedom, for one, is the foe of equality, especially equality in poverty. "In much wisdom is much vexation, and he who increases knowledge increases sorrow," says Ecclesiastes (1:18). There is much vexation in much freedom as well, and those who increase it—the liberators—may increase sorrow for millions, at least in the short run.

But the short run, the first ten to fifteen years of wrenching post-Communist transition, is all that matters in politics—and not just in Russia. The darling of the Western intelligentsia and the one-time model post-Communist leader, President Václav Havel of the Czech Republic, is serving out his second term in office, abandoned and often depressed in Prague Castle, irrelevant, even a bit of a joke for his people, who are angry at the cronyism and corruption that they blame on the new economic order. "All the Communists who stole were allowed to keep their wealth, and today they are captains of industry," a Prague worker complained to an American reporter in 1999. Havel "should have left at the height of his career," the worker added. "He gave people hope but did not fulfill it."[16] Last year, 49 percent of Czechs polled thought Havel should resign, and only slightly over half approved of the fall of communism. A third explicitly regretted the demise of the Communist regime.[17]

The most painful, most personal disappointment to Havel must be the emergence—ten years after he led the anti-Communist "velvet revolution"—of the Communist Party of Bohemia and Moravia as the most popular party in the Czech Republic. The party's leaders—gray, mediocre apparatchiks, very much like Gennady Zyuganov's colleagues in the Communist Party of the Russian Federation—represent everything that Havel detested on aesthetic and moral as well as political grounds all his life.

༄

A great deal in Yeltsin's sorry public image at the time of his resignation is traceable to these genetic handicaps of liberators. Yet for much, perhaps most, he had only himself to blame. That as millions suffered, millions of others gained enormously from political and economic freedom does not absolve Yeltsin of responsibility for blunders in the strategy of economic reforms and for abetting corruption and a brief but pernicious reign of the so-called oligarchs, the Russian robber-barons, whose presence became synonymous with crooked deals, rigged markets, fraudulent "auctions," and the incestuous relationship between political power and the privatized economy.

There seemed to be two Yeltsins coexisting in the public eye—occasionally overlapping, sometimes clashing and retreating, but always remaining distinct and resilient. One was Yeltsin the leader and the visionary. The other was Yeltsin the politician—an avid and very competent greasy-pole climber, obsessed with power and its many gaudy trappings, petty, and jealous of competitors' popularity. In many ways he ran the Kremlin like a Byzantine court (or like the *obkom*, a provincial party committee, where he spent seventeen years). It was rife with intrigue, backstabbing, favorites and outcasts, sudden firings and hirings, demotions and promotions.

Yet in addition to the "built-in" features of a historic Yeltsin, as always in the social sciences, observers' biases were at work as well. As he readied his old-fashioned camera to photograph the remnants of the Casa Bertini, Shelley's house in the wooded hills near Lucca, Richard Holmes, who is likely the finest literary biographer in the English language today, set the field of focus and aperture to "ten foot to infinity." He wrote later that this was precisely the range for a conscientious biographer: "ten foot to infinity."[18] In the case of Yeltsin, the depth of vision was a few inches at best.

Much of what passed for reporting on Yeltsin fell within the genre of political entomology: like insects, political leaders are watched through a magnifying glass within the tiny confines of their personal foibles, petty passions, and daily stupidities, in almost total isolation from their policies, ideologies, agendas—and from their countries at large.

This was history as practiced by those whom Isaiah Berlin called "the glass and plastic" historians, who "regard all facts as equally interesting" and whose product is contaminated by "craven pedantry and blindness."[19] In an essay about Chaim Weizmann, Berlin supplied an antidote:

> Greatness is not a specifically moral attribute. It is not one of the private virtues. . . . A great man need not be morally good, or upright, or kind, or sensitive, or delightful, or possess artistic or scientific talent. To call someone a great man is to claim that he has intentionally taken . . . a large step, one far beyond the normal capacities of men, in satisfying, or materially affecting, central human interests.[20]

As with Berlin's definition of liberty, this formula remains, for the most part, unheeded.

⁕

No matter what happens in the short run, ultimately History appears to recognize only choice, not luck or accident. The great French socialist and Prime Minister Léon Blum noted that "life does not lend itself to the simultaneous retention of all possible benefits, and I have often thought that morality consists uniquely perhaps in having the courage to choose."[21] This might be one of those rare cases where, *pace* Machiavelli, private morality and statesmanship intersect. Making critical choices may not be a sufficient condition for greatness, but it is most certainly a necessary one.

Sooner or later, therefore, a search for a historic Yeltsin must confront the matter of choice. Did Yeltsin, not to put too fine a point on it, know what he was doing? Or did he, as the currently fashionable Russian and Washington lore directs us to believe, wake up with a hangover after non-stop drinking in Belavezhskaya Pushcha on December 8, 1991, and decide to dissolve the Soviet Union? And did he introduce capitalism by freeing the prices on January 2, 1992, in much the same manner: impulsively, even capriciously, concerned only with petty political gain and unaware of the gravity of the consequences?

I believe that the preponderance of evidence demonstrates consistent and considered choices for liberty in Yeltsin's three central decisions about the Russian domestic empire, democracy, and the market economy. Of these three choices, which laid the foundation of post-Communist Russia, that of economic freedom is generally treated as something almost accidental. Yet it was precisely here that personal choice was both absolutely central and hardest to make. Democratization and the dissolution of the empire had been set in train by Gorbachev (the former more or less consciously, the latter inadvertently). Not so changes in the economy; by the end of 1991, after four years of tinkering, the market and private property were still a taboo, dealt with by articles in the criminal code.

The choice of economic liberty was unique also because Yeltsin had to abandon the strategy that had served him so well before. Until then, he had sensed the direction of Russian public opinion and followed, as well as guided and molded, it. Yet if democracy were clearly in tune with the sense of the majority, and if the abandonment of the Soviet Union, at least for the moment, seemed a fair price to pay for Russian liberty and prosperity, neither the freeing of prices nor the privatization of the economy was being clamored for by tens of millions. With the market revolution, Yeltsin was, so to speak, on his own.

In the end—after years of debates, recommendations, commissions, and resolutions—it was one man's ability to make a choice and to take the responsibility that tipped the scale. The market economy happened in Russia because Yeltsin wished it to happen (as it did not happen in neighboring Ukraine because its president, Leonid Kravchuk, decided to have a peaceful and uncomplicated presidency).

As Yegor Gaidar remarked to me years later, the freeing of prices, which would turn millions of Russians into paupers overnight (no matter how impoverished they already were because of shortages and inflation that made worthless most of their savings), was something that Yeltsin knew Russia "needed" but, he was equally certain, "could not support"—at least not by the majorities to which he was accustomed. For the first time, as an astute Russian journalist noted at the time, Yeltsin the "populist" and Yeltsin the revolutionary became adversaries.[22]

This was, literally, Yeltsin's first major "unpopular" decision. He would confess later that for "two whole months" he and his advisers had searched for "more acceptable," "less onerous" ways to begin the reforms without freeing the prices—but could not find any.[23] No politician makes such choices lightly, least of all someone who until then had been close in status to the nation's savior, basking in the adoration of millions.

On October 28, 1991, Yeltsin went to the Congress of People's Deputies of Russia to seek a mandate for the price liberalization and privatization plan (which, as many in Russia and the West would soon so conveniently forget, was granted by an 876 to 16 vote). In one of the best speeches he ever made, Yeltsin declared that the time of "small steps" was past. We must in deeds, he went on, not words, begin extricating ourselves from "the swamp that pulls us deeper and deeper." Only a "large-scale reformist breakthrough" could save Russia's economy from disintegration, her people from poverty, and her state from collapse.[24]

He called the "unfreezing" of prices the "hardest" measure; but the entire experience of "world civilization," Yeltsin said, had proved that fair prices could not be set by the bureaucrat, only by the market. He counted on the "support and understanding" of the people of Russia, support that they had so generously given him in the past. Together, the previous August, they had defended "political freedom"; now it was time for economic freedom, freedom for enterprises and entrepreneurs, for people to work as much as they wanted and to get as much for their labor as they earned.[25] "Today, we must make a decisive choice," Yeltsin concluded.

> To do so requires the will and wisdom of the people, the courage of political leaders, the knowledge of experts. Your president has made this choice. This is the most important decision of my life. I have never looked for easy roads in life, but I understand very clearly that the next months will be the most difficult. If I have your support and your trust, I am ready to travel this road with you to the end. The time has come for practical actions in the name and for the benefit of every Russian family, in the name and for the benefit of the Russian state.[26]

On December 29, four days before price controls were to be lifted, Yeltsin addressed the nation in a televised speech, in which he placed the economic revolution at the center of the general "decommunization" of Russia. Along with prices set by the state, "we are abandoning mirages and illusions," Yeltsin said.[27] It was clear that the Communist utopia "could not be built." It was not Russia that had been defeated; it was Communism. Along with the state-owned economy, Russia was "ridding" itself of "the militarization of our life," of the "antihuman economy" devoted almost entirely to military production. Russia had stopped "constant preparation" for war "with the whole world." The "iron curtain" that had been there "between us and almost the whole world" was no more.[28]

We have inherited "a devastated land," a "gravely ill Russia," Yeltsin concluded, but "we must not despair." No matter how difficult things are at the time, "we have a chance to climb out of this pit." Our people are "no worse, no lazier than any other. It is necessary only to help people find themselves in this new life."[29]

⁂

Of course, liberty, even if consciously chosen, is not democracy (although it is a necessary condition for democracy)—and a liberator is not a democrat. What label, what shorthand will History settle on in the case of Yeltsin? Here was the man who ordered troops into Chechnya in December 1994 and for a year and a half prosecuted a war there—incompetently, cruelly, and with complete disregard for the country's public opinion. (Five years later, this time with public opinion on his side, he allowed his handpicked successor to unleash another savage attack on Chechnya.) Yeltsin weakened the nascent constitutional order and cheapened free political discourse with his cynical palace games. He was responsible for a great deal of the alienation of the people from power in the new Russia.

He was also someone who allowed complete freedom of speech and political organization for his most outrageous and crudest critics; who, except for three days in August 1991 and two weeks in October 1993, never closed down a single opposition newspaper; who sought popular mandates for his policies and his office in a referendum and free elections open to those same critics. In the 1996 presidential race, he quite literally risked his life for victory—ignoring the doctors' warnings, suffering a heart attack a few days before the final vote, and undergoing quintuple bypass heart surgery four months later.

He was rife with authoritarian habits and urges—and bound by self-imposed and self-enforced constraints. He thirsted for power and was zealous to acquire and hold it. Yet both the mode of acquisition of that power (by two free elections) and at least some of the uses to which he put it—greatly weakening the state's stranglehold over society and the economy, and Moscow's over Russia—were utterly novel for that country.

The Russia that Yeltsin left behind on the last day of the year 1999 reflected the contradictions of its founding father. It was a hybrid: a polity still semiauthoritarian, corrupt, and mistrusted by the society, but also one that was governable, in which the elites' competition for power was arbitrated by popular vote, and in which most of the tools of authoritarian mobilization and coercion appeared to have been significantly dulled. Yeltsin's legacy is a collection of necessary, although far from sufficient, conditions for a modern capitalist democracy: free elections; freedom of political opposition; demilitarization of state and society; decentralization of the traditionally unitary state; a largely privatized economy; and a still small and weak but increasingly assertive civil society, sustained by civil liberties, freedom of the press from government censorship, and an increasingly independent and assertive judiciary. The political organism that he forged is full of severe defects, both genetic and acquired, yet capable of development and of peacefully thwarting Communist restoration without succumbing to authoritarianism.

Perhaps most important of all, Yeltsin freed Russia from what the great English poet Robert Graves (in an entirely different context) called "the never changing circuit of its fate"[30]—the history that after four centuries appeared to have become destiny: imperialism, militarism, and rigid centralization interrupted by episodes of horrifyingly brutal anarchy. He gave Russia a "*peredyshka*," a time to catch its breath. The traditional attributes of the Russian state—authoritarianism, imperialism, militarism, xenophobia—are far from extinguished. Yet more and higher hedges have been erected against their recurrence under Yeltsin's *peredyshka* than at any other time in Russian history.

Brutalized—the rulers and the ruled alike—by terror and lies, gnarled by fear and poverty, paralyzed by total dependence on the state, the Russians' journey from subjects to a free people will be neither easy nor fast. Yet, like a convalescing invalid, Russia under Yeltsin began to hobble away from the prison hospital that the czars and commissars built, with its awful food, stern nurses, short visiting hours, and ugly uniforms.

She is not out of the hospital yard yet. But if she can no longer be stopped, Yeltsin's name, next to Gorbachev's, will be inscribed by History among those of the greatest liberators.

14

Poor Democracy
2001

The single largest category of political newcomers in the post–Cold War era, poor democracy has proved to be both a hopeful and a frustrating affair. Bypassing the centuries of gradual political and economic developments that cumulatively led to the triumph of liberal capitalism and modern democracy in their richer cousins, poor democracies find themselves confronting enormous problems that elsewhere were resolved (and safely forgotten) a long time ago, or that have never arisen before. How to reconcile "primitive" capitalism and modern democracy? How quickly to separate state and economy, political power and private property? What are the ramifications of a capitalism by majority? Which attributes of modern democracy are vital for continuing progress, and which, while desirable, are secondary? Despite all the huge obstacles they face daily and despite many temporary reversals, poor, "preliberal" democracies have shown themselves to be remarkably resilient and very well worth not only criticism, but also support and encouragement.

The post–Cold War era has produced something new in world history: an abundance of poor democracies. There are today some seventy nations with a gross domestic product below $10,000 per capita and with the basic attributes of democratic government. These regimes have been greeted in the West mostly with scorn and condescension. In reading about them, we learn of their economic failures, their democratic deficiencies, their gloomy prospects. But their existence can also be seen as a hopeful sign, even a remarkable success story, and as a tribute to the universal appeal of freedom and self-government.

Until 1989, democracy was rare in "less-developed nations." Stable democracy seemed to be a luxury only rich nations could afford, the icing on the cake of a five-digit per-capita GDP. To be sure, the correlation was never perfect. An assortment of poor countries—India, the island nations of the English-speaking Caribbean, Venezuela—had been democracies for decades. Almost all the states of Central and South America had had democratic interludes sandwiched between periods of military dictatorship. And in the course of the 1980s, a few poor countries held breakthrough elections that launched durable democracies—notably El Salvador in 1982. But protodemocratic regimes that sprang up in the Third World tended to be torn apart by the magnetic tensions of the bipolar Cold War circuit. Within a few years, most devolved into leftist or rightist dictatorships, often beset by guerrilla insurgencies.

Now all that has changed. While the end of the Cold War did not in itself introduce democracy in poor nations, it greatly improved the odds for democratic stabilization. No longer assets in a global struggle, poor countries were left to their own devices—and many succeeded in establishing tenuous and flawed, but real, democracies, in Central and South America, Southeast Asia, and Africa, as well as in the former Soviet bloc.

✍

Poor democracies are barebones democracies. They face huge economic challenges, and their civic cultures are underdeveloped by the standards of the West. Yet, for all their conspicuous faults, they feature basic individual rights and political liberties. Their people enjoy freedom of speech, the right to petition government, freedom of assembly, and the freedom to travel abroad. The opposition can organize and participate in politics, criticize the government, distribute canvassing materials, and compete for local and national office in free and more or less fair elections, whose results, in the end, reflect the will of the majority. Finally, poor democracies have newspapers free of government censorship. These characteristics distinguish poor democracies both from nondemocracies (such as Burma, China, Cuba, North Korea, Saudi Arabia, Turkmenistan, and Vietnam) and from pseudodemocracies—regimes decked out in the institutional trappings of democracy, yet falling short on one or more of the criteria suggested above (for instance, Azerbaijan, Egypt, Kazakhstan, or Malaysia).

In economic terms, the poor democracies cover an enormous range: from Nigeria, Bangladesh, and India (with per-capita GDPs of $440 or below, according to World Bank figures for 1999), to Peru, Russia, Jamaica, and Panama (between $2,000 and $3,000), to Poland, Chile, Hungary, and the Czech Republic (between $4,000 and $5,000), and, in the upper crust, Argentina ($7,555), South Korea ($8,500), Barbados ($8,600), Malta ($9,200), and Slovenia ($10,000). (For comparison, the rich democracies enjoy per-capita GDPs over $20,000: Canada, Italy, and France are between $20,000 and $24,000; the United States is at $32,000; and Switzerland and Luxembourg are at $38,000 and $43,000, respectively. The intermediate category—democracies with per-capita GDPs between $10,000 and $20,000—includes Portugal, Spain, Greece, and Israel.) Even excluding ministates and protectorates, poor democracies are now more numerous than regimes of any other type.[1] For most of the past century, history was shaped by the global struggle between democracy and totalitarianism acted out by some of the world's largest industrial and military powers: the United States, Germany, Japan, Russia, and China. The story of the twenty-first century, by contrast, could be greatly influenced by the evolution of the poor democracies.

As we have already seen, the poor democracies and their wealthy cousins arrived at democratic institutions by very different paths.[2] Beginning in the Middle Ages, the Western European road to democracy was paved with slow gains in rights and immunities, as nobles secured independence from the king, and towns, the church, universities, and corporations grew progressively freer from local lords. Over centuries, a system of mutual rights and obligations took shape in the feudal relations of vassalage. Gradually, customary arrangements acquired the force of law: the sanctity of contracts freely entered into; the impartiality of courts; the self-policing of corporations, guilds, and professional associations. Local self-government preceded national democracy by centuries.

In many respects, the poor democracies' experience has been the opposite. Here, the institutions, ethical norms, and practices of modernity failed to develop under the *ancien régime*. And if most poor democracies lack a democratic culture, the formerly Communist nations are at a special disadvantage. Except in a few Central European nations, such as Estonia and the Czech Republic, the "software" of liberal capitalist democracy never existed. It has been said that the post-Communist societies have had to start out as "democracies without democrats," for the totalitarian state systematically destroyed, corrupted, or subverted even nonpolitical voluntary associations— the very groupings that promote and help internalize self-restraint and compliance with rules: church, neighborhood, profession, and, at the height of Stalinism, family itself.

The revolt against the totalitarian or authoritarian state that gave birth to the poor democracies was, in most instances, a national rather than a local affair. A powerful national consensus formed in favor of personal and political liberty. This led to the embrace of the principles of democratic governance and the swift adoption of institutions through which they could be effected. Far from being an outgrowth of local self-government, democratization in these countries was an exercise in superimposing borrowed political structures—enthusiastically borrowed, to be sure—upon societies whose everyday social arrangements had been inherited largely intact from antidemocratic regimes.

✑

Another crucial distinction between the richer and poor democracies is in the linkage of property and political power. In Western Europe, the medieval unity of economic and political power eroded over centuries, until the economic and political spheres became largely (although never entirely) separate. In most poor democracies, this critical divergence is only beginning, haltingly, to take place. Political power translates into ownership or economic control, and vice versa, to the benefit of the elder, the tribal chief, the mayor, the governor, the *kolkhoz* chairman, or the factory manager.

Long experience of self-rule at the level of the town, the congregation, the guild, the local charity, together with the separation of the economic and political realms, forms the tallest hedge a culture can place against lawlessness and graft. One hesitates before stealing from a till one has freely voted to fill, or breaking rules one has freely agreed to uphold. The most immediate and conspicuous effect of the poor democracies' shortcut to political modernity has been corruption, which to a varying but very high degree plagues all of them.

Of course, even in the West, these formidable safeguards were no guarantee against the fraud and corruption of early capitalism:

> An impatience to be rich, a contempt for those slow but sure gains which are the proper reward of industry, patience, and thrift, spread through society . . . [and] took possession of the grave Senators of the City . . . Deputies, Aldermen. It was [easy] and . . . lucrative to put forth a lying prospectus announcing a new stock, to persuade ignorant people that the dividends could not fall short of twenty percent. . . . Every day some new bubble was puffed into existence, rose buoyant, shone bright, burst and was forgotten.[3]

Written by Thomas Macaulay about London at the end of the seventeenth century, in the aftermath of the Glorious Revolution, this could have been written about any number of poor democracies. For that matter, there remain well-publicized pockets of corruption in modern rich democracies: New York and Chicago through most of the last century; Marseilles or Palermo today.

But in the poor democracies, corruption is pervasive and systemic. It is a central issue in the national politics of Peru and Mexico, Colombia and Venezuela, Brazil and the Czech Republic, Bulgaria and Romania, all the countries of the former Soviet Union, the Philippines, Turkey, India, South Korea, Nigeria, and South Africa.

Most of these countries were corrupt for centuries before they became democratic (or capitalist). There is, furthermore, a matter of perception: Government bureaucrats under dictators, and party elites under communism, tended to steal and consume inconspicuously, certainly without media attention, while the new class that has succeeded them is far less secretive and is relentlessly pursued by television and newspapers. (Hence, perhaps, the American businessman's enthusiasm for nondemocratic China, where graft is centralized and strictly rank-rationed, workers are docile, secrets are protected by the police, and the lines of authority are etched by fear in the hearts of underlings, ensuring a bribe's effectiveness—by contrast with, say, Russia, a poor democracy where fear of government has been mostly forgotten, the media are brazen and hungry for scandal, prerogatives are hopelessly confused, and secrets have a half-life of two days.)

Where democracy arrived suddenly, state wealth, formerly appropriated by the dictator or the party and guarded with guns by the army and secret police, was delivered into the custody of a much less cohesive group of first-generation democratic politicians. We have already noted that, occurring in an institutional vacuum, privatization, whether in Mexico, Brazil, India, the Czech Republic, or Russia, necessarily brought together the newly empowered (often, newly legalized) and very hungry entrepreneur and the impoverished bureaucrat—with the predictable result.[4]

☙

Another defining attribute of poor democracies (as we have already noted with regard to Russia)[5] is their historically unprecedented combination of elections by universal suffrage with early, crude, and brutal capitalism—what Marx called the capitalism of "primary accumulation."

In the West, capitalism preceded universal suffrage by at least a century. In most poor democracies, certainly those of the post-Communist variety, democracy has been the paramount societal goal, with capitalism a distant second item on the agenda. (In some countries, we have been treated to the sight, never before beheld, of modern democracy essentially without modern capitalism—for example, in Ukraine between 1991 and 1995.) This has produced a novel socioeconomic organism: capitalism whose key elements require approval by the voters—elements as basic as private ownership of large industrial enterprises, the right to buy and sell land and to hire and fire workers, and market prices for rent and utilities.

Where the foundations of modern capitalism are being laid for the first time in countries governed by majority rule, the consequences for both capitalism and democracy are profound. The experience of the poor democracies is a reminder of the fundamental heterogeneity of capitalism and democracy: The former institutionalizes inequality, while the latter institutionalizes equality. Amalgamated in the West by the weight of time and custom, capitalism and democracy have an especially tense, often tenuous, coexistence in poor democracies. One result is a remarkable opportunity in the early twenty-first century to revisit the rough and ready days of early capitalism, whose "blood-stained story of economic individualism and unrestrained capitalist competition," in the words of Isaiah Berlin,[6] has faded from the memory of the West. That story involves, among other things, the brutality with which the rich democracies rid themselves of surplus classes, most conspicuously the subsistence farmers and the independent artisans made obsolete by the Industrial Revolution. The pioneer of large-scale industrial capitalism, merry old England, where eight out of ten subsistence farmers were forced off the land in just thirty years between about 1780 and 1810, traveled the road to industrialization over the bodies of farmers and urban poor—pauperized, arrested as vagabonds, branded, hanged, or shipped to the colonies. The author of the classic account of the various paths to modern democracy, Barrington Moore, wrote that "as part of the industrial revolution, [England] eliminated the peasant question from English politics. The admitted brutality of the enclosures confronts us with the limitations on the possibility of peaceful transition to democracy and reminds us of open and violent conflicts that have preceded its establishment."[7]

In their leap to modernity and global capitalism, the poor democracies have had to start out with backward, autarkic, often militarized state-owned economies. Their surplus labor is concentrated in the civil service and obsolete industries: shipyards, steel mills, mines, or defense. In the 1980s, an estimated 30 percent of the Soviet economy was assumed to be value-subtracting, meaning that a finished product was worth less than the raw materials and labor that went into making it. A 1998 survey by the McKinsey Global Institute (the best study of the Russian economy to date) confirmed that estimate, finding 30 percent of Russian enterprises, employing 50 percent of the industrial workforce, to be "not worth upgrading because they were either subscale or relied on obsolete technology."[8]

Admittedly, Russia, with its extraordinary isolation and the militarization of its economy, is an extreme example; but every poor democracy that has implemented market reforms has experienced an initial large drop in GDP. The result has been surplus workers in obsolete bureaucracies and industries—be they Brazilian civil servants, Romanian miners, or the dock workers of Gdansk—creating an enormous political problem. For unlike the predemocratic capitalist West, the poor democracies have not brutally "eliminated" these millions of people from politics, but instead have given them the right to shape the institutions and practices of emerging capital-ism. They vote.

The dynamics of what I have already labeled capitalism-by-majority are by now well known.[9] Parliaments, often dominated by leftist populists, adopt budgets with ever greater "social spending" and subsidies for loss-making public or nominally private enterprises with politically sensitive constituencies, such as farmers or coal miners. In the absence of tax rev-enues even remotely commensurate with skyrocketing expenditures, budget deficits burgeon (Poland, leader of the post-Communist transition, today runs a budget deficit of 8 percent of GDP), national currencies weaken, interest rates rise, and governments become heavily indebted to the international financial institutions.

In the worst-case scenario, the vicious circle closes, as governments seek to make ends meet by selling debt at astronomically high rates of return and increasing already unrealistically high taxes. There follow depressed equity prices, stifled direct investment in the economy, capital flight, the shift of ever more economic activity into "gray" or "black" markets—and the further shrinking of the tax base. The government is confronted with a Hobson's choice, reigniting inflation by printing money or reducing already meager welfare benefits and cutting government services, with the attend-ant risk of losing elections to the left (in the post-Soviet regimes, the "ex-," "reformed," or "neo-" Communists).

The principal agent seeking to reconcile democracy and capitalism in poor democracies is the state. This is an enormous task. Almost always impoverished (and often near-bankrupt), the state is saddled with the task of simultaneously promoting modern capitalism open to the global economy and coping with the huge political problems such a strategy engenders in a democracy. Thus, in 1999, Brazil sought to reduce the budget deficit (much of it due to the salaries, benefits, and pensions of a bloated civil service) by taxing pensions and imposing painful, across-the-board public-sector cuts. To overcome the same problem, in the spring of 2000, Argentina cut the wages of public-sector workers by 10–15 percent.

Much to the annoyance of Western journalists and experts, the capitalism-by-majority practiced by poor democracies has turned out to be a very tricky business, characterized by slow and zigzagging market reforms, incomplete privatization, a less than wholehearted embrace of globalism, and, at best, extreme difficulty in reducing huge budget deficits resulting from social spending and the subsidization of failed industries.

℘

Given these heavy handicaps, it would be easy to conclude that the poor democracies, however numerous, are a flash in the pan, destined to go down in history as a hopeful but short-lived post–Cold War phenomenon, too exotic to be stable, lacking the "software" of democracy, corroded by corruption, and torn apart by the tensions between democracy and capitalism.

Yet the evidence indicates otherwise. Democracy has endowed these countries with remarkable strength and flexibility. This was made plain in the 1997–98 "emerging markets" financial crisis. Poor democracies like Russia, Brazil, and South Korea survived rather easily, while the nondemocracy Indonesia saw state authority collapse amid riots and anti-Chinese pogroms, and the pseudodemocracy Malaysia reached for scapegoats and kangaroo trials to save the regime.

Even where poor democracies have been systematically subverted, their democratic elements have proved difficult to extinguish. Cases in point are countries whose political systems combine antidemocratic and democratic practices and institutions, with neither side scoring a permanent victory—for instance, Belarus, Zimbabwe, Haiti, and Pakistan. They also include "soft" one-party states or military dictatorships, like Mexico until Vicente Fox's victory in 2000, which ended seventy-one years of one-party rule, or Turkey until the Welfare Party victory and Necmettin Erbakan's premiership in 1996, where the opposition is permitted to exist but never to win the majority in the national parliament or to hold the highest executive office for long.

In 2000, in addition to Mexico, two such regimes passed the ultimate test of a democratic transfer of power in Ghana and Yugoslavia, where the opposition was able to dislodge a government by majority vote, ending, respectively, the nineteen-year and thirteen-year rules of one party or an elected autocrat.

Despite continuing setbacks, the case of Zimbabwe thus far has been among the most heartening. A deafening agitprop campaign and open harassment of the opposition by the government failed in the face of determined and at times heroic voter resistance. First, in a referendum in

February 2000, Zimbabweans defeated a draft constitution, which would have legitimized President Robert Mugabe's life term in office and authorized the seizure of land belonging to white farmers. Then, in parliamentary elections in June 2000, came the spectacular success of the Movement for Democratic Change and, four months later, an attempt to impeach Mugabe, who had ruled the country since its independence in 1980. Belarus may be another instance of deadlock between democracy and authoritarianism. "*Sen'ya—Miloshavich, zaytra—Luka*" ("Today Milosevic, tomorrow Lukashenko"), read a poster carried by a Minsk protester last October.

Countries like Yugoslavia and Ghana have tested and confirmed the correctness of Joseph Schumpeter's classic minimalist definition of democracy as "free competition for a free vote."[10] In his *Capitalist Revolution*, Peter Berger elaborated: In democracies, "governments are constituted by majority votes in regular and uncoerced elections, in which there is 'genuine competition' for votes of the electorate; and those who are engaged in such competition are guaranteed freedom of speech and freedom of association." The end result is the "institutionalized limitation of the power of government."[11]

Freedom to vote for opposition candidates has turned out to be not only a necessary but often the sufficient condition for an initial democratic breakthrough. More or less fair elections, a press free of government censorship, real choices before the voters, and mostly honest tallying of the results may be key to the exercise of popular sovereignty, even in the absence of (or with glaring deficiencies in) such components of mature liberal democracy as independent and impartial courts, the separation of powers, and checks and balances.

Among the most spectacular confirmations of this theory are Solidarity's parliamentary victory in Poland in 1989 and the upset of the Sandinista government by the United National Opposition in Nicaragua in 1990. Even when competitive elections and an honest count are confined to a few pockets within a dictatorial regime, they can portend earth-shattering change—as in the mighty strides made by proindependence and anti-Communist candidates in elections in the Soviet republics between 1988 and 1991, or the election of Boris Yeltsin to the Congress of People's Deputies in March 1989 with 92 percent of the Moscow vote after Yeltsin had been expelled from the Politburo. Variations on this scenario were played out in February 2000 legislative elections in Iran, when reformers and moderates won a number of districts and carried Tehran decisively, and again in the June 2001 presidential election, when the allegedly proreform President Mohammad Khatami was reelected with 76 percent of the national vote. Similarly, in March 2001 municipal elections in Ivory Coast, opposition candidates for mayor won in most cities after an almost forty-year monopoly by the ruling party. (On the other hand, in 2001 elections in Uganda and Benin, the lack of a clean vote count precluded what might have been two more democratic brea throughs.)

❦

What are the policy implications? First, the strength of the democratic impulse in poor democracies should never be underestimated. Again and again, liberty's appeal has proved powerful enough to overcome great obstacles. Elites, professing to know how the masses really feel, have time and again predicted disillusionment with democracy and its abandonment by the citizens of poor nations. Yet, in the past decade, with just a few exceptions (in Venezuela and in several African nations where democracy has been brutally and cynically subverted by warlords fanning tribal strife), poor democracies have resisted slipping back into authoritarianism.

Second, after almost a century of modern democracy, many Western experts and journalists have forgotten that democracy is not an all-or-nothing affair, but a system toward which a political culture may advance in fits and starts, amid contradictory impulses, by minute but cumulatively momentous steps. Experience has shown again and again that progress can defy enormous odds. This reality suggests that the term "illiberal democracy," popularized by Fareed Zakaria, is misleading. "Preliberal democracy" would be more accurate.

Third, we can revise the criteria by which the progress of poor democracies is measured. So pervasive has the Marxist interpretation of history become that economic growth is often considered the sole measure of progress. With rare exceptions, Western media coverage of poor democracies is shaped by GDP fetishism.

As always in matters of liberty, ordinary people have proved far wiser, and infinitely more patient, than intellectuals. The poor democracies have shown remarkable resilience under the harsh conditions of primitive capitalism. The voters in the poor democracies seem to have grasped—as have few journalists or experts—the essence of Isaiah Berlin's adage, "Liberty is liberty, not equality, or justice, or culture, or human happiness or a quiet conscience."[12] Democracy itself, conceptually uncoupled from economic hardship, is cherished by consistent and solid majorities.

Corruption is a huge problem, and political cultures formed over centuries and misshapen in recent decades by particularly dehumanizing and irrational political and economic systems cannot be remade overnight. But the proper response to the inadequacies of poor democracies is neither to give up on their democratic prospects nor to refrain from pointing out their shortcomings. Rather, it is to encourage their democratic development while refusing to reduce their complex reality to a single issue or measure their progress by a single criterion. In addition, analysts must learn to recognize gradations of corruption—to differentiate between levels potentially fatal to democracy and liberal capitalism (the Nigerian or, until a few years ago, the Sicilian level) and pernicious but nonlethal degrees (the Indian, Mexican, or Turkish).

Finally, in assessing the viability and prospects of this or that poor democracy, we tend to focus on the state, which is readily analyzable, rather than on other more elusive yet crucial parts of the picture: civil society and those aspects of economic and social development that lie beyond the state's reach. The case of one rich democracy, Italy, suggests the limitations of this approach. A leading member of Silvio Berlusconi's parliamentary coalition, which won the May 13, 2001, elections, described the contrast between "public" Italy—which he called "bad" and "embarrassing," its legal system a "joke," its armed forces "just collecting their pay," its police "pitiful"—and "private" Italy, which he called "very good," "admired all over the world," and which, in the last half-century, has boasted the most vibrant, least recession-prone economy in Europe.[13] Some poor democracies may follow the "Italian path" to modernity, enduring a dysfunctional state—corrupt, wasteful, meddlesome, universally despised, and cheated by the taxpayers—while enjoying a vigorous private economy and strong and dynamic local democracy.

The progress of the poor democracies in the coming years is our best hope for diminishing poverty and violence in the world. If the West is serious about assisting them, Western leaders, and international financial institutions must be prepared to travel a long and tortuous road. It may help to remember that, unlike the West at a comparable stage of economic development, these poor countries are practicing an early capitalism that is strengthened and made more equitable by democracy, step by painful step. Surely the poor democracies—inspired, after all, by the example of the older and wealthier democracies—deserve aid and encouragement, not neglect or disdain.

Part V

The Putin Restoration

15

The YUKOS Affair
2003

Launched by the reformist regime from the institutional and normative void inherited from the Soviet economic and political collapse, Russian capitalism was forged in the largest privatization of state economic assets in history. Yet with the decaying Soviet socialism as its maternity ward and the corrupt Soviet functionaries as its midwives, the newly born market economy was linked to the state by myriad crooked "deals." In addition to the debates about large personal wealth and the role of the state in the economy that exist in every poor democracy, the "original sins" of Russian capitalism continue sharply to divide the society. Yet the choice of YUKOS as a scapegoat signaled an intent that went beyond a welcome attempt at the objective legal examination and final settlement of the troubling issues. Instead, the "YUKOS affair" seemed to herald a sharp turn toward economic and political recentralization.

In the early morning of October 25, 2003, masked agents of the Russian security agency, the FSB, stormed the plane of Mikhail Khodorkovsky, CEO and principal owner of Russia's largest private oil company, YUKOS, arrested him, and conveyed him to a Moscow prison. He was charged with tax evasion, fraud, forgery, and embezzlement.

Khodorkovsky's arrest and imprisonment were only the latest of the Russian government's actions against YUKOS's executives and owners. On July 2, 2003, on a warrant from the prosecutor general of the Russian Federation, Moscow police arrested Platon Lebedev, a principal shareholder and director of the Menatep holding and investment company. Menatep owns 61 percent of YUKOS, and Khodorkovsky is the majority owner of Menatep.

Lebedev was charged with embezzling state assets in the 1994 privatization of Russia's largest phosphate extraction and enrichment plant, Apatit, on the Kola Peninsula, 750 miles northeast of Moscow. Subsequently, the Russian government has issued additional charges against Lebedev, including "tax evasion," "abuse of trust," and "failure to comply with a court order." Lebedev's petitions for bail have been repeatedly denied.

Despite assurances by the government that the action against Menatep and YUKOS is nothing more than a "routine investigation," the choice of the target and the timing of the prosecution belie such claims. Instead, what has come to be known in Russia as "the YUKOS affair" is a reflection of a deep division among the elite, as well as the public at large, concerning the relationship between the state and the private economy, wealth, and democracy.

The Russian government created YUKOS in April 1993 by integrating several state-owned production, refining, and distribution companies. The company's name is a combined acronym of the original constituent companies: Yuganskneftegaz, one of the largest oil producers in the Tyumen' region of Western Siberia, and KuybyshevnefteOrgSintez, a major refinery and petrochemical plant in Kuybyshev (now Samara), a city on the Volga.

Khodorkovsky's Menatep acquired YUKOS at a "loans-for-shares" auction in December 1995. Having inherited an empty treasury from the Soviet Union and being unable, as in any revolution, to collect taxes, the government was desperate to pay pensions to retirees and salaries to teachers and doctors. With presidential elections looming, the Kremlin sought huge instant loans from the top private banks. As collateral, the government offered controlling stakes in key industrial enterprises. When the state defaulted on the loans a year later, the companies became the property of the creditors.

In a country still clawing its way out of the Soviet economic collapse, the hundreds of millions of dollars raised at the auctions were an astronomic sum. At the time, barely two years had passed since the outbreak of a mini–civil war in Moscow in October 1993. Within days of the auctions, the Communist-led "popular patriots" gained a plurality in the Duma election, and a Communist candidate was widely predicted to win the summer 1996 presidential election half a year later. (By the rules of the auctions, the owners of the collateral state shares were not to take possession of the properties until the fall of 1996. Had a Communist won, the lenders would have lost every kopeck.)

With political risks so high, no reputable foreign investor was willing to spend hundreds of millions of dollars for the privilege of owning potentially profitable but then mostly loss-making enterprises and face the sullen and technologically backward workforce, Communist-dominated unions, and additional hundreds of millions of dollars in technological overhauls. For the Russian privatizers, then, the choice in 1995 was not between pristinely clean foreign corporations and banks spoiling for direct investment in Russian industry on the one hand and the home-grown entrepreneurs with dubious connections and practices on the other. Instead, they had to choose between the latter and the thieving, corrupt, and incompetent Soviet functionaries in ministries and committees who had run most of these "crown jewels of the Soviet economy" (the obligatory journalistic cliché) deep into the ground.

Menatep "loaned" the government $159 million in exchange for 45 percent of YUKOS's shares. Shortly thereafter, the company purchased another 33 percent for $150 million in an investment tender. The transactions were conducted through an intermediary company, Laguna, since Menatep was the organizer of the auction. Thus, Menatep purchased YUKOS at an auction that it ran through a company it created.

Uniquely in world history, private property and capitalism emerged simultaneously in post-Soviet Russia. At the time, the laws and mores that, in more fortunate lands, predated modern capitalism by centuries had to be created from scratch on a slate wiped clean by seventy years of totalitarian Marxism-Leninism and absolute state ownership of the economy. In what Russia's leading liberal economist Evgeny Yasin called "the revolutionary chaos,"[1] no large business in Russia was "clean" by today's standards—and the larger the company, the greater the violations it likely committed.

In the case of approximately a dozen Menatep-like business empires in post-Soviet Russia, the list of violations was undoubtedly very long. During the 1990s, Russia's fledgling entrepreneurs routinely trampled on the rights of minority shareholders, created shell companies for transfer payments, and leveraged their bribe-greased connections with government officials in a race against equally rough and aggressive competitors to snatch up the choicest pieces of state property. At the time, when full remittance of several dozen taxes would have absorbed well over 100 percent of a business's profit, tax evasion was the only strategy allowing an entrepreneur to pay salaries and invest in his business.

Given the wide array of abuses committed by the vast majority of Russia's capitalists during the 1990s, the case that state prosecutors have constructed against Lebedev is surprisingly, even insolently, flimsy. A front firm allegedly linked to Lebedev bought a 20 percent stake in Apatit in 1994 for $225,000 and pledged to invest $280 million.[2] In 1996, the Murmansk regional government sued the firm for reneging on the investment commitment. The case was settled in 2002, with the firm agreeing to pay $16 million in penalties. Ignoring the settlement, prosecutors have resurrected the case and charged Lebedev with embezzling $280 million.

✑

Despite all its unsavory baggage, the choice of YUKOS as the scapegoat for the misdeeds of the 1990s makes little sense—unless one assumes that it has been picked not for what it has done but for what it has become.

In the past five years, YUKOS has traveled the farthest of any post-Soviet industrial giant away from the mores and practices of the 1990s. In 1999, YUKOS became the first Russian megafirm to switch to international accounting standards. Two years later it became the first Russian oil company to report its quarterly financial statements in accordance with U.S. Generally Accepted Accounting Principles (GAAP). The company has several dozen Western accountants permanently on staff. Its 2002 annual report has been audited by PriceWaterhouseCoopers.[3] Independent directors constitute a majority of the company's board.[4] Today, YUKOS is considered the most transparent of Russia's largest industrial corporations. Meanwhile, as YUKOS started to be publicly traded, the company's ownership diversified considerably, with Menatep's share falling from 85 percent to 61 percent.

When Menatep took over YUKOS in 1996, the company suffered from the same problems that were hobbling the rest of Russia's energy sector. With salary arrears mounting and oil output declining precipitously, the company was on the brink of bankruptcy. Four years later, the firm had enough cash to become the first Russian oil company to pay dividends to its nearly 60,000 shareholders—the ruble equivalent of $300 million in 2000, $500 million in 2001, and $700 million in 2002.

By 2002, YUKOS accounted for 18 percent of Russia's total oil production, pumping an average of 1.4 million barrels a day. The company's output grew by 17 percent in 2001 and by 19 percent in 2002, and is projected to increase by another 19 percent this year. Pursuing his dream of creating Russia's first global private economic player, Khodorkovsky engineered the purchase of another private Russian oil firm, Sibneft. Approved by the Russian State Anti-Monopoly Committee and completed on October 4, 2003, the complex equity-and-cash transaction has created the world's fourth largest oil producer. Today YukosSibneft pumps 2.3 million barrels a day, commands reserves of 19.4 billion barrels, and, prior to Khodorkovsky's arrest, was worth $43 billion.[5] Recently, ExxonMobil has been reported interested in acquiring between 40 and 50 percent of YukosSibneft for an estimated $25 billion—the single largest direct foreign investment in Russian history.[6]

Following YUKOS, Sibneft, and other privately owned companies and helped by their investing an estimated $5 billion in new technology, exploration, and drilling, Russia has increased its daily extraction of oil by 40 percent in the past five years, from an average of 5.9 million barrels in 1998 to 8.6 million barrels this past August.[7] On several occasions since 2001, Russia has pumped more oil in a given month than Saudi Arabia.

Since the 1998 financial crisis, the value of YUKOS's shares has increased more than tenfold, including 250 percent growth in 2001 alone.[8] In September 2002, Khodorkovsky, who owns 36 percent of the company's stock, was ranked first on *Fortune* magazine's "Global 40 Richest Under 40" list, with an estimated worth of $7.2 billion.[9] He was thirty-nine years old at the time.

In December 2002, Standard & Poor's rated YUKOS "BB with stable outlook," and in January 2003, Moody's Investor Service assigned the oil company a rating of "Ba2." At the time, these were the highest long-term and foreign currency issuer ratings of any private Russian company.[10] Last year, YUKOS garnered awards for "Best Manager" (Khodorkovsky), "Best Investor Relations," "Best Website," and "Best Annual Report" from the Association for the Protection of Investors' Rights, which includes twenty-seven of the largest Russian and foreign institutional investors in the Russian market with an equivalent of $10 billion under management.[11]

Khodorkovsky also won the 2002 "Entrepreneur of the Year" prize, awarded annually by Russia's leading business daily, *Vedomosti*, which is published jointly by the *Financial Times* and the *Wall Street Journal*. The same year, the Russian government named YUKOS the "Best Company for Compensation and Social Payments Programs," as well as recognizing it for the "Implementation of Social Programs at Enterprises and Organizations."[12]

❦

Khodorkovsky likes to describe himself as three generations of Rockefellers rolled into one.[13] Having been a robber baron, a respectable industrialist, a leading philanthropist, and, perhaps, a national political figure—all in the span of ten years—he is not far from the truth.

Although the number of private Russian charities has skyrocketed from zero in 1988 to seventy thousand today, with 2.5 million Russians actively helping an estimated 30 million of their fellow citizens,[14] YUKOS's contributions and Khodorkovsky's personal donations are beyond parallel in post-Soviet history. YUKOS gave the ruble equivalent of $45 million to charity in 2002 and is projected to donate an equivalent of $50 million this year.[15] According to Hugo Erikssen, the director of YUKOS's International Information Department, in addition to charitable disbursements by YUKOS, the company's core shareholders will donate between $100 million and $150 million in 2003. (Leonid Nevzlin, Menatep's second largest shareholder with 8 percent of the equity, is the leading contributor to Jewish charities in the territory of the former Soviet Union.)[16]

In early 2002, $10 million went to establish the Open Russia Foundation for the support of educational and cultural projects in Russia and abroad. Its projects include the first permanent exhibition of artwork from St. Petersburg's Hermitage Museum to be held outside Russia, in the historic Somerset House in London.

In November 2001, YUKOS donated $500,000 to the U.S. Library of Congress for its Rule of Law Program, which brings Russian judges to American communities, where they are hosted by senior federal judges and observe firsthand the U.S. judicial system. At the same time, another half-million dollars was given to the library to administer resident fellowships for Russian scholars and students.

When the billionaire investor and speculator George Soros decided last year to end a decade of charitable giving in Russia, YUKOS stepped in with a $1.15 million contribution to the U.S. nonprofit Eurasia Foundation for the support of "small business and community development."[17]

The corporation has instituted a home mortgage program for its employees and plans to spend up to $15 million in 2003 to subsidize loans extended by participating banks at special low rates.[18] YUKOS purchases drugs and state-of-the art diagnostic equipment for hospitals in its "company towns"— Nefteyugansk, Khanty-Mansiysk, Angarsk, Achinsk, and Tomsk. In the same cities, the company runs "social cafes" where anyone can get a free hot meal.

YUKOS also provides stipends to the children of its employees if the children are enrolled in college and receive straight A's two semesters in a row, and awards stipends to A-students in universities and institutes with majors related to the oil industry.[19]

Khodorkovsky is convinced that the export of raw materials (Russia's major source of foreign earnings and tax revenue today) is incapable of turning the country into a world-class industrial power and securing a high standard of living for most Russians. To achieve these objectives, Russia must transform itself from an industrial to a postindustrial society—a trajectory possible only in the presence of a progressive and modern home-grown scientific, managerial, and technological elite, which Khodorkovsky calls the "creative minority."[20]

It is to create such an elite that, in March 2000, YUKOS launched a nationwide program called Pokolenie.ru (or "Generation.ru") to provide Internet skills and access to Russian high school teachers and students. Managed by the Federation for Internet Education (FIE), Pokolenie.ru opens and equips regional centers where forty teachers at a time spend two weeks acquiring Internet skills to pass on to their students. Their travel, room, and board are paid by YUKOS.[21] By last spring, there were Internet centers in thirty-four out of Russia's eighty-nine regions, and 56,600 Russian educators received FIE diplomas after completing the course.

Started in 1996 in the oil-producing regions of Russia, another of YUKOS's educational programs, "New Civilization," is designed to educate high school students in the principles of democracy, market economics, and civic responsibility. Classes participate in a role-playing activity in which they "invent" their own country, determining its political system, electing its government, introducing a currency, even opening a stock exchange.[22] The students compete for the "most effectively governed" state, with the winners representing the school at a district competition. According to the program's website, each school is "transformed into an independent 'children's repub-lic,'" establishing "economic, political, cultural, and educational ties with the 'countries' in neighboring schools."[23] By 2003, over two hundred thou-sand Russian high school students had participated in New Civilization, and the number was expected to reach five hundred thousand by 2005.

❧

The choice of YUKOS (among dozens of equally culpable corporations) as the whipping boy for the excesses of the early post-Soviet "primary accumulation" is hard to explain in terms of the core long-term interests of Russia's state and society, be they the diminution of corruption, greater trans-parency, social responsibility of large businesses, or foreign investment. As leading Russian political philosopher Igor Kliamkin put it, "If the war on the oligarchs is begun with one of the most successful, effective, and transparent companies, then success, effectiveness, and transparency are no longer the priorities of the state."[24]

Those who engineered the assault on YUKOS were likely guided by another set of priorities. In the short run, they hoped to bolster the chances of the progovernment centrist party, United Russia, in the December 7, 2003, parliamentary elections. The attack on YUKOS was expected to help United Russia in two ways. First, it was to scare the top Russian entrepre-neurs into giving more to United Russia and less to opposition parties. Khodorkovsky was reportedly concerned about the possibility of a two-thirds progovernment majority in the next Duma—the so-called "constitu-tional majority" required by the 1993 constitution to effect changes in the "foundation" of Russia's economic and political systems. Among the possi-ble "federal constitutional laws" Khodorkovsky seemed to be most wary about and determined to oppose are renationalization, the extension of the president's tenure to include a third four-year term, and the imposition of a "development fee," or "rent," for the use of natural resources.

To prevent any faction from gaining control of the Duma, Khodor-kovsky gave amply to the major opposition parties since the beginning of this year—the Communists on the left and the liberals of the Union of

Rightist Forces and Yabloko on the right. (He is reportedly underwriting Yabloko's entire campaign budget.) In exchange, YUKOS placed more than a dozen people on these parties' national candidate lists. At the same time, Khodorkovsky repeatedly refused the Kremlin's "requests" to finance United Russia.[25]

The other, more important, reason for the YUKOS crackdown was an apparent belief that a sustained and well-publicized attack on a prominent "oligarch" would add voters to United Russia's count. Based on a selective reading of public opinion polls, this was not an unreasonable hope.

Tensions between democracy, which is institutionalized equality, and capitalism, which is institutionalized inequality, are a permanent feature in the public attitudes of countries that combine these systems. Wariness and resentment of "big business," private wealth, and the role they play in democratic politics are characteristic of all capitalist nations, but are especially acute in the younger "poor democracies"[26] of Eastern Europe, Asia, and Africa.

In Russia, suspicion of and hostility toward big business have been intensified by almost three-quarters of a century of socialist autarky and incessant anticapitalist propaganda, the stresses of adjusting to the rapid transformation of most of the economy from state-owned to private, while the inevitable unsavory details of a transformation of such a magnitude ˙ were reported daily in a press free from government censorship.

In July 2003, 77 percent of Russians viewed "big capitalists" somewhat or completely negatively.[27] In a country where for almost four generations private wealth (apart from carefully hidden Communist Party *nomenklatura* possessions) by definition could only be acquired by breaking the law, 88 percent of respondents in the same poll believed that large private fortunes had been earned "mostly" or "totally dishonestly."[28]

Perhaps most enticing to those behind Khodorkovsky's and Lebedev's arrests was the less overwhelming but still solid public support for the "need" to revise the results of privatization: 44 percent for privatization as a whole, and 33 percent for "parts" of privatization. Additionally, the prosecution of the "big capitalists" who benefited from privatization was approved unconditionally by 57 percent of those polled, while 31 percent supported criminal charges in "exceptional cases."[29]

Of course, like anyone else, Russians are perfectly capable of holding contradictory opinions simultaneously. When asked last year if the liberal economic reforms (with privatization as their centerpiece) should have been started, the share of those who said "yes" was almost three times larger than of those who responded negatively: 62 percent versus 22 percent.[30] In 2002, 84 percent of those polled wished to work at a private firm or enterprise, as compared to 19 percent in 1990.[31] This past summer, 53 percent of those surveyed felt that their country should "create favorable conditions" for the development of big business, and only 22 percent thought that it should not.[32]

The public is almost evenly divided on whether private businessmen have been "good" for Russia: 45 percent consider their activity "useful for the country," and 40 percent, harmful.[33] (Commenting on these numbers, Yuri Levada, the dean of Russian sociologists and pollsters, said that "45 percent is not at all bad, not at all. With our poverty and our [Soviet] upbringing, the number could have been much lower.")[34]

Directly bearing on the attack on YUKOS, a strong plurality of 48 percent believed that "redivision" (*peredel*) of large properties today would "harm" Russia, and only 12 percent felt that their country would benefit from such an act; the rest were uncertain.[35] Furthermore, smaller pluralities in a mostly undecided population thought that the YUKOS affair would "worsen the political situation" in Russia (30 percent); "damage Russia's image in the West" (36 percent);[36] or "diminish Putin's prestige" (41 percent).[37]

The selective reading of public attitudes may explain not only the eagerness of the anti-YUKOS plotters but also Putin's silence for almost three months between Lebedev's and Khodorkovsky's arrests. During this time, the Russian president said nothing to domestic audiences about YUKOS—and his responses to foreign reporters' queries about the case were omitted from transcripts on government websites and television. When Putin finally spoke, two days after Khodorkovsky's arrest, he warned against "hysteria and speculations" and expressed confidence that the court "had a reason" to order the arrest.

Putin's reluctance to interfere likely stems from surveys of voter preferences in the March 2004 presidential elections. While in all polls Putin is far more popular than all other potential candidates, he slipped in spring of this year to just below the 50 percent mark for the first time since his election in 2000.[38] If Putin were to receive less than half of the vote, the Russian constitution would require a second-round runoff election. For someone accustomed to approval ratings in excess of 70 percent and addicted to popular adulation, the possibility of carrying less than half the electorate is an affront. Reportedly near-obsessive about his daily poll numbers and often hesitant and indecisive to the point of paralysis, Putin may hope that the attack on YUKOS will add just enough popularity for him to avoid the humiliation of a runoff.[39]

∽

Yet the YUKOS affair extends well beyond proximate political battles. In the end, it is about competing visions of Russia's fledgling capitalism and its relations with the state.

The institutional and normative void inherited from the Soviet collapse is still far from filled, and both the elites and society at large are sharply divided on what to fill it with. Among the key contested issues are the relationship between the state and the privatized economy, in which over 70 percent of the country's GDP is now produced; the competing claims on the enormous wealth that the privatized economy has generated and continues to generate daily; and the role of "big capital" in Russian politics and society.

Russia's economic revolution was also the largest denationalization of property in history. With no other source of capital inside the country— foreign investors having prudently stayed out for fear of a Communist comeback, and no Marshall Plan–like massive assistance from the West ever having materialized—Russian large capital could and did originate only through the privatization of the Soviet state, which owned everything.

Born out of decaying Soviet socialism, with corrupt Communist Party functionaries and thieving bureaucrats as its midwives, Russian capitalism continues to be bound to the state by myriad "deals," outdated regulations, and nefarious connections between businessmen and local and federal officials. Yet it was inevitable that sooner or later the most advanced, export-oriented, and cosmopolitan segment of the Russian business elite would come to resent the status quo and attempt to claim more independence, as well as a presence in civil society and politics unmediated by the state.

To secure such a modus vivendi, however, Russian business must overcome very tall obstacles. The steepest among them may be the confluence of political authority and property. This is not just a Russian predicament. Perhaps more than anything else, the blending of power and ownership distinguishes poor democracies from the older capitalist nations. In the West, from the end of the Middle Ages onward, the state's control over private possessions steadily eroded until the king "was the lord in the political sense but not in the sense of an owner," as two lawyers reportedly explained to Frederick II of Prussia in the mid-eighteenth century.[40] In poor democracies, which mostly came into being in the last twenty years of the twentieth century, political power still tends to translate, directly or indirectly, into ownership, or at least control, by the elder, the factory director, the tribal chief, the mayor, or the governor.[41]

The difficulty in breaking up the unity of power and ownership, which is the source of some of poor democracies' most recalcitrant problems (corruption first among them), is much aggravated by Russia's legacy of patrimonialism: a political system in which the ruler or rulers are "both sovereigns of the realm and its proprietors," and "political authority is exercised as an extension of the rights of ownership."[42]

Between the fifteenth and the middle of the seventeenth centuries, Russia was a full-fledged patrimonial state. For the local functionaries, patrimonialism translated into a rule that was to become the perpetual motto of successive Russian bureaucracies: "That which I manage, on it I feed." (Indeed, *kormlenie*, or "feeding," was the official designation of the means by which czars' district prefects were expected to support themselves and their families during their time in office.)

After gradually receding over the course of a hundred years, patrimonialism was further diminished under Catherine the Great. The noblemen were no longer automatically the conscripts of the state, and the crown began to surrender its monopoly on the land by giving the nobles titles to their estates. The state's grip on the economy weakened gradually throughout the nineteenth century, particularly after the liberal reforms of Czar Alexander II (1861–65). Patrimonialism continued to erode in the first decade and a half of the twentieth century when Russia's was among the fastest-growing economies in the world.

Yet patrimonialism returned with vengeance in the Soviet state. For sixty years, from 1929 to 1989, the state owned everything and employed everyone. Anyone who has lived or traveled in the Soviet Union—with its underground trade in automobile parts, records, jeans, or books—will instantly recognize the description of private economic activity written by Giles Fletcher, an Englishman who went to Russia in the sixteenth century:

> And if [the Russian people] have any thing, they conceale it all they can, sometimes conveying it to Monasteries, sometimes hiding it under the ground, and in woods, as men are woont to doo where they are in feare of forreine invasion. In so much that many times you shall see them afraid to be knowen to any [Boyar] or Gentleman of such commodities as they have to sell. I have seen them sometimes when they have layed open their commodities for [sale] (as their principall furres & such like) to looke still behind them, and towards every doore: as men in some fear, that looked to be set upon, & surprised by some enimie. Whereof asking the cause, I found it to be this, that they [feared lest] some Nobleman or [Boyars' sons] had been [present], & so layed a traine for the prey upon their comodities perforce. This maketh the people (though otherwise hardened to beare any toile) to give themselves much to idlenes and drinking; as passing for no more, than from hand to mouth.[43]

Today, the boyar and the nobleman have been replaced by the bureaucrat and the policeman, and robbery by bribery, but the idea of the ultimate dependence of private business on the state's good graces persists. After four generations of limitless power, many in the still largely Soviet-era Russian bureaucracy, which easily survived the 1991 "velvet revolution," are still incapable of accepting an economic system in which property and wealth are not directly conferred (or withdrawn) by the state or, at least, controlled by it.

"If we don't like you, how can you be rich?" is the message that the state bureaucracy intends to send to Khodorkovsky, other "oligarchs," and hundreds of thousands of owners of small and middle-sized businesses.

❧

YUKOS's first offense was its increased transparency, as well as its newfound but stubborn respect for Russian and international laws. International accounting standards and audits by top Western accounting firms leave few, if any, "slush" funds for bribery. YUKOS was attacked, many Russian analysts believe, because, after years of wholesale buying of government bureaucrats and Duma deputies, it began to set an example of a big business determined to operate "by the book." "Our bureaucracy cannot stand clean and legal business," observed three leading Russian political experts in a long commentary on the YUKOS affair.

> They are interested in keeping businesses in the "shadows". . .
> [and] in pushing them into an illegal, criminal space. Because an
> "oligarch" who is the subject of a thick dossier in the prosecutor's
> office is much easier to command and to use as a money bag.[44]

YUKOS broke another cardinal rule of the bureaucratic "great game" by openly contributing to opposition political parties to advance its interests and shape the laws—instead of following the age-old Russian and Soviet tradition of ignoring the laws and bribing those who implement and enforce them. In a country where long-term planning—economic, financial, and political—has been all but extirpated by four hundred years of brutal authoritarianism and totalitarian ownership of the economy, YUKOS dared plan for decades ahead without consulting state ministers and committee chairmen.

The YUKOS affair, then, is a battle in a war of two economic cultures. One is labeled by Russian observers "great-power statist" (*derzhavno-etatistskaya*), and the other, "liberal-oligarchic."[45] Though hardly perfect from the Western point of view, the latter nevertheless has shown the capacity for change and progress since its inception a decade ago. It has produced fiscal discipline, low inflation, lower corporate and income taxes, the extension of private property rights to urban real estate and agricultural land, the diminution of bureaucratic interference in the private sector, continuing privatization of state assets, improvements in corporate governance, and greater transparency.

By contrast, the "great-power statists" seek to increase the government's control over the economy and, inevitably, civil society. Concentrated among federal and local elected authorities and bureaucrats, they are supported by a significant segment of the Russian public, including the one-quarter to one-third of the electorate that votes Communist. Added to the "statist" constituency in the last three years have been many retired or still serving secret service officers who under Putin came to occupy an unprecedented multitude of executive positions in the federal and regional governments. (The alleged masterminds of the YUKOS affair are veterans of the KGB/FSB—deputy heads of presidential administration Igor Sechin and General Viktor Ivanov.)

Their campaign for recentralization is said to be bankrolled by partially privatized companies with controlling or significant state ownership, like the natural gas monopoly Gazprom, Russia's largest oil company Lukoil, and another oil major, Rosneft. Notoriously wasteful and corrupt, they have contributed obediently and generously to the Kremlin bureaucrats' favorite parties and are said to be behind the newly formed People's Party, a left-populist entity with dangerous nationalist overtones.

Another reportedly key underwriter of the attack on YUKOS is Russia's third largest bank, Mezhprombank. Although private, this institution is as close to the ideal of "state capitalism" as any Russian enterprise. The bank's principal shareholder and former CEO, Sergei Pugachev, began his career in the Kremlin's Presidential Property Administration, which manages the huge tracts of real estate inherited from the czars and general secretaries. Later, Mezhprombank was rewarded with the government accounts that brought billions of rubles in state revenues. Rumored to be very close both to the hierarchy of the Russian Orthodox Church and to the Putin-led St. Petersburg political machine, Pugachev's bank has recently extended a $100 million credit line to the perennially struggling Gazprom. Lately, the bank is rumored to be considering entering Russia's very lucrative arms exports business.

Yet even with this heavy artillery behind them, the victory of the "statists" is not assured. During the 1990s, Russia has made long strides in the past three years toward further freeing the entrepreneur and the consumer from state control. In the legislative pipeline are measures aimed at further debureaucratization and reduction of state ownership or control over the nodal points of Russia's economy and society—housing and utilities, pensions, and banking, as well as a civil service reform and the breakup of the two remaining state monopolies in railroads and natural gas. The on-and-off military reform is aimed at cutting in half the size of the Russian armed forces (already reduced to one-fourth of their strength in the Soviet Union) and will abolish perhaps the most hated manifestation of state power over society—the three-century-old conscription.

The "statists" needed a decisive success over not just a giant private conglomerate but a symbol of a more open, rapidly modernizing Russian capitalism. As likely the best-known private Russian company inside and outside the country, YUKOS fits the bill. If successful, the attack on YUKOS may presage the scaling down or even the abandonment of liberal reforms, and a shift in the Kremlin's priorities. Some Russian observers foresee an increasing reliance by the state on the "power bureaucracies" (siloviki), that is, the secret services, the police, and the military. Another serious danger is the adoption of the left populism of the People's Party as a state ideology based on Orthodox Christianity, and the mobilization of the electorate for "class warfare."[46]

While stopping short of across-the-board renationalization, new policies may include a massive "redistribution" (pereraspredelenie) of the privatized economy, with key industrial sectors and the most profitable megacompanies reverting to state control or being taken away from the current owners and given to more "loyal" entrepreneurs.

⌐⌐

The longer Lebedev and Khodorkovsky are in jail, the more the traditional Russian ailments that had begun to recede are likely to surface again: the lack of responsibility for oneself, one's business, and one's country; the inability to make long-term work and personal plans; bribery and tax evasion.

Like innumerable generations of Russians before them, today's Russian entrepreneurs are again made to feel like guests in their own country at the sufferance of the powers that be. Leading businessmen are bound to resume, or to increase, investing money abroad, stashing it in Swiss banks—or buying foreign soccer clubs, like Sibneft's principal owner, Roman Abramovich, who in August of this year purchased London's Chelsea club for $94 million.

Abramovich's decision two months later to unload half of his stake in Russian Aluminum, the world's third-largest aluminum producer, for $2 billion, coupled with his sell-off of Sibneft, could be a harbinger of things to come.

No matter who wins, the outcome of the YUKOS affair will represent a major choice among the many that Russia and the Russians must make today. This is a judgment about the nature and the extent of state control over the economy and about the role of big business and personal wealth in what is still a very poor and state-bound society.

The stakes perhaps are the highest where the evolution of individual rights, including the right to own property, are concerned. Throughout history, such rights have "trickled down," from barons protected from arbitrary arrests and confiscations by the crown, to towns and cities autonomous from the feudal lord, to universities and guilds free from outside interference, to individuals getting their day in court.

It may be politically incorrect to say so in this proud and victorious republic of ours steeped in democratic chauvinism, but the historical record is unambiguous: Where the barons (including oil ones) are safe from state despotism, and where the rich can get a fair court hearing in their disputes with the government (or one another), there eventually will be impartial justice for the ordinary citizen seeking to protect his or her rights or property.

Where an arbitrary and patently subverted judicial process against some of the country's most successful, civic-minded, and progressive entrepreneurs is deployed with impunity, the rights of everyone are uncertain, at best. On Russia's long and rocky road to dignity and prosperity, the YUKOS affair may signal a costly and frustrating detour.

16

Institutions, Restoration, and Revolution

2005

Charting the institutional pathways of the Putin restoration reveals structural deficiencies and lacunae in the system forged in the early 1990s, especially in its legislative, federal, and legal aspects. Any democracy is a work in progress, and Russia's post-Putin progress hinges on some urgent corrections that would put limitations on the executive, restore federalism, and strengthen the independence of legislative and judicial branches of power. In the meantime, as in every restoration, the clash between reaction and the enduring legacy of the revolution is likely to continue.

It is true, of course, that every great revolution is followed by a restoration, but this generality tells us little about the particulars. It does not explain, for instance, why in the Russian case the deviation from the values and ideas of the 1991 revolution has been far more pronounced than in Eastern and Central European countries, whose own "restorations"—which in many cases brought former Communists back to power and witnessed sharp, leftward turns in economic policy—were much milder and did not raise concerns about recurrent authoritarianism.

While the closely related issues of the genesis, goals, and resilience of the Putin restoration are complex and invite an array of analytic approaches,[1] the restoration's institutional context is especially important. Some key political and social structures and processes have clearly facilitated the authoritarian drift, while other systemic features thus far have resisted the Kremlin's agenda, adhering to the legacy of the 1991 revolution. An understanding of the systemic strengths and weaknesses of the Putin restoration is indispensable to gauging the sustainability of Russia's present direction.

The Federal Assembly

If there is an overarching theme to the Kremlin's policies, it is the exploitation of institutional loopholes and ambiguities in order to erode checks and balances and replace the separation of powers with what President Vladimir Putin likes to call "the vertical of power." The stealthy subjugation of the legislative and judicial branches to the executive begins with the country's parliament.

The Federation Council. Stipulating only that the upper chamber of the federal assembly consist of two representatives ("senators") from each of Russia's eighty-nine regions and that they be elected to four-year terms, the 1993 constitution is silent on the actual mode of election to the Federation Council, except to say that it is to be determined by "federal laws." Although such laws require a "constitutional majority" of three hundred votes (two-thirds of the lower chamber, or Duma) to pass, the lacunae have invited tampering.

In the first legislature (1993–95), senators were directly elected by the regions' populations. Between 1996 and 2001, the chamber was made up of regional governors and presidents (speakers) of local parliaments ex officio—a less democratic but nevertheless tolerable practice, as both the governors and the speakers were elected to the region-wide offices by the voters of their regions directly.

Shortly after Vladimir Putin was elected president in 2000, the Duma passed a law at the Kremlin's urging that filled the Federation Council with unelected representatives from each region: one appointed by the region's governor and the other by the local legislature.

In February 2005, in an overt violation of the separation of powers, Putin told the leaders of the Federation Council that fifty senators whose terms expired that year (slightly less than one-third of the 178-member chamber) should not be reappointed. "I am convinced," Putin said, "that the personnel should be reshuffled to make the chamber's work and personnel more stable."[2] Given Putin's recent proposal to eliminate the direct election of the governors (described below), the "reshuffling" means that senators sent to Moscow by the governors will almost certainly be selected by the Kremlin.

The State Duma. The same exploitation of a constitutional gap has been perpetrated in the Duma. Apart from specifying the size of the lower, and more powerful, chamber of the parliament at 450 deputies and setting their term of office at four years, the 1993 constitution, again, leaves the details to be determined by "federal laws."

To facilitate the emergence of political parties after seven decades of the one-party state, the original federal law established that half of the Duma's deputies should be elected "wholesale," as it were, as members of parties which receive the most votes nationwide. Of the 225 seats thus filled, a party receives a share proportionate to the percentage of the national party-list vote it garnered. To qualify for Duma membership, a party must poll no less than 5 percent of the national party-list vote. The other half of the Duma is filled by individual candidates who win a majority of votes in the country's 225 electoral districts.

In the wake of the Beslan massacre of September 1–3, 2004, in which hundreds of hostages, most of them children, were killed by terrorists in southern Russia, President Putin proposed that all Duma deputies be elected by party lists. While party-list-only elections are practiced in a number of established democracies (for instance, Israel and Italy), the elimination of single-mandate races in today's Russia, where less than 1 percent of the population belongs to a party, is a blow to democratic self-government at a national level.

Compared to the individual races, a number of requirements for a party to qualify for the ballot (including the collection of 200,000 signatures, no more than 10,000 of which can be from any one region, or a deposit of 39 million rubles—approximately $1.3 million) make party-list competition far more expensive, cumbersome, and vulnerable to interference by state and federal authorities. In addition, beginning in 2007, a new election law will raise the threshold for entry to the Duma from 5 percent to 7 percent of the national party-list vote, thus making it still more difficult to qualify for membership in the parliament.

Public opinion polls have established a strong and consistent preference for single-mandate representation. Since 1997, between two and five times as many respondents have favored direct election as those who support the party-list system.[3] In September 2004 the breakdown was 50 percent to 9 percent.[4] On May 19, 2005, following the Duma vote, President Putin signed into law a bill eliminating the single-mandate system in Russia.

Local Self-Government

Too big and diverse to be governed democratically as a centralized, unitary state, Russia was held together through most of its history first by the authoritarianism of the czars and then the one-party dictatorship of the Soviet Union. Whenever the "center" collapsed, the country literally fell apart. Tyranny and anarchy were the only alternatives until 1995, when President Boris Yeltsin authorized direct popular elections of the regional governors. A new Russian state was born: decentralized and democratic yet whole, and consisting of self-governing provinces.

In another post-Beslan measure, Vladimir Putin proposed that governors should be "nominated" by the Kremlin rather than directly elected by their constituents, and on December 12, 2004, signed into law the corresponding legislation passed by the federal assembly.[5] Again, the government used the absence of an explicit mention of gubernatorial elections in the country's constitution to violate the spirit (and almost certainly the letter) of the basic law. This breach is even more obvious than in the case of the federal assembly "reforms" and has been widely recognized as such by Russian observers.[6]

According to the Russian constitution, "the citizens of the Russian Federation have the right to elect and be elected to . . . bodies of local self-government" (article 32, part 2). Self-government is to be exercised, among other means, through "elections," while the structure of self-government "shall be determined" by the population of the regions (articles 130, part 2, and 131, part 1).[7] It is further stipulated that the then existing eighty-nine regions "have all the powers of state" except for those that are held either by the federal government or jointly shared between it and the regional authorities (article 73). Nowhere does the detailed list of the president's duties and powers (articles 83 and 84) include the "nomination" of the governors.

In this break from the country's basic law, Putin has embarked on a very dangerous experiment of attempting to recreate a unitary state, risking

Russia's destabilization and perhaps even disintegration.[8] The official reasons for the "reform"—to protect people from their bad choices, to prevent the election of inept or corrupt individuals, and to reign in governors' rapacity or dictatorial tendencies—are seen by leading Russian critics as a cure that is worse than the illness and a fig leaf for what the Kremlin really seems to want: "strict subordination to the center."[9] Can Russia really be governed as a unitary state? In the words of one Russian analyst: "A definite no . . . The vertical of power, so cherished by the administration, will begin to buckle under the weight of corruption, popular dissent, and administrative inefficiencies."[10]

The people agreed. Polled on September 18, 2004, five days after Putin announced his intention to abolish gubernatorial elections, 61 percent of respondents in a national survey said governors should be elected by the citizens of the regions, while only 25 percent supported their appointment "by the leadership of the country."[11]

The Legal System and Judicial Independence

Perhaps no other key institution has been so affected by the retreat from the revolutionary achievements of the previous decade as Russia's legal system. The post-Soviet legal revolution ended the state's monopoly on dispensing justice, giving courts a measure of independence.[12]

The 1993 constitution established every Russian citizen's equality before the law and his or her right to defend personal "rights and liberties" in court (articles 18, 19, and 46). It declared judges "independent," irremovable, and immune from prosecution (articles 121, 122, and 123). Court proceedings, it held, are to be conducted "on an adversarial and equal basis" between the defense and the prosecution (article 123, part 3). Self-incrimination is no longer required of the defendant (article 51).[13]

The courts' jurisdiction was thus vastly expanded, and their rulings on hundreds of thousands of lawsuits brought by people against local and federal authorities helped bolster freedom of religion and even grant exemptions from the military draft. Trials by jury were introduced, and the share of acquittals increased sharply. Emerging as the ultimate arbiter and the most effective instrument of the post-Soviet legal overhaul, the Constitutional

Court of the Russian Federation has ruled against the government in a number of landmark cases and has been vital to the emergence of civil society from the state's shadow.[14]

The legal revolution was formalized in the 2001 criminal procedural code, which proclaimed judicial independence and the equality of prosecution and defense; granted courts (rather than prosecutors) the sole power to sanction arrests, searches, and detentions; and guaranteed the right to an attorney and the writ of habeas corpus.[15]

A direct assault on judicial independence began on September 30, 2004, when the Federation Council passed legislation changing the composition of the Supreme Qualification Collegium, which appoints members of federal courts, including the Supreme Court and Supreme Arbitration Court, and which alone has the power to dismiss them.

Until then, eighteen of the Supreme Qualification Collegium's twenty-nine members had been elected every four years by the All-Russian Congress of Judges; ten so-called "representatives of public organizations" were appointed by the Federation Council, and one by the Russian president. Under the proposed structure, the collegium would be reduced to twenty-one members, of which the Congress of Judges would only "recommend" ten judges for nomination by the president and approval by the Federation Council, while the Federation Council speaker would continue to appoint ten members and the president, one. With the consent of a majority of the collegium, the Russian president would be able to dismiss any of the eleven judges he nominates or appoints, and the Federation Council would have the same power over "its" members. It is almost certain that the same takeover by the executive will be attempted in the regional qualification collegiums.

In addition to its "colliding with the constitution," in the words of the Collegium chairman Valentin Kuznetsov (who said he had learned of the proposed changes only when Russian journalists called him for comments),[16] the measure violates the 1998 European Charter on the Statute for Judges, to which Russia is a signatory. The charter states that for "every decision affecting the selection, recruitment, appointment, career progress, or termination of office of a judge, the statute envisages the intervention of an authority independent of the executive and legislative powers within which at least one half of those who sit are judges elected by their peers."[17]

The chairman of the Supreme Court, Vyacheslav Lebedev, has declared that the proposed change "would break Russia's separation of powers, giving the legislative (and executive) command over the judiciary."[18] (As of this writing, the Federation Council's law has not yet been taken up by the State Duma.)[19]

The contrast between the legal environment of the 1990s and that of today is highlighted by a comparison of cases of alleged espionage. In 1995 the Federal Security Service (FSB) arrested Alexander Nikitin, a former navy captain and environmental activist, and charged him with "high treason" for alleged espionage and disclosure of state secrets. Nikitin pleaded not guilty, insisting that he obtained information from unclassified and publicly available sources.

Basing his defense on the constitutional right to "freely seek, receive, pass on, produce, and disseminate information," as well as the constitutional ban on the application of unpublished laws and the retroactive application of the law, Nikitin obtained a favorable procedural ruling by the Constitutional Court and successfully undermined the legality of the state's case. The Nikitin case marked the first acquittal in Russian history on a charge of treason brought by state security agencies.[20]

A few years later, the trials of two scholars arrested and accused of very similar crimes followed a markedly different procedure with an opposite outcome. Both Igor Sutyagin, an arms-control scholar with the United States and Canada Institute in Moscow, and Valentin Danilov, a professor and expert on satellite technology at the Krasnoyarsk State Technical University, were charged by the FSB with selling state secrets to foreign companies. Both defendants insisted that the information they had communicated was based entirely on open sources.

In Sutyagin's case, the court switched juries to include individuals whom, the defendant's lawer argued, had connections to the secret services, and barred much of the cross-examination. Although the judge in the Sutyagin case ruled that the prosecution had failed to identify the state secrets the defendant allegedly sold to his foreign employers, the scholar was found guilty in April 2004 and sentenced to fifteen years of hard labor.

Danilov was acquitted by a jury in December 2003, but six months later the Supreme Court overturned the verdict, siding with the prosecution, which alleged "improper pressuring of the jury" by Sutyagin's attorney.[21]

The espionage charge was reinstated, and Danilov was rearrested. At a second trial, which was held in the fall of 2004 and closed to the public, the presiding judge banned the defense from presenting evidence that showed that the information passed by Danilov to a Chinese company was unclassified. The list of jurors was never published, and Danilov alleged that they were "acting under pressure."[22] The scientist was found guilty and received a fourteen-year sentence.

In 2003, the government started legal proceedings against the principal owners of YUKOS, Russia's largest private company, including its CEO Mikhail Khodorkovsky, for alleged fraud. The case subsequently expanded to incorporate charges against the company itself for nonpayment of taxes.[23]

Undoubtedly, there are legitimate legal concerns about how enormous private wealth was accumulated in a relatively short time in Russia during the 1990s.[24] Yet, regardless of the factual basis of the prosecution's case against YUKOS and its owners, in both instances what could have become a great precedent for dispassionate and scrupulous investigation and fair competition between prosecution and defense has increasingly deteriorated into a travesty scripted by the prosecution.

In a clear violation of the 2001 criminal procedural code, Khodorkovsky was denied bail, despite personal guarantees given by leading liberal politicians and entrepreneurs. Attorney-client privilege and confidentiality, guaranteed by the new code, were denied, and Khodorkovsky's attorneys were harassed and their offices searched. At the end of 2004, the procurator general's office issued warrants for two senior YUKOS lawyers, who fled abroad. Two members of the YUKOS team who stayed in Russia have been arrested and charged with fraud, money laundering, and tax evasion.

In one of many instances of judicial negligence or bias, it took the presiding judge in the YUKOS trial only three days to examine hundreds of volumes of tax documents and rule for the prosecution. Judges who attempted an objective examination were dismissed or reassigned from the case by the chairman of the Moscow city court. The trials have resulted in a new Russian expression to describe a crooked legal process: a *Bassmanniy sud*, or "Bassmanniy court," after the name of the Moscow court district in which most of the original proceedings against YUKOS were held.

The Institutional Legacy of the Revolution

Yet the institutional legacy of the revolution is far from extinguished. Contrary to the grotesquely misinformed taxonomies that place Russia in the same category of "unfree" nations as totalitarian North Korea, Libya, Cuba, and Turkmenistan,[25] or the dictatorships of Uzbekistan and Pakistan,[26] democratic institutions—although eroded and often subverted—are far from dead in the country. Like the flaws in the "enabling" institutions listed above, they are indispensable to a responsible analysis of Russia's prospects.

People in Russia today are free to travel abroad, leave the country, emigrate, and return. Christians, Muslims, and Jews pray unmolested and side by side in churches, mosques, and synagogues. Following the dramatic growth in their number during the 1990s, houses of worship continue to multiply, as do the religious schools, kindergartens, and adult education courses they run.[27]

Nicolai Petro, a leading student of local self-governance in post-Soviet Russia, estimates that there are 350,000 nonprofit, nongovernmental organizations in Russia today.[28] He also notes that "there is not a region in Russia with fewer than a dozen registered political parties and twice as many political associations."[29] According to Daniil Meshcheryakov, the executive director of the Moscow Helsinki Group, Russia's most prominent human rights organization, the participation of young professionals in the human rights movement is increasing and "the wave of initiative comes from the bottom."[30]

Although much criticized—sometimes deservedly so—and often honored in the breach, Russia's 1993 constitution nevertheless is an astonishing breakthrough in the country's political history. The basic law declares "man, his rights, and liberties" to be of "the highest value," and their recognition, observance, and protection, a "duty of the state." Among other "foundations" of the new Russian state are private property, "ideological diversity," and "multipartyness" (mnogopartiynost). No official state ideology or religion may be established. Throughout the rest of the constitution, separate articles guarantee freedom of religion, speech, demonstrations, and mass media.

Far from being powerless, as it is often portrayed, the Russian parliament has in its possession some powerful constitutional tools. Thus, during the opposition plurality of 1995–99, when the Duma was the de facto headquarters of the leftist "popular patriots," the parliament managed to block government-sponsored legislation for years. The successful opposition killed such vital measures as post-Soviet tax and labor codes, the breakup and privatization of the state-owned "natural monopolies" (gas, electricity, railroads), and the partial privatization of the housing and pension systems. On several occasions (including three times in the spring and summer of 1997), the parliament has mustered two-thirds majorities in both houses to override presidential vetos of bills that prohibited the purchase and sale of agricultural land or restricted religious freedom.

In matters that constitutionally are the legislature's prerogative, the Duma was far from shy during the 1990s in ignoring the Kremlin's wishes, as, for instance, in 1994, when it amnestied the leaders of the August 1991 *putsch* and the October 1993 uprising in the center of Moscow. In early 1999, the Duma initiated Yeltsin's impeachment, although it failed to garner the necessary three hundred votes on any of the four articles.

Thus, the absence of an effective legislative counterbalance to the Kremlin today stems not from any systemic deficiency of the constitutional arrangements but from the results of the 2003 election, in which the pro-Kremlin party, United Russia, won a majority of seats, the Communist vote was almost halved, and right-of-center liberal parties failed to overcome the 5 percent threshold. The opposition was reduced to about one-fourth of the chamber. In effect, both the executive and the legislative branches of the Russian government came to be dominated by the same "party of power," as it is known in Russia.

Yet such unity may prove to be shaky. Already in February of this year, United Russia abstained in the Duma on a vote of no-confidence in the government. With the voters increasingly disappointed in United Russia, and with more and more Russians understanding the need for a viable political opposition, the 2007 parliamentary election may weaken United Russia and strengthen the opposition on the left and on the right.

Of course, for that to happen, access to the polls and vote-counting will need to be fair and honest. If, on the other hand, the regime decides to resort to rigging on a national scale (which will be easy to prove by comparing the preelection surveys and exit polls to the official results), it may face a far greater danger of mass protests, such as followed the vote falsification in Georgia, Ukraine, and Kyrgyzstan.

Public Resistance

The public reaction to the regime's sharp turn toward authoritarianism in September and October 2004 was far from muted. In the following months there were more than a dozen conferences, roundtables, pickets, and rallies criticizing Putin's "reforms."[31] On December 12, the Civic Congress in Moscow gathered 1,500 prodemocracy and human rights activists from all over Russia. The tough declaration adopted by the Congress demanded that the government "adhere" to the constitution.[32]

An umbrella prodemocracy opposition group of leading liberal politicians and activists, called "Committee 2008," was formed to prepare for the next presidential election. On February 15, the leaders of the committee gathered in Moscow to discuss the formation of an opposition political party.

In February 2005, hundreds of thousands of protesters all over Russia rallied against the replacement of in-kind welfare benefits with inadequate monetary equivalents. During a national protest day on February 12, between 250,000 (the official estimate) and 800,000 (the organizers' number) took to the streets. During the previous week, there was a demonstration near the Kremlin to protest the abolition of the direct election of governors, a rally in the center of St. Petersburg to protest the lack of coverage of political opposition by the city's state-owned television channel, and protests in dozens of cities across the country by transportation workers against the rising price of gasoline.

At the same time, a new student opposition movement sprang up. Calling itself *Idushchie bez Putina*, or "Walking without Putin" (a reference to a government-supported youth movement *Idushchie Vmeste*, or "Walking Together"), the group is led by Roman Dobrokhotov, a twenty-one-year-old student at the Moscow State Institute of International Relations. Modeled on the Ukrainian prodemocracy youth group *Pora!* ("It's Time!"), which was the backbone of street protests during the prodemocracy Orange Revolution in Ukraine in the late fall–winter 2004–5, *Idushchie bez Putina* is planning street protests.

"Our values are liberal democracy, civil rights, and freedom," said Dobrokhotov, who wore an orange shirt at a press conference in the Moscow headquarters of the liberal Yabloko party. "In the first four years of Putin's regime," he continued, "people had hope. Nowadays, people understand that under authoritarian rule, development is impossible. This government, this system, is not suitable for them."[33] Seeking to create a "student protest movement," *Idushchie* sees its mission as being "in the vanguard of social opposition to Putin's regime."[34]

Freedom of Speech

With the very notable exception of Mikhail Khodorkovsky, all the key opposition leaders in Russia remain at liberty, including some of the most vocal critics of the regime: Duma deputy Sergei Glaziev, former co-chair of the left-nationalist Rodina Party; Irina Khakamada, former co-chair of the right-liberal Union of Rightist Forces (SPS), a 2004 presidential candidate, and leader of a new opposition party, Our Choice; Boris Nemtsov, former co-chair of SPS and an adviser to newly elected Ukrainian President Viktor Yushchenko; Vladimir Ryzhkov, a liberal opposition leader in the Duma; Georgy Satarov, a former top political adviser to President Yeltsin and the founder and president of INDEM, a liberal think tank; Gennady Zyuganov, chairman of the Communist Party of the Russian Federation and a deputy in the Duma; and Eduard Limonov, the leader of National-Bolsheviks, an ultra-leftist Stalinist party with anti-Semitic overtones.

Last March, at a press conference in Moscow, former prime minister Mikhail Kasyanov declared Russia to be on the "wrong track" and moving in an "incorrect" direction that "negatively affects the economic and social development of the country."[35] Strongly hinting at the possibility of running as an anti-Kremlin candidate in the 2008 presidential election, Kasyanov said that "what's important is not who is elected in 2008, but that whoever [it] is spearheads a movement toward democratic values."[36] Kasyanov's statement was reported and exhaustively analyzed by all the major Russian newspapers.[37]

The freedom of speech can occasionally be extended even to the Chechen pro-independence resistance. On March 8, Ekho Moskvy, a national radio station specializing in interviews with independent political experts and opposition figures, broadcast comments by Akhmad Zakayev, a leader of the Chechen resistance, who is wanted in Russia on charges of terrorism and whose extradition from Great Britain the Russian government has unsuccessfully sought for years. Reacting to the killing of Chechnya's rebel leader and former president Aslan Maskhadov, Zakayev said that "Maskhadov's death will lead to an outburst of terrorism in Chechnya and all over Russia."[38]

Last year, a popular national public organization, the Union of Soldiers' Mothers, which has helped thousands of conscripts since 1989 avoid the draft or be discharged by providing legal and medical counseling services, decided to become a political party. The Union of the Committees of Soldiers' Mothers, which intends to run for Duma seats in 2007, had its founding congress in November 2004 in Moscow. The gathering was attended by 164 delegates from fifty regions.

In response to the Ministry of Defense's announced intention to sharply reduce the number of exemptions from the draft,[39] the Union of the Committees of Soldiers' Mothers began preparations for a national referendum on the draft, the exemptions, and the transition to all-volunteer armed forces.

Hated by the Russian military brass, the organization has been trying to mediate a peaceful resolution to the Chechen crisis. In March of this year, the leaders of the group traveled to London for talks with Akhmad Zakayev. The representatives of the Union of Soldiers' Mothers and Zakayev agreed at the meeting that the conflict could not be settled by force and blamed Moscow's "shortsighted and criminal policies" for the war in Chechnya and "the terrorism it triggered."[40]

The Opposition Press

Although in the past few years, following "hints" from the Kremlin, some publishers and advertisers have "toned down" their content or closed their outlets altogether, many—indeed most—have not. Today one finds in Russia a robust print media across the entire political spectrum. Among the publications on the right and left that vehemently and openly oppose the regime are the left-nationalist and reactionary *Zavtra*, which carries vicious anti-Putin cartoons; the left-liberal *Novaya Gazeta*; and the right-liberal *Novoe vremya* and *Moskovskie Novosti*, the latter still funded by Mikhail Khodorkovsky's Open Russia Foundation. Anyone with enough money can start a newspaper or a magazine. Of the country's thirty-five thousand local newspapers and magazines, seven thousand are privately owned.[41]

Thus far, no Russian journalist has been jailed for his or her writing, and all the most vociferous and adamant critics of the regime are free to publish, including Evgenia Albats, Masha Gessen, Maria Lipman, Valeria Novodvorskaya, Leonid Radzikhovsky, and Viktor Shenderovich. Similarly, such independent and highly respected scholars and experts as Pavel Felgengauer, Alexander Golts, Nikolai Petrov, Andrei Piontkovsky, Lilia Shevtsova, and Dmitry Trenin—all of whom have been critical of the post-Beslan "reforms"—do not seem to have any difficulty in getting their views published, as well as broadcast and televised.

A rather unexpected source of antigovernment criticism is the tabloid *Moskovskiy Komsomolets*, which is Moscow's most popular newspaper, with a readership of approximately 1.5 million.[42] Along with lurid crime stories and elite gossip, delivered in a style reminiscent of the *New York Post*, *Moskovskiy Komsomolets* offers a good daily selection of the most important national, political, and economic news, often in sharp contrast with the official "line." In January 2005, the tabloid ran a series of mock "letters to the president" filled with "vituperative criticism" of Putin's policies.[43]

Although the circulation of other independent newspapers and magazines is much smaller (far less than the audiences of the government-controlled television), they are read daily by several million members of the country's elite and middle class, whose influence in politics and the economy is far in excess of their numbers.

Television and Internet

Even while television has come to be dominated by the Kremlin (with all of the major national television channels—Channel One, RTR, and NTV—taken over by the state or state-owned companies), it is a far cry from the uniformity of the Soviet days. Government policies are not exempt from criticism, and the nightly news broadcasts invariably lead with stories about violent crime (with terrorism now added to the mix), natural disasters, poverty, corruption, incompetence, and other instances of general malfeasance by local officials.

Although nowhere near its former no-holds-barred broadcasts under Yeltsin, the private NTV network, which used to be owned by the Media Most empire of self-exiled media mogul Vladimir Gusinsky, provided "thorough and quite sympathetic" coverage of Ukraine's Orange Revolution, despite the Kremlin's open disdain for (and fear of) the movement.[44]

A smaller private national network, REN TV, strays even farther in providing objective news. In the words of one Russian observer, the network "has not been transformed into a propaganda mouthpiece."[45] (Anyone with knowledge of Russian and access to the MHz cable network in the Washington, D.C., metropolitan area could judge for himself by watching REN TV's 24 Hours daily news program, starting at 1:00 p.m. EST).[46]

In addition to the four Moscow-based television networks, there are seven hundred fifty local, broadcast or cable stations—about eight in every region—of which almost two hundred are privately owned.[47] Generally, they are more independent in their programming than the national networks. "For my money, [local networks] are better than the central channels," the director of the Center for Media and Law at Moscow State University told an American reporter. "They are more objective, less biased, and they try harder to show all sides of an issue."[48]

An Institutional Balancing Act

Whatever else history's verdict on the Putin presidency may be, his regime has proved an important diagnostic tool for uncovering, or confirming, several systemic illnesses of Russia's body politic—as well as its healthy segments capable of withstanding the centripetal pressures.

Some of the institutional deficiencies and vulnerabilities that provided targets of opportunity for the authoritarian project stem from constitutional ambiguities and incomplete or absent laws, including those governing elections to both chambers of the federal assembly and regional governorships. In other cases, such as the post-Soviet legal system, the laws are explicit and adequate, yet they are ignored and subverted because of society's indifference or the absence of effective mechanisms of societal control over implementation.

At the same time, although often weakened, restricted, and subverted by the authorities, a number of institutions bequeathed by the 1991 revolution have proved resilient. They include relative freedom of speech, press, and demonstrations, and a general tolerance of opposition and dissent—all of which have proved indispensable in 2003–5 for the victorious prodemocracy mobilizations in the protoauthoritarian societies of Georgia, Ukraine, and Kyrgyzstan. In Russia's case, these liberties are rooted in the 1993 constitution, which, although in obvious need of clarifying amendments, is nevertheless far from outliving its usefulness.

In the end, an institutional analysis of Russian politics reveals a contradictory system engaged in a dangerous balancing act. Such incoherence cannot be sustained for long. Either the regime must evolve toward full-blown "classic" authoritarianism that succeeds in dismantling all the key democratic structures—or there will be a reaffirmation and renewal of the revolutionary legacy of the division of powers, freedom of all media, growing judicial independence, and the erosion of state's control over private property.

The next few years will be decisive in resolving this uncertainty.

17

Chechnya: New Dimensions
of an Old Crisis
2003

The withdrawal of Russian troops from Chechnya at the end of 1996 and the de facto independence of the "Republic of Ichkeria" from Russia did not end a conflict that began as a secular war for national self-determination. Instead, it acquired an increasingly fundamentalist dimension. Between 1997 and 1999, most of the key Chechen warlords, who held the real power in the tiny country, turned toward a radical interpretation of Wahhabism—a celebration of death and suicide as weapons against the infidels—and Chechnya was declared an "Islamic republic," ruled according to the Koran-based Sharia law. Links with al-Qaeda were established and grew closer. Three of the September 11 pilots were recruited in an al-Qaeda training camp in Afghanistan, where they had come to "fight the Russians in Chechnya."

Another war began in August 1999, and, despite massive and brutal Russian assaults, the conflict is far from extinguished. Can it be? An analysis of other prolonged guerilla wars of independence, in which combatants have been separated by ethnicity, religion, or both—the French and the Algerians, the Turks and the Kurds, the Sinhalese and the Hindus (Tamils) in Sri Lanka, the Hindus and Muslims in Kashmir, and the Israelis and the Palestinians—shows that a permanent satisfactory solution is very rare, and peace comes only with surrender by one of the sides. In the case of Chechnya, the only hope appears to be the "deinternalization" of the conflict, and a courageous and creative effort at a negotiated solution by Moscow.

The seizure on October 23–26, 2002, of a Moscow theater, in which 120 of the 800 people taken hostage by fifty Chechen terrorists died, briefly drew the world's attention to the far greater tragedy of Russia's war in Chechnya: the daily torment and relentless misery of the Chechen people, victimized by the indiscriminate brutality and corruption of incompetently led Russian troops and by the extortion and arbitrary executions by guerrilla warlords. Punctuated by two invasions by Russian troops in 1994 and 1999, the bloody stalemate in Chechnya is now in its twelfth year.

In the past six years, gradually accumulating evidence points to significant changes in the nature of the conflict and the agenda of the Chechen resistance. Graphically displayed during the hostage crisis in Moscow, the new dimensions complicate the bitter contest and are likely to increase the already formidable obstacles to a peaceful settlement.

While continuing to condemn the massive human rights abuses by the Russian troops in Chechnya and to press Moscow toward a political solution, the world—first and foremost the United States, which thus far has found in Russia a steady and reliable ally in the war on terrorism—ought to notice the new evidence and adjust both policy recommendations and expectations of the timing and the shape of the resolution.

The takeover of the Moscow theater during a performance of the musical *Nord-Ost* stemmed from eleven years of a complex and evolving conflict. Formerly a part of the Chechen-Ingush Autonomous Republic, Chechnya declared independence from Russia in November 1991. A nation of fearless Muslim warriors, the Chechens had fought Russian troops for several decades in the nineteenth century and were the last people of the northern Caucasus to be incorporated into the Russian empire, after the 1817–64 Caucasian War.

Accused by Stalin of welcoming the Germans in World War II, the entire Chechen nation of 489,000 people was deported to Soviet Central Asia in 1944; an estimated 200,000 died there of hunger and disease. Nikita Khrushchev allowed the Chechens to return to their motherland in 1956. In November 1991 Chechnya's freely elected president, Dzhokhar Dudaev, declared independence, which was not recognized by Russia or any other state.

In the spring and summer of 1993 Dudaev dissolved the parliament and ordered the killing of scores of protesters in Chechnya's capital, Grozny. Thence he ruled as a brutal, erratic, and increasingly paranoid dictator, his small army of "bodyguards" murdering his enemies, both real and imagined.

Soon Chechnya became a lawless enclave, bristling with weapons bought from corrupt Russian generals and paid for with profits from the oil field near Grozny. Trains passing through Chechnya were routinely robbed; Russian newspapers advised passengers how to barricade themselves in the compartments to survive. Knowing that they would never be extradited to Russia, criminals, including fugitives sought for murder and armed robbery, flocked to the mountain republic. An illicit drug and arms trade flourished, as did the counterfeiting of rubles. The "Chechen mafia" became one of the largest and most violent segments of the Russian criminal underworld.

✺

Seeking to reclaim what it considered Russian territory and end the violent anarchy that threatened to spread to the rest of the northern Caucasus, Russia invaded Chechnya in December 1994 and attempted to take Grozny in Stalingrad-like house-to-house battle. Well-supplied, skillful, experienced, and immensely brave Chechens slaughtered ill-trained Russian draftees by the hundreds. After the Russians resorted to indiscriminate bombing from air and missile attacks, Grozny was finally secured a month and a half later. As many as 30,000 civilians and at least 1,800 troops were killed, while the resistance fighters made an orderly retreat and regrouped in the mountains.

The siege of Grozny epitomized Russia's first campaign to pacify Chechnya, the ineptitude and brutality of the Russian troops, who routinely massacred Chechen civilians, and the courageous, steadfast, and tactically superior resistance, which inflicted heavy casualties on the enemy.

Soon guerrillas began striking outside Chechnya. In June 1995 more than 200 fighters seized a hospital in the southern Russian city of Budyonovsk, 125 miles north of Chechnya. They held more than 2,000 patients and medical personnel hostage as they demanded the withdrawal of Russian troops from Chechnya. After the Russian troops failed twice to dislodge the Chechens (who used patients, among them pregnant women from the maternity ward, as shields), Prime Minister Victor Chernomyrdin negotiated by phone with the group's leader, Shamil Basaev; the guerrillas were transported to the Chechen border and released. The 120 killed included police, troops, hostages, and several guerrillas.

Half a year later, Chechens captured the town of Kyzlyar in Dagestan and retreated to the nearby village of Pervomayskoe with more than two thousand hostages. After a two-week siege, the Chechens broke through the cordon in a fierce night battle and escaped to Chechnya with more than a hundred captives, whom they later exchanged for Chechen prisoners and the bodies of their killed comrades.

Although most Russians opposed Chechnya's independence, the war soon became widely unpopular. Mounting casualties were daily reported on Russian television networks: tens of thousands of Chechens dead and hundreds of thousands displaced, and at least 5,800 Russian soldiers killed. As he sought reelection in a close race against a Communist candidate for the presidency, Boris Yeltsin promised to end the war.

In May 1996, Yeltsin and the leader of the Chechen resistance, Zelimkhan Yandarbiev (who replaced Dudaev, killed a month before), signed a cease-fire agreement in the Kremlin. Although both sides repeatedly violated the cessation of hostilities (with Chechens retaking Grozny in a lightning attack), in the predawn hours of August 31 in the Dagestani city of Khasavyurt, the secretary of the Kremlin's Security Council, General Alexander Lebed, and the chief of the general staff of the Chechen resistance, Aslan Maskhadov, signed an agreement that stipulated an immediate withdrawal of all Russian troops. By January 1, 1997, not a single Russian soldier remained in Chechnya. Although Chechnya's final political status was to be resolved in the next five years, it became de facto independent. Russia granted Chechnya its own constitution and "full control over finance" and "natural resources."

∾

Elected president shortly thereafter, Aslan Maskhadov witnessed the disintegration of the Chechen state within three years of assuming power. Strengthened by the violence and devastation of the previous half-decade, the traditional, clan-based loyalties proved immeasurably stronger than allegiance to central authorities in Grozny.

Chechnya dissolved into murderous anarchy. Warlords and their heavily armed gangs made the country into a Somalia of the Caucasus. In addition to expanding an already prominent role in Russian and international organized crime, Chechnya turned kidnappings for ransom into an industry. At least 1,100 people were seized in the border areas outside Chechnya. The victims included international relief workers, Russian and foreign journalists, employees of private Russian and foreign companies, wealthy Chechens, and even ordinary citizens. To expedite the payment of ransom, severed limbs were often mailed to relatives of the prisoners. The abducted were frequently starved and tortured to death. (The handful of international relief organizations still operating in Chechnya require staff to be accompanied everywhere by armed security guards.)

One gang known for its extreme cruelty and rapacity was headed by the man who led the hostage-takers in Moscow, Movsar Baraev. He inherited the band from his uncle Abri Baraev, who was killed earlier in 2002, and was responsible for scores of murders and kidnappings, including the 1998 abduction for ransom and the subsequent beheading of three Britons and a New Zealander who worked for a private telecommunications company.

Slavery became widespread. Some of the kidnapped were sold into indentured servitude to Chechen families. For years the slaves, as they were openly called, endured starvation, beatings, and often maiming and mutilation.

Despite the Maskhadov administration's concerted effort, the republic of Ichkeria, with a lone howling wolf on its national flag, was not recognized by a single nation save Taliban-ruled Afghanistan. In support of the utter fiction of Chechnya's continuing membership in the Russian Federation, Moscow continued to send hundreds of millions of rubles for "rehabilitation," as well as pensions and funds for schools and hospitals. Grozny authorities instantaneously stole all transfers and divided the funds among the favored warlords.

The years between 1996 and 1999 marked the beginning of the transformation of what had been a generally conventional, secular, ethnic, irredentist movement with aims limited to securing Chechnya's independence.

First came attacks on Russian troops in neighboring Dagestan, Ingushetia, and Ossetia. In April 1998, near the border of Ossetia and Ingushetia, a Chechen detachment attacked a motorcade of top officers of the Russian general staff and the leadership of the North Caucasus Military District; four generals were killed. A month later, kidnappers captured the representative of the president of the Russian Federation in Chechnya, Valentin Vlasov. Unable to send armed police into Chechnya to search for Vlasov

because of the Khasavayurt agreements, the Russian government authorized intermediaries to negotiate his release after five months in captivity for
a ransom of a reported $4 million. In 1999 the representative of the Min-
istry of Internal Affairs of the Russian Federation in Chechnya, Major General Gennadiy Shpigun, was abducted at the airport in Grozny. His body
was found a year later.

Finally, in August and September 1999, 1,200–2,000 fighters invaded
Dagestan from Chechnya with the goal of establishing an "Islamic republic
of North Caucasus." They were repelled by primarily local troops and mili-
tia supported by the overwhelming majority of the multiethnic and predominantly Muslim population of Dagestan. Shamil B..aev's appeal to the
Dagestani population "to rise up and end 140 years of occupation by the
Muscovite infidels" fell on deaf ears.[1]

Soon after, the newly appointed prime minister of the Russian Federation, Vladimir Putin, ordered the second invasion of Chechnya by 80,000
federal troops. Since then, an estimated 80,000 Chechens have been killed
(including elected or appointed Chechen officials assassinated by the rebels
for cooperating with the federal government); another 35,000 have "disappeared" and are presumed dead. The number of refugees in neighboring
Ingushetia is estimated at 110,000; 18,000–20,000 live in tent cities. At
least 4,000 Russian soldiers were killed (Russian and foreign human rights
groups put the number as high as 14,000).

✧

Although hardly visible to the outside world behind the smoke of Russian
carpet-bombing, and overshadowed by the Russian-made humanitarian crisis, a significant shift began in the mid-1990s, and especially after 1996, in
the outlook and agenda of some of the key elements of the Chechen resistance. At the heart of this transmogrification was an evolution that closely
resembled a change in the movement for the independence of Palestine (the
West Bank and Gaza, occupied by Israel in 1967).

Although in both Palestine and Chechnya the secular and religious
components have coexisted in the movement for independence, the Islamic
element steadily strengthened at the expense of the secular objectives.

By 1999, secular agenda and symbols all but disappeared among the key leaders of the Chechen resistance. Dzhokhar Dudaev had been a major general in the Soviet Air Force, a former member of the Communist Party of the Soviet Union, and, by all appearances, an atheist, whose face was shaven save for a neat, tiny moustache. He had invoked Islam solely to boost his own legitimacy in the fight against the Russians and would hardly have recognized the movement that he started. From a primarily secular national liberation, Chechnya's war for independence increasingly looked like part of the worldwide jihad, as the top Chechen commanders grew long beards and started quoting the Koran.

Since 1996 the resistance leaders and their troops have been switching their traditional allegiance from the Sufi branch of Islam to a radical interpretation of Wahhabism that celebrates death and suicide as weapons against the infidels. Converts included the top warlords Shamil Basaev, who led the takeover of the hospital in Budyonnovsk in 1995 and claimed responsibility for masterminding the Moscow theater hostage-taking, and Salman Raduev, Dzhokhar Dudaev's son-in-law and the leader of the Kyzlyar raid in 1996. (Captured by Russian troops in March 2000 and sentenced to life in prison for terrorism, Raduev died in December 2002.)

"Under the influence of . . . Arab mujahadeen," observed a Middle East policy analyst, "Basaev . . . appeared to have metamorphosed gradually from a Chechen nationalist to a Chechen Muslim."[2] His stated objective became a Chechen theocracy like that established by the leader of the nineteenth-century Chechen resistance to the Russian empire (and Basaev's namesake), the ruthless and cunning Shamil (1797–1871),[3] a red-bearded imam who went everywhere with an axe-wielding executioner. (For a historically accurate sketch of Shamil, see one of Leo Tolstoy's finest novellas, *Hadji Murat*.)

In a videotaped statement aired on the second day of the Moscow standoff by the Qatar-based Al Jazeera satellite television network, the hostage-takers spoke against the backdrop of a green banner of Islam with white Koranic verses. The women wore Arab-style *hijab* (a head-to-toe black dress with only eyes uncovered), which Chechen women had not been seen wearing before.

Even before President Maskhadov declared Chechnya an Islamic republic in November 1997, Chechnya introduced Islamic courts, which began sentencing those who violated the Koran-based Sharia law. In April of that year, in the first of the executions broadcast on Chechnya's state-run television, a man's throat was slit by a group of hooded men. Subsequent executions by firing squad took place in Grozny's central Friendship of Peoples Square in the presence of thousands of spectators.

In response to statements by President Yeltsin and the Duma, horrified by what they labeled "barbaric," "medieval," and "impermissible" acts in what was nominally still part of Russia, the Chechen presidential spokesman said, "The disapproval by Russia and the West of our actions—shooting by a firing squad and public executions—means that we're heading in the right direction. There is no doubt that only the laws of Allah and norms of Sharia will be in force in Chechnya."[4] The Chechen vice president, Vakha Arsanov, added: "Hearing [the Russian protests] makes me laugh. I spit on Russia. . . . Russia means nothing to us; we are an independent state."[5]

✍

Al Jazeera's broadcast of the videotaped statement of the terrorists in the Moscow theater highlighted the international dimension of the Chechen resistance: The network had established itself as a conduit for messages from the al-Qaeda leadership. The tape also reflected the prominence that the Chechen cause had gained among fundamentalist Islamic militants. "Hundreds" of Arab volunteers, many of them veterans of the 1979–88 war in Afghanistan, came to fight in Chechnya.[6] The most prominent was the Saudi-born commander Samir bin Saleh al Suwailem (known by the nom de guerre Khattab), who, together with Basaev, led the 1999 invasion of Dagestan. (Khattab was reported killed in April 2002.)

As early as December 1996, al-Qaeda's second in command, the Egyptian Ayman al-Zawahiri, tried clandestinely to enter Chechnya, allegedly to find a new base for the organization after Sudan expelled the al-Qaeda leadership. Arrested in Dagestan with two Arab companions, Zawahiri spent six months in prison in the Dagestani capital, Makhachkala, was found guilty of entering Russia without a visa, and was released in May 1997. In a handwritten statement in Arabic, made public by the Russian authorities with other trial documents this past October, Zawahiri claimed to be a "businessman" who had entered Dagestan "to study the local market and to build contacts for our business."[7] In a file stored on a laptop computer found in an al-Qaeda safe house in Kabul after the fall of the Taliban regime, Zawahiri wrote, "God blinded [the Dagestani authorities] to our identities."[8]

In November 2002 the testimony at the Hamburg trial of Mounir Motassadeq, a Moroccan accused of assisting the September 11 hijackers, established a connection between some of the hijackers and the Chechen cause. The young men, who were said to be "obsessed with jihad" and who "cheerfully" sang songs about martyrdom, "always talked about Kosovo, Afghanistan, and Chechnya."[9] In the fall of 1999, the three September 11 pilots—Mohammed Atta, Marwan al-Shehhi, and Ziad Jarrah—left Hamburg for the al-Qaeda training camp near Kandahar, Afghanistan, with the intention of "fighting the Russians in Chechnya."[10] They were told that there were "enough fighters" in Chechnya.[11] Instead, according to German investigators, while in Afghanistan, the al-Qaeda leadership ordered the three to "begin laying plans" for what became the September 11 attack.[12]

An audiotape attributed to Osama bin Laden and broadcast in November 2002 by Al Jazeera mentioned Chechnya in the long list of Muslim grievances: "As you look at your dead in Moscow, also recall ours in Chechnya."[13] Chechnya is constantly invoked by fundamentalist Islamic leaders in Pakistan. Along with Palestine, Chechnya has become the focal point in the call to war to the death against the West by Islamic extremists in Britain.

In 1999, at least a hundred al-Qaeda fighters joined hundreds of Chechens in the Pankisi Gorge on the Georgian side of the Chechen-Georgian border.[14] According to the Georgian investigators and U.S. intelligence sources, the "[al-Qaeda] militants split their time between helping the Chechens in their war against Russia and helping the [al-Qaeda] international organization in its war against the United States."[15] One of the teams reportedly planned to blow up a U.S. or Western installation in Russia, and another unit developed poisons "for possible attacks against Western targets in Central Asia."[16]

In October 2002 the U.S.-trained Georgian special forces captured fifteen Arab fighters in the Pankisi Gorge and immediately extradited them to the United States. Among them was the Egyptian Saif al-Islam al-Masry, a member of the al-Qaeda military committee. Trained by the Iran-supported Hezbollah terrorist group in southern Lebanon and dispatched by al-Qaeda to Somalia in the early 1990s, he was mentioned in the federal indictment of a prominent Muslim charity, the Illinois-based Benevolence International Foundation, as an officer of the foundation's "Chechen branch."[17]

Last fall France opened a special judicial inquiry into connections between French Muslim extremists and Chechnya. According to the presiding judge, "Chechnya could become the new Afghanistan. It could serve as a new laboratory for [terrorist] attacks as Afghanistan once did."[18]

Although it continues to resist an internationally brokered solution to the Chechen crisis, Russia is beginning to recognize the conflict's international dimension. Immediately after the October 2002 seizure of the theater, the ambassadors from all Arab nations with embassies in Moscow were called to the Foreign Ministry and sharply rebuked for not offering assistance in the negotiations with the terrorists. Russia also requested the extradition from Qatar of the cosigner of the May 1996 agreement, Zelimkhan Yandarbiev, whose phone conversation with the hostage-takers Russian authorities claim to have intercepted.[19]

A month later President Putin launched an unprecedented public attack on Saudi Arabia. At the conclusion of his meeting with President George W. Bush in Tsarskoe Selo near St. Petersburg in November 2002, he said that "we should not forget about those who finance terrorism" and pointed out that the majority of the September 11 hijackers were Saudi citizens. "We should not forget about that," Putin repeated.[20]

⁓

The Khasavyurt agreement, scuttled by the Chechen militants, offered Chechnya de facto independence and secular statehood in return for the end of revolt and terrorism.

The struggle for a secular independent state has been submerged by a fundamentalist agenda that seeks not peace but victory in an endless jihad. In 1996 the top Chechen guerillas began forming *jamaats*, at once military detachments and fundamentalist religious communities, with the explicit goal of conquering neighboring Dagestan and joining it with Chechnya into an Islamic state.

Two months before the invasion of Dagestan, Chechnya's president, Aslan Maskhadov, told an interviewer: "After the [1994–96] war I was tired, I was dreaming about a respite, as was the rest of the Chechen nation. But even then it looked like war was imminent. With dismay I listened to the speeches of a variety of [Chechen] politicians and [military] commanders. These calls for holy war, the liberation of the Caucasus, flying green flags [of Islam] over the Kremlin. I knew everything was heading toward war."[21] After the August invasion of Dagestan was repulsed, Shirvani Basaev, Shamil Basaev's brother, said: "The assault on Dagestan was just a rehearsal. It was nothing to do with oil or territory. This is jihad."[22]

According to one of the most knowledgeable Russian journalists, Andrei Babitsky—who spent months with the rebels in the 1990s and whose imprisonment by Russian troops on charges of assisting the enemy caused an international uproar—Movsar Baraev was one of the *jamaats*.[23] The fighters called themselves mujahadeen and espoused "extreme fundamentalist Islam and a struggle under the slogan of jihad."[24]

Throughout both wars against the Russians, the Chechens rightly prided themselves on tactical acumen. Most soldiers not only escaped with their lives but carried away their wounded and dead while inflicting maximum damage on the enemy. For all their spectacular daring, the Chechen attacks, including the largest hostage-taking operations in Budyonovsk, Kyzlyar, and Pervomayskoe, were never about suicide.

By contrast, on the Al Jazeera tape, which was virtually indistinguishable from those of the Al Aqsa Martyrs Brigade or Hamas, the black-clad Chechens talked of little else. "I swear by God we are more keen on dying than you are keen on living," one said.[25] A woman in *hijab* added: "We have chosen to die in Moscow and we will kill hundreds of infidels. Even if we die, thousands of our brothers and sisters are ready to give their lives to free our motherland."[26]

In interviews they gave to Russian radio and television inside the theater during the *Nord-Ost* takeover, the terrorists confirmed the tape's morbid tenor. "Our group is called Islam's suicide brigade," Movsar Baraev said. "Our dream is to become martyrs of Allah."[27] "We have come to die," an unidentified hostage-taker told an interviewer. "Our motto is freedom and paradise. We already have freedom as we've come to Moscow. Now we want to be in paradise."[28]

Two months after the Moscow hostage-taking, the Chechen resistance effected its first "classic" suicide bombing when, on December 27, 2002, two vehicles loaded with more than a ton of explosives crashed into the courtyard of the government headquarters in Grozny, killing 72 people and wounding 110.

In the words of a Russian journalist, Anna Politkovskaya, known for her brave reporting from and condemnation of the Russian war on Chechnya (the Moscow hostage-takers requested her by name as a negotiator[29]), a new generation of "sons" is increasingly taking over the armed resistance in Chechnya. Aged twenty-five to thirty, this generation has come of age during war, has seen nothing but war, and has "known nothing but a Kalashnikov and the woods since they finished [high] school."[30]

In both Chechnya and Palestine in the past few years, power has shifted from elected leaders (Maskhadov and Arafat) to fundamentalist warlords and heads of terrorist networks. According to Politkovskaya, Maskhadov's options are limited: choose "the frenzied radicalizations of the 'sons' or be swept away, and very soon."[31] Whether Maskhadov genuinely opposes the fundamentalist agenda or clandestinely approves of and supports it, he is perceived by a majority of Russians in much the same way as Israelis perceive Arafat: either responsible for the terrorist attacks or unable to control the jihad radicals.

In either case, after the terrorist attack in Moscow, the Russians no longer consider Maskhadov a viable negotiating partner. Asked after the *Nord-Ost* hostage-taking if Moscow should negotiate with Maskhadov or with someone else, only 17 percent named Maskhadov, while 42 percent thought that Moscow should seek out someone else. Just as the White House turned away from Arafat in June 2002, since October of the same year the United States no longer insists on Maskhadov as Russia's interlocutor.[32]

✑

The illuminating analogies between Chechnya and other separatist movements are not limited to Palestine. The search for a solution to the Chechen stalemate might benefit from a look at the outcomes of several recent wars of national self-determination that are comparable in intensity, seeming intractability, length, and cruelty.

Offering a Compromise: Turkey and the Kurds. From 1987, when a state of emergency was introduced in the country's southeast, to 2002,

Turkey waged a war on Kurdish leftist separatists (the Kurdistan Workers Party, or PKK), seeking independence for the country's 12 million Kurds— about one-fifth of the country's population. Between 25,000 and 35,000 Kurds and at least 5,000 Turkish soldiers and police died. An estimated 3,000 Kurdish villages were destroyed; 2–3.5 million Kurds were displaced.

In addition to the scale of violence, the similarities between the Chechen and the Kurdish conflicts extend to the length and intensity (though not the details) of historical grievances against the central authorities. Since the early 1920s the Turkish state has sought to suppress or eradicate every sign of Kurdish national identity. The Kurdish language and culture have been banned. Teaching Kurdish in schools is a criminal offense. Radio and television broadcasting in Kurdish is prohibited, as are plays and movies. Children have been thrown in jail for playing Kurdish songs on a tape recorder. Local registrars routinely refuse to issue birth certificates for babies with Kurdish names.

Human rights abuses have been massive and systematic. Prisoners have been tortured; women have been routinely sexually humiliated or raped.[33] (Ending torture is a key requirement for Turkey's entry into the European Union.) In 2001 twenty-eight Kurdish boys, ages ten to fifteen, were arrested and charged with terrorism for allegedly chanting pro-Kurdish slogans. Six were kept in jail for a month until their first court hearing.[34]

Turkey's war on the Kurds was conducted behind a total information blackout; no newspaper journalists, let alone television cameras, were allowed anywhere near the battle zones. Using criminal penalties for "insulting" or "belittling" the armed forces, the security forces, parliament, the president, or the judiciary, Turkish authorities charged—and courts sentenced—journalists to lengthy prison terms for merely mentioning the conflict and the Kurdish resistance. (In 1999 more journalists were imprisoned in Turkey than in China.) In 2000 criminal charges were brought against five campaigners for prisoners' rights for using the words "Kurdish women" in their speeches.

The violence generally subsided after the capture of the PKK leader Abdullah Ocalan in 1999. Three years after Ocalan called on his followers to end violence and limit demands to cultural autonomy and linguistic rights rather than independence, Turkey removed the prohibitions against broadcasts in Kurdish and appears ready to grant the Kurds limited autonomy.[35]

Negotiating Autonomy: Sri Lanka and the Tamils. In September 2002, the government of Sri Lanka reached an agreement with the rebels who fought for the secession of the predominantly Tamil northern and eastern regions from the Sinhalese-majority state. The Liberation Tamil Tigers of Eelam, who pioneered suicide bombings that killed more than 1,500 people and conscripted children as fighters, agreed to "substantial regional autonomy" within a newly created federal state. The war lasted nineteen years and resulted in 65,000 deaths and the displacement of 1.6 million of the island state's population of 18 million.[36]

"Walking Away": France and Algeria. Marked by cruelty on both sides, the 1954–62 war in Algeria included widespread and systematic torture of suspects and prisoners by the French, the destruction of eight thousand villages in pacification campaigns, and the forcible relocation of more than 2 million Algerians into areas controlled by the French. Paris resorted to collective punishment, concentration camps through which more than 100,000 Algerians passed, and security sweeps (*ratissages*), comparable to the infamous Russian *zachistki* from which many seized Chechens never returned. Three thousand Algerians "disappeared" in police custody.

In the end, an estimated 300,000 Algerians died at the hands of both occupying troops and the Front de Libération Nationale (FLN) guerillas, as did 24,000 French soldiers. The French withdrawal was followed by the torture and execution by the FLN of tens of thousands of pro-French "collaborators" and "traitors," including the so-called *harkis*, Algerian soldiers who fought alongside the French.

Religion, Territory, and the "Internationalization" of a Conflict: Kashmir and Palestine. Unlike the three cases above, not even a putative solution has been found to the conflict in the Muslim-majority state of Kashmir in India, which separatists seek to join with neighboring Pakistan and where 80,000 people have died since 1947. Likewise, in the war for independence of the Israeli-occupied West Bank and Gaza (Palestine), an estimated 25,000 Palestinians and Israelis have died since the territories came under Israeli control in 1967.

A comparison of Turkey and Sri Lanka with Algeria, Kashmir, and Palestine yields several factors that were decisive in bringing about the mutually acceptable end of violence. First, a compromise is more likely in conflicts where the religious factor is either nonexistent (both the Turks and the Kurdish are Muslim; both the armed forces and the PKK are secular in their ideology) or secondary to standard ethnic issues (as with the Buddhist Sinhalese majority and the Hindu Tamils, whose grievances included an inferior status of the Tamil language vis-à-vis the official Sinhala and discrimination in college admissions and state employment).

By contrast, in Algeria, Kashmir, and Palestine, the movements for national liberation became religious wars between Muslims and Christians, Muslims and Hindus (Kashmir), and Muslims and Jews (Israel), even if they began as generally secular movements (Algeria and Palestine). Demands for ethnic equality can be negotiated; the war of religions has thus far ended in defeat or stalemate.

Ending a conflict by walking away is immeasurably harder when the disputed territory is contiguous than when it lies far away from the country's borders. Thus only Algeria achieved full independence; although it had been part of France for more than a century, it was separated from it by the Mediterranean. Relinquishing contiguous territory was unacceptable to either Sri Lanka or Turkey.

Islamization, and consequently internationalization (as in Kashmir and Palestine), led to a change of agenda as secular proindependence movements morphed into fronts of the worldwide jihad, with volunteers and funds from all over the Muslim world.

By contrast, the Kurds' proindependence quest drew little, if any, support from Muslim fundamentalists. The Sri Lanka settlement followed the termination of outside assistance. First, India stopped supplying the Tamil insurgents with arms, ammunition, and logistical support after the assassination of former prime minister Rajiv Gandhi by the Tamil Tigers in 1991. Then the Tamil diaspora in the United States, Canada, Europe, and India ended financial support after the United States, Britain, and India declared the Tigers a terrorist organization.

Furthermore, in the nonreligious and thus noninternationalized or deinternationalized conflicts in Turkey and Sri Lanka, the countries' territorial integrity was not negotiable as far as the national authorities were concerned. The separatists in the end accepted political or cultural autonomy rather than total independence. Such a compromise seems distant in Kashmir or Palestine as long as irredentist movements are dominated by the proponents of world jihad. The limits of autonomy can be negotiated; liberation from the infidels, by definition, may not be compromised.[37]

✍

With the Islamization and internationalization of the Chechen proindependence movement, a carefully crafted and mutually acceptable settlement along the Sri Lankan lines appears out of the question. In addition to the same two obstacles, the Turkish solution—decapitation of the movement and the end of insurgence in exchange for the life of the supreme leader—is even less plausible because of the decentralization of the Chechen resistance, the Chechen code of honor that equates surrender with betrayal, and the apparent commitment of its top commanders to suicide.

The French model is not applicable because the overwhelming majority of Russians, including some of the war's most vocal and courageous opponents, cannot conceive of compromising the country's territorial integrity. Declaring Chechnya "autonomous" and "walking away" are perforce unacceptable to Russian public opinion because Moscow already "walked away" in Khasavyurt in 1996, with resulting periodic raids on Russian territory, the death of more than 300 people in the bombing of three apartment buildings (one in Moscow) in August 1999, and the invasion of Dagestan.

Immediately after the *Nord-Ost* hostage takeover, most of the friends in Moscow with whom I spoke over the phone advocated *stena*, a wall along the border with Chechnya. Interviewed several days later by an American reporter, a middle-class Muscovite, too, "believed [that] the possible solution . . . may well be 'to build a Chinese wall' around Chechnya, trapping the people and the problem inside, where it can't infect the rest of Russia."[38] But the Russian *stena* for Chechnya is hardly more practical than a similar plan in Israel: an estimated 800,000 Chechens live in Russia outside of Chechnya (40,000–400,000 in Moscow).

At the heart of the conflict is the Chechens' legitimate desire for self-rule and the repeated and savage historical injustice dealt the Chechen people by Russia and the Soviet Union. No solution is likely until the injustice is acknowledged and corrected.

The settlement may not be achieved without a profound change on the part of the Russians. With public opinion consistently far more inclined toward ending the war than otherwise, on the Russian side the solution is primarily a matter of strong, creative, and courageous leadership.

Only a strong leader can declare a war lost. Vladimir Putin appears well-suited for such a role: Because of the country's economic progress and the rise in the standard of living (now in its fourth consecutive year) and his uncanny ability to "connect" with the majority of the Russian people, his popularity is enormous and consistent. If anyone can forge a painful exit from Chechnya, Vladimir Putin is the man.[39]

Yet the obstacles are formidable. In many respects, Chechnya has brought Putin to power. From almost complete obscurity Putin became the country's most popular politician during the fall and winter of 1999–2000 because his steely public resolve to win the war in Chechnya reassured a nation paralyzed with grief and fear in the wake of the 1999 invasion of Dagestan and the apartment bombings. Those who witnessed Putin at the U.S.-Russian summits report the apparently genuine fury when the question of Chechnya was raised.

Second, regardless of the final details, an exit from Chechnya will call for enormous political sacrifice and perhaps physical courage. Following a decisive reelection victory in 1996, Yeltsin "walked away" from Chechnya to fulfill a key campaign promise. For all his popularity, Putin may not want to jeopardize his reelection in 2004.

Finally, an inevitably painful compromise in Chechnya (again, regardless of the shape of the accord) would just as inevitably subject Putin, as it did Yeltsin, to relentless hatred by Russian nationalists and "popular patriots." Should the economy falter, he may even face attempts at impeachment, as Yeltsin did in 1999. In the worst case, he may be subjected to assassination plots, like the ones that nearly killed de Gaulle after the Algerian settlement.

Yet even the most propitious changes "on the ground" are not likely to succeed alone in the absence of change in the larger context of the Russo-Chechen conflict. If "Palestinization" of the Chechen conflict has advanced as far as it appears, especially in Islamization and internationalization, the road to its solution is similar to those likely to bring peace to Palestine and Israel.

As with its Palestinian counterpart, the conflict must be, first and foremost, deinternationalized. Such a development may only come after a sharp setback for the global fundamentalist militant Islamic International following a sustained and successful war against al-Qaeda and, concomitantly, a change in the Middle East's political landscape, beginning in Iraq and Iran.

By stanching the flow of money, weapons, ammunition, and volunteers, deinternationalization is likely to lead over time to the weakening of the radical Islamic component of the Chechen struggle, its detachment from the world jihad, and a return of the Chechen resistance to an agenda that can be managed in good-faith negotiations.

History is littered with examples of people's legitimate aspirations for ethnic equality, national dignity, or social justice hijacked, cynically exploited, misdirected, and in the end subverted by ruthless fanatics in pursuit of their own ideological or power agendas. Compounded by the savagery of the Russian retaliation, the Chechen conflict has traveled far in a most inauspicious and hopeless direction. Both in Russia and in Chechnya only a complex and fortuitous combination of many factors may reverse that course—most important, the deinternationalization and de-Islamization of the Chechen resistance and a genuine, strong, and creative impulse toward a negotiated solution in Moscow.

Only time will tell if Chechnya and Russia will be lucky enough to be delivered from the present vicious circle by such an alignment of the heavens—highly improbable today, but far from impossible even in the near future.

18

The Battle over the Draft
2005

Among the structural reforms that the Putin restoration froze or subverted, few are as urgent and as fervently hoped for by the Russian people as the phasing out of conscription and a transition to all-volunteer armed forces. Three centuries old, the draft is the biggest obstacle to a modern army: mobile, highly motivated, knowledge-based, and founded on a mutual respect between the officers and men. Instead, the draft renders the Russian army an almost completely dysfunctional mass of corrupt and negligent officers, and brutalized and brutalizing conscripts, an increasing number of whom are functionally illiterate, drug users, or have criminal records. Peacetime injuries, deaths, and desertion are almost daily occurrences. A prison for most and a torture chamber for many, the army's performance in the two Chechen wars (1994–96 and 1999–present) has shown it to be utterly incapable of achieving victory other than with hugely disproportionate casualties. More than a matter of military preparedness, the continuing existence of the draft is perhaps the starkest reminder that the Putin regime, which advertises itself as "modernizing," is unwilling (with all the means available in a time of unprecedented prosperity) to part with one of the ugliest and most damaging relics of the state's domination of society.

On December 29, 2004, Russia's minister of defense, Sergei Ivanov, announced plans to eliminate draft deferments for college students. Predictably, the popular reaction was so uniformly negative and furious that the abolition of deferments was postponed—but it has not been eliminated from the Kremlin's agenda.

This confrontation between the state, determined to preserve the draft, and the society, which fears and detests it, is only the most recent clash over the three-century-old institution—and it will not be the last. For the draft is one of the last vestiges of the formerly omnipotent Soviet state, the epitome of the absolute command over society it wielded with mindless and often self-defeating cruelty.

Post-Soviet Russia's break with the past will not be complete without the shedding of the conscript army. For that reason alone, the political battle over the draft is worth watching carefully as a weathervane of Russia's direction.

The Long Roots of the Draft

Until the late 1980s, the paramount goal of the Russian and Soviet states for almost two centuries was the expansion and defense of the empire. The very birth of a modern Russian state under Peter the Great (1698–1725) was in many respects an extension of the czar's principal goal of building a modern—by eighteenth-century standards—army. From the construction of St. Petersburg on the bones of countless serfs to forbidding male nobles to marry until they passed rudimentary arithmetic and geometry exams, Peter's reforms were ultimately aimed at winning wars. Over two centuries later, Stalin's much bloodier "revolution from above"—which robbed, starved to death, and enslaved millions of peasants and introduced breakneck industrialization—was also justified by war preparation.

Introduced by Peter in 1705, the conscription law required every twenty peasant households to provide one draftee who would serve in the czar's army for thirty years. It was the first systematic military induction in Europe, where kings relied mostly on mercenary armies. Until the French Revolution almost a century later, Russia was the only European country with compulsory military service of twenty-five years. Russia's army remained the largest in the world.

The system survived unchanged until 1874 when, as part of the reforms of Alexander II, the length of service was drastically reduced and all male citizens, regardless of social class, became eligible for conscription.

After seizing power in 1917, the Bolsheviks were initially determined to rely on a "volunteer army of workers and peasants." Yet only a year later, amidst a raging civil war, the chairman of the Revolutionary Military Council, Leon Trotsky, introduced universal conscription—buttressed by instant

executions of deserters (sometimes entire platoons, companies, or even reg-
iments), draft evaders, and violators of discipline. Thus secured, the seemingly inexhaustible supply of poorly trained, poorly fed, poorly armed but
multitudinous conscripts made the complete disregard for soldiers' lives a
cornerstone of Soviet military doctrine. In the "human wave" strategy, the
enemy was to be overwhelmed by relentless attacks until victory was
achieved—regardless of the casualties.

Because of conscription the Soviet Union survived the disastrous first
two years of the war with Nazi Germany, when up to five million Soviet soldiers were estimated to have been killed or captured. (According to various
estimates, the Soviets lost between five and ten soldiers for each German
casualty.)

Thus, just as the victory over Napoleon in 1812–14 appeared to the
czarist court and the generals to have vindicated Peter's century-old
rekrutchina (military conscription), so did the vanquishing of Nazi Germany
confirm to the Soviet leadership the essential soundness of the extant social
organization: The glory of the country was equated with the might of its
army; one of the society's key reasons for existence was to supply the military with whatever was necessary in blood and treasure; and conscription
was the backbone of the army.

✐

One of the key results of the democratic anti-Communist revolution of
1991 was an unprecedented demilitarization for a country not defeated
on the battlefield or occupied by the victors. Under Russia's first post-
Soviet president, Boris Yeltsin, defense spending was slashed by 90 percent, from at least 30 percent of the GDP to between 2 and 3 percent.
Between 1992 and 2001, the 2.7 million troops that Russia inherited from
the Soviet Union's 5-million-strong armed forces were reduced by half
to 1,365,000.[1]

Yet every attempt to switch to a professional army was scuttled by the lack
of funds to pay competitive salaries to volunteer soldiers[2] and by the fierce
resistance of the generals and their supporters among the leftist "popular
patriotic" plurality in the 1995–99 Duma, who viewed the abolition of the

draft as treason. Unable to collect taxes—and thus impoverished like every revolutionary government before it—and unwilling to take on yet another battle against the "patriots" amidst the endless economic and political crises, the Kremlin failed again and again to dispose of the draft.

cↃꝋ

Unlike their allies among the nationalists and the leftists, for the Russian officer corps the preservation of the draft is less a matter of highfalutin sloganeering about "the glory and the honor of the Motherland" than a confluence of institutional inertia and, particularly for those in the senior ranks, job security.

Cutting the ground troops by almost half—from today's impoverished, incompetent, sullen, and sluggish army of 1,000,000–1,250,000 men (no one knows for sure) to a professional, well-trained, and highly mobile modern force of 500,000–650,000—would require a drastic reduction in the bloated upper echelons. Even after Yeltsin's periodic mass dismissals, the generals, who served for thirty to forty years to gain the power and the privilege that gold stars on the epaulettes confer, still number an incredible 2,000.[3] (In addition, as of the fall of 2004, the top-heavy Russian military had more colonels than lieutenants.)[4]

The all-volunteer force will also put an end to what is, in effect, the extralegal status of draftees. Contract soldiers, who could quit at any time should the army fail to live up to its part of the bargain, would no longer tolerate the prison-like living conditions, awful food, and lack of recreation, as well as the constant verbal and physical abuse. They could no longer be ordered to build a dacha for a general or work in a bakery, a brick-making plant, or a city sanitation department, or to harvest potatoes at a local farm in exchange for a bribe paid to a commanding officer.

Perhaps most importantly, having climbed through the ranks of what, in essence, is a nineteenth-century army with tanks and missiles, most of Russian senior officers today lack the skills to lead a professional army, in which authority would have to be earned by knowledge, skills, physical fitness, and respect for fellow soldiers—and not maintained by fear of punishment and abuse.

"Our generals know only one science: how to conscript a huge number of civilians, organize the most primitive military training, and then grind the hastily slapped-together units in a war," writes Russia's leading independent military analyst, Alexander Golts. A professional army, he continues, would

> inevitably force a cardinal change in the training of the armed forces, a cardinal modernization of the entire system of military education. To attempt to do so for the current leaders of the Russian armed forces would be tantamount to preparing their own resignations. . . . For them, the preservation of the slave conscript army is a matter of self-preservation.[5]

ゆ

Russia's new military doctrine no longer views the United States and NATO as the enemy. Gone, too, are the commissars (*politruks*), and with them, the indoctrination sessions in Communist ideology and the evils of imperialism, conducted in the ubiquitous "Lenin's rooms" at every military base. Yet the Soviet-style draft still daily reproduces the Soviet-style army, which humiliates and torments the conscripts.

The unbridgeable gap in status and education between officers and the conscripts in the czarist army, so vividly portrayed in the stories and novels about the Russian imperial army by Leo Tolstoy and Alexander Kuprin, did not diminish in the Soviet Union. In the absence of professional noncommissioned officers (especially the veteran sergeants who play a central role in the U.S. Army's socialization of its men, the inculcation of skills, and respect for authority and regulations), the Russian army barracks are ruled by the second-year draftees known as *dedy*, or "grandfathers."

The result is a monstrous routine called *dedovshchina*—the word that strikes terror in the hearts of millions of Russian parents and their draft-age sons and forces them to seek any and all means to avoid conscription. Entirely at the *dedy*'s mercy, the draftees are brutally hazed, forced to perform meaningless and degrading tasks, and robbed of their personal possessions, money, and food parcels. The daily humiliation and often savage beatings of first-year recruits have been recorded in harrowing detail in letters smuggled out of bases and given to kind civilians to mail. Sometimes they reach the aggrieved and outraged parents after the sender has already died from abuse, committed suicide, or disappeared without a trace.

According to Defense Minister Ivanov, during a ten-month period in 2002, 531 soldiers were killed in noncombat situations,[6] including one-third by suicide.[7] Yet the national antidraft organization, the Committees of Soldiers' Mothers (which later merged into the Union of the Committees of Soldiers' Mothers), estimated the total number of *dedovshchina*'s victims for the same year to be around 3,000.[8]

Military prosecutors annually investigate about 2,000 cases of abuse—a number which most likely represents only a fraction of such incidents because conscripts rarely complain, fearing further retribution from the *dedy*, while the officers routinely cover up these crimes.[9] A leading advocate of military reform, former first deputy prime minister Boris Nemtsov, has claimed that the total number of abused every year is closer to 20,000.[10]

Desertion is rampant. According to the deputy chief of the general staff, 2,270 servicemen fled their units between January and June 2002. The Soldiers' Mothers estimate that 40,000 soldiers per year desert or attempt to desert—a number which represents about one in fifteen of all conscripts serving at any given time.[11] In August 2002, two soldiers deserted in Chechnya after murdering eight comrades in retaliation for systematic hazing. In another case that attracted national attention three years ago, fifty-four soldiers left their units' firing ranges and marched thirty-five miles to a Soldiers' Mothers chapter in the southern city of Volgograd in order to protest regular beatings by the officers.

⁂

Along with airing many other dirty secrets of the Soviet regime, the liberalization of the late 1980s resulted not only in public awareness of the horrors of *dedovshchina*, but the emergence of informal support groups of the mothers of conscripts who were killed, maimed, vanished, or deserted from their units. Soon, the Committees of Soldiers' Mothers became one of the largest, best-organized, and most active civic organizations, now consisting of nearly three hundred local branches throughout the Russian Federation.

By publicizing the abuse, the organization seeks to force the authorities to abide by the laws and to reform the army. The Soldiers' Mothers also provide legal services and counseling on deferments, arrange medical consultations in cases where exemptions were not granted despite illness or deformity, as well as bring lawsuits against the Ministry of Defense.

Yet tens of thousands of future conscripts and their relatives still choose to bypass the system rather than to challenge it. Bribery is pandemic, as parents and grandparents pool resources to pay off college officials in order to ensure college entry and the deferment. President Putin's representative to the G8, Igor Shuvalov, estimates that Russians spend some $7 billion a year on bribes to get their children into institutions of higher education—much, if not most, of the sum going to shielding boys from the army.[12] Members of medical commissions are routinely bribed to disqualify a draftee as physically unfit.

Some of the future conscripts' relatives have even called for a kind of a "draft tax"—with the price of deferral officially established and payable to the state instead of going to bribes—to help fund a professional army. Speaking in support of the scheme, the mother of a thirteen-year-old boy from Rostov-on-the-Don recently told a major Russian daily that her "buyout" money could then be used to "pay [to feed, to house, and to equip] a boy who is in good health and wants to serve in the army."[13]

The first Chechen war (1994–96) turned the dread and loathing of the draft into near-hysteria. Assured by then defense minister Pavel Grachev and his generals that a victory over the Chechen separatists could be achieved by "a battalion" of Russian troops, President Yeltsin ordered the December 1994 assault on the capital of the breakaway province, Grozny.

The result was a massacre of the raw, untrained draftees, thousands of whom were trapped in the streets and mowed down by machine guns and grenade launchers, as the Russian commanders kept sending more and more troops into the ambush. The official estimates of the casualties in the first Chechen war vary between 4,000 and 5,500. Independent observers put the number at 8,000 killed, and the Soldiers' Mothers, at 14,000.[14]

The prospect of dying in Chechnya increased draft avoidance manyfold, turning into resisters even those groups of youths who ordinarily served willingly (mostly from villages and smaller towns). With terror and fear—the key instruments of totalitarian control—having melted away, hiding from the draft was no longer impossible. Many of those who failed to obtain college deferments or medical disqualifications simply did not bother to reply to the summons; others "went underground" by moving in with distant relatives or friends; still others, who were served the summons, failed to present themselves at the collection points on the day of the draft.

Yet the end of the war in 1996 was not enough to diminish the fear of the draft. Today, an estimated 30,000–40,000 young men ignore the call-up letters every year.[15] In recent years, the military has managed to draft no more than 11 percent of all eligible men. The quality of the draftees, now virtually void of middle-class youths, has also deteriorated drastically, as the military is compelled to draft those who can barely read, have criminal records, or use drugs.[16]

Just as importantly, the radical demilitarization of state and society, as well as the first signs of economic revival after the crisis inherited from the Soviet Union, resulted in an exodus of junior and mid-level officers. In contrast to the Soviet days, when their salaries were among the highest and they had priority in the allocation of scarce apartments, these officers were no longer part of Russia's most prestigious institution. They began leaving the army in droves. Almost one-third of all officers who retired from active duty in 2000 were under the age of thirty.[17] By 2002, nearly half of all platoons were without leaders.[18]

The already limited involvement of junior officers in the daily life of the barracks diminished even further, and the reliance on *dedovshchina* for the maintenance of discipline became even more prevalent, bringing with it more fatalities, desertions—and a still greater reluctance of the future draftees to serve.

Coinciding with Putin's appointment as prime minister of the Russian Federation in August 1999, the second Chechen war, which began with the invasion of the Russian province of Dagestan by Chechen militants seeking to establish the "Islamic Republic of Northern Caucasus," further highlighted the inadequacy of the draft-based system. Although, like Yeltsin before him, Putin had been told that the battle-ready troops stood by waiting for his command to attack, it took almost a month for the federal units to gather and drive at most one to two thousand invaders back into Chechnya. As Putin angrily acknowledged three years later, "There was nobody to send to war."[19]

Mindful of the bloody fiasco in December of 1994, the Ministry of Defense (MOD) sought to mollify public opinion by substituting volunteer contract soldiers (*kontraktniki*) for some draftees in the battlefront units. Attracted by the promise of a monthly salary of nearly $1,000 (or, at the time, about three times the average national wage), *kontraktniki* soon constituted 20 percent of combat units.

Yet in a sequence that has been repeated many times before, having made a step forward toward a volunteer army, the government proceeded— in Lenin's famous phrase—to take two steps backwards. As soon as the worst of the fighting was over, the volunteers received only one-third of the promised wages. They responded by rioting and by quitting en masse.

✍

Regarding the draft, Putin's behavior fits the broader pattern of his regime: from the seemingly enthusiastic adoption and implementation of the key Yeltsin-era structural reforms, blocked by political opposition or impeded by the state's empty coffers,[20] to a slowdown after the first two and a half years, followed by freeze and, in some areas, reversals after Putin's 2004 reelection.

The newly elected president came out swinging in November 2000, when the Kremlin announced, without specifying the deadline, a reduction of the troops by 470,000 men and the retirement of 380 generals after the cuts were implemented.[21]

Half a year later, around the first anniversary of his presidency, Putin declared that a "professional army is the goal to which it is possible and necessary to strive. . . . I think we can gradually reduce the draft and bring it to the minimum . . . around 2010."[22]

The Kremlin's show of solidarity with the United States after the September 11, 2001, terrorist attacks highlighted a radical change in Russia's strategic environment and the need for an overhaul in the composition and structure of its military establishment. Overruling his generals (and the Ministry of Foreign Affairs), Putin declared support for the U.S.-led war on Islamic terrorism. He ordered intelligence and logistic cooperation in preparation for the U.S. war on the Taliban regime in Afghanistan and allowed the unprecedented overflight of Russia's territory by U.S. and NATO transport planes, as well as the deployment of U.S. and NATO troops at former Soviet bases in Central Asia. A month later, the president's press service announced that Putin had approved a plan to "phase out the conscription system" and "go to a contract army."[23]

In November of the same year, the president seemed to endorse the "fast track" program, advocated by the then co-chairmen of the Union of Rightist Forces (SPS), Boris Nemtsov and Yegor Gaidar,[24] when he invited them to take part in a Kremlin meeting with the leadership of the Ministry of Defense and the general staff. The president ordered the government to prepare a comprehensive reform program for his review no later than July 1, 2002. In April 2002, in his "state of Russia" address to the Federal Assembly, Putin for the first time presented the transition to an all-volunteer military as his top priority.

The case for a radical reform was bolstered in spring 2003 by the images of the U.S. invasion of Iraq, broadcast nightly on Russian television. The contrast between the professional U.S. army and the Soviet-style (and, in many instances, Soviet- and Russian-trained) conscript Iraqi force—which employed the outdated World War II strategy of stationary deployments, trenches, and dug-in tanks and artillery—became "exhibit A" for the proponents of an all-volunteer force.

The Iraqi army's collapse after three weeks of fighting and the astoundingly minor losses inflicted upon the U.S. forces and those of its allies underscored the strategic and tactical incompetence of the top Russian official military experts and generals, whose widely publicized predictions had confidently forecast prolonged trench warfare with tens of thousands of casualties among the Americans.

"For ten years we have been talking ad nauseam about what a 'modern army' should be and how to create it," a leading Russian pollster close to the Kremlin told me in May 2004, "and, lo and behold, here it was, in flesh and blood, on our television screens for everyone to see, with its helmet-mounted cameras, laptops with satellite links, and knee-pads!" He was at once wistful and angry.

Lessons of Iraq notwithstanding, the Kremlin was already beating a retreat. When it was finally adopted in July 2003 (a year after Putin's original deadline), the "Special Federal Program to Transform the Staffing of the Armed Forces Primarily with Contract Servicemen" did call for the reduction of compulsory service from two years to one in 2007 and for the introduction of professional sergeants; yet the program set no date for the end of the draft. Instead, it envisioned fully replacing only 145,500 conscripts (or around 21 percent of the 700,000 drafted privates and sergeants currently in the army) with volunteers in eighty "combat-ready" units by 2007.

A year before, the pro-Kremlin majority in the Duma made a mockery of the "Law on Alternative Service." Conscientious objectors were to serve three and a half years instead of two for conscripts. They would have no say in the choice of occupation and would most likely serve outside their home regions and possibly within military units—where they were certain to be brutally hazed.

In refusing to eliminate the draft, the Kremlin defies the longstanding and strong preference of a vast majority of Russians. In a national poll a year ago, 87 percent of Russians thought that "youths today do not want to serve in the army."[25] Asked in early 2005 if they wanted to see their son, brother, husband, or other close relative serve in the military, 67 percent of Russian citizens said no, and only 28 percent answered in the affirmative.[26] In the same poll, 62 percent of the respondents supported the transition to a contract army, as compared to 31 percent who wished to preserve the draft.[27]

Yet so apparently determined is the regime not to allow any significant force reduction that it is willing to change the arrangement that has been in place for half a century. With the approaching 2007 deadline for reducing the term of conscription from two years to one year, Defense Minister Ivanov—who is President Putin's confidant and putative successor—announced that he intended to scrap college deferments in order to make up for halving the numbers of conscripts serving at any given moment.

Even leaving aside the waste and ineffectiveness associated with a mostly conscripted force, Ivanov's arithmetic is suspect. According to the July 2003 "program," in the same year, 2007, kontraktniki are supposed to replace 145,000 conscripts, and, a year later, the army is to be reduced by 200,000,[28] thus making the increase in the call-up unnecessary.

Nor can the failure to make the transition to a fully volunteer army be any longer excused by a lack of funds. Although the changeover is estimated to cost $4.3 billion,[29] with the price of oil skyrocketing Russia clearly can afford it. What better use could there be for some of the $33 billion (as of this writing) "stabilization fund," built on oil superprofits, or for the record $149.6 billion in foreign currency and gold reserves in Russia's Central Bank?

Between 1999 and 2003, the defense budget more than doubled, and it grew again by 28 percent in 2005. Yet the Ministry of Defense has been stinting where increased spending was most needed: The salaries of the future *kontraktniki* are still below the minimum necessary to attract a sufficient number of volunteers.[30]

It is hard to think of a more explosive social issue in today's Russia than the elimination of draft deferments, which could overnight turn millions of college students and their largely middle-class parents into political opposition and, perhaps, send them into the streets. When asked in February 2005 whether deferments should be granted to college students, 83 percent of those surveyed agreed.[31] Moreover, a plurality of the Russian citizens (46 percent) believes that the changes in the draft exemptions must be decided not by a government decree, but by a national referendum.[32]

The Soldiers' Mothers, who in late 2004 forged a political party,[33] quickly began collecting signatures for a national referendum on the draft, exemptions, and the transition to a professional army. Facing a nightmarish scenario of students and their parents joining the retirees, who at the time were demonstrating in every major city against the necessary but bungled monetization of in-kind social security benefits, the government retreated. Ivanov promised to keep deferments in place "for now."

On the principle of conscription, however, the government remains unyielding. Ivanov has already declared that conscription as such will never be completely phased out. Resuming the offensive in June of this year, the MOD declared that, instead of abolishing college deferments, the state will achieve the same objective by closing down the so-called "military departments" in 199 out of 229 Russian colleges and universities.[34] These "departments" conduct military training and confer the ranks of junior officers on graduates, thus shielding them from being drafted as privates.

❦

With the government flouting public opinion and all but goading the middle class and college students, Alexander Golts was right to surmise that "the contract army may be one of the hottest issues in the next presidential campaign."[35]

Yet the matter is much broader than a proximate political battle. After the radical demilitarization of post-Soviet Russia, the society and the economy are no longer mere resource appendages to the military-industrial complex at the service of an expansionist totalitarian state. The impoverished, abusive, and dehumanizing conscript army is too heavy a baggage to carry into the peaceful, democratic, and prosperous Russia in which most Russian people would like to live.

The draft is a symbol of the contest between the Russian state and society for a democratic control over a central institution—the army. It is here that the Kremlin, now in the throes of counterrevolutionary restoration, has chosen to make a stand. The outcome of this clash will go a long way toward defining Russia's path for years to come.

19

Putin's Risks
2005

By eroding many of the key achievements of the revolution and by freezing or reversing most of the badly needed structural reforms, the Putin restoration poses serious risks to the stability and potentially even the territorial integrity of Russia. In effect, the regime has weakened or altogether removed some of democracy's key shock absorbers and raised the center of political gravity to the very top, making the Russian state far less capable of navigating the difficult road ahead. From the housing and welfare reforms to the national electricity system on the verge of major breakdowns, the ubiquitous and unprecedentedly brazen corruption and completely dysfunctional armed forces, the growing tension between the Kremlin and the provinces, and the threat of terrorism from Chechnya and the increasingly ungovernable North Caucasus, the years since 2003 have been a time when many a precious opportunity has been wasted and many a potential danger made more acute.

Western and Russian observers alike have watched with mounting concern as President Vladimir Putin has tried to consolidate the Kremlin's control over Russia's politics and economy. From the campaign against the YUKOS oil company to the elimination of regional elections, Putin—a growing chorus of critics argues—is leading the country toward authoritarianism.

But the Kremlin's authoritarian project carries even greater risks than commonly appreciated. Although officially justified as necessary to "strengthen" state and society, these policies, in fact, are likely to do the very opposite, destabilizing Russia's politics, economy, and national security. In evaluating the current situation, some leading analysts in Moscow privately spoke last fall of a "GKchP-2 scenario"—a reference to the unsuccessful

August 1991 hardliner putsch, whose perpetrators sought to prevent the breakup of the Soviet Union but instead brought about its speedy collapse.

The cumulative effect of Putin's recentralization has been to raise the center of political gravity to the very top at precisely the time when the Russian state will need every available ounce of stability and maneuverability to absorb severe shocks and navigate sharp turns. The regime's course is made even more perilous by its efforts to remove or obscure the road signs of societal feedback, which Russia's increasingly emaciated democratic politics and constrained media are less and less capable of providing.

✍

Since 2000, public opinion polls have consistently shown that, more than anything, Russians want their government to sustain a steady improvement in the standard of living, maintain law and order, and protect them from terrorism. At the heart of Vladimir Putin's high approval ratings has been his ability to "deliver," de facto or symbolically, but convincingly—on all three points. Early on he "connected" with the majority of Russians by projecting the image of an energetic and caring advocate for the people's well-being, a determined opponent of corruption, and a tough but competent defender against terrorism. Today, because of its choices, the regime is increasingly vulnerable on all three fronts.

Prepared by the structural reforms of the 1990s and spurred by the currency devaluation and high oil prices, Russia's remarkable economic growth of the past six years has expanded well beyond the energy sector. Yet the shift in Putin's economic policy toward greater state control or ownership and, with it, the customary incompetence, corruption, and waste, may already be dampening the expansion.

According to Putin's senior economic adviser, the radical liberal economist Andrei Illarionov, the "effectiveness" of Russian economic policy has been "declining" because of the "movement toward state intervention" and because "out of a pool of choices, bureaucrats tend to make decisions that have a higher rate of return for themselves, not for the country (redistributing rent rather than implementing responsible economic policies)."[1]

As a result of the Kremlin's "utterly incompetent interference," Russia's economic growth has failed to keep pace in the past year with the rising price of oil, falling behind by almost two percentage points, according to Illarionov's calculations.[2] Had it not been for high oil prices, Illarionov argues, "Russia most likely would have had a recession."[3]

The continuing detention and trial of Mikhail Khodorkovsky, the former CEO of Russia's largest private company, YUKOS, and the systematically malicious judicial extermination of Russia's most modern, most transparent, and most profitable enterprise have further damaged the country's economic prospects. Regardless of the veracity of the charges against Khodorkovsky, who was arrested in October 2003, the blatant procedural violations and the brazen bending of the court to the Kremlin's will have violated the letter as well as the spirit of the progressive 2001 criminal procedural code.[4]

Illarionov has called the entire YUKOS affair "the swindle of the year" and a "serious mistake" that boosted illiberal forces in the country, with "dire consequences for . . . industry, the authorities, and for the country as a whole."[5] The prosecution of Khodorkovsky has sent a clear signal to federal and local authorities everywhere that they can blackmail and extort local businesses with impunity. A rigged bankruptcy "auction" at which YUKOS's key production unit, Yuganskneftegaz, was sold to a front company at half its actual value, followed by its quick resale to the state-owned Rosneft oil company, has further eroded the integrity of financial and legal institutions and underscored the vulnerability of corporations to the arbitrariness of executive power.

The predictable consequence of the YUKOS affair has been the chilling of entrepreneurial activity in Russia, with billions of rubles in potential investments transferred for safekeeping abroad. Down to just $2 billion in 2003, capital flight from Russia is estimated to have reached $16.9 billion between January and September of 2004.[6]

An uncertain, and worsening, legal regime resulted in little foreign investment in 2004 outside the oil and gas sectors. Yet even here, with oil prices near record levels, some of the largest potential players are increasingly unwilling to commit funds. Recently, Lee Raymond, the CEO of ExxonMobil—which in the fall of 2003 came very close to investing in a 25 percent share of YukosSibneft (at the time Russia's largest private company)—said that it was "pretty difficult for people to think [of] putting large sums of money in [Russia] as an investment."[7]

⁓

The perception of Putin's commitment to the bettering of the Russian people's lot has been considerably tarnished by the August 2004 welfare reform, which replaced myriad in-kind entitlements with cash allowances for over 30 million Russians, including the disabled, the elderly, World War II veterans, and survivors of the Nazi blockade of Leningrad and the Chernobyl disaster. Ranging in benefits from subsidized telephone service to free bus rides, dentures, wheelchairs, and prescription drugs, the system was notoriously poorly targeted, wasteful, corrupt, and very much in need of overhaul. Yet the peremptory manner in which the law was passed by the Duma, the size of the cash supplements, and a generic mistrust of the state bureaucracy have combined to make the majority of Russians unhappy or, at the very least, suspicious of the "reform."

Critics argue that replacing "privileges" with a monthly 450-ruble entitlement (about $14) and supplementary allowances ranging from 600 to 2,400 rubles amounts to a de facto reduction of benefits for vast numbers of recipients. An additional concern is that the new system will not keep up with inflation, which may reach 11 percent this year. To add insult to injury, the passage of the reform was accompanied by massive increases in salaries for top federal officials.

In the end, Russians felt shortchanged. Almost twice as many told pollsters that they expected their families to be worse off after the reform as felt that they would gain from it.[8] Only 35 percent of Russians approved of the reform, while 55 percent were opposed.[9]

This shift in the perception of the state's priorities has been compounded by the 2005 state budget. Amidst record surpluses, appropriations for the "social sector" (housing, medical care, education) register minuscule growth—and even a de facto reduction after inflation. In October of last year, according to trade union officials, more than a million state sector workers, including teachers, doctors, and scientists, took part in a strike demanding a 50 percent increase in their salaries, which for the most part are below the national average of 5,000 rubles ($180) per month.

The evidence of Russians' growing discontent with their government's economic policies is all the more arresting because the general level of well-being, which is by far the single most important explanation of Putin's popularity,[10] is still very high by the lights of the past fifteen years. In November 2004, 61 percent of those surveyed reported their incomes to be "middle-of-the-road," good, or very good, and 72 percent said that they had either adjusted or expected to adjust "in the nearest future" to the epochal changes that have swept Russia since the collapse of the Soviet Union.[11]

Yet despite the improvement, over half of Russians reported to the pollsters that the government cannot tame inflation, and four in ten felt the Kremlin does not care about the "social protection" of the population.[12] While slightly over one-third agreed that the past year brought changes for the better in Russia, their share was virtually the same as in March 2000, when Putin was first elected to the presidency, while the number who felt the change had been negative almost doubled, from 16 percent to 30 percent.[13]

Designed to deflect criticism from the government, the populist propaganda class war on the country's richest citizens—a campaign that has been a staple of Kremlin public relations for the past fourteen months, centered on the YUKOS affair—does not seem to have gained traction in public opinion. In November of last year, only 33 percent of Russians expressed annoyance toward (18 percent), contempt for (7 percent), or hatred of (8 percent) the people "who became rich in the past ten to fifteen years," while 27 percent expressed "respect" (15 percent) or "interest" (12 percent), and the rest reported having "no special feelings" toward them.[14]

☙

The government also seems to be failing in "delivering" on another of its key promises: that of political stability. In October 2004 only 22 percent of Russians surveyed felt that in the past few years Russia had become stable, while 67 percent agreed there was no stability in the country.[15] Most ominously, over half of the population reported the political situation in Russia as "tense,"[16] and 45 percent reported an increase in their "dissatisfaction with the authorities."[17]

As a result, what has been aptly labeled "resigned acceptance of an incomplete democracy"[18] may be shifting in favor of concerted political action. While in 2000 less than half of the people indicated support for political pluralism, two-thirds did last fall, with the numbers of "don't knows" dropping from 24 percent to 13 percent.[19] In the words of leading independent political analyst Dmitry Oreshkin, "The feeling that there are no real alternatives to Putin upsets the people. I think the number of citizens who think this way will grow."[20]

Much of the rising political unrest and dissatisfaction in Russia can be traced to Putin's pursuit of measures that equate security with control and thus gravely weaken key institutions outside the executive branch—foremost, his September 13, 2004, plan for changes in Russia's political structure, announced in the aftermath of the September 1–3 Beslan massacre.[21]

Speaking before his cabinet of ministers and the governors of most of Russia's provinces, Putin put forward a blueprint for what he called "a cardinal restructuring . . . of the executive power in the country . . . with the aim of strengthening the unity of the country."[22] The reimposition of direct political control over the provinces has riled local elites. Despite their voicing no public protest and, in some cases, even paying lip service to Putin's plan, the governors are said to be seething, especially in rich and ethnically non-Russian regions. For the first time since the late 1980s, there was even talk in Moscow in the fall of 2004 about groups of provinces uniting into ten to twelve "states" and declaring their "autonomy" or even independence from Moscow.

With provincial elites in passive resistance, Putin's "reform" lacks popular support as well. In a national poll conducted shortly after the September 13 speech, almost two-thirds of those surveyed thought that the governors should be elected, rather than appointed.[23] Rejecting a key official justification of the reform, six in ten respondents felt that the appointment of governors would leave the present level of corruption undiminished and might even raise it.[24] At the same time, 50 percent told pollsters that a Duma deputy would serve their interests better if he or she were elected directly rather than on a party list, while only 9 percent preferred election by party list alone.[25]

According to persistent rumors among the Moscow cognoscenti, the gap between the Kremlin and the rest of the country will grow wider still. The appointment of governors is said to be followed by a second, as yet unpublicized, phase of federal reform, which envisions a drastic reduction in the number of provinces, their merger into larger entities, and the abolishment of non-Russian ethnic "autonomous republics." Such steps are all but certain to provoke popular resistance, which in the larger areas, especially the predominantly Muslim ones, has the possibility of becoming violent. One of quite a few horrifying prospects is the potential transformation of 3.7-million-strong, majority-Muslim Tatarstan in the heart of Russia into another Chechnya.

෴

After adopting a slew of promarket reforms from 2000 through 2003—including land privatization; a radical simplification of the tax code and the reduction of personal and corporate income taxes to some of the world's lowest flat rates; partial pension privatization; the liberalization of currency laws; and a package of laws on the breakup of the state electricity monopoly—the Putin administration has slowed its pursuit of structural reforms or abandoned them altogether. Among the desperately needed but unfinished or subverted measures are a radical administrative reform that would free small and medium businesses from bureaucratic blackmail; enforcement of compliance with the 2001 criminal procedural code, including the strengthening of courts' independence and the protection of the rights of defendants; and stronger guarantees of property rights, especially for acquisitions made during the 1990s. The glacial pace of Russia's military reform, which aims to create a much smaller, all-volunteer force, has left intact the widely hated draft, which has rendered parts of the Russian defense establishment dysfunctional and utterly unprepared to deal with a large-scale terrorism threat.[26]

Apart from hampering long-term economic growth, the postponement or abandonment of the gradual privatization of state monopolies in the impoverished housing, utilities, and health care sectors is bound to increase social tensions. Of greatest concern is the delay in the privatization of electricity generation plants and the gradual decontrol of wholesale and retail prices of electricity. The reform, approved by the Duma a year and a half ago after exhaustive review and debates, was designed to attract badly needed private capital to the worn-out and archaic industry. In the absence of investment and renovation, another severe winter is almost certain to bring more blackouts and fatalities.[27]

With the governors appointed rather than elected, however, henceforth the Kremlin, and not the local authorities, will be the lightning rod for any popular indignation and demonstrations caused by natural and manmade disasters, from floods and pollution to industrial accidents and lack of heat and electricity in the winter.

✑

President Putin's image as a competent and energetic defender against rapacious bureaucrats has also been undermined by the regime's inability to reduce, let alone eliminate, corruption. The openly voiced consensus judges official venality today to be beyond anything seen in either the Soviet Union or post-Soviet Russia.

At the outset of Vladimir Putin's presidency in 2000, pollsters asked Russians whether they expected that there would be more or less thievery and corruption after his election. At the time, 36 percent believed that malfeasance would diminish, while 46 percent thought it would remain at approximately the same level.[28] When the question was again put to the Russian people following Putin's reelection four years later, the share of optimists was down to 29 percent, while those who predicted no change climbed to 58 percent.[29]

In 2000, a 47 percent plurality of Russians named corruption as the main obstacle to the implementation of "democratic and market reforms"; the next most frequently cited factor was the lack of a "thought-through" program, mentioned by 42 percent.[30] In 2004, after four years of Putin, concern about corruption has not diminished in a statistically significant way (it is cited by 42 percent of respondents), but its relative prominence has increased as the absence of a coherent reform program, still in second place, is now cited by only 30 percent.[31]

While it is true that most Russians are accustomed to ubiquitous graft and venality and have stomached them for a long time, no one should bet on their tolerating corruption indefinitely, especially after they begin to identify it as a barrier to their country's vital political and economic progress. In this context, the example of neighboring Ukraine is portentous: In a country by all accounts even more corrupt than Russia, popular revulsion over official wrongdoing became one of the key driving forces behind last year's popular protest against the perpetuation of the ruling regime. In Russia, too, acquiescence may give way to a mass movement for change.

cℐo

Whatever damage is done to Vladimir Putin's popularity by his recent political and economic choices, the regime's inability to end the festering Chechen crisis—and the future terrorist attacks facilitated by it—represents an even greater threat to Russia's stability.[32]

The Russian people first rallied around Putin in October 1999 following the invasion of Dagestan by fundamentalist Chechen warlords seeking to establish "an Islamic Republic of Northern Caucasus." Recently appointed prime minister and projecting competence, energy, and determination, Putin promised to go to the source of the attacks and end them once and for all. Today, by contrast, in the bloody wake of the 2002 *Nord-Ost* and the 2004 Beslan terrorist attacks[33] the number of Russians who express no faith in the government's ability to shield them from terrorism has grown by half, from 50 percent to 76 percent.[34]

Following the storm of media criticism about the Kremlin's handling of Beslan, when the incompetence, corruption, and callousness of the authorities receiving unprecedented coverage, that heinous attack produced surprisingly little by way of "rallying around the flag." While 18 percent of Russians reported that they felt better about Putin after Beslan, 21 percent said their attitude toward the president had somewhat or significantly worsened.[35] Another large-scale terrorist attack with the number of casualties on the order of *Nord-Ost* or Beslan is almost certain to produce a sharp drop in, if not indeed a meltdown of, Putin's approval ratings.

The damage will be greater still if Shamil Basaev, Chechnya's principal al-Qaeda-linked warlord and the reputed mastermind of the Beslan attack, succeeds not merely in perpetrating further suicide bombings or conventional attacks against Russian civilians, but in a large-scale massacre that kills thousands or tens of thousands—sabotaging, for instance, a hydroelectric power station, dam, or chemical or nuclear facility, or detonating one of thousands of nuclear weapons that remain scattered around the country.[36]

The intensity of popular indignation and revulsion after such an attack would be so much stronger because of a disjuncture between Russian public opinion on the Chechen crisis and the government's policy. Contrary to the Kremlin's widely disseminated claims, more people traced the Beslan tragedy to the war in Chechnya (39 percent) than either to international terrorism (27 percent) or "enemies in the West" (12 percent).[37]

In sharp dissonance with the official policy of "no negotiations," a consistent majority of Russians (54–59 percent) has for the past three years favored the avoidance of civilian casualties "at any cost," including acquiescing to terrorists' demands.[38] Even more importantly, 55 percent indicated in a poll last September that for the war in Chechnya to end, "some sort" of negotiations with the insurgents would have to be started, compared to 32 percent who thought the continuation of military operations offered the best prospects for peace.[39]

All in all, as many people in a poll in October 2004 blamed the "mistaken policies of the Russian authorities" for the spate of terrorist attacks (35 percent) as they did "plots by hostile forces" (34 percent), with the remainder attributing equal responsibility to both factors.[40]

Yet not only does the Kremlin stubbornly refuse to take notice of the popular mood, it has aggressively attempted to use Beslan to end the debate on Chechnya and impugn the motives of those who favor a different course. In an interview that was widely interpreted as defining the Kremlin's policy, the deputy head of the presidential administration, Vladislav Surkov, averred that Chechen terrorists are "servicing political technologies" of Russia's unnamed enemies, who, he claimed, had sought for two centuries to "blow up Russia's southern borders." Surkov went on to say that he sensed "the smell of treason" in the mere suggestion of alternatives to the Kremlin's current approach and labeled their advocates "a fifth column."[41]

As further terrorist attacks occur, the majority of Russians who today favor negotiations and insist on avoiding casualties at any cost may become galvanized into protesting nationwide. Their demands may include not only the immediate abandonment of Chechnya to the insurgents (as Russia did in 1996) but also the shedding of the entire North Caucasus south of the Stavropol region, with perhaps a wall along the new border. Demoralized by yet another loss, with the president's popularity sharply down and protests threatening to become violent, the authorities may retreat in panic.

Such a hasty withdrawal would be an unmitigated disaster. Chechnya is almost certain to fall to jihadist warlords and become a fundamentalist Muslim enclave and a haven for world Islamic terrorism, like Afghanistan under the Taliban. The abandonment of the North Caucasus, which is home to over a dozen ethnic groups, risks an explosion of Yugoslavia-like proportions.

✐

Taken together, Vladimir Putin's economic, political, and security policies may, in the end, damage his popular image, which until a year ago seemed coated in Teflon.[42] The number of Russians who see more failures than achievements during Putin's stay in office has grown to one-fifth of the electorate, while the percentage of those who consider the president to be serving the interests of people like themselves has slipped to 44 percent.[43]

Between March 2003 and October 2004, the number of those who thought Putin knew the mood of the society diminished from 66 percent to 53 percent, while the share of those who were convinced he did not know grew from one-quarter to over one-third.[44] Although a solid majority still approves of Putin's performance, the margin fell 20 percent between December 2003 and September 2004, from 84 percent to 66 percent.[45] More ominously, more Russians think the country is on the wrong track than the right one: 51 percent to 38 percent, respectively.[46] The dynamic of these attitudes is just as telling; in January 2004, the numbers were almost exactly reversed: 37 percent and 50 percent.[47]

Of course, as crises mount and the president's popularity falls, the Kremlin may try to discard its milder version of plebiscitarian authoritarianism (that is, the one held together largely by the leader's political dominance based on immense popularity) in favor of a classic dictatorship based on systemic coercion and violence. But even if President Putin wished to establish such a regime (which today still is very much of an open question), would he be able to?

The Kremlin lacks practically all of the key instruments of successful modern authoritarianism. It has no mass party or, at least, mass movement. The progovernment United Russia party is widely perceived as mostly a collection of opportunists who will jump ship the moment the going gets tough. United Russia also lacks a clearly and consistently articulated unifying ideology.

The loyalty of the armed forces—another sine qua non of a sustainable dictatorship—is very much in question. The strong apolitical tradition of the Russian military, so evident in its reluctance to participate in the political conflicts of August 1991 and September–October 1993, argues strongly against the likelihood of its decisive support for the regime, especially if violence becomes necessary.

At the same time, the Kremlin's inability, or reluctance, to effect military reform has prevented the creation of a competent, modern force that could become a major stabilizing factor in a crisis. Instead, deeply demoralized by the continuing Chechnya debacle and corroded by corruption and brutal hazing, the military is likely incapable of mustering the coherence and esprit de corps necessary to become a key power player on anyone's side.

That leaves the secret services as the putative dictatorship's most likely enforcer and guardian. In the past few years, President Putin has placed many of his former colleagues throughout the executive branch, making the KGB/FSB the single most common institutional affiliation among the top government officials. Yet in addition to the less than certain ability of the secret services to secure and hold power without the support of the armed forces, their reliability in a major crisis is far from assured.

Until recently considered the least corrupt of all Russian institutions, the FSB and other "power" agencies appear by all private accounts today to be catching up in rapaciousness to their widely despised policeman colleagues in the Interior Ministry. In fact, in the opinion of some of Russia's leading political observers, much in the Kremlin's new economic policy, especially in its dispatch of President Putin's top aides to the boards of directors of some of Russia's most lucrative companies,[48] may be little more than a massive go at the trough after the "lean years" of the 1990s, when the leaders of the secret services seethed at the sight of private entrepreneurs ("appointed billionaires," in Putin's famous phrasing) growing rich.[49]

If so, those whose loyalty has been rewarded once and who thus acquired a taste for high living may in the future be swayed by higher bidders. The "vertical of power," which the Kremlin has spent so much time and effort engineering and advertising, may yet prove to be corroded to the core.

Yet perhaps the greatest obstacle against a classic dictatorship in Russia is the legacy of the revolution of 1991. With over 70 percent of the economy in the nonstate sector, the restoration of a Soviet-style dictatorship is extremely unlikely.

Although fear of the state is a force to reckon with in Putin's Russia, it is not going to take hold easily after almost twenty years of freedom of speech and protest. In newspapers and magazines (and occasionally still on television), opinion leaders on the right and on the left attack the regime with abandon and ferocity. Every leading publication and most opposition parties, movements, groups, and even individuals have websites, while Internet penetration is estimated to be at least 15 percent of the population and is growing by leaps and bounds.[50]

The levels of literacy, urbanization, and education—factors that traditionally militate against the establishment and survival of dictatorships—are all very high for a country with Russia's per-capita GDP. The cultural autarky of the Soviet Union has followed the command economy into the trash heap of history, and Russian elites are very cosmopolitan. In every poll, those under thirty years of age are almost united in their support of democracy and private property. Like their peers everywhere, they are largely apolitical, yet they have mobilized impressively to defend their vital interests in the past, as in the August 1991 and the 1996 presidential elections.

✍

A totalitarian regime, like the one that ruled Russia until the late 1980s, owns and manages everything. When it collapses, much of what constitutes a modern state—its institutions, economy, and society—collapses with it, leaving behind enormous fissures and piles of postrevolutionary rubble. Vladimir Putin was elected because he personified to most Russians the hope of using state power and resources to clear the field for rank-and-file citizens, while nurturing the new institutions of private property, democracy, and the post-Soviet legal system.

In the first three years of his presidency, Putin appeared to be living up to these expectations and, helped by a rapidly expanding economy and high oil prices, he was rewarded with astronomical ratings. But beginning with the Kremlin's assault on the YUKOS oil company in 2003, he seemed increasingly unable to choose between the two competing halves of his identity: that of the former KGB lieutenant colonel, and that of the former top aide to the late Anatoly Sobchak, Russia's leading anti-Communist and mayor of St. Petersburg.

The trauma of Beslan must have made the familiar and the traditional all the more irresistible to Putin. Consequently, the Kremlin now appears to be inclined to make the state the most powerful player in Russian politics, to repossess at least some of the economy's commanding heights, and to turn an evolving federation into a rigid unitary state. Yet with all the key elements of modern authoritarianism swept away or eroded by the 1991 revolution, these tasks may prove far more arduous and, in the end, dangerous than the Kremlin imagines. Having set out to strengthen the Russian state at any cost, Putin instead may risk its destabilization and even its unraveling.

20

Russia's Oil: Natural Abundance and Political Shortages

2006

Between 1999 and 2004 the largely privatized oil industry grew by leaps and bounds, making Russia the world's second-largest producer. Yet the change in economic policy, which now seeks to achieve the dominant state role in energy production and distribution, has jeopardized exploration, extraction, and transportation capacity. Russia's future as a reliable and growing supplier of the world's expanding demands is increasingly in question.

With 6–10 percent of the world's known reserves, Russia pumped on average 9.4 million barrels of oil a day and exported around 7 million last year—second only to Saudi Arabia and occasionally outstripping the desert kingdom in monthly production. In the past six years, the high prices for crude oil have added at least 15 percent to the country's gross domestic product, brought billions of dollars to the treasury, boosted personal incomes by almost one-third, and significantly enhanced Russia's position in the world.

Capitalizing on these developments, President Vladimir Putin placed "energy security" at the center of the meeting of the seven leading capitalist democracies and Russia in St. Petersburg this July—the first G8 summit to be hosted by a Russian leader.

There is little doubt that Russia will remain one of the world's leading oil exporters for many years. Yet, unless arrested or reversed, several structural tendencies may significantly jeopardize the country's ability to meet the world's rapidly growing demand for oil.

The most troubling areas are transportation, taxation, domestic consumption, investments, and, especially, ownership. In the end, all of these issues are linked to the ideological change in economic policy over the past four years and thus are unlikely to be addressed effectively until the country alters its political direction.

Transportation

Without exception, Russia's largest deposits of hydrocarbons lie in extremely inhospitable terrain thousands of miles away from terminals from which they can reach key consumers. The state-owned monopoly, Transneft, operates over 29,000 miles of pipelines.[1] Yet, despite its vast reach, the pipeline system is increasingly inadequate and constitutes the most obvious obstacle to a stable and increasing export capacity.

Today, of the 7 million barrels per day that Russia produces for export, only about 4 million can be transported via the pipelines, and the rest are shipped by the far more expensive, slow, and cumbersome means of rail.[2] As a result, between 1999 and 2003, the average cost of transporting oil has doubled from approximately $5 per ton (approximately 7.35 barrels) to around $10 per ton.[3]

The bottlenecks are multiplying. By 2007, Russia's production for export may exceed its shipping capacity by 220 million to 294 million barrels per year.[4] The aging of the Russian pipelines—one-third are over thirty years old, and another third are older than twenty years—adds urgency to the need for a massive modernization, new construction, and increased efficiency.

In response to such a need, in 2002–3 a consortium of the top Russian private oil companies, led by YUKOS, Sibneft, TNK, and Surgutneftegaz, lobbied the government to allow them to build Russia's first private pipeline, which would carry an estimated 1 million barrels per day over 960 miles, from the main fields in western Siberia across the White Sea to the port of Murmansk on the Barents Sea, for export primarily to the United States.

Because of the Gulf Stream, Murmansk is Russia's only northern port that does not freeze in winter. It is deep enough for the largest tankers (deadweight of over 200,000 tons), making the cost of transportation to the United States competitive with that from the Middle East. The pipeline was not going to cost Russia's treasury a single ruble: Estimated by the members of the consortium to cost between $3.5 billion and $4.5 billion, the project was to going to be financed entirely by private investment.

Although the Russian oil majors had offered for Transneft to be the new pipeline's sole manager, with other companies (state-owned as well as private) having unhindered access to the route, after some hesitation and conflicting signals—and despite high-level lobbying from the U.S. government—the Kremlin decided against a private pipeline. The decision—among the first signs of changing economic policy—amounted to an effective veto of private construction of pipelines in Russia and the affirmation of the Transneft monopoly.

Yet apart from the usual and well-founded concerns about waste and corruption associated with total state ownership of a vast and vital sector of the economy, the choice of Transneft as the sole operator and owner of the Russian pipelines raises serious questions about the availability of resources commensurate with the required volume of new construction, on the one hand, and the state monopoly's ability to deploy these resources most effectively by building infrastructure where the markets need it most, on the other.

Despite the revenue windfall of the past five years, Transneft is far short of having the necessary funds for the approximately 4,000 miles of new pipelines the monopoly said it intended to lay down in the next six years. The price of such construction is estimated at $24 billion, but given the increasing cost of maintaining the aging system, Transneft is not likely to be able to invest more than $600 million a year.[5] It can try to raise the money on the financial markets, but if past world experience serves, banks and investment funds tend to be leery of the length of time, complexity, and risks associated with pipeline construction. Thus, Transneft is unlikely to raise more than $2 billion to $2.5 billion, while the traditional capitalization of such projects—by oil companies themselves in exchange for a share in the ownership—appears to be ruled out by the western Siberia–Murmansk ban.[6]

Eastern Siberia–Pacific Ocean

Those skeptical of Transneft's ability to provide for the needed export capacities point to the firm's top project: the 2,500-mile pipeline from Taishet in eastern Siberia to the port of Nakhodka in the Perevoznaya Bay on the

Pacific Ocean. While direct access to Asian (especially Chinese, Japanese, and South Korean) markets and to the West Coast of the United States holds enormous promise, the venture today appears to be a giant boondoggle-in-the-making: built in the wrong place, carrying a huge price tag, plagued by slow construction as well as environmental and legal concerns, and, in the end, likely to make the oil almost too expensive to be profitable.

Projected to convey 588 million barrels a year, the pipeline will cost between $11.5 billion (by the government's estimate) and $15 billion (by that of independent Russian analysts).[7] The span of the pipeline will make the oil very expensive by world standards: between $6.40 a barrel (Transneft's estimate) and $9.80 (independent experts).[8] Transneft wants the costs to be borne by Russian taxpayers and has lobbied the government for tax relief until the pipeline becomes profitable.

Although Prime Minister Mikhail Fradkov "signed off" on the project in December 2004, the construction has yet to start, making very unlikely the planned completion in 2008 of the first 1,500-mile segment to the railroad station of Skovorodino, from which slightly over one-third of the oil is to be taken by rail to China. (The Chinese oil monopoly, China National Petroleum Corporation, or CNPC, has reportedly offered Transneft a *liwu*, or "gift," of $400 million, ostensibly to conduct a "feasibility study" of the link to China.)[9]

In addition to the cost and length of the pipeline, the eastern Siberia–Pacific Ocean route has already raised serious environmental and legal concerns. With millions of barrels of oil carried over hundreds of miles of unique tundra and taiga preserves in an earthquake-prone area, the pipeline will come within half a mile of Lake Baikal, the world's largest natural freshwater reservoir, designated a World Heritage Site by UNESCO.[10] The route will terminate in the Perevoznaya Bay, which the Russian government's own environmental watchdog, the Federal Service for Environmental, Technological, and Atomic Inspection, deems too shallow to accommodate an oil terminal, and will thus be a threat to "land and sea nature reserves."[11]

The project may become legally complicated as well, since the license for developing the largest oilfields of eastern Siberia (Yurubcheno–Takomskoe) belongs to YUKOS, a company that is being systematically destroyed by the authorities for the political transgressions of its founder and former CEO, Mikhail Khodorkovsky, who is serving an eight-year prison sentence in eastern Siberia, not far from the pipeline's proposed route. Few in Russia doubt that the authorities will succeed in taking the license away from YUKOS in the same shameless exercise of unchecked executive power they displayed in their prosecution of YUKOS and Khodorkovsky.[12] Yet YUKOS may seek recourse in European and U.S. courts, delaying foreign funding and making the designated customers apprehensive of purchasing oil that may well turn out to be stolen.

The plan's biggest flaw, however, is Transneft's apparent unawareness of a shortage of the oil the pipeline is designed to deliver. There is simply not enough oil in eastern Siberia to justify so hugely expensive an undertaking. Even with all of the currently known major oilfields in eastern Siberia coming fully "on stream" by 2015, production will be no more than 287 million barrels per year—or less than half of the planned amount.[13] To make up for the shortfall, Transneft is likely to fill the pipeline by "borrowing" from the oilfields of western Siberia. Such a strategy will add 1,250 miles to the route's length and may bring the cost per barrel as high as $12.[14] (In addition, the largest producer of oil in the eastern part of western Siberia, Tomskneft, still belongs to YUKOS.)

Domestic Consumption

Another structural impediment to Russian oil exports is the way energy is consumed domestically. Badly outdated and, in many cases, nearly worn-out thirty- to forty-year-old equipment, continuing state subsidies, and price controls result in highly inefficient use of fuel—gas, coal, and oil. (Fuel oil, also known as "residual fuel oil," or "*mazut*," accounts for 20 percent of Russian energy consumption. Last year, 56.4 million tons of fuel oil were produced—12 percent of the total Russian production of 470.2 million tons, or 3.455 billion barrels.)[15] Russia's consumption of energy per dollar of GDP is estimated to be two and a half to five times higher than it is in more developed capitalist nations.[16]

To attract the investment needed to upgrade the country's electricity production—which along with gasoline accounts for most domestic oil usage—an ambitious and elaborate reform was designed between 2000 and 2003 by Anatoly Chubais, the CEO of the electricity monopoly RAO-UES, and approved by the parliament after a long and detailed examination. The largest privatization of electricity in history, the UES restructuring was to include the breakup and sale of the monopoly's power generating plants, a gradual price deregulation, and, eventually, the emergence of private, competing generator wholesale and retail companies.[17]

Along with other key structural reforms—health care, utilities, housing, and education—the privatization of electricity was gradually frozen by a Kremlin bent on recapturing the economy's "commanding heights" after President Putin's reelection in 2004. The state continues to monopolize both the generation and the distribution of electricity, with no more than 15 percent of energy (mostly gasoline fuel) sold at market prices. In the absence of price incentives to conserve energy and to invest, the squandering of Russian electricity and oil continues unabated, greatly aided by obsolete technology. To sustain the current rate of economic growth, by 2015 Russia will have to increase oil production for domestic consumption by 955 million barrels—or reduce exports.[18]

Taxes, Foreign Participation, and Ownership

In addition to encouraging waste by precluding large-scale privatization, price liberalization, and the modernization of domestic energy production, distribution, and consumption, the ideologically driven statist economic policy is an obstacle to "greenfield" investments in the exploration and development of new oil deposits vital to the continuing growth of exports. While stable high prices tend to provide an economic incentive to funding exploration, taxes in Russia today virtually negate this stimulus. In addition to paying export duties and a "mineral resources" tax, Russian oil companies are subject to a 90 percent tax on the profits when the per-barrel price of the oil they export exceeds $25. (Russia's dominant brand, "Urals," which is "heavier" and more "sour" than the top "light sweet" oil because of its higher content of nonhydrocarbons and serum, fetched on the average around $50 per barrel in 2005.)

Furthermore, major foreign oil companies, generally eager to put up money for exploration in exchange for a share of exports, are effectively barred from the largest and therefore most profitable fields. A "Law on the Subsoil" (*Zakon o Nedrakh*), which was introduced in the Duma last year but has not yet been passed, bars companies without Russian majority ownership from fields containing over 1 billion or more barrels of oil deposits.

Once the law is adopted, the largest remaining privately owned Russian oil company, TNK-BP (which is 50 percent owned by British Petroleum) may be forced either to reduce the BP ownership or give up on the development of the largest eastern Siberian fields, the Verkhnechonskoe, which could produce between 29 million and 37 million barrels a year. (TNK-BP owns a majority of shares in the company that holds the field's development license.)

Private Oil Companies: A Brilliant Success

Yet the greatest impediment to maintaining the present level of investment and growth appears to be the gradual change in ownership from private to state-owned or "state-affiliated" oil companies.

There was a time when the editorial pages of elite U.S. newspapers were overflowing with righteous indignation about the privatization of the Soviet oil industry. Together with other "crown jewels" of Soviet industry, oil wealth was said to be taken away from the oh-so-innocent and civic-minded Soviet state and given to the nasty bunch, soon to be known as the "oligarchs," at "knockdown" prices. "Looted" was the cliché of choice to describe the fate of the privatized Soviet oil companies, and David Ignatius of the *Washington Post* and William Safire of the *New York Times* fulminated especially frequently and voluminously against the "looters."[19]

The future "oligarchs" were certainly no choir boys. They were hungry and extremely ambitious men in their early thirties. As in every revolution, the state was weak and new institutions virtually nonexistent. There were no rules to play by, and, on the way to the riches, one bribed the state officials, strong-armed the competition, and rode roughshod over minority shareholders because everyone seemed to be doing it. The privatization was not fair by any measure, even the most lenient ones. (For instance, Mikhail Khodorkovsky's financial group, Menatep, purchased 33 percent of the then state-owned YUKOS at an auction that Menatep itself ran through a front company.)[20]

Yet the real choice at the time was not between ownership by these rough men on the one hand and the abstract "state" or "clean" investors on the other, as imagined by U.S. columnists. The "state," in reality, stood for corrupt, incompetent, and thieving Soviet-era bureaucrats who had run oil production virtually into the ground. (Throughout the 1980s, there was serious talk among the experts about the Soviet Union's, and then Russia's, becoming net importers of oil.) After sixty years during which private entre-preneurship had been a criminal offense, there were simply no "clean" investors with enough money, and foreigners were hardly breaking down the doors to buy Russian state oil companies at a "fair price." Instead, they prudently stayed away from spending hundreds of millions of dollars on assets in a country that was teetering on the brink of Communist restora-tion, with a sullen workforce which had not been paid in months, if not years, no independent courts to enforce contracts, declining output, and aging, often broken-down equipment.

The actual alternatives were the continuing de facto ownership of the oil industry by the bureaucrats or its transfer to the often unsavory but energetic entrepreneurs willing to risk the millions of dollars—in the case of Mikhail Khodorkovsky, the 159 million dollars—that they "loaned" to the state in 1995 in exchange for the shares of major state-owned enter-prises. (By the conditions of the loans-for-shares auctions, in the case of the state's widely expected default, the owners of the collateral could not assume possession until after the 1996 presidential election, which the Communist Party candidate was, at the time, generally expected to win.)

When the Russian privatizers—led by Anatoly Chubais and protected by Boris Yeltsin against the Communist-led "people's patriots" in the Duma—chose the future "oligarchs," critics decried the imminent "strip-ping of the assets." Chubais countered that one does not steal from oneself. He hoped that, instead, the new private owners would try to maximize their personal profit by maximizing production.

Chubais has since proved right beyond any doubt. When Menatep took over YUKOS in 1996, salaries had not been paid for four months, output was declining, and the company was on the verge of bankruptcy. Four years later, YUKOS became the first Russian company to pay dividends to its nearly 60,000 shareholders: the ruble equivalent of $300 million in 2000, $500 million in 2001, and $700 million in 2002.

Between 2000 and 2004, YUKOS doubled oil production.[21] After it reported quarterly financial statements in accordance with U.S. Generally Accepted Accounting Principles (GAAP) in 2001 and had its annual reports audited by PricewaterhouseCoopers one year later, the company's capitalization increased twenty-fold.[22] YUKOS's top executives boasted that in the late 1990s and early 2000s, the company's taxes accounted for 5 percent of the national budget. YUKOS began giving millions of dollars to charity, launched a nationwide Internet education project, and provided stipends for employees' children who were getting good grades in colleges.[23]

YUKOS's brilliant success epitomized the larger story of Russia's privatized oil industry. Between 1999 and 2004, private-sector production grew 47 percent.[24] According to the Russian official statistical agency, Rosstat, of the $41.4 billion in net profits earned between 1999 and 2004, the private oil companies reinvested $36.4 billion—or 88 percent—in exploration, drilling, and modern technology.[25] During the same period, state-owned companies increased production by 14 percent, with the largest, Rosneft, essentially stagnant, its output barely holding its own from year to year.[26]

Nevertheless, last year Rosneft (whose chairman is Putin's deputy chief of staff and confidant, Igor Sechin) went on a shopping spree, buying several private oil companies. Its biggest acquisition was YUKOS's main oil-producing component, Yuganskneftegaz, which was seized by the state for alleged tax evasion and sold at a rigged auction to a front company, which was bought a few days later by Rosneft. (Reportedly, a consortium of Chinese banks gave Rosneft a $6 billion "loan" against future oil deliveries to China.)

In the same year, another star private producer, Sibneft, was bought by Gazprom, the giant natural gas monopoly and by far the most opaque and corrupt of major Russian firms. Gazprom's production has grown at no more than 2–3 percent over the past five years, during which the price of gas has skyrocketed. The natural gas behemoth has not invested in a major "greenfield" development in years. (It is widely believed in Moscow that the fate of YUKOS and Mikhail Khodorkovsky had a lot to do with the willingness of Sibneft's principal owners to sell.)

Thus, some of the most productive assets of the Russian oil industry have been transferred from the most transparent and efficient companies (YUKOS and Sibneft) to the least transparent and efficient: Rosneft and Gazprom. The state's share of oil production increased from less than 10 percent to 30 percent in the last two years. After expanding, on average, 8 percent per year in the previous seven years, the extraction grew by only 2.4 percent in 2005.

Stagnation and High Risks?

Driven by private investment and high prices, the 1999–2004 Russian oil boom greatly profited the country and the world. Yet continuing success is increasingly threatened by the government's economic policy of quasi-nationalization, which amounts to a short-term redistribution of oil wealth and asset control, instead of the crucially needed long-term strategy of creating new riches and new resources.

"The era of quick recovery and success of the Russian oil sector, led by private initiative and openness, is over," concluded Vladimir Milov, a leading independent Russian expert on trends in the energy market. "It has been replaced by a new era of state domination, non-transparency, high risks and stagnation."[27] One cannot but agree with this pessimistic conclusion—certainly as a tendency if not yet the reality "on the ground."

It is this disturbing possibility that ought to have been a key item in the discussion of the Russian contribution to "energy security," which President Vladimir Putin was so keen on making the centerpiece of the G8 summit. Yet precisely because this alarming trend has been a result of the policy set at the very top of the Kremlin administration, such a discussion did not take place in St. Petersburg and is not likely to happen at other meetings of the G8 until after 2009—the year after the Russian presidential election.

21

The United States and Russia: Ideologies, Policies, and Relations 2006

Having reached a level of solidarity not seen since the end of World War II, what looked like a permanent alliance between the United States and Russia began to unravel in the second half of 2003. Why the change? The coincidence with the U.S. invasion of Iraq and the sharp alteration of the Kremlin's domestic political and economic priorities is not accidental. These events signaled the emergence of divergent and increasingly incompatible ideological agendas. In Washington, the tragedy of September 11 transformed the ex-"realists" into "neoconservatives" and produced an activist foreign policy agenda in which democratization is seen as the key means of fighting a global war on terrorism. In Moscow, the ideology of restoration gave rise to a postimperial "pragmatism" in foreign policy, omnivorous and concerned mostly with short-term gains. A collision and Cold War II are unlikely because of some core national security interests (and the corresponding "strategic assets" that each country possesses and the other needs) and because of the seemingly irreversible changes that separate Russian foreign policy goals from their Soviet counterparts. But so long as the regimes' ideologies continue to diverge, U.S.-Russian relations are not likely to improve, and they may well worsen between 2007 and 2009, when new administrations come to the White House and the Kremlin.

Charles de Gaulle famously said that countries have no friends, only interests. He forgot to add: interests as perceived and interpreted by the elites and—in democratic regimes and in cases of long-term and expensive policies—by public opinion.

In turn, perception and interpretation of national interests are determined by the ideology of the regimes—that is, by their leaders' ideas of how their countries should live and what they should strive for. Thus, the relations between one country and another usually reflect the regimes' ideologies. The latter dictate foreign policy goals and shape dealings with other countries, depending on the roles they play in the attainment of these objectives.

Relations between the United States and Russia today are no exception. No cabal, plot, or personal ill will is to blame for the fact that their ties have deteriorated markedly in the past three years and are likely to continue to get worse before they improve. Instead, the current state of affairs is the result of each side's pursuit of its ideologically determined strategic agendas and of its perceptions of the other's reaction to the implementation of these agendas.

The ideology that guides the foreign policy of the Bush administration has been shaped by two interrelated factors, both traceable to the tragedy of September 11, 2001. The first is a preoccupation with Islamic extremism, the risk of another terrorist attack in the United States, and, especially, with the possibility of a transfer of weapons of mass destruction (first and foremost, nuclear) from unstable, anti-American, or fundamentalist states to terrorist organizations.

The other ideological "birthmark" of the Bush White House is its neoconservatism. There is much nonsense in the talk about the supposedly near-Bolshevik orthodoxy of the "neocons," their alleged "philosophy," and the unanimity of their views. Any objective observer would find all of this unrelated to reality. Neoconservatism is, at most, a sensibility, a set of general beliefs, not a coherent doctrine, much less, in James Q. Wilson's words, "a program of action."[1]

Yet to the extent that there are principles of a neoconservative foreign policy, three seem to be central. First, a world in which liberty is triumphant is a world in which America's security is much easier to maintain. A free world is America's best defense. This correlation has been the thrust of nearly every major national security statement by President George W. Bush in the past five years, including, most recently, his commencement address at the United States Military Academy at West Point, where he said, "We have made it clear that the war on terror is an ideological struggle between tyranny and freedom."[2]

Of course, neoconservatives are far from being the first to emphasize the connection between the spread of liberty and U.S. security. The link has always been a major theme of U.S. foreign policy, including Jimmy Carter's human rights crusade and Ronald Reagan's fervent and so effectively expressed belief in the eventual victory of freedom over totalitarian tyranny. This leitmotif's most powerful expression was President John F. Kennedy's 1961 inaugural address, in which he wished to "let every nation know, whether it wishes us well or ill, that we shall pay any price, bear any burden, meet any hardship, support any friend, oppose any foe to assure the survival and success of liberty." But the Bush administration reemphasized the urgency of this goal.

Second, a regime's foreign policy is an extension of its domestic behavior. Hence, the character of the regimes is crucial in determining their place in U.S. foreign policy and their relations with Washington. Following from these principles is the third element of the neoconservative foreign policy: its activism. As far as the Bush White House is concerned, demolished together with the Twin Towers on September 11 was the school of thought called foreign policy "realism," which postulated stability as the overarching goal, and which this White House inherited and initially adopted from the "realists" of George H. W. Bush's administration.[3] The maintenance of the status quo suddenly turned out to be an unacceptable risk. America, which only a month, a week, a day before had rested on the laurels of the victory in the Cold War and seemed so invulnerable, so utterly self-sufficient, suddenly found itself on the hard and cold earth: bleeding, shaken but defiant, and looking for allies—genuine allies, not business partners like Saudi Arabia, where fifteen of the September 11 hijackers originated.

❧

It was then that Russia suddenly burst upon the scene—crisply and competently, as if it had waited for this moment and had done all its "homework." From President Vladimir Putin's call to Bush minutes after the attack in New York (the first expression of condolences by a foreign leader on that day), to the permission by Moscow for overflights of Russian airspace by U.S. and NATO planes on the way to Afghanistan, to Moscow's effective acceptance of U.S. bases in the former Soviet Central Asia, to the sharing of Russia's vast intelligence sources in Afghanistan and the links to the anti-Taliban Northern

Alliance, Moscow acted decisively and generously in every instance, without preconditions or diplomatic horse-trading. Along the way, Russia closed the Lurdes military complex in Cuba, which had been its largest military base and electronic listening post in the Western Hemisphere, and shut down the eavesdropping post and naval base in Cam Rahn Bay, Vietnam.

When the character of political regimes became essential to the conduct of U.S. foreign policy, Russia in the fall of 2001 looked promising: a country with political freedoms, real opposition, and many political parties; freedom of religion; free press; uncensored culture; and a stream of free-market reforms. It was a coincidence of some basic values and, as a result, of some key (although even then far from all) national interests that seemed to have given post-9/11 U.S.-Russian relations the character of a long-term, strategic partnership, perhaps even an alliance.[4] There followed a rapprochement between Moscow and Washington—unprecedented since the end of World War II—which included the first-ever visit of a Russian leader to a U.S. president's home.[5]

⚜

Yet it was precisely this neoconservative focus on the nature of domestic political systems that was to become an issue between Moscow and Washington when Russia began to modify significantly its ideological priorities and, as a result, its international behavior.

Beginning approximately with the second half of 2003, it became clear that the Putin Kremlin was no longer dedicated to the continuation of the strategic "line" of the revolutionary 1990s in politics and economics—albeit in a much-advertised "cleaner," "more civilized," and "socially responsible" fashion. On the contrary, it seemed that the ideology of the regime was increasingly shaped by deep shame for what was now referred to as the "chaos" of the previous decade and, most of all, for the weakening of the Russian state.

In this emergent perspective, the policies of the 1990s were seen not as a consequence of a free and conscious, although far from perfectly implemented, choice of the majority of the Russian people—a choice confirmed by the election of Boris Yeltsin to the presidency of a still-Soviet Russia in June

1991; the April 1993 referendum on economic and social policies; and the results of the June–July 1996 presidential and the December 1999·Duma elections, which removed the choking grip of the leftist "popular patriotic" majority on the Russian parliament. Instead, these and other fateful events were seen as products of a vast plot, in large measure forced on Russia from outside, paid for by super-rich "oligarchs," and implemented by venal (or, at best, shortsighted and weak) political leaders.

The traditional postulates of Russian state philosophy were returning in force: The state is tantamount to society; all that is good for the state is automatically good for the country; and the strengthening of the state means the strengthening of society. (Only two Russian leaders, Alexander II and Boris Yeltsin, understood that the weakening of the Russian state might be beneficial for Russian society in the long run. Peter the Great [1682–1725] and Joseph Stalin [1929–53] epitomized the opposite tendency.)

From this perspective, a state functionary, a bureaucrat (of course, enlightened, intelligent, hardworking, and a model of probity), is a far more effective and consistent agent of progress than a free press (so corrupt, sensationalist, and concerned with profits instead of the good of the country); a voter (so naïve, uneducated, and fickle); an independent judge (such a bribe-taker); or, God forbid, a private entrepreneur.

The Kremlin now saw the radical decentralization of politics and economics undertaken in the 1990s as wrong in principle and harmful to the country's interests. The situation had to be redressed by establishing an unchallenged preponderance of the executive branch over the legislature and the judiciary, bringing television and much of the print media under state control or ownership, restoring Moscow's authority over the formerly self-governing provinces, reclaiming the "commanding heights" of the economy, and returning the "diamonds" in the country's economic crown to their rightful owner: the state.

⟡

The changes in foreign policy have followed logically. As with domestic reforms, the generally pro-Western vector of the previous regime was attributed not to the commonality of interests, the "all-human values" search for "a path to the common European house," or the making for Russia of a place in the "civilized world." All these Gorbachev-Yeltsin desiderata were now perceived solely as a result of the weakness brought about by the collapse of the Soviet Union—an event President Putin declared "a major geopolitical disaster of the twentieth century."[6]

The integration of Russia into the family of Western capitalist democracies was no longer accepted even as a distant goal. Hence, the 1990s efforts to bring Russian domestic and foreign behavior in line with this objective have been discontinued. For instance, where Russia could, it would resurrect and strengthen the former Soviet ties. Those of the newly independent states that assisted this effort would be rewarded. Those that opposed it would be punished.

Of course, this does not amount to the re-creation of Soviet foreign policy. The restoration of a "common political and economic space" on the formerly Soviet territory fits rather well into the imperative of national security of all large continental powers, from ancient Babylon, Persia, China, and Rome to the United States until the 1970s: stability, and friendly (better yet, vassal) states along the borders are to be maintained by all manner of bribery and roguery. Hence, Moscow's support of the Belorussian autocrat Alyaksandr Lukashenka—the equivalent of what U.S. decision-makers used to call (as FDR said of the Nicaraguan dictator Anastasio Somosa in the 1940s) "a son of a bitch but our son of a bitch."

In contrast to that of the Soviet Union, Russia's foreign policy today is pragmatic. It is aimed at creating the greatest possible freedom of action, positioning oneself "above the fray" for a greater advantage. Not to bind oneself with abstract principles ("Western civilization," "democracy," "liberty," "human rights"), but to maneuver. Not to enter "ideological" alliances, but to "work" with other nations bilaterally. Again, very much unlike the USSR, long-term results are far less important than the role in the international process that Russia manages to arrogate for itself today and the dividends that accrue in the process. In Napoleon's words, which Lenin liked to repeat, "*On s'engage et puis on voit!*" ("First, one gets into a fight and then one sees what to do next!") In short, realpolitik.

To follow the fashion for business terminology in the current Russian political parlance, a key instrument of this strategy is asset-leveraging—that is, the most effective (although often risky) deployment of available assets.

The character of the political regimes is unimportant; the comparative advantages are paramount: nuclear technology for civilian use, conventional arms, and, of course, energy resources. Another integral part of Russia's post-2003 behavior in the world is engaging in a diplomatic arbitrage between conflicting actors in international affairs. Again, disregarding the substantive merits of their cases, Moscow seeks to arrogate for itself an indispensable role in conflict resolution, with the goal of gaining maximum international prestige and, where possible, gaining or expanding export markets.

This approach is illustrated by Russia's recent steps in the Middle East. The delivery to Syria of tactical air-defense missiles last year is viewed in Moscow as a means of restoring its influence in the Middle East after the collapse of the Soviet Union. The visit of the leaders of the terrorist organization Hamas to Moscow earlier this year was seen as a step in the same direction—as well as an attempt at diplomatic arbitrage in the hope of obtaining important concessions (for instance, the recognition of Israel's right to exist and a denunciation of terror), and thus achieving the reputation of an indispensable mediator between East and West.

The *locus classicus* of this strategy is Moscow's relations with Tehran. Russia has almost completed the $1 billion construction of the Bushehr nuclear power plant and continues to oppose any sanctions aimed at forcing Iran to halt uranium enrichment, which is a key step toward making a nuclear bomb. Despite insistent requests by Washington, Russia resumed arms sales to Tehran, which were suspended by Yeltsin in the summer of 1995. The most recent arms deal, signed in December 2005, will provide Iran with mobile air defense missile systems, MiG fighter jets, and patrol boats. The estimated size of the transaction is $1 billion, with the delivery to be completed by 2008.

With Russia's gold and hard currency reserves approaching $300 billion, the money, although important, is hardly Moscow's primary objective. Nor, unlike the Soviet Union, is Russia driven by ideological opposition to U.S. "imperialism" or to its closest Middle Eastern ally, Israel. While the Kremlin staunchly defends Iran's right to a "peaceful development of nuclear energy" and resists all "nondiplomatic measures of pressure" on Tehran, on April 25 a Russian rocket launched from a Russian cosmodrome in the Far East carried into orbit an Israeli spy satellite which undoubtedly will "monitor" that very "peaceful" effort by Iran. Instead, Moscow's Iranian policy is an instance of the same overarching purpose: the enhancement of Russia's role in the world. According to a leading Russian expert on Iran, Russia

> has a unique and historic chance to return to the world arena once again as a key player and as a reborn superpower. If Russia firmly stands by Iran in this conflict [with the United States] Russia will immediately regain its lost prestige in the Muslim world and on the global arena at large . . . and no lucrative proposals from the United States can change this situation strategically.[7]

Hence, too, Russia's diplomatic arbitrage between the United States, Britain, France, and Germany, on the one hand, and Iran on the other. For as long as possible, Moscow delays the "moment of truth" when it will have to choose sides, postponing the "sale" of Russia's support in order to bid up the value of its diplomatic assets.

✐

In other times, this policy might have not caused serious complications in relations with the United States. After all, Washington did get used to (although never without irritation) the diplomacy of France, which tried to compensate for the loss of its superpower status after World War II by practicing similar pragmatism and arbitrage in its relations with the opposing sides in the Cold War.

But the times are different—and so are the values. The post-9/11 activist foreign policy of the United States, which perceives the promotion of liberty and democracy as the key strategic means of ensuring America's security, cannot but be increasingly at odds with the Kremlin's postimperial "restoration," the essence of which is political and economic recentralization at home and an omnivorous realpolitik abroad. Even on the territory of the former Soviet Union, where under different circumstances the United States might have been more inclined to indulge Russian interests, Moscow's opposition to democratization and liberalization in the post-Soviet space and its support for some of the region's most repressive governments (Belarus and Uzbekistan) cannot but cause serious friction with the United States. The Kremlin, for its part, tends to view new pro-Western regimes (for instance, in Georgia and Ukraine) as inherently anti-Russian.

As a result of the growing divergence in values, the ships of U.S. and Russian foreign policies began to drift away from each other. That they have not yet moved as far apart as to lose visual contact is due to the anchors of each side's strategic assets that are central to the other's national interests.

For the United States, Russia is crucial to the global war on terrorism, nuclear nonproliferation, the world's energy security, and the containment of a resurgent authoritarian China, which increasingly threatens the interests of the United States and its allies in Southeast Asia.

In Russia's strategic calculations, America is featured, first, as an ally in the struggle against domestic terrorism emanating from North Caucasus. Second, Washington is expected to show an "understanding" of Russia's "special role" (and, therefore, "special interests") in the post-Soviet territory, where 25 million ethnic Russians live outside Russia, and where most of the people and industry are kept warm, lit, and working by Russian oil, gas, and electricity, until recently provided essentially on credit. Third, Moscow hopes for the decisive assistance of the United States in Russia's integration into the world economy.

But perhaps the key American resource, the most desirable thing the United States can give Russia, is esteem and equality. No matter how much America is castigated in the pro-Kremlin or Kremlin-owned newspapers or television channels, no matter what is being said about "Asia" or "Eurasia" as new national destinations, today, as under Lenin, Stalin, Khrushchev, Brezhnev, Gorbachev, and Yeltsin, for the people as well as the elite, a parity with America—be it in strategic nuclear missiles or corn, meat, or steel, democracy or coal, outer space or Olympic medals—and its appreciation of Russia have always been a key legitimizing domestic political factor. When it comes to Russia's national self-respect, no one else—not Europe, nor Asia, nor yet Germany, China, France, or Japan—even comes close.[8]

❧

This list of core mutual interests is hardly new. A novel development is the erosion of the assets' value, no longer sufficiently sustained and renewed by ideological commonality. The anchor chains have started to rust.

From Washington's point of view, in the past year Russia's reputation as a partner in the antiterrorism campaign has been significantly compromised by Moscow's attempt at forging its own position vis-à-vis Hamas; by the sale of air-defense systems to Syria, a terrorism-sponsoring dictatorship; and by the export of fighter jets and helicopters to Sudan, which is on the State Department's list of terrorist states and which practices genocide against its own population.

In nuclear nonproliferation, Russia's assistance in restraining a former Soviet client, North Korea, has proved disappointing. Still more frustrating for the United States was Russia's reluctance to join the opposition to Iran's effort to develop nuclear weapons. It is possible that here Russia has already passed the point of no return, where no amount of hedging could avert serious losses when Moscow is forced to abandon its position.

Unwilling to jeopardize the G8 summit in St. Petersburg, Russia in the end is likely to vote with the United States, Britain, and France for sanctions against Iraq in the UN Security Council, or at least to abstain. Iran is almost certain to respond by formally abandoning the Nuclear Nonproliferation Treaty and thus trigger a set of punitive measures that are likely to target not only civilian nuclear projects, but also cooperation with Tehran in conventional defense, finance, or investment in non–nuclear energy development, such as natural gas.[9] In all these areas, Russia today is invested more deeply than anyone else,[10] and it is hard to imagine a scenario in the unfolding Iranian saga in which Moscow can avoid very considerable long-term damage to its prestige (not to mention its purse).

In energy security, the change of economic policy has resulted in the Kremlin's scuttling the Western Siberia–Murmansk pipeline that would have carried oil from Russia's largest field to its only all-year-round, deepwater port for export to the United States. Erasing the prospect of a significant substitution for oil imports from the Persian Gulf, the Kremlin's action was, in effect, a veto on all private alternatives to the state-owned pipeline monopoly, Transneft, which is notoriously inefficient and corrupt and already incapable of handling the current output, let alone any future growth in Russian oil production.[11]

A few years later, concerns about the reliability and expansion of Russia's energy supplies were heightened by the de facto renationalization of the country's two most modern, transparent, and profitable private companies,

YUKOS and Sibneft. The increase in production fell from an average of 8 percent between 1999 and 2004 to 2 percent in 2005. In the same year, for the first time since 1999, the volume of Russian oil exports fell in absolute terms.

No sooner had Europe gotten over the shock caused by the sudden decrease in the flow of Russian natural gas in January 2005 (when gas exports to Ukraine were interrupted because of the price dispute and the siphoning off of "European" gas by the Ukrainians), when in April the heads of the state-owned Transneft and natural gas monopoly Gazprom threatened Europe with the decrease of Russian energy supplies (and their transfer to the East, mostly China) if the Europeans continued to be less than enthusiastic about Gazprom's efforts to acquire retail assets in the West. A few days later, Vladimir Putin repeated the warning.[12]

Finally, even if one takes with a very large grain of salt the Sino-Russian protestations of friendship, the massive and incessant flow of weapons and defense technology from Moscow to Beijing—the largest buyer of Russian weapons and defense technology—renders illusory any common U.S.-Russian position vis-à-vis China.

✐

A parallel drop in the value of U.S. strategic assets in Russia has been just as steep. Instead of "sensitivity" for Russia's "special interests" in the post-Soviet territory, Moscow saw these "interests" neglected or challenged by antiauthoritarian and anticorruption "color revolutions" (like the one of "roses" in Georgia and the "orange" in Ukraine) which are perceived as aimed against Russia and inspired, if not orchestrated, by Washington. (Permeated by cynicism, so typical of postrevolutionary restorations, be it Charles II in England or Napoleon III in France, the Kremlin leadership seems to have completely forgotten Russia's very recent history and appears incapable of imagining a mass popular protest not engineered and paid for "from outside.") After the lightning-fast acceptance of the former Soviet republics of Estonia, Latvia, and Lithuania into NATO, Moscow interprets the U.S "sponsorship" of future Ukrainian and Georgian memberships[13] as the establishment of NATO's monopoly over Russia's "sphere of influence."

The hopes for support of Moscow's antiterrorist fight have been largely frustrated as well. Instead of offering help—at least moral support or silence—the State Department, U.S. nongovernmental organizations, and mass media continue to expose and criticize human rights violations in Chechnya and refuse (as do most Russians) to see the "Chechnization" of the war as a lasting solution. In addition, following the example of Great Britain, Washington has shown no desire to cooperate with Moscow on the extradition of those whom Russia accuses of assisting Chechen terrorists.

Almost as disappointing for Moscow was the devaluation of Washington's third strategic asset: help with integration into the global economy. On the contrary, America turned out to be perhaps the largest roadblock to Russia's membership in the World Trade Organization (WTO). Among around thirty issues that U.S. businesses want to have resolved before Russia's admission, two are particularly important: enforcement of copyright protection in the entertainment industry and the end of rampant piracy of intellectual property (music, films, and computer programs), which cost U.S. businesses about $2 billion in 2005 alone; and access to Russian retail banking and insurance, including the unlimited ability to open branches in Russia.[14] Here the White House follows rather than leads powerful economic interests, yet the Kremlin, which is by now used to lording it over entrepreneurs, blames Washington for the failure to pacify America's "oligarchs."

The difficulties with the WTO have reopened the old wound of the Jackson-Vanik Amendment. The 1974 legislation denies the normal Most Favored Nation (MFN) trade status to countries with nonmarket economies that restrict their citizens' right to emigrate. Post-Soviet Russia removed all the restrictions on foreign travel and immigration and was found to be in formal compliance with the emigration provision of the amendment in 1994. Even after the effective renationalization of the two largest private oil companies, YUKOS and Sibneft, at least 65 percent of the country's GDP today is generated in the private sector.[15] Still, unlike China, which was granted MFN status in 2000 despite its clear noncompliance with both requirements, the affront to Russian national dignity continues in violation of the letter of America's own laws.

Corroding in and of themselves, all these unfulfilled expectations eat away at the most important American resources: equality and respect for Russia. As a result, there have been calls in Moscow to force the United States into arms control negotiations by accelerating the construction and deployment of the Topol-M (SS-25) multiwarhead intercontinental ballistic missiles. As the current Russian cache of strategic weapons is many times over what is required for effective deterrence, the main objective seems to be making the United States reckon with Russia as an equal. "Of course, no one is planning to attack Russia," one of the advocates of this strategy explained on Russian television last March. "But they also refuse to conduct negotiations with her."[16] Two months later, in his 2006 state of Russia speech to the joint session of the chambers of the Federal Assembly, President Putin endorsed this position.

✐

Built into the ideology of the regimes, the alienation between the United States and Russia will not diminish till at least 2009, when new administrations take over in both countries. Until then, the tension is.likely to increase because of the political calendars in both Moscow and Washington.

In the United States, Russia has been "lost" every four years, as the contenders for the presidency rake the White House incumbents over the coals for the many failures on Russia's road to free-market economy and liberal democracy. This time the cycle will start earlier because of the December 2007 Duma election, in which there are almost certain to be more than enough violations of democratic procedures to justify censure. For his part, Putin's anointed successor for the presidency will have to return fire—in addition to the dose of anti-Americanism initially prescribed for the 2008 campaign by his "political technologists."

Yet the probability of a frontal confrontation and a new Cold War remains very remote for at least three reasons. First, despite the erosion, the countries' geopolitical assets are still very weighty, as the bedrock issues of antiterrorism, nuclear nonproliferation, and energy will continue to force them to seek common ground and at least limited partnership.[17]

Second, the "restorationist" foreign policy notwithstanding, the three basic elements of the 1992–93 national consensus on the foreign policy and defense doctrine remain largely the same. Russia is to stay a *nuclear* superpower and the *regional* superpower, but it seems to have settled for the role of one of the world's great states, rather than a global superpower engaged in a worldwide competition with the United States. While these desiderata will continue to cause occasional sparring with the United States, they are no longer dedicated to the attainment of goals inimical to the vital interests of the United States and are not likely to ignite a relentless antagonistic struggle to the bitter end.

Lastly, despite the muscular rhetoric emanating of late from the Kremlin, unlike the Soviet Union twenty years ago and China today, Russia is not a "revisionist" power. It does not seek radically to reshape the geopolitical "balance of forces" in its favor. Moscow may rail at the score, but it is unlikely to endeavor to change the rules of the game. For that, one needs a different ideology and, as a result, a different set of priorities. Yet even in today's Russia, flush with petrodollars, the share of GDP devoted to defense (around 3 percent) is not only at least ten times smaller than it was in the Soviet Union, but also below the 1992–97 average in a Russia that inherited an empty treasury from the Soviet Union and was, like every revolutionary government, unable to collect taxes. Calculated in purchasing power parity, Russia's defense expenditures in 2005 ($47.77 billion) were less than one-eleventh of what the United States spent ($522 billion).[18]

Changed sharply since 2001, U.S.-Russian relations have followed the trajectories of shifting ideological priorities in Moscow and Washington. Formerly coinciding or running in close parallel, the paths began to diverge or even cross. This state of affairs will continue until one or both sides revise the vision of their nations' interests.

Although a massive confrontation and a descent into a new Cold War are highly unlikely, the situation, in all probability, will get worse. The ships will not collide. But there will be a great deal of tossing, rocking, pitching, and seasickness. Don the lifejackets and stay calm.

Epilogue as Prologue

Here we are, gentle reader, about to part ways in October 2006. It has been fifteen years and slightly over a month since the Glorious Revolution of 1991. Glorious because, mindful of the country's horrifically violent history, the revolution was self-limiting, for the first time in Russian history sacrificing ideology to consensus and free dialogue. Launched amid economic collapse and the chaos of a dying dictatorship and a spent economic system, it did not deteriorate into a bloody anarchy and pogroms. Glorious, most of all, because, having defended their right to be treated as free and thinking people, the Russians never surrendered it to a new tyranny. The essence of the revolution—de-Bolshevization (politics and the legal system); privatization (economy and culture); de-militarization (defense and foreign policy); and the end of the Cold War confrontation with the West—was preserved and shaped by the government's policies in the 1990s.

They became tired, to be sure. Exhausted by a young, poor democracy's cacophony, and longing for the slower and the familiar amid the dizziness of change, they seemed to approve of one giant beast, the Kremlin bureaucracy, as it set out to subdue other roamers of the postrevolutionary jungle, ostensibly to bring order, law, and prosperity.

There is no telling today when the Russians will see that a measure of maddening chaos is a price of freedom; that frightening indeterminacy and constant flux are a consequence of democracy; that no one will relieve them of the burden of responsibility for themselves and their country without exacting too high a price; and that only many beasts—"oligarchs," tycoons, fat cats among them—no matter how ugly and greedy but secure in their liberty and property, almost despite themselves increase the probability of liberty and property for all, as freedom of speech, free newspapers and television, and truly competitive politics cannot exist without large private property owners unafraid of the state.

Mass modern democracy is full of taxing paradoxes. Understanding and accepting them require wisdom and strength. Neither can be borrowed from outside. Both will have to come from within the people themselves. In the meantime, the caravan, which opened this book, has slipped into old ruts and veered into yet another dead-end alley.

So Russia's age-long quest to reconcile the strength of state with the dignity of man will continue. That, after reading this book, one will enjoy this drama is too facile to say. Frustration mixed with occasional amazement and inspiration is more likely. But in suggesting where to look on the enormous stage, this book may have eased the viewing. Most of all, if these pages accomplished what they should have, there ought to be at least some empathy and a sense that, once started, the self-liberation of a great people and a great country cannot be stopped, only interrupted.

Therefore, no epilogues yet. Only prologues.

Bibliographical Note

I am indebted to the American Enterprise Institute, which since 1998 has published my *Russian Outlook* quarterly essay, and to the following magazines for permission to use in this volume the materials they have published:

Commentary ("What *Glasnost* Has Destroyed")

Demokratizatsiya ("In Search of a Historic Yeltsin") Reprinted with permission of the Helen Dwight Reid Educational Foundation, 1319 18th Street, NW, Washington, DC 20036-1802

Harper's Magazine ("Restauration") Copyright © by Harper's Magazine. All rights reserved. Reproduced by special permission.

The National Interest ("A Private Hero for a Privatized Nation")

The Weekly Standard ("Poor Democracies")

World Affairs ("Two Requiems for *Perestroika*")

Notes

Preface

1. As quoted in Frank Kermode, "Lives of Dr. Johnson," *New York Review of Books*, June 22, 2006, 31.

2. As quoted in Bernard Bailyn, *The Ideological Origins of the American Revolution* (Harvard/Belknap: Cambridge, 1992), x.

3. G. M. Trevelyan, *Garibaldi and the Making of Italy* (London: Longmans, 1911), 297.

Chapter 1: What *Glasnost* Has Destroyed

1. *Moscow News*, "Fighting Stalinism," September 11, 1988, 3.

2. *Pravda*, "Otevety istorika" [Answers of a Historian], July 26, 1988, 3.

3. A. Chernyak, "Edoki po statistike I v zhizni" [Food Consumers in Statistics and in Real Life], *Pravda*, September 1, 1988, 3.

4. Yu. Rytov, "Kak zhivyotsya pensioneru" [How the Pensioner Fares], *Izvestiya*, August 20, 1988, 1 and Yu. Rytov, "Na choym derzhitsya defitsit" [What Sustains the Scarcity], original copy in author's possession.

5. Ibid.

6. *Izvestiya*, "Nuzhna Pomoshch" [Help Is Needed], September 21, 1988, 6.

7. As this was the only question about the United States's position vis-à-vis the Soviet crisis, Yeltsin's response should play prominently back home. Chernyak, "Edoki po statistike I v zhizni."

8. Alexander Bekker, "Where's the Beef?" *Moscow News*, July 17–24, 1988, 13.

9. Zoriy Balayan, "Kogda bolezn' obgonyaet lekarstva" [When Disease is Faster than Medicines], interview with Minister of Health Care of the Soviet Union Yevgeniy Chazov, *Literaturnaya gazeta*, February 3, 1988, 11.

10. A. S. Zaychenko, "SSha-SSSR: lichnoe potreblenie" [USA-USSR: Personal Consumption], *SShA: Ekonimika, politika, ideologiya*, no. 12 (1988): 15.

11. As of 1989, the Soviet Union reports only eighty AIDS cases and only one acknowledged death from AIDS. But there is a potential here for an immense catastrophe. A country the size of the Soviet Union needs at least a billion disposable syringes a year. The plan for 1988 was 100 million; the actual production, 4.5 mil-

lion. The shortage is so severe that it is a common practice to use the same needle to draw blood from several patients. Often, sterilization procedures are observed imperfectly or ignored altogether. As a result, 3.8 percent of the Soviet population—over ten million people—suffer from hepatitis B, the disease that is transmitted exactly the same way as AIDS.

12. A song in the required repertoire of the Soviet grade school contains the stanza:
Our golden childhood
Grows brighter every day.
Under a lucky star,
We live in the motherland.

13. G.A. Yagodin, Chairman of the USSR State Committee on Education, speech at the XIX All-Union party Conference, *Pravda*, June 30, 1988, 9.

14. O. Drunina, "K chemu privodit bezdushie" [What Heartlessness Has Caused], *Trud*, January 19, 1988, 2.

15. Ibid.

16. Evgeny Chazov (USSR minister of health), speech at the Nineteenth All-Union CPSU Conference, reported in *Pravda*, June 30, 1988, 4. See also Mark D'Anastasio, "Soviet Health System, Despite Early Claims, Is Riddled by Failures," *Wall Street Journal*, August 18, 1987, 1.

17. *Pravda*, "Rebionok bez prismotra?" [Anybody Minding the Child?] (interview with V. I. Kulakov, director of All-Union Mother and Child Scientific Research Center), August 10, 1987, 4.

18. *Literaturnaya Gazeta*, October 5, 1988, 6.

19. S. Polevoy, "Bez prizora" [Without Supervision], *Pravda*, October 8, 1988, 6; Yu. Shekochikhin "Lev prygnul!" [The Lion Has Jumped!], *Literaturnaya Gazeta*, July 20, 1988, 13.

20. V. Yaroshenko, "Printsy i nishchie" [Princes and Paupers], *Pravda*, October 12, 1988, 2.

21. Vladimir Omlinskiy, "Ten" [Shadow], *Literaturnaya Gazeta*, September 7, 1988, 12.

22. A. Novikov, "U poroga voyny" [At the Threshold of the War], *Komsomol'skaya Pravda*, August 24, 1988, 3.

23. Ibid. See also Mikhail Simiryaga, "23 avgusta 1939 goda [August 23, 1939], *Literaturnaya gazeta*, October 5, 1988, 14.

24. Ibid.

25. *Literaturnaya Gazeta*, "Istoria i literatura" [History and Literature], May 18, 1988, 2.

26. *Literaturnaya Gazeta*, August 24, 1988, 5

27. *Literaturnaya Gazeta*, "Kto vinovat?" [Who Is to Blame?], March 8, 1988, 2.

28. Aleksandr Tsipko, "Istoki Stalinisma" [The Sources of Stalinism], part 4, *Nauka i Zhizn'*, no. 2 (February 1989): 53–61.

29. Vasily Seliunin, "Istoki," *Novy Myr*, May 1988, 162–89.

30. *Pravda*, October 5, 1988, 4.

31. Andranik Migranyan, "Dolgiy put' k evropeyskomu domu" [A Long Road to the European Home], *Novy Myr*, July 1989, 184.

32. M. Gorky, "Nesvoevremennye mysly" [Untimely Thoughts], *Literaturnoe Obozrenie*, no. 9 (1988): 103, and no. 10 (1988): 106.

33. V. I. Lenin, "The Tasks of the Youth Leagues," speech at the Third All-Russian Congress of the Komsomol, October 2, 1920, in *Collected Works*, v. 41 (Moscow: Politizdat, 1963): 309, 313.

34. Vladimir Lakshin, "Nravstvennost', spravedlivost', gumanism" [Ethics, Justice, Humanism], *Kommunist* 10 (July 1989): 41

35. Vasily Grossman, *Vsyo techyot* [Forever Flowing], *Oktyabr'* 6 (June 1989): 73, 105.

36. *Sovetskaia Molodezh*, "Sdelka" [The Deal], July 7, 1989, 3.

37 *Izvesitiya*, "Kakoy idee my sluzhim?" [What Idea Do We Serve?], August 23, 1989, 3.

38. *Pravda*, August 26, 1988, 3.

Chapter 2: Moscow Diary: January 12–17, 1991

1. *Le Figaro*, "Le Seul Espoir: Boris Eltsin" [The Only Hope: Boris Yeltsin], January 18, 1991, 21.

2. Yeltsin is referring to a statement signed on January 13 in Tallinn by the four presidents: Anatoly Gorbunovs of Latvia, Boris Yeltsin of Russia, Vitautas Landsbergis of Lithuania, and Anatoly Ruutel of Estonia.

3. Most likely, Yeltsin had in mind defense, foreign relations, and finance.

4. Yeltsin means the three Baltic republics plus Georgia and Armenia.

5. Yeltsin used the word "rayteeng," which, together with "spohnsohr" and "rehgeeohn" ("region"), are the most frequently encountered linguistic manifestations of a new détente and *perestroika*.

6. Of the fifteen republics of the Soviet Union, only Belorussia and Ukraine are, formally, members of the United Nations.

7. I was wrong. As far as I could establish, the Moscow bureaus of the three U.S. television networks ignored the press conference. The *New York Times* at least mentioned it and quoted Yeltsin's comment on Gorbachev's turn to the "iron hand" solution. The *Washington Post* printed not a word of or about it. The most popular Soviet daily, *Izvestiya*, published a detailed account in the center of page two.

8. The next day, a member of the Estonian parliament, Mikk Titma, told his colleagues, "If Yeltsin had not supported Estonia, I am not sure we would be meeting here today"; quoted in *Izvestiya*, January 15, 1991, 2.

Chapter 3: Two Requiems for *Perestroika*

1. John Reed, *Ten Days That Shook the World* (New York: Boni and Liveright, 1919). The author, a founding member of the Communist Party of the USA,

provided one of the first eyewitness accounts of the October Revolution, to the original of which Lenin wrote the introduction. Reed died in Moscow and became the only American buried in the Kremlin Wall.

2. Yakovlev's August 20, 1990, television address announcing the presidential decrees "on the restoration of rights of all those repressed in the years 1920–30–40–50" is among the most moving documents of *perestroika*. One is reminded of the cadences of Lincoln's Gettysburg address (which Yakovlev, undoubtedly, had read): "It is not they [political prisoners] whom we forgive, it is ourselves. We are guilty because they lived, for years, oppressed and maligned. It is we who are being rehabilitated, not those who thought differently, had different ideas, different convictions." And on the Soviet regime: "History has not known so concentrated a hatred toward the human being."

3. Ryzhkov, *Perestroika*, 33, 94.

4. Yakovlev, *Muki*, 343.

5. Ryzhkov, *Perestroika*, 236.

6. Yakovlev, *Muki*, 100.

7. Ryzhkov, *Perestroika*, 166.

8. Yakovlev, *Muki*, 42.

9. Ibid., 337.

Chapter 4: The Strange Case of Russian Capitalism

1. Igor Kliamkin, *Polis*, no. 4 (1994), 62.

2. The estimates of the share of GDP consumed by the Soviet military-industrial complex varied from 15 percent to 30 percent and could be conservatively assumed to be at least 20 percent. Counting family members, between one-quarter and one-third of the Russian population was connected with the defense establishment.

3. *RFE/RL Newsline* [daily publication of Radio Free Europe/Radio Liberty], February 6, 1998.

4. *RFE/RL Newsline*, September 25, 1997.

5. Joseph R. Blasi, Maya Kroumova, and Douglas Kruse, *Kremlin Capitalism* (Ithaca, N.Y.: Cornell University Press, 1997), 190, table 2.

6. Of course, far from being confined to Russia, the simultaneity of the introduction of modern capitalism and democracy is an increasingly general phenomenon. See chapter 14, "Poor Democracy."

7. Thomas Babington Macaulay, *The History of England* (New York: Penguin Books, 1986), 51.

8. Of the political and economic elites in Poland, Hungary, and Russia in 1988, one-third remained in the same positions in 1993; John Higley, Judith Kullberg, and Jan Pakulski, "The Persistence of Post-Communist Elites," *Journal of Democracy* 7,

no. 2 (1996): 133–47. The political comeback of the *nomenklatura* was formalized in parliamentary and presidential elections in Poland (in 1993 and 1995) and in parliamentary elections in Hungary (1994) and Russia (1995).

9. Blasi, Kroumova, and Kruse, *Kremlin Capitalism,* 148.

10. Maxim Boycko, Andrei Shleifer, and Robert Vishny, *Privatizing Russia* (Cambridge: MIT Press, 1995), 11, 65.

11. Blasi, Kroumova, and Kruse, *Kremlin Capitalism,* 179.

12. Ibid.

13. According to the first deputy prime minister at the time, Oleg Soskovets, 35 percent of all Russian enterprises were "technically bankrupt in June 1996"; ibid., 178.

14. *PlanEcon Report,* "Russian Economic Monitor," December 31, 1997, 10. Economist Igor Birman contended that, seeking to lower their taxes, employees of many "commercial organizations" report salaries two and a half to three and a half times lower than they actually are. The Russian state statistical administration (Goskomstat) estimated that hidden salaries account for 20–25 percent of the total; Anatoly Druzenko, "Na Rusi zhyvetsya luchshe, chem schitaetsya" [Life in Russia Is Better than Given Credit For] (interview with Igor Birman), *Izvestiya,* December 4, 1997, 2.

15. Steve Liesman, "Surprise: The Economy in Russia Is Clawing Out of Deep Recession," *Wall Street Journal,* January 28, 1998, 11.

16. Between 1992 and 1996, Anatoly Chubais directed the largest privatization effort in history, comprising 77 percent of mid-sized and large enterprises and 82 percent of small shops and retail stores. Russian entrepreneurs started nine hundred thousand new businesses. Virtually nonexistent until 1991, by the end of 1997 the private sector of the Russian economy accounted for around 70 percent of the GDP; Blasi, Kroumova, and Kruse, *Kremlin Capitalism,* 26, and Stanley Fischer, *The Russian Economy at the Start of 1998* (Cambridge: John F. Kennedy School of Government, Harvard University, 1998), 2.

17. Yegor Gaidar, *The Days of Defeats and Victories* (Moscow: Vagrius, 1997), 365.

18. *Novoye vremia,* no. 48 (1996), 7.

Chapter 5: Russia's New Foreign Policy

1. For more on the legal challenges to the draft, see chapter 7, "From State-Owned Justice to a Law-Based State."

2. For further developments between Russia and Chechnya, see chapter 17, "Chechnya: New Dimensions of an Old Crisis."

3. Boris Yeltsin, "Teleobrashchenie Prezidenta RF Boris El'tsina" [Televised Address by the Russian Federation's President Boris Yeltsin], *Natsional'naya Sluzhba Novostei,* June 12, 1997, 2, http://www.nns.ru/chronicle/obr1206.html (accessed June 13, 1996).

4. *OMRI* [Open Media Research Institute] *Daily*, October 5, 1993.

5. Ibid.

6. Robert Seely, "Ex-Soviet Nations Give Support," *Washington Post*, October 5, 1993.

7. Ibid.

8. "Dogovor o druzhbe, sotrudnichestve i partnyorstve mezhdu Rossiyskoy Federatsiey i Ukrainoy" (Treaty of Friendship, Cooperation, and Partnership between the Russian Federation and Ukraine), Natsional'naya sluzhba novostey, June 2, 1997, http://www.nns.ru.

Chapter 6: Land Privatization: The End of the Beginning

1. Richard Pipes, *The Russian Revolution* (New York: Alfred A. Knopf, 1990), 494.

2. Alexander Yakovlev, *Omut pamyati* [The Maelstrom of Memory] (Moscow: Vagrius, 2001), 396.

3. A. Sizov, "Sverim tsifry" [Let's Compare the Numbers], *Kommunist* 15 (October 1989): 63.

4. Stephen K. Wergen and Vladimir Belen'kiy, "The Political Economy of the Russian Land Market," *Problems of Post-Communism* 45, no. 4 (July–August 1998): 59.

5. Vasily Uzun, "Agrarian Reform in Russia in the 1990s: Objectives, Mechanisms, and Problems," in *Russian Views of the Transition in the Rural Sector*, ed. L. Alexander Norsworthy (Washington: World Bank, 2000), 34.

6. Ibid.

7. Ibid., and Wergen and Belen'kiy, "Political Economy," 65.

8. Andrei Lazareveskiy, "Nes'edobniy buterbrod" [The Inedible Sandwich], *Ekspert* 15 (April 16, 2001), http://www.expert.ru/economy/2001/04/15ex-zemlya/.

9. Zvi Lerman and Karen Brooks, "Russia's Legal Framework for Land Reform and Farm Restructuring," *Problems of Post-Communism* 43, no. 6 (November–December, 1996): 58.

10. *Rossiyskaya Gazeta,* "Boris Yeltsin: Zemlya dolzhna postepenno perekhodit' v ruki nastoyashchih khozyaev" [Boris Yeltsin: Land Must Gradually Pass Into the Hands of the Genuine Owners], September 20, 1997, 1.

11. *RFE/RL Newsline,* "Yeltsin Criticizes Duma's Stance," September 30, 1997.

12. Bronwyn McLaren, "Russia Holds First Sale of Private Land," *Moscow Times*, March 6, 1998, 2.

13. "Grazhdanskiy Kodeks Rossiyskoy Federatsii, Glava 17: Pravo Sobstvennosti i Drugie Veshchnye Prava na Zemlyu" [The Civil Code of the Russian Federation, Chapter 17: The Right of Land Ownership and Other Real Estate Rights on Land], in Pavel Krasheninnikov, *Pravo Sobstvennosti i Inye Veshchnye Prava na Zemlyu. Vvodnyi Commentariy k Glave 17 Grazhdanskogo Kodeksa RF* [The Right of Ownership

and Other Real Estate Rights. An Introduction to Chapter 17 of the Civil Code of the Russian Federation] (Moscow: Statut, 2001), 10.

14. Yegor Chegrinetz, "Land and the Law: Chapter 17 of the Statute Book," *Russian Property Online,* May 3, 2001, www.rupron.com/static (accessed June 20, 2001).

15. Pavel Krasheninnikov, interview with the author, Moscow, May 31, 2001.

16. Chegrinetz, "Land and the Law."

17. Krasheninnikov, *Pravo sobstvennosti,* 4.

18. Ibid., 9.

19. Two months later, in the second and third (final) reading, the legislation was passed by the lower house with solid majorities of 254 to 121 and 252 to 123, respectively.

20. *Washington Post,* "Putin Backs Russian Land Reform," January 31, 2001, A16.

21. Vladimir Putin, "President Putin's Address to the Federal Assembly," Federal News Service, April 3, 2001, 7.

22. Fond Obschestvennoye Mneniye (FOM, Foundation for Public Opinion), "Svobodnaya kuplya-prodazha: za i protiv" [Freedom of Buying and Selling: For and Against] and "Vopros o zemle" [The Land Question], Moscow, March 29, 2001, www.fom.ru (accessed April 10, 2001). In the eighteen- to thirty-five-year-old group, 63 percent were for buying and selling land with or without restrictions, while 28 percent supported the ban on all such transactions. For those older than fifty, the corresponding figures were almost exactly the opposite: 32 percent and 59 percent. Of college graduates, 68 percent approved of buying and selling, and 27 percent were for the ban. Among those with less than high school education, the respective numbers were 24 percent and 66 percent.

23. *ITAR-TASS,* "Russia: Official Says Land Use Decisions May Be Given to Regions," January 30, 2001, wnc.fedworld.gov/cgi-bin (accessed April 11, 2001).

24. Putin, "Address," 8.

25. Peter Baker, "Critic's Voice Adds Clout to Putin's Reform Plans," *Washington Post,* May 10, 2001, A27.

26. Krasheninnikov, interview with the author.

27. Anatoly Epshtein, "Good and Bad in the New Code," *Russian Property Online,* June 6, 2001, www.rupron.com/static (accessed June 20, 2001).

28. Nikolay Vladimirov, "Vyrashchivayte krokodilov!" [Raise Crocodiles!] *Moskovskie Novosti,* February 13–19, 2001, 11.

29. Vyacheslav Nikonov and Viktoria Abramenko, "Land and Freedom We Have Checked, Russia Does Have Money!" *Trud,* March 2, 2001, 2.

30. Krasheninnikov, interview with the author.

31. See, for example, Valeriy Konovalov, "Zemlya neulovimaya" [The Elusive Land], *Izvestiya,* February 22, 2001, 6. The article reveals the existence of an illegal land market in the black-soil Stavropol region.

32. Yevgenia Borisova, "Kremlin's Land Code Goes before Duma," *St. Petersburg Times,* June 15, 2001.

33. Anna Raff, "Kasyanov Promises a 'Different Country,'" *Moscow Times,* April 27, 2001.

34. Borisova, "Kremlin's Land Code."

35. Ivan Rodin, "Duma Oboshlas' bez Kommunistov" [The Duma Managed without the Communists], *Nezvisimaya Gazeta,* June 16, 2001, www.ng.ru/printed/politics (accessed June 18, 2001).

36. Ibid.

37. Yevgeniya Borisova, "Putin Asks Council for Hand with Land Code," *Moscow Times,* January 31, 2001.

38. *RFE/RL Newsline,* May 10, 2001, 2.

39. Gennady Zyuganov, interview with the Ekho Moskvy radio station on May 23, 2001, Federal News Service transcript.

40. *RFE/RL Newsline,* June 7, 2001, 3.

41. Ibid.

42. NTV International, "Russian Communists in the Last-Ditch Attempt to Keep Land Sales Off Agenda," *BBC Worldwide Monitoring,* June 15, 2001.

43. Agence France-Presse, "Red Flags Fly As Russian Deputies Discuss Land Bill," June 15, 2001 (accessed June 18, 2001).

44. *Chattanooga Times,* "Fists Fly as Russian Lawmakers Approve Limited Sales of Land," June 16, 2001, A3.

45. Robyn Dixon, "Capitalist Heads Prevail in Russia," *Los Angeles Times,* June 16, 2001, A3.

46. Raff, "Kasyanov Promises."

47. RIA Oreanda, "Mikhail Kasyanov Thanked Deputies for Giving First Reading to Land Code," June 16, 2001.

48. In January 2003, the Duma adopted the federal law "On Agricultural Land Transactions," finally allowing buying and selling of agricultural land.

Chapter 7: From State-Owned Justice to a Law-Based State

1. Peter H. Solomon Jr. and Todd S. Foglesong, *Courts and Transition in Russia* (Boulder: Westview Press, 2000), 7.

2. Ibid.

3. Ibid.

4. Peter H. Solomon Jr. and Todd S. Foglesong, "The Procuracy and the Courts in Russia: A New Relationship?" *East European Constitutional Review* 9, no. 4 (Fall 2000): 106, www.law.nyu.edu/eecr/vol9num4/features/nikitinarticle5.html (accessed November 21, 2006).

5. Peter H. Solomon, "Law and Courts in Post-Soviet Russia," paper presented December 3, 1999, at the Paul H. Nitze School of Advanced International Studies, Johns Hopkins University, Washington, D.C., 2.

6. Solomon and Foglesong, *Courts and Transition*, 32.

7. Ibid., 36.

8. Ibid., 16–18.

9. Ibid., 71.

10. Ilian G. Cashu and Mitchell A. Orenstein, "The Pensioners' Court Campaign: Making Law Matter in Russia," *East European Constitutional Review* 10, no. 4 (Fall 2001): 70, http://www.law.nyu.edu/eecr/vol10num4/special/cashuorenstein.html (accessed November 16, 2006).

11. Solomon and Foglesong, *Courts and Transition*, 69.

12. Ibid., 68.

13. Ibid., 69.

14. Cashu and Orenstein, "The Pensioners' Court Campaign," 69.

15. Ibid.

16. Ibid., 70.

17. Reuters, "Jehovah Witnesses Registered under New Law," May 7, 1999.

18. *Washington Post*, "Russian Court Rejects Pentacostalist Ban," May 29, 1999, A20.

19. Scott P. Boylan, "The Status of Judicial Reform in Russia," *American University International Law Review* 13, no. 5 (1998): 1327–44.

20. Peter H. Solomon, "The Persistence of Judicial Reform in Contemporary Russia," *East European Constitutional Review* 6, no. 4 (Fall 1997): 55.

21. Daniel Williams, "Where 'State Interests' Rule," *Washington Post*, June 29, 2000, A20. For more on draft evasion, see chapter 18, "The Battle over the Draft."

22. Ekaterina Larina, "Alternatively Speaking," *Russia Journal*, February 25, 2002, 3. The law was adopted in July of 2002 and is still in place.

23. Elena Barikhnovskaya, "How the Constitutional Court Is Reforming Criminal Procedure: The Nikitin Case," *East European Constitutional Review* 9, no. 4 (Fall 2000): 99.

24. Solomon and Foglesong, *Courts and Transition*, 150.

25. Damian S. Schaible, "Life in Russia's 'Closed City': Moscow's Movement Restrictions and the Rule of Law," *New York University Law Review* 76, no. 16 (2001): 344–46.

26. "Postanovlenie Konstitutsionnogo Suda Rossiyskoy Federatsii 13 Dekabrya 2001 goda" [Decision of the Constitutional Court of the Russian Federation, December 13, 2001], ks.rfnet.ru (the official website of the Russian Constitutional Court). The author is grateful to Judge Stephen F. Williams of the U.S. Court of Appeals, D.C. Circuit, for drawing attention to the case.

27. Ibid.

28. Viktor Tereshkin, "The Nikitin Case through the Eyes of the Acquitting Judge," *East European Constitutional Review* 9, no. 4 (Fall 2000): 92.

29. Barikhnovskaya, "How the Constitutional Court," 100.

334 NOTES TO PAGES 99–102

30. Mikhail Matinov and Yuri Schmidt, "The Nikitin Case and Russia's Legislative and Social Reforms," *East European Constitutional Review* 9, no. 4 (Fall 2000): 97. The authors were the defense attorneys.

31. Ibid.

32. Tereshkin, "The Nikitin Case," 92.

33. Ibid., 93.

34. "O Vnesenii Dopolneniya i Izemeneniy v Federal'nyi Konstitutsionnyi Zakon 'O Sudebnoy Sisteme Rossiiskoy Federatsii'" [On an Amendment and Changes in the Federal Constitutional Law "On The Judicial System of The Russian Federation"], December 17, 2001; "O Vnesenii Izmeneniy i Dopolneniy v Zakon Rossiyskoy Federatsii 'O Statuse Sudey v Rossiyskoy Federatsii'" [On Changing and Amending the Law of the Russian Federation "On the Status of Judges in the Russian Federation"], December 15, 2002; "O Vnesenii Izmeneniy i Dopolneniy v Federal'nyi Konstitutsionnyi Zakon 'O Konstitutsionnom Sude Rossiyskoy Federatsii'" [On Changing and Augmenting the Federal Constitutional Law "On the Constitutional Court of the Russian Federation"], December 17, 2001; "O Vvedenii v Deystvie Ugolovno-Protsesual'nogo Kodeksa Rossiyskoy Federatsii" [On Implementing the Criminal Procedural Code of the Russian Federation], December 22, 2001, www.adki.ru (accessed February 22, 2002).

35. "Ugolovno-Protsessual'nyi Kodeks Rossiyskoy Federatsii" [The Criminal Procedural Code of the Russian Federation], article 29, www.akdi.ru/gd/proekt (accessed February 22, 2002).

36. Ibid., article 94.

37. "Federal'nyi Zakon of Vvedenii v Deystvie Ugolovno-Protsessual'nogo Kodeksa Rossiyskoy Federatsii" [The Federal Law on the Bringing into Force the Criminal Procedural Code of the Russian Federation], article 14, section 3, December 22, 2001, www.akdi.ru/gd/proekt (accessed February 1, 2002).

38. Dmitry Kozak, "Remarks by Deputy Chief of Presidential Staff Dmitry Kozak at a Luncheon of the American Chamber of Commerce in Russia," Federal News Service, 7.

39. Anna Bondarenko, "Legal Revolution," www.therussianissues.com (accessed March 15, 2002). The newspapers quoted in the article are *Kommersant, Vremya Novostei,* and *Izvestiya.*

40. "Ugolovno," article 109.

41. Ibid., article 237.

42. Ibid., articles 314 and 316.

43. Ibid., article 106.

44. Ibid., articles 30 and 31.

45. By the end of 2003, jury trials were adopted in eighty-three regions, and in five more regions during 2004. The Republic of Chechnya is the only region where the introduction of juries has been delayed until at least January 1, 2007; Kristi O'Malley, "Not Guilty Until the Supreme Court Finds You Guilty: A Reflection on

Jury Trials in Russia," *Demokratizatsiya*, Winter 2006, www.findarticles.com/p/
articles/mi_qa3996/is_200601/ai_n16537202 (accessed November 16, 2006).

46. "Ugolovno," article 14.

47. Ibid.

48. Ibid., article 15.

49. Ibid.

50. Kozak, "Remarks," 4.

51. "Ugolovno," article 246.

52. Ibid., articles 53 and 86.

53. Ibid., article 49.

54. Ibid., article 165.

55. Ibid., article 75.

56. "Federal'nyi Konstitutsionnyi Zakon, O Vnesenii Izmeneniy i Dopolneniy v
Federal'nyi Konstitutsionniy Zakon 'O Konstitutsionnom Dude Rossiyskoy Federatsii'" [The Federal Constitutional Law, On the Introduction of Changes and Amendments to the Federal Constitutional Law "On the Constitutional Court of the Russian
Federation"], December 17, 2001, akdi.ru/gd/proekt (accessed January 30, 2002).

57. For more on the Sutyagin case, see chapter 16, "Institutions, Restoration, and
Revolution."

58. Thomas Jefferson to Edmund Randolph, August 18, 1779, *The Portable Thomas
Jefferson*, ed. Merrill D. Peterson (New York: Penguin, 1977), 480. As quoted in
Schaible, "Life in Russia," 369n.147.

Chapter 8: In Search of a Russian Middle Class

1. See, for example, *Moskovskie Novosti*, "Professionaly Ekstra-Klassa Diktuyut
Usloviya" [Top Professionals Dictate Their Conditions], April 9–16, 1996, 4; and L.
Belyaeva, "'Novye srednie' v Rossii," *Svobodnaya Mysl'* 7, no. 1476 (July 1998): 34–45.

2. *Pravda*, "Semeyniy buydjet: Dokhody i raskhody" [Family Budget: Income
and Expenses], May 19, 1989.

3. Goskomstat, "Distribution of Population by Average Per Capita Money Income.
January to September 1998 and 1999," www.gks.ru.

4. Alexey Savin, "Dokhody srednego klassa rastut" [The Income of the Middle
Class Is Growing], *Izvestiya*, May 12, 1999, 6; and Paul Starobin and Olga
Kravchenko, "Russia's Middle Class," *Business Week*, October 16, 2000, 79.

5. Starobin and Kravchenko, "Russia's Middle Class," 79.

6. Professionals constitute 22 percent of Moscow's population, as compared
with 9 percent nationwide. U.S. Information Agency, Office of Research and Media
Reaction, *Russia's Would-Be Middle Class* (Washington, D.C.: Government Printing
Office, January 1998), 2.

7. *RFE/RL Newsline*, "Russia's Middle Class Growing," November 2, 2000.

8. Between January and August 1999, and the same period of 2000, the real (that is, inflation-adjusted) average monthly wage in Russia increased by 50 percent to 2,099 rubles, or $76. Goskomstat, "Nominal and Real Average Monthly Wages," www.gks.ru.

9. According to the distribution of "official" (declared) incomes put out by the federal statistical agency, the Goskomstat, in September 1999 those with incomes between one and two-tenths and two times the cost of living comprised 29 percent of the population. The estimate has been revised upward to account for the 12 percent increase in the average "official" income after September 1999; Goskomstat, "Distribution of Population by Average Per Capita Money Income."

10. Goskomstat, "Main Socioeconomic Indicators of the Living Standard of the Population," www.gks.ru.

11. For more on the stunning changes in Russian gastronomy, see chapter 11, "Restauration."

12. *Expert Magazine* and COMCON Research Company, "Stil' zhizni srednego klassa" [The Lifestyle of the Middle Class], October 2000, http://www.comcon-2.com/ (accessed November 1, 2000).

13. Andrew Jack, "Russia's Desktop Revolution," *Financial Times,* March 7, 2000, 10.

14. Andrew Jack, "Mobile License Deal Stuns Moscow," FT.com, May 30, 2000.

15. Reuters, "Screens Blank, So Russians Turn to Cable TV," August 31, 2000.

16. Steve Liesman, "Surprise: The Economy in Russia Is Clawing Out of Deep Recession," *Wall Street Journal,* January 28, 1998, 11.

17. Erlen Berenshteyn, "Sredniy klass gotovit ekonomicheskiy rost" [The Middle Class Is Forging Economic Growth], *Novoe vremya* 5 (February 1998): 19.

18. Gregory Feifer, "People's Carmaker Evolves," *Moscow Times,* May 30, 2000.

19. *RFE/RL Newsline,* "More and More Cars Clogging Moscow Roads," October 25, 2000.

20. Starobin and Kravchenko, "Russia's Middle Class," 85.

21. John Varoli, "A Little Levitttown on the Neva," *New York Times,* July 13, 2000, D1, D8.

22. Lee Hockstader, "The Russian Invasion," *Washington Post,* August 15, 1994, A12.

23. *Washington Post,* "Travel Fever," August 2, 1997, A14.

24. *New York Times,* "Round and Round They Go. And Where They Stop and Shop," April 12, 1998, 5.

25. Larisa Piyasheva and Igor Birman (economists), "My zhivyom luchshe, chem schitaetsya, no khuzhe, chem khotim" [We Live Better than Is Assumed but Worse than How We Want to Live], interview by Anna Ostapchuk and Evgeniy Krasnikov, *Moskovskie Novosti,* December 14, 1997, 18; and Anatoly Chubais (former first deputy prime minister), "Soyuz pravykh—zavtrashnyaya vlast" [A Union of the

Right Is Tomorrow's Power], interview by *Novoe vremya* 49 (December 1999): 13. See also chapter 4, "The Strange Case of Russian Capitalism."

26. Ekaterina Terpigoreva, "Nevziraya na vizy" [Visas Notwithstanding], *Novoe vremya* 30 (July 2000).

27. Chubais, "Soyuz pravykh," 13.

28. *Katalog knig* [Book List] (Moscow: Presstorg, 2000).

29. Anatoliy Golubobskiy, "Zapovednik" [A Preserve], *Itogi,* April 21, 1998, 38.

30. Robert Brustein, "Moscow Nights," *New Republic,* October 16, 2000, 42–43.

31. *Vash Dosug* [Your Leisure], October 19–26, 2000, 9–21.

32. *Expert Magazine* and COMCON Research Company, "Lifestyle of the Middle Class."

33. Belyaeva, "'Novye srednie' v Rossii," 35.

34. U.S. Information Agency, Office of Research and Media Reaction, *Russia's Would-Be Middle Class,* 11.

35. Anatoly Novikov, "Ya, melkiy lavochnik" [I, a Small Store Owner], *Moskovskie novosti,* March 31–April 7, 1996, 40.

36. Celestine Bohlen, "Small Entrepreneurs Tired of Russian Politicians," *New York Times,* December 16, 1999, A3.

37. Ibid.

38. Starobin and Kravchenko, "Russia's Middle Class," 79, 84.

39. *Expert Magazine* and COMCON Research Company, "Lifestyle of the Middle Class."

40. U.S. Information Agency, Office of Research and Media Reaction, *Russia's Would-Be Middle Class,* 12.

41. Masha Gessen, "Pervyi raz v sredniy klass" [For the First Time—Into the Middle Class], *Itogi,* April 21, 1998, 14.

42. Novikov, "Ya, melkiy lavochnik."

43. *New York Times,* "How Russians Voted in the Runoff," July 4, 1996, A8. The national poll was conducted by Minofsky International and CESS Ltd. Other polls revealed still larger leads for Yeltsin in these age groups.

44. *New York Times,* "Russian Voters Speak Out on Issues," June 18, 1996, A4. The balance of the votes was cast for the other nine candidates in the first round.

45. Viktor Sheynis, "Proyden li istoricheskiy rubezh?" [Have We Passed a Historic Watershed?] *Polis,* no. 1 (1997): 88.

46. Center for Strategic Planning, *Strategiya razvitiya Rossiyskoy Federatsii do 2010 goda* [Strategic Development of the Russian Federation to the Year 2010], Moscow: June 2000, 57.

47. Ibid.

48. *Economist,* "Russian Love in a Cold Climate," August 15, 1998, 37–38.

49. Larisa Naumenko, "Life Revolves around Charity Work," *Moscow Times,* October 21, 1999, 24.

50. U.S. Information Agency, Office of Research and Media Reaction, *Russia's Would-Be Middle Class*, 17.

Chapter 9: An Anchor in the Mud: Three Novels as a Guide to Practicing Freedom and Constructing a New Self

1. Butov's use of both Cyrillic and Latin letters in the title is deliberate.

2. Boris Pasternak, *Zimnyaya noch* [A Winter Night], in *Izbrannoe v dvukh tomakh* [Selected Works in Two Volumes), vol. 1 (Moscow: Khudozhestvennaya literatura, 1985), 406–407.

3. Fyodor Dostoevsky, *Zapiski iz podpol'ya* [Notes from Underground] (Letchworth, England: Bradda Books, 1974), 15.

4. Ibid., 17.

5. Joseph Brodsky, *On Grief and Reason* (New York: Farrar, Straus and Giroux, 1995), 237.

6. Robert Graves, "The Naked and the Nude," in Robert Graves, *Collected Poems 1975* (New York: Oxford University Press, 1988), 189.

7. Fyodor Dostoevsky, *Polnoe sobranie khudozhestvennykh proizvedeniy* [Complete Works of Fiction], vol. 11 (Moscow: Litizdat, 1929), 50.

Chapter 10: A Private Hero for a Privatized Nation: Boris Akunin's Mysteries

1. Guy Chazan, "Russian Authors Start to Eschew Potboilers," *Wall Street Journal—Europe*, February 22, 2002, www.cdi.org/russia/johnson/6092.htm (accessed December 28, 2006).

2. Alexandra Koneva, "Igor Zakharov: The Man behind the Books," www. capitalperspective.ru/septem... 2_october2001/profile (accessed May 16, 2002).

3. Brian Killen, "Émigré Enigma Wins Booker Prize, " *Moscow Times*, December 7, 2000, 4.

4. All the books in the Fandorin series have been published by Zakharov [Moscow]: *Azazel', Turetskiy gambit* [The Turkish Gambit] and *Leviafan* [The Leviathan] in 1998; *Smert' Akhillesa* [The Death of Achilles] and *Osobye porucheniya* [Special Assignments] in 1999; *Statskiy sovetnik* [State Councilor] and *Koronatsiya* [The Coronation] in 2000; *Lyubovnik smerti* [Death's Lover] and *Lyubovnitsa smerti* [Death's Mistress] in 2001; and *Almaznaya kolesnitsa* [The Diamond Chariot] in 2003.

5. S. F. Platonov, *Uchebnik Russkoy istorii* [A Textbook on Russian History] (St.Petersburg: Nauka, 1994), 371. (This is the second edition of a textbook published in 1909.)

6. Adam Ulam, *Russia's Failed Revolutions* (New York: Basic Books, 1981), 134.

7. Platonov, *Uchebnik*, 390.

8. See, for example, Donald Rayfield, *Anton Chekhov: A Life* (London: Flamingo/Harper-Collins, 1997), 111.

9. As quoted in Yury Lebedev, *Russkaya literatura XIX veka. Chast' vtoraya* [Russian Nineteenth-Century Literature, Part 2] (Moscow: Prosveshchenie, 1994), 276.

10. The great Russian philosopher Sergey Bulgakov called the intelligentsia "the creation of Peter the Great"; Sergey Bulgakov, "Heroism and Asceticism," in *Landmarks: A Collection of Essays on the Russian Intelligentsia*, ed. Boris Shragin and Albert Todd (New York: Karz Howard, 1977), 25.

11. Vladimir Nabokov, *Lectures on Russian Literature* (New York: Harcourt, Brace, Jovanovich, 1981), 3.

12. Vladimir Nabokov, *Nikolai Gogol* (New York: New Directions Books, 1971), 29.

13. *Landmarks: A Collection of Essays on the Russian Intelligentsia*, ed. Boris Shragin and Albert Todd (New York: Karz Howard, 1977).

14. For the first, and most laudatory, detailed exposition and citation in the Soviet Union see Igor Kliamkin, "Kakaya ulitza vedyot k khramu?" [Which Street Leads to the Church?], *Novy Myr*, November 1987, 150–88.

15. Boris Shragin, "An Important Lesson," the introduction to Shragin and Todd, eds., *Landmarks*, xxxi.

16. Ibid.

17. Mikhail Gershenzon, "Preface to the First Edition," in Shragin and Todd, eds., *Landmarks*, 1–2.

18. Bulgakov, "Heroism and Asceticism," 45.

19. Bogdan Kistyakovsky, "In the Defense of Law," in Shragin and Todd, eds., *Landmarks*, 137.

20. Semyon Frank, "The Ethic of Nihilism," in Shragin and Todd, eds., *Landmarks*, 156.

21. Kistyakovsky, "In the Defense," 137.

22. Frank, "The Ethic."

23. Fyodor Dostoevsky, *Zapiski iz podpol'ya* [Notes from Underground] (Letchworth, England: Bradda Books, 1974), 30–31.

24. *Koronatsiya* [The Coronation], 258–59.

25. Alexander Griboedov, *Gore ot uma* [Woe from Intelligence] (Moscow: Detskaya Literatura, 1967), act I, scene 2, and act II, scene 1, pp. 14, 31.

26. Arkady Ostrovsky, "Taking Literature to the Middle Classes," *Financial Times*, April 9, 2001, 8.

27. *Turetskiy gambit*, 38.

28. *Lyubovnitsa smerti*, 158.

29. Nabokov, *Lectures on Russian Literature*, 254.

30. Anton Chekhov to A. S. Suvorin, December 27, 1889, in A. P. Chekhov, *Sobranie sochineniy v dvenadsati tomakh* [Collected Works in Twelve Volumes] (Moscow: Khudozhestvennaya Literatura, 1963), 11:388. Emphasis is Chekhov's.

31. Chekhov, "Nevesta," in Chekhov, *Sobranie*, 8:495.

32. Chekhov to N. I. Orlov, February 22, 1899, in Chekhov, *Sobranie*, 12:274.

33. Nabokov, *Lectures on Russian Literature*, 247.

34. Rayfield, *Anton Chekhov*, 275.

35. Alexander Kuprin, "To Chekhov's Memory," in Maxim Gorky, Alexander Kuprin, and Ivan Bunin, *Reminiscences of Anton Chekhov* (New York: B. W. Huebsch, 1921), 71, 48.

36. Chekhov to A. N. Plesheev, October 4, 1888, in Chekhov, *Sobranie*, 11:251–52.

37. Kuprin, "To Chekhov's Memory," 43; Rayfield, *Anton Chekhov*, 86; and Ivan Bunin, "A. P. Chekhov," in Gorky, Kuprin, and Bunin, *Reminiscences*, 95.

38. Kuprin, "To Chekhov's Memory," 46–47.

39. Bunin, "A. P. Chekhov," 102–3.

40. Quoted in Maxim Gorky, "Anton Chekhov," in Gorky, Kuprin, and Bunin, *Reminiscences*, 18–19.

41. Rayfield, *Anton Chekhov*, 257.

42. Chekhov to A. S. Suvorin, January 7, 1889, in Chekhov, *Sobranie*, 11:317–18.

43. Vladimir Putin, "Poslanie Prezidenta Rossiyskoy Federatsii V. V. Putina Federal'nomy Sobraniyu Rossiyskoy Federatsii" [The Message of President of the Russian Federation V. V. Putin to the Federal Assembly of the Russian Federation], April 18, 2002, http://president.kremlin.ru/eng/speeches/2002/04/18/0000_type70029type82912_70662.shtml (accessed November 17, 2006).

44. Ostrovsky, "Taking Literature."

45. "Boris Akunin: V blizhayshie mesyatsy dolzhno opredelit'sya, po kakomu puti poydyot Rossiya" [Boris Akunin: The Next Few Months Will Determine the Road Taken by Russia], interview on *The Itogi Show* on the NTV network, April 29, 2001.

46. Ibid.

47. David Hoffman, "A Literary Spring in Russia," *Washington Post*, July 12, 2002, A14.

48. N. Lapin, ed., *Kak chuvstvyut sebya, k chemu stremyatsya grazhdane Rossii. Osnovnye fakty i vyvody analiticheskogo doklada* [How the Citizens of Russia Feel and What They Aspire To. The Main Facts and Conclusions from the Analytical Report] (Moscow: Russian Academy of Sciences, 2002), 2–8.

Chapter 11: Restauration: The Art of Eating Returns to Russia

1. See chapter 1, "What *Glasnost* Has Destroyed."

2. See chapter 8, "In Search of a Russian Middle Class."

3. In 2001, for the first time since the late 1920s, Russia had enough grain not only to feed its people and cattle without millions of tons of American, Canadian, and Argentine wheat, but to export at least 5 million tons.

Chapter 12: Is Russia Really "Lost"?

1. Fritz W. Ermath, "A Scandal, Then a Charade," *New York Times,* September 12, 1999.

2. "The Future of Foreign Policy: Interviews with Coit Blacker and Condoleezza Rice," *Stanford Journal of International Relations* 1, no. 2 (Spring–Summer 1999): 40, http://www.stanford.edu/group/sjir/1.2.06_blacker_rice.html (re-accessed November 22, 2006).

3. As quoted in Steven Mufson, "Albright Defends Russia Policy," *Washington Post,* September 17, 1999.

4. A. Chernyak, "Edoki po statistike i v zhizni" [Food Consumers in Statistics and in Real Life], *Pravda,* September 1, 1988, 3. See also chapter 1, "What *Glasnost* Has Destroyed."

5. Yu. Rytov, "Kak zhivyotsya pensionru" [How Pensioners Fare], *Izvestiya,* August 20, 1988, 1. Even before the full bloom of *glasnost,* Soviet poverty was hardly a secret to perceptive Western scholars and analysts. See, for instance, Mervyn Matthews, *Poverty in the Soviet Union: The Life Styles of the Underprivileged in Recent Years* (Cambridge: Cambridge University Press, 1986), and Aaron Trehub, "Poverty in the Soviet Union," *Radio Liberty Research* (RL 256/88), June 20, 1988.

6. V. Radayev and O. Shkaratan, "Vozvrashchenie k stokam" [The Return to the Sources], *Izvestiya,* February 16, 1990.

7. "Vasiliy Selyunin, "Soviet Reformer Fears Collapse of the Economic House of Ration Cards, *Glasnost* 2, (January-March), 1990, 57.

8. P. Voroshilov and A. Solovyov, "Konstruktivniy dialog s shakhtyorami" [A Constructive Dialogue with Miners], *Izvestiya,* July 19, 1989.

9. Vladimir Treml, "Document on Alcoholism in the USSR Put in Perspective," *Radio Liberty Research* (RL39/85), February 1985, 2.

10. Vladimir Treml, "Gorbachev's Anti-Drinking Campaign: A Noble Experiment or a Costly Exercise in Futility?" *Radio Liberty Supplement* (RL2/87), March 18, 1987, 8.

11. Ibid.

12. Barrie R. Cassileth, Vasily V. Vlasov, and Christopher Chapman, "Health Care, Medical Practice and Medical Ethics in Russia Today," *The Journal of the American Medical Association* 273, no. 20 (May 24–31, 1995): 1570. For earlier data from the *glasnost* era, see chapter 1, "What *Glasnost* Has Destroyed."

13. This tragic datum was first revealed in the late 1980s. See chapter 1, "What *Glasnost* Has Destroyed."

14. In 2001, Russia exported 5 million tons of grain.

15. Harley Balzer, "Russia's Middle Classes," *Post-Soviet Affairs* 14, no. 2 (April–June 1998): 172, 173, 176.

16. U.S. Information Agency, Office of Research and Media Reaction, *Is Economic Reform in Russia Dead?* opinion analysis (Washington, D.C.: Government Printing Office, March 15, 1999), 2.

17. Indeed, the ruble was to remain within the R27–R32 range throughout the fall of 2006, when this essay was last edited.

18. U.S. Information Agency, *Is Economic Reform in Russia Dead?* 3.

19. Ibid.

20. U.S. Information Agency, Office of Research and Media Reaction, *Many Russians Still Admire America, But More and More Disapprove of U.S. Foreign Policies*, opinion analysis (Washington, D.C.: Government Printing Office, February 23, 1999), 2.

21. U.S. Information Agency, Office of Research and Media Reaction, *Is Russia Turning the Corner? Changing Russian Opinion, 1991–1996*, by Richard Dobson (Washington, D.C.: Government Printing Office, September 1996), 55, table 25.

22. U.S. Information Agency, Office of Research and Media Reaction, *How Unsteady is Russian Democracy?* by Steven Grant (Washington, D.C.: Government Printing Office, May 1997), 2.

23. RFE/RL, "Russian Human Rights Movement on the Rise," briefing report, September 9, 1999.

24. For details of the courts' ruling against the authorities and of the Nikitin case, see chapter 7, "From State-Owned Justice to a Law-Based State."

25. This, more or less, is what happened.

26. Evgeny Primakov, "Russia Must Be a Star Player on the World Arena" (excerpts from a speech given at the conference of the Council of Foreign and Defense Policy, March 14, 1998, 1; distributed by the Information Department of the Embassy of the Russian Federation).

27. For details, see chapter 5, "Russia's New Foreign Policy."

28. For details see chapter 5, "Russia's New Foreign Policy."

29. Konstantin Simis, *USSR: The Corrupt Society* (New York: Simon and Schuster, 1982), 248.

30. Nikolai Ryzhkov, *Perestroika: Istoriya Predate'lstv* [*Perestroika*: The History of Betrayals] (Moscow: Novosti, 1992), 94.

31. James M. McPherson, *Abraham Lincoln and the Second American Revolution* (Oxford University Press, 1990), 16.

Chapter 13: In Search of a Historic Yeltsin

1. Leon Aron, *Yeltsin: A Revolutionary Life* (New York: St. Martin's Press, 2000).

2. Aleksandr Gertzen (Herzen), *O Razvitii revolutsionnykh idei v Rossii* [On the Development of Revolutionary Ideas in Russia] (Moscow: Gosudarstvennoe Izdatel'stvo Khudozhestvennoi Literatury, 1958), 115.

3. Stanislav Govorukhin, "Voyna s Prestupnost'yu" [War on Crime], *Sovetskaya Kul'tura* via *Novoe Russkoe Slovo*, August 19–20, 1989.

4. Nikolai Kostomarov, *Rossiyskaya istoriya v zhizneopisaniyakh eyo glavneyshikh deyateley* [Russian History in Biographies of Its Foremost Figures] (Moscow: Kniga,

1991), vol. 1, 565. The author is grateful to Sir Rodric Braithwaite, Britain's former ambassador to the Soviet Union and Russia, for pointing out this passage.

5. Ilya Mil'shtein, "Neudachnik na trone" [A Loser on the Throne], *Novoe vremya* 2, no. 3 (January 23, 2000): 23.

6. Oksana Dmitrieva, interview in *Moskovskie Novosti*, February 15–21, 2000, 15–21.

7. Robert Conquest, *Reflections on a Ravaged Century* (New York: Norton, 1999), 103

8. L. Velikanova, "Kogda sbudut'sya nadezhdy nadezhdy na otdel'nuyu kvartiru" [When the Hopes for an Apartment of One's Own Will Be Fulfilled], *Literaturnaya gazeta*, June 6, 1990, 11.

9. G.A. Yagodin, Chairman of the USSR State Committee on Education, speech at the XIX All-Union Party Conference, *Pravda*, July 2, 1988, 9.

10. Vasiliy Selyunin, "Soviet Reformer Fears Collapse of the Economic House of Ration Cards," *Glasnost* 2 (January–March 1990).

11. See also chapter 5, "Russia's New Foreign Policy."

12. See Chapter 7, "From State-Owned Justice to a Law-Based State."

13. Ibid.

14. In August 1999, Yeltsin formally asked the Duma to abolish the death penalty in Russia.

15. Isaiah Berlin, "Two Concepts of Liberty," in his *Four Essays on Liberty* (Oxford: Oxford University Press, 1969), 125.

16. Steven Erlanger, "Havel Finds His Role Turning From Czech Hero to Has-Been," *New York Times*, November 4, 1999, A12.

17. *RFE/RL Newsline—Central and Eastern Europe*, February 10 and November 17, 1999.

18. Richard Holmes, *Footsteps: Adventures of a Romantic Biographer* (New York: Vintage Books, 1996), 148.

19. Isaiah Berlin, "Winston Churchill," in *Personal Impressions*, ed. Henry Hardy (New York: Penguin, 1982), 17.

20. Isaiah Berlin, "Chaim Weizmann," in *Personal Impressions*, 32.

21. Tony Judt, *Burden of Responsibility: Blum, Camus, Aron, and the French Twentieth Century* (Chicago: University of Chicago Press, 1998), 83–84.

22. Valeriy Vyzhutovich, "My boyalis' shokovoy terapii, i prishli k shokovoy khirurgii," [We Feared Shock Therapy, But Have Come to Shock Surgery], *Izvestiya*, October 29, 1991, 1.

23. Boris Yeltsin, address to the nation, December 29, 1991 (Moscow Central Television, FBIS-SOV-91-250, December 30, 1991), 29.

24. Boris Yeltsin, speech to the Congress of People's Deputies of the Russian Federation, October 28, 1991, in *Sovetskaya Rossia*, October 29, 1991, 2.

25. Ibid.

26. Ibid.

27. Yeltsin, address to the nation, 27.

28. Ibid.
29. Ibid., 28.
30. Robert Graves, "To Juan at the Winter Solstice," in *Collected Poems, 1975* (New York: Oxford University Press, 1988), 137.

Chapter 14: Poor Democracy

1. World Bank, "World Development Indicators 2001," April 11, 2001, http://web.worldbank.org/WBSITE/EXTERNAL/DATASTATISTICS/0,,content-MDK:20398986~menuPK:232599~pagePK:64133150~piPK:64133175~the-SitePK:239419,00.html (accessed November 22, 2006).
2. See chapter 4, "The Strange Case of Russian Capitalism," 44.
3. Thomas Babington Macaulay, *The History of England* (New York: Penguin Books, 1986), 490.
4. See chapter 4, "The Strange Case of Russian Capitalism," 46.
5. See chapter 4, "The Strange Case of Russian Capitalism."
6. Isaiah Berlin, *Four Essays on Liberty* (Oxford: Oxford University Press, 1969), xlv.
7. Barrington Moore, *Social Origins of Dictatorship and Democracy* (Boston: Beacon Press, 1967), 429.
8. McKinsey Global Institute, *Unlocking Economic Growth in Russia* (London: McKinsey and Company, October 1998), 8.
9. See chapter 4, "The Strange Case of Russian Capitalism," 48.
10. Joseph A. Schumpeter, *Capitalism, Socialism and Democracy* (New York: Harper and Row, 1975), 271.
11. Peter L. Berger, *The Capitalist Revolution* (New York: Basic Books, 1986), 74–75.
12. Isaiah Berlin, "Two Concepts of Liberty," in his *Four Essays on Liberty*, 125.
13. The author's notes of the presentation at the American Enterprise Institute in March 2001.

Chapter 15: The YUKOS Affair

1. Evgeny Yasin in Sergei Karaganov, Otto Latsis, Yuri Levada, Viktor Pleskachevskiy, Georgiy Satarov, Liliya Shevtsova, Pavel Teplukhin, and Evgeny Yasin, "Papka na oligarkhov" [The Dossier on the Oligarchs], *Novoe vremya*, August 24, 2003, 14.
2. Daniel Kimmage, "Table, Chair, YUKOS," *RFE/RL Newsline*, July 14, 2003.
3. YUKOS Oil Company, *YUKOS 2002 Annual Report*, Moscow, 2003, 42, http://2002.yukos.com/eng/dir_1/1.html (accessed July 24, 2006).
4. Alex Nicholson, "Independent Directors Find Seat on the Board," *Moscow Times*, October 2, 2003, 14.

5. Catherine Belton, "Mikhail Khodorkovsky," *Business Week,* February 11, 2002, www.businessweek.com/magazine/content/02_06/b3769614.htm (accessed November 17, 2006); YUKOS Oil Company, *YUKOS 2002 Annual Report,* 2, 10. The merger unraveled after Khodorkovsky's arrest, and Sibneft was later acquired by Gasprom, the Russian natural gas monopoly, majority-owned by the government.

6. Like the Yukos-Sibneft merger, the ExxonMobil-YukosSibneft deal fell victim to Khodorkovsky's arrest.

7. Energy Information Agency, "World Crude Oil Production," *RFE/RL Newsline,* September 2, 2003, 2, table 1.1c.

8. Belton, "Mikhail Khodorkovsky."

9. *Fortune,* "Global 40 Richest Under 40: Snapshot," September 16, 2002, http://money.cnn.com/magazines/fortune/fortune_archive/2002/09/16/328569 (accessed July 25, 2003).

10. Menatep, "Company News," www.groupmenatep.com/company_news/awards_2.cfm (accessed September 8, 2003).

11. Ibid.

12. Ibid.

13. Stefan Wagstyl, "The Road To Recognition," *Financial Times,* February 6, 2002.

14. *Economist,* "Russian Love in a Cold Climate," August 15, 1998, 37–38.

15. Peter Baker, "Soros's Mission in Russia Ends, $1 Billion Later," *Washington Post,* June 10, 2003; YUKOS Oil Company, "YUKOS Deputy Chairman Mikhail Trushin Discusses the Company's Many Social Programs," *YUKOS Exclusive,* www.yukos.com/exclusive/28.asp (accessed September 13, 2003).

16. The Russian government later charged Nevzlin with being an accessory to murder, and he fled Russia.

17. *Impact Russia,* "YUKOS and Eurasia Foundation Launch $1.15 Million Development Partnership," Summer 2002, www.eurasia.org/offices/moscow/Impact%20Russia%20Summer%202002.pdf (accessed September 14, 2003).

18. YUKOS Oil Company, *YUKOS 2002 Annual Report,* 27.

19. YUKOS Oil Company, "Corporate Citizenship," www.yukos.com/cc/edu/scholarships/ (accessed September 13, 2003).

20. Mikhail Khodorkovsky, "What Russia's Intellectual Potential Means for the Country's Economy," *YUKOS Review,* no. 5, September–October 2001, www.yukos.com/pdf/YUKOS_Review5.pdf (accessed September 15, 2003).

21. Igor Naydenov, "Gibloe mesto" [A Rotten Place], *Moskovskie Novosti,* August 8–14, 2003, 8.

22. Ibid.

23. YUKOS Oil Company, "A Five-Year-Old 'New Civilization,'" *YUKOS Exclusive.* www.aei.org/admin/internet/publications/www.yukos.com/exclusive/15.asp (accessed September 14, 2003).

24. As quoted by Evgeny Yasin in Sergei Karaganov, et al., "Papka na oligark-hov," 23.

25. Dmitry Oreshkin, "O chem molchat oligarkhy" [What the Oligarchs Are Silent About], *Moskovskie Novosti*, July 15–21, 2003, 7.

26. For a discussion of this category of nations, see the previous chapter.

27. Rossiyskoye Obschestvennoye Mneniye i Isledovaniye Rynka (ROMIR) [Russian Public Opinion and Market Research], "Rossiyane o vozmozhnosti peres-motra privatizatsii i krupnom kapitale" [Russian Citizens on the Possibility of the Revision of the Privatization's Results and on Big Capital], survey conducted July 9–14, 2003.

28. Ibid.

29. Ibid.

30. Center for the Study of Socio-Cultural Changes, Institute of Philosophy, Rus-sian Academy of Science, *Kak chuvstvuyut sebya, k chemu stremyatsya grazhdane Rossii?* [How Are Citizens of Russia Feeling and What Are Their Goals?], Moscow, 2002, 3, table 5.

31. Ibid., table 8.

32. Anastasiya Naryshkina, "Delo YUKOSa glazami Rossiyan" [The YUKOS Affair as Viewed by Russian Citizens], *Izvestiya*, July 24, 2003, 2.

33. Ibid.

34. Ibid.

35. Fond Obschestvennoye Mneniye (FOM, Foundation for Public Opinion), "YUKOS i peredel krupnoy sobstvennosti" [YUKOS and the Redivision of Large Property], conducted August 30–31, 2003, http://bd.fom.ru/report/map/d033511 (accessed September 4, 2003).

36. Vserossiyskiy Tsentr Izucheniya Obschestvennogo Mneniya [VTsIOM, Rus-sian Center for Public Opinion and Market Research] "Delo YUKOSa glazami Rossiyan" [The YUKOS Affair as Viewed by Russian Citizens], conducted July 17–21, 2003, www.wciom.ru/vciom/new/public/ 030724.htm (accessed Septem-ber 10, 2003).

37. Fond Obschestvennoye Mneniye (FOM, Foundation for Public Opinion), "YUKOS i peredel krupnoy sobstvennosti."

38. Fond Obschestvennoye Mneniye (FOM, Foundation for Public Opinion), "Reytingi politikov" [The Politicians' Ratings], conducted May 17, 2003, http://bd.fom.ru/report/cat/policy/rating/of031903 (accessed May 25, 2003).

39. In the event, Putin was reelected in 2004 with 71 percent of the vote.

40. Richard Pipes, *Russia Under the Old Regime* (London: Penguin Books, 1974), 65.

41. See chapter 14, "Poor Democracy."

42. Pipes, op. cit., xxii. See also chapter 4, "The Strange Case of Russian Capi-talism," 44.

43. Giles Fletcher, *Of the Russe Commonwealth* (Cambridge: Harvard University Press, 1966), 47.

44. Boris Makarenko, Mark Urnov, and Lilya Shevtsova, "My ne sdayom imena v arendu" [We Do Not Rent Out Our Names], *Moskovksie Novosti*, August 5–11, 2003, 6.

45. Ibid.

46. Gleb Pavlovsky, "O negativnykh posledstviyakh 'letnego nastupleniya' oppozitsionnogo kursu prezidenta RF men'shinstva" [On the Negative Consequences of the "Summer Offensive" of a Minority Opposed to the Policy of the President of the Russian Federation], September 2, 2003, http://2003.novayagazeta.ru/nomer/2003/67n/n67n-s00.shtml (accessed September 7, 2003).

Chapter 16: Institutions, Restoration, and Revolution

1. For one of the most impressive examinations of this issue, see Lilia Shevtsova, "Otkat, ili kak Vladimir Putin nachinaet vtoroe prezidentsvo" [Retreat, or How Vladimir Putin Begins His Second Presidency], *Briefing* 7, no. 1, Moscow Carnegie Center, January 2005, www.carnegie.ru/ru/pubs/briefings/71911.htm (accessed July 24, 2006).

2. Francesca Mereu, "President Says 50 Senators Must Go," *Moscow Times*, February 14, 2005.

3. Fond Obschestvennoye Mneniye (FOM, Foundation for Public Opinion), "Vybory v Gosdumu po partiynym spiskam" [The Election to the State Duma by Party Lists], September 23, 2004, http://bd.fom.ru/report/cat/services/parliament2/duma/of043706 (accessed February 15, 2005).

4. Ibid.

5. The "nomination" is a euphemism and in fact amounts to appointment. If a regional legislature fails to approve the president's gubernatorial "nominee" twice, he can appoint an acting governor; if the legislature persists and rejects his candidate for the third time, it can be dissolved.

6. See, for example, Vitaly Tretyakov, "Putin's Choice as Russia's Choice," *Russia in Global Affairs* 2, no. 4 (October–December 2004): 41; and Konstantin Sonin, "It's Time to Change the Constitution," *Moscow Times*, November 30, 2004.

7. For a strong constitutional analysis, see Robert Coalson, "Mayoral Elections: Democracy's Last Stand?" *RFE/RL Russian Political Weekly* 5, no. 9 (March 4, 2005): 1.

8. For more on the dangers of the Putin restoration, see chapter 19, "Putin's Risks."

9. Nikolai Petrov, "The Shape of Strings to Come," *Moscow Times*, March 4, 2005.

10. Alexei Sitnikov, "A Brief History of Russian Federalism," *Moscow Times*, February 4, 2005.

11. Fond Obschestvennoye Mneniye (FOM, Foundation for Public Opinion), "Gubernatory: Izbirat' ili naznachat?" [Governors: Elect or Appoint?], September 23, 2004, http://bd.fom.ru/report/map/of043704 (accessed February 12, 2005).

12. For details, see chapter 7, "From State-Owned Justice to a Law-Based State."

13. Ibid.

14. Ibid.

15. Ibid.

16. Peter Finn, "Putin Close to Winning New Power Over Judiciary," *Washington Post*, October 2, 2004.

17. See Council of Europe, *European Charter on the Statute for Judges*, DAJ/DOC (98) 23, July 8–10, 1998, www.coe.int/t/e/legal_affairs/legal_co-operation/legal_professionals/judges/instruments_and_documents/charte%20eng.pdf (accessed November 21, 2006).

18. Ben Wetherall, "President Putin Calls for Russian Judiciary to Help 'Curb' Oligarchs' Influence as Gazprom Moves for Yukos," World Markets Research Centre, December 1, 2004.

19. According to a 2005 fact-finding mission on the status of the law by the International Bar Association (IBA), a majority of Duma members felt that "the proposals would not pass in their current form"; International Bar Association, *Striving for Judicial Independence: A Report into the Proposed Changes to the Judiciary in Russia*, June 2005, 29, http://www.ibanet.org/images/downloads/2005_06_June_Report_Russia_Striving%20for%20Judicial%20Independence_Final_English.pdf (accessed October 27, 2006).

20. For details, see chapter 7.

21. Susan B. Glasser, "Russian Court Reverses Space Expert's Acquittal," *Washington Post*, June 10, 2004.

22. Steven Lee Myers, "2nd Russian Jury Convicts a Physicist Who Was Acquitted of Spy Charges," *New York Times*, November 6, 2004.

23. For more on the YUKOS judicial persecution, see chapter 15, "The YUKOS Affair."

24. For an analysis of the political and economic issues in the "YUKOS affair," see chapter 15.

25. Freedom House, *Freedom in the World 2005* (New York: Freedom House, 2005).

26. Glenn Kessler and Robin Wright, "Bush's Words on Liberty Don't Mesh with Policies," *Washington Post*, January 21, 2005.

27. For instance, in the past five years, the number of registered Jewish communities in Russia has grown from 80 to 180, and more than 80 synagogues, community centers, and Jewish schools are currently under construction. In recent months, new synagogues have opened in Yekaterinburg, Khabarovsk, and Birobijian; Avraham Berkowitz, "Jews in Russia Today: Is There a Future?" (presentation to AEI's U.S.-Russia Working Group, Washington, D.C., March 16, 2005).

28. Nicolai Petro, "Russia's Doing Just Fine," *Providence Journal*, October 30, 2003. The chairwoman of the Moscow Helsinki Group, Ludmilla Alexeyeva, has put the number of NGOs at 350,000. (See Ludmilla Alexeyeva, "Putin's Definition of Democracy?" *Washington Post*, June 8, 2004.) Petro, a professor of political sci-

ence at the University of Rhode Island, is also the author of a pioneering study of local self-governance and civic society in the Novgorod region of post-Soviet Russia, *Crafting Democracy* (Ithaca: Cornell University Press, 2004).

29. Petro, "Russia's Doing Just Fine."

30. Robert Coalson, "Out from Behind the Mask," *RFE/RL Russian Political Weekly* 5, no. 7 (February 18, 2005), http://www.rferl.net/reports/rpw/2005/02/7-180205.asp (accessed November 21, 2006).

31. Maria Lipman, "How Russia is Not Ukraine," *Policy Outlook*, Carnegie Endowment for International Peace, January 2005.

32. Ibid.

33. Francesca Mereu, "Youth Groups Say It's Time to Oppose Putin," *Moscow Times*, February 25, 2005; and Steven Lee Myers, "Mounting Discontent in Russia Spills into the Streets," *New York Times*, February 12, 2005.

34. Mereu, "Youth Groups Say It's Time to Oppose Putin."

35. Neil Buckley, "Kasyanov Hints At Run for Russian Presidency," *Financial Times*, March 2, 2005.

36. Ibid.

37. See, for example, Anna Nikolayeva, Olga Proskurnina, Aleksandr Bekker, and Aleksey Nikolskiy, "Democrat Kasyanov Has Challenged the Kremlin," *Vedomosti*, February 25, 2005, www.vedomosti.ru (accessed February 25, 2005); Andrey Bagrov, "The Premier's 'Ex'-Hour," *Kommersant*, www.kommersant.ru/doc.html?DocID=550172&IssueId=23336 (accessed February 25, 2005); and RIA Novosti, "Three Candidates For 2008 Presidential Election Emerge," February 28, 2005.

38. Peter Finn, "Separatist Leader in Chechnya Is Killed," *Washington Post*, March 9, 2005.

39. For more on the draft and the opposition to it, see chapter 18, "The Battle over the Draft."

40. Ibid.

41. U.S. Department of State, Bureau of Democracy, Human Rights, and Labor, *Country Reports on Human Rights Practices*, February 25, 2004, 2–3, www.state.gov/g/drl/rls/hrrpt/2003 (accessed February 12, 2005). Since then, the Kremlin orchestrated ownership takeover of the top national independent newspapers *Izvestiya*, *Nezavisimaya Gazeta*, and *Kommersant* by businesses linked to or "friendly" to the government.

42. Maria Lipman, "How Russia is Not Ukraine."

43. Ibid.

44. Ibid.

45. Ibid.

46. MHz is also available nationwide on channel 9407 on the Dish Network.

47. U.S. Department of State, Bureau of Democracy, Human Rights, and Labor, *Country Reports on Human Rights Practices*, 2–3.

48. Michael Wines, "Russia's Media Variety Survives Network's Travail," *New York Times*, April 28, 2001.

Chapter 17: Chechnya: New Dimensions of an Old Crisis

1. Brian Glyn Williams, "The Russo-Chechen War: A Threat to Stability in the Middle East and Eurasia," *Middle East Policy* 8, no. 1 (March 1, 2001): 6.

2. Ibid.

3. Ibid.

4. Said Isaev, "Chechnya to Live by Sharia Laws Only," *ITAR-TASS*, September 17, 1997.

5. Colin McMahon, "Executions Remind Uneasy Russia of Chechnya's Islamic Path," *Chicago Tribune*, September 12, 2002, 14.

6. Williams, "The Russo-Chechen War," 4.

7. Mark Franchetti, Christina Lamb, and Ben Aris, "Kremlin Probes Al-Qaeda Links," *Ottawa Citizen*, October 27, 2002, A1.

8. Ibid.

9. Dirk Laabs, "Holy War Planning Described," *Los Angeles Times*, November 13, 2002, 4.

10. Anton Notz and Hugh Williamson, "Court Hears 9/11 Pilots Had Links with Chechens," *Financial Times*, October 30, 2002, 7.

11. Ibid.

12. John Crewdson, "9/11 Suspect Backs Theory on Al Qaeda," *Chicago Tribune*, October 23, 2002, 1.

13. Agence France-Presse, "Text of Reputed Bin Laden Audiotape Broadcast by Al Jazeera," November 13, 2002.

14. Peter Baker, "15 Tied to Al Qaeda Turned over to the U.S.," *Washington Post*, October 22, 2002, A17.

15. Ibid.

16. Ibid.

17. Ibid.

18. Elaine Sciolino and Desmond Butler, "Europeans Fear that the Threat from Radical Islamists Is Increasing," *New York Times*, December 8, 2002, 32.

19. Yandarbiev was assassinated by two Russian agents in Doha on February 13, 2004.

20. Vladimir Putin, "Remarks Following Discussions with President Vladimir Putin of Russia and an Exchange with Reporters in St. Petersburg, Russia," *Public Papers of the Presidents*, November 25, 2002.

21. *Gazeta Wyborcza*, June 17, 1999, 3, as quoted in Williams, "Russo-Chechen War," 7–8.

22. Jill Doughtery, "Putin Marks Victory in Dagestan; Russia Bombs Chechen Bases," CNN, August 26, 1999, www.cnn.com/WORLD/europe/9908/26/russian/dagestan (accessed December 16, 2002).

23. Andrei Babitsky, "Who is Movsar Baraev?" *RFE/RL Russian Political Weekly*, October 24, 2002, 3–4.

24. Ibid.

25. *BBC News*, "Hostage-Takers 'Ready to Die,'" October 25, 2002, www.news.bbc.co.uk/1/world/europe/2360735.stm (accessed December 12, 2002).

26. Ibid.

27. *The Week*, November 2, 2002, 11.

28. *BBC News*, "Hostage-Takers 'Ready to Die.'"

29. Politkovskaya was assassinated in 2006 in Moscow, and as of February 2007 the perpetrators have not been found and brought to justice.

30. Anna Politkovskaya, "The 'Sons' Rise in Chechnya," *Washington Post*, November 3, 2002, B7.

31. Ibid.

32. Aslan Maskhadov was killed in Chechnya in March 2005.

33. U.S. Department of State, "Turkey," in *Country Reports on Human Rights Practices—2001* (Washington, D.C.: Government Printing Office, March 4, 2002), 5–8.

34. Ibid.

35. In 2004, however, the PKK called off the cease-fire, and violence in the Kurdish regions flared up again. On October 1, 2006, leaders of the PKK declared another unilateral cease-fire, but Turkish officials dismissed it as "another publicity stunt," while armed forces chief General Yasar Buyukanit vowed to fight on "until the last guerrilla is eradicated"; Paul de Bendern, "Turkey's Kurds Back Cease-fire," Reuters, October 30, 2006, http://today.reuters.co.uk/news/articlenews.aspx?type=reutersEdge&storyID=2006-10-30T115617Z_01_NOA042908_RTRUKOC_0_TURKEY-KURDS-CEASEFIRE.xml&pageNumber=0&imageid=&cap=&sz=13&WTModLoc=NewsArt-C1-ArticlePage2 (accessed November 21, 2006).

36. The war between Sri Lankan troops and Tamil Tigers resumed in 2006. In July of that year, the Tigers formally repudiated the 2002 cease-fire.

37. In 2003, India and Pakistan signed a cease-fire agreement, followed by reciprocal high-level visits to New Delhi and Islamabad. In February 2005, bus service across the Line of Control was started for the first time in sixty years. In October 2005, following a major earthquake in the region, India and Pakistan jointly took the unprecedented step of opening the militarized border for emergency relief deliveries.

38. Susan Glasser, "Russian Crisis Brings War Home," *Washington Post*, November 3, 2002, A20.

39. Instead, Putin chose "chechenization" of the conflict by ceding control over Chechnya to the brutal dictatorship of Ahmad Kadyrov and, after he was assassinated in 2004, to his son Ramzan. Although for now the Kadyrov rule seems to

have "pacified" Chechnya, the instability, terrorism, and Islamic radicalism have spread to other areas of North Caucasus, especially Dagestan, Ingushetia, and North Ossetia. (See chapter 19, "Putin's Risks.")

Chapter 18: The Battle over the Draft

1. See, for example, Dale Herspring, "Putin and Military Reform," in *Putin's Russia*, ed. Dale Herspring (New York: Roman & Littlefield, 2003), 189. See also chapters 5 ("Russia's New Foreign Policy") and 12 ("Is Russia Really 'Lost'?").

2. In 1993–95, some fifty thousand contract soldiers left the army because of the low pay, with their salaries less than twice the national subsistence minimum. See, for example, Herspring, "Putin and Military Reform," 191–92.

3. Fred Weir, "In Russia, An Army of Deserters," *Christian Science Monitor*, September 30, 2002.

4. Alexander M. Golts and Tonya L. Putnam, "State Militarism and Its Legacies," *International Security* 29, no. 2 (Fall 2004): 154.

5. Alexander Golts, "Militaristy otstupili? Net, oni manevriruyu" [Have the Militarists Retreated? No, They Are Maneuvering], *Ezhenedel'nyi Zhurnal*, January 20, 2005.

6. Golts and Putnam, "State Militarism," 148.

7. Vladimir Isachenkov, "Russia Battles Hazings, Desertions in Military," *Los Angeles Times*, October 13, 2002.

8. Ibid.

9. Sharon LaFraniere, "Russia's Battered Military," *Washington Post*, May 20, 2001.

10. Boris Nemtsov, "Reforma: po generalski ili po umu?" [The Reform: According to the Generals or According to Logic?], interview by Vladimir Voronov, *Novoe vremya*, August 3, 2003.

11. Weir, "In Russia, An Army of Deserters."

12. Judith Ingram, "Kremlin Adviser Says Russia is Vital to G8," *Moscow Times*, July 1, 2005.

13. *Izvestiya*, "Vypusknikov vuzov zastavyat sluzhit' v armii" [College Graduates Will Be Forced to Serve in the Army], June 10–12, 2005.

14. Diederik Lohman, "Russia," *Human Rights Watch Report* 14, no. 8 (November 2002): 6–7.

15. Golts and Putnam, "State Militarism," 136; and Lohman, "Russia," 7.

16. In 2003, Boris Nemtsov estimated that 15 percent of the draftees had difficulty reading and writing, while one-fourth experimented with drugs (Nemtsov, "Reforma," 9).

17. Leonid Polyakov, "Military Reforms in Russia," *Toward Understanding of Russia*, ed. Janusz Bugajski (New York: Council on Foreign Relations, 2002), 89.

18. Ibid.

19. As quoted in Golts and Putnam, "State Militarism," 135.

20. Among the measures backed by Putin's sky-high popularity because of economic revival, the rapidly growing treasury revenues from rising oil prices, and the results of the 1999 Duma elections that for the first time since 1993 produced a pro-Kremlin and proreform plurality in the parliament, were the flat 13 percent income tax, privatization of urban and later agricultural land, the progressive criminal procedural code, the creation of private pension accounts, and the laws on breaking up and privatizing the government electricity monopoly.

21. Maura Reynolds, "Putin Order Cuts Military by 600,000," Los Angeles Times, November 10, 2000.

22. Polyakov, "Military Reforms," 89.

23. Alexander Golts, "The Russian Volunteer Military—A New Attempt?" European Security 12 (2004): 56.

24. The SPS program envisioned the abolition of the two-year conscription from spring 2002 and its replacement with a six to eight months' training course. The transition to an all-volunteer force was to be finished by the fall of 2002. The plan called for competitive salaries for the volunteers, private pensions, and free college education. Vestnik [Institute of the Economies in Transition], "Voennaya reforma" [Military Reform], November 8, 2002; and Nemtsov, "Reforma," 9–11.

25. Fond Obschestvennoye Mneniye (FOM, Foundation for Public Opinion), "O sluzhbe v armii," [About Service in the Army], national poll, July 3–4, 2004, http://bd.fom.ru/report/cat/socieas/army/d042711 (accessed February 4, 2005).

26. Levada Center, "Rossiyane ne khotyat, chtoby ikh blizkix prizyvay v armiyu" [The Russians Don't Want Their Close Relatives to Be Drafted into the Army], nationwide poll, January 21–24, 2005, www.levada.ru/press/2005020902.html (accessed February 4, 2005).

27. Ibid.

28. Golts, "Militaristy otstupili?"

29. Herspring, "Putin and Military Reform," 196.

30. Vestnik, "Voennaya reforma."

31. Fond Obschestvennoye Mneniye (FOM, Foundation for Public Opinion), "Armeyskaya sluzhba i otsrochki dlya studentov" [Army Service and Deferments for Students], February 10, 2005, http://bd.fom.ru/report/cat/societas/army/d050616 (accessed March 1, 2005).

32. Levada Center, "Rossiyane ne khotyat."

33. See also chapter 16, "Institutions, Restoration, and Revolution."

34. Izvestiya, "Vypusknikov vuzov zastavyat sluzhit' v armii" [College Graduates Will Be Forced to Serve in the Army], June 10–12, 2005.

35. Golts, "The Russian Volunteer Military," 62.

Chapter 19: Putin's Risks

1. Stefan Wagstyl, "Kremlin Man But No Fan of State Control: These are Tough Times for Andrei Illarionov," *Financial Times*, October 7, 2004; and Andrei Illarionov, "Letter to the Editor," *Financial Times*, October 9, 2004. Andrei Illarionov resigned in protest on December 27, 2005.

2. *Kommersant*, "Sovety potustoronnego" [The Advice of the Denizen of the Other World], October 8, 2004; and *New York Times*, "Advising Vladimir Putin," January 6, 2005.

3. *Kommersant*, "Sovety potustoronnego."

4. For more on the YUKOS persecution, see chapters 15 ("The YUKOS Affair") and 16 ("Institutions, Restoration, and Revolution"). In May 2005, Mikhail Khodorkovsky was convicted and sentenced to nine years in labor camps. He is serving the sentence near the town of Chita in eastern Siberia, three thousand miles from Moscow.

5. Wagstyl, "Kremlin Man," and C. J. Chivers, "Putin Demotes Adviser Critical of the Kremlin," *New York Times*, January 4, 2005.

6. EIU ViewsWire, "Russia Finance: Capital Flight's Two-Way Ticket," January 6, 2005.

7. Lee Raymond, interview by Charlie Rose, *The Charlie Rose Show*, PBS, December 7, 2004.

8. Levada Center, "Lgoty ili pribavka k pensii?" [Privilege or Addition to the Pension?], August 19, 2004, www.levada.ru/press/2004081901.html (accessed December 2, 2004).

9. Ibid.

10. Richard Rose, Neil Munro, and William Mishler, "Resigned Acceptance of an Incomplete Democracy: Russia's Political Equilibrium," *Post-Soviet Affairs* 20, no. 3 (2004): 195–217.

11. Levada Center, "Sotsial'no-politicheskaya situatsiya v noyabre 2004" [Sociopolitical Situation in November 2004], December 2, 2004, www.levada.ru/press/2004120202.html (accessed January 5, 2005).

12. Levada Center, "Pretenzii Rossiayn k deyatel'nosti pravitel'stva" [Russian People's Grudges toward the Activity of the Government], December 12, 2004, www.levada.ru/press/2004120101.html (accessed December 17, 2004).

13. Fond Obschestvennoye Mneniye (FOM, Foundation for Public Opinion), "Putin na postu prezidenta" [Putin as President], October 7, 2004, http://bd.fom.ru/report/cat/president2/putin/three_year/tb044007 (accessed November 14, 2004).

14. Ibid.

15. Fond Obschestvennoye Mneniye (FOM, Foundation for Public Opinion), "Situatsiya v Rossii: Stabil'nost' i peremeny" [The Situation in Russia: Stability and Change], October 14, 2004, www.fom.ru (accessed November 14, 2004).

16. Levada Center, "Sotsial'no-politicheskaya situatsiya v noyabre 2004."

17. Fond Obschestvennoye Mneniye (FOM, Foundation for Public Opinion), "Sotsial'nyi protest: nastroeniya i deystviya" [Social Protest: Moods and Actions], November 4, 2004, http://bd.fom.ru/report/cat/civil_society/tb044409 (accessed December 3, 2004).

18. Rose, Munro, and Mishler, "Resigned Acceptance."

19. Georgy Ilyichev and Olga Tropkina, "Dve treti grazhdan Rossii za to choby byla oppozitsiya" [Two-Thirds of Russian Citizens Are in Favor of Having an Opposition], Izvestiya, November 8, 2004.

20. Ibid.

21. For details see chapter 16, "Institutions, Restoration, and Revolution."

22. Vladimir Putin, "Vystuplenie na rasshirennom zasedanii pravitel'stva s uchastiem glav sub'ektov Rossiyskoy Federatzii" [speech, expanded session of the government with the heads of the subjects of the Russian Federation], September 13, 2004, www.kremlin.ru/appears/2004/09/13/1514 (accessed September 15, 2004).

23. Izvestiya, "Ne doshlo" [They Didn't Get It], September 27, 2004. The referenced poll was conducted by the Fond Obschestvennoye Mneniye (FOM, Foundation for Public Opinion).

24. Ibid.

25. Ibid.

26. See the preceding chapter.

27. In the unusually cold Moscow winter of 2005–6, the government-controlled electricity monopoly United Energy Systems (UES) was faced with a severe lack of gas to power its generating plants and warned that the increased demand could lead to shutdowns. At a conference in Moscow in March 2006 attended by the author, the chairman of UES Anatoly Chubais foresaw a catastrophe within three years unless UES were privatized and upgraded.

28. Levada Center, "Posle izbraniya Vladimira Putina vorovstva i korruptsii v rukovodstve stranoj stanet bol'she?" [After the Election of Vladimir Putin Will Thievery and Corruption Grow?], www.levada.ru/postelections05.html (accessed December 9, 2004).

29. Ibid.

30. Levada Center, "Korruptsiya—glavnoe prepiatstvie reformam" [Corruption—the Main Obstacle to Reforms], April 13, 2004, www.levada.ru/press/2004041301.html (accessed November 12, 2004).

31. Ibid.

32. See chapter 17, "Chechnya: New Dimensions of an Old Crisis."

33. On the Nord-Ost crisis, see chapter 17, "Chechnya: New Dimensions of an Old Crisis."

34. Levada Center, "Rost terrorizma v Rossii" [The Growth of Terrorism in Russia], October 4, 2004, www.levada.ru/press/2004100403.html (accessed November 9, 2004).

35. *Izvestiya*, "Ne doshlo.

36. Shamil Basaev was reported by the Russian authorities to have died in an explosion in July 2006. As of the end of 2006, however, his remains were not positively identified. See, for example, Vladimir Voronov, "Neopoznanie Basaeva" [The Non-identification of Basaev], *Novoe vremya*, December 3, 2006, 12–13.

37. Levada Center, "Kak pokonchit' s terrorizmom v Rossii" [How to Finish Off Terrorism in Russia], September 16, 2004, www.levada.ru/press/2004091602.html (accessed November 11, 2004).

38. Ibid.

39. *Moscow News*, September 22–28, 2004. The polling is by the Levada Center.

40. Levada Center, "Kak pokonchit' s terrorizmom v Rossii."

41. "Vladislav Surkov: Putin ukreplyaet gosudarstvo, a ne sebya" [Putin Strengthens the State, but Not Himself], *Komsomol'skaya Pravda*, September 29, 2004.

42. ROMIR Monitoring, "Grazhdane Rossii o prezidente" [Citizens of Russia on the President], September 16–21, 2004, www.romir.ru/socpolit/socio/09_2004/president1.htm (accessed December 7, 2004). Of those surveyed, 21 percent trusted President Putin "fully," and 52 percent "trusted him more than they mistrusted him"; 25 percent mistrusted Putin fully or "completely." In November 2004, Putin was admired (4 percent) and liked (30 percent), as well as someone about whom "nothing bad could be said" (69 percent); Levada Center, "Sotsial'no-politicheskaya situatsiya v noyabre 2004."

43. Fond Obschestvennoye Mneniye (FOM, Foundation for Public Opinion), "Putin na postu prezidenta."

44. Ibid.

45. Tatiana Skorobogatko, "The People Support Putin, But Reject His Policy," *Moscow News*, September 22, 2004; and Levada Center, "Uroven' odobreniya deyatel'nosti V. Putina na postu prezidenta Rossii" [The Level of Support for V. Putin in the Post of President], www.levada.ru/prezident.html (accessed January 7, 2005).

46. Levada Center, "Sotsial'no-politicheskaya situatsiya v noyabre 2004."

47. Alexander Kolesnichenko, "The Despair Syndrome," WPS Monitoring Agency, December 6, 2004, www.wps.ru (accessed December 3, 2004). The numbers cited are from a Levada Center survey.

48. Putin aide Viktor Ivanov is chairman of the board of directors of a strategically valuable defense company, Almaz-Antey, and of the Russian airline Aeroflot. Deputy chief of the Kremlin administration Igor Sechin is chairman of the board of the state-owned oil company Rosneft, which recently acquired Yuganskneftegaz, the main production unit of YUKOS. Putin's chief of staff, Dmitry Medvedev, is chairman of the board of the state-owned energy giant Gazprom. Deputy chief of the Kremlin administration Vladislav Surkov is chairman of the board of the state-owned oil pipeline monopoly Transnefteprodukt.

49. See, for example, Leonid Radzikhovskiy, "Osedlye chekisty" [The Settled Chekists], *Ezhenedel'nyi Zhurnal*, September 27–October 3, 2004, 23.

50. Fond Obschestvennoye Mneniye (FOM, Foundation for Public Opinion), "Oprosy 'Internet v Rossii,' Leto 2004" [Surveys "Internet in Russia," Summer 2004], http://bd. fom.ru/report/map/projects/internet/internet08/o040801 (accessed November 14, 2004).

Chapter 20: Russia's Oil:
Natural Abundance and Political Shortages

1. Isabel Gorst, "The Energy Dimension in Russian Global Strategy," speech given at the James A. Baker III Institute for Public Policy, Rice University, Houston, Texas, October 2004, 1.

2. U.S. Department of Energy, Energy Information Administration, *Country Analysis Brief—Russia*, January 2006, 4, www.eia.doe.gov/emeu/cabs/Russia/Oil_exports. html (accessed October 12, 2006).

3. Tsentr Strategicheskikh Razrabotok [Center for Strategic Research], "O vozmozhnykh variantakh razvitiya infrastruktury po eksportu nefti v Rossii" [On Possible Options of the Development of Export of Oil in Russia], Moscow, October 2004.

4. Ibid.

5. Ibid.

6. Vladimir Milov and Ivan Selivakhin, "Problemy Energeticheskoy Politiki" [Problems of Energy Policy], Working Paper No. 4, Moscow Carnegie Center, Russia, 2005, 18; and "O Vozmozhnykh Variantakh."

7. Peter Finn, "Russia Approves Divisive Pipeline Plan," *Washington Post*, March 7, 2006; "O Vozmozhnykh Variantakh"; and Milov and Selivakhin, "Problemy Energeticheskoy Politiki," 20.

8. Milov and Selivakhin, "Problemy Energeticheskoy Politiki," 19.

9. Valeria Korchagina, "China Offers $400M for Oil Pipeline," *Moscow Times*, March 23, 2006.

10. Finn, "Russia Approves Divisive Pipeline Plan."

11. Stephen Boykewich, "Transneft's Pipeline Faces More Scrutiny," *Moscow Times*, March 27, 2006.

12. More on YUKOS and Khodorkovsky is in chapters 15 ("The YUKOS Affair") and 16 ("Institutions, Restoration, and Revolution").

13. Milov and Selivakhin, "Problemy Energeticheskoy Politiki," 19, table 2.

14. Ibid.

15. International Energy Agency, "Share of Total Primary Energy Supply in 2003. Russia," Key World Energy Statistics, 2005, www.iea.org/statist/index.htm (accessed April 7, 2005); and Edgewater Group Ltd., "Crude Oil and Oil Products," 2005, www.edgewatergroup.org/en/products.php (accessed April 7, 2005).

16. Milov and Selivakhin, "Problemy Energeticheskoy Politiki," 6.

17. See Leon Aron, "Privatizing Russia's Electricity," *Russian Outlook*, Summer 2003, www.aei.org/publication17983 (accessed October 16, 2006).

18. Milov and Selivakhin, "Problemy energeticheskoy politiki," 9.

19. See, for example, David Ignatius, "Who Robbed Russia?" *Washington Post*, August 25, 1999; and William Safire, "Welcome to Kremlingate," *New York Times*, September 9, 1999.

20. For details, see chapter 15, "The YUKOS Affair."

21. Andrei Illarionov (an adviser to the president of Russia), "Kampaniya protiv biznesa—eto kampaniya protiv Rossii" [The Campaign Against Business Is a Campaign Against Russia], interview by Vitaly Tsiplyaev, *Argumenty I Fakty*, November 30, 2005, 6.

22. Ibid.

23. For details, see chapter 15, "The YUKOS Affair."

24. Vladimir Milov, "Neftianoe gosudarstvo" [The Petrostate], interview with *Novaya Gazeta*, December 22, 2005, http://2005.novayagazeta.ru/nomer/2005/96n/n96n-s15.shtml (accessed October 16, 2006).

25. As quoted by Vladimir Milov, "Russian Energy Policy in a Broader Context," presentation at the U.S.-Russia Working Group luncheon at the American Enterprise Institute, Washington, D.C., March 16, 2006.

26. Ibid.

27. Vladimir Milov, "Russia Ill-Equipped to Lead on Global Security," *Financial Times*, January 24, 2006, http://news.ft.com/cms/s/eeb4cda8-8d0e-11da-9daf-0000779e2340.html (accessed October 16, 2006).

Chapter 21: The United States and Russia: Ideologies, Policies, and Relations

1. James Q. Wilson, *On Character* (Washington, D.C.: AEI Press, 1995), 8.

2. George W. Bush, "President Delivers Commencement Address at the United States Military Academy at West Point," Office of the White House Press Secretary (Washington, D.C.: May 27, 2006), www.whitehouse.gov/news/releases/2006/05/20060527-1.html (accessed May 30, 2006).

3. Three weeks before the Soviet Union was undone by the national liberation movements in the Soviet republics and the democratic revolution in Russia at the end of August 1991, in Kiev, President George H. W. Bush solemnly warned the Ukrainians of the dangers of "suicidal nationalism." Labeled the "Chicken Kiev speech," that oration has become "exhibit A" for the critics of "realism."

4. See Leon Aron, "Russia's Choice," *Russian Outlook* (Winter 2002), www.aei.org/publication13639/ (accessed June 16, 2006).

5. Vladimir Putin stayed at the Crawford Ranch on November 14–15, 2001.

6. Vladimir Putin, "Annual Address to the Federal Assembly of the Russian Federation" (Moscow, April 25, 2005), www.kremlin.ru/eng/speeches/2005/04/25/2031_type70029type82912_87086.shtml (accessed June 16, 2006).

7. Radzhab Safarov (director, Iranian Studies Center, Moscow), as quoted in Alissa J. Rubin and Kim Murphy, "Russian Bridge to Iran Has Twists," *Los Angeles Times*, May 4, 2006.

8. Despite periodic "spiking" of the anti-American sentiment because of Iraq or unfair treatment of Russian skiers and figure skaters at the Olympics, in March 2006, 66 percent of the Russians polled described their attitude toward the United States as "good" or "very good," versus 17 percent who classified their sentiment as "bad" or "very bad"—a proportion that virtually has not changed since December 2001. Levada Center, "Sotsial'no politicheskaya situatsiya v Rossii v marte 2006 goda" [Social and Political Situation in Russia in March 2006], April 11, 2006, www.levada.ru/press/2006041104.html (accessed April 15, 2006). As to their feeling about the American people, the share of those who thought well of them has hovered around 80 percent from February 2000 to September 2004. Levada Center, "Rossiya i SShA" [Russia and the USA], www.levada.ru/russia.html (accessed April 15, 2006).

9. "Should no agreement be reached, the West would do everything in its power to isolate Iran economically, financially, technologically and diplomatically, with the full support of the international community"; Joschka Fischer, "The Case for Bargaining With Iran," *Washington Post*, May 29, 2006. The author was Germany's foreign minister and vice chancellor from 1998 to 2005.

10. For instance, with Russia and Iran together controlling almost half of the world's proven reserves of natural gas, the Russian state-owned natural gas pipeline monopoly Gazprom has sought to become the largest partner and investor in Iran's natural gas exploration and transportation.

11. For details and analysis, see Leon Aron, "Russian Oil: Natural Abundance and Political Shortage," *Russian Outlook* (Spring 2006), www.aei.org/publication24251/ (accessed June 16, 2006).

12. Natalya Grib and Petr Sapozhnikov, "Evropa na brovyah: Moskva grozit povernut' truby na vostok" [Russia Is Threatening to Turn the Pipelines East], *Kommersant*, April 25, 2006, www.kommersant.ru/content.html?IssueId=30077 (accessed April 26, 2006); and Andrew E. Kramer, "Putin Talks of Sending Oil to Asia, Not Europe," *New York Times*, April 27, 2006. The United States responded by Secretary of State Condoleezza Rice's promoting in Ankara a gas pipeline from Azerbaijan to Turkey, bypassing Russia, and by its reception in the White House of Azerbaijani President Ilham Aliev, who inherited power from his father, the longtime strongman Geydar. Less than two weeks later, in an effort to persuade Kazakhstan President Nurlsultan Nazarbayev to export oil through Azerbaijan and

Georgia to Turkey (the Baku–Supsa–Ceyhan pipeline), instead of via Transneft to the Russian Black Sea port of Novorossiysk, Vice President Dick Cheney suspended neoconservative principles in his own attempt at realpolitik. Cheney praised "strategic partnership" with Kazakhstan and professed friendship and "great respect" for Nazarbayev, a likely president-for-life, who received 91 percent of the vote in the last year's election, after which one of his main political opponents was shot to death by the Kazakh security forces and the other arrested. Glenn Kessler, "Rice Warns against Russian Gas Monopoly," *Washington Post*, April 26, 2006; and Peter Baker, "Cheney Switches from Scowls to Smiles," *Washington Post*, May 6, 2006.

13. See, for example, Vasily Sergeev, "Bush prinyal Ukrainu v NATO" [Bush has accepted Ukraine into NATO], *Gazeta*, April 26, 2006, www.rambler.ru/news/politics/260005285/7757456.html (accessed April 27, 2006).

14. Marina Pustilnik, "Russia-WTO: A Failed Courtship?" *Moscow News*, April 14, 2006. The International Intellectual Property Alliance claims that Russia is the world's largest distributor of pirated optical disks and estimates that there are about fifty-two illegal optical plants in Russia, producing up to 400 million disks a year; Christopher Swanning, "IP Vital to Russia WTO Hopes," *Financial Times*, May 3, 2006, http://news.ft.com/cms/s/da3b5d12-da41-11da-b7de-0000779e2340.html (accessed June 16, 2006)

15. Anders Aslund, "The Folly of Renationalization," *Moscow Times*, May 23, 2006.

16. An entry in the author's travel diary, Moscow, March 22, 2006. The expert, Alexei Arbatov, was a Duma deputy from a liberal party, Yabloko, until 2003.

17. For instance, in June 2006, Russia and the United States reached an accord extending for seven more years the 1992 Cooperative Threat Reduction Agreement—a multibillion-dollar program, paid for by the United States, to secure or destroy the Soviet Union's biological, chemical, and nuclear weapons.

18. Julian Cooper, "Military Expenditure in 2005 and 2006: Federal Budgets of the Russian Federation," research note, 15, table 5: "Trend of Russian Military Spending in Real Terms: 'National Defense' Plus Military Pensions"; Stockholm International Peace Research Institute (SIPRI), www.sipri.org/contents/milap/cooper_russia_20060130 (accessed August 11, 2006), and Alexey Ventsiolovskiy, "Kvartiry, l'goty, samolyoty" [Apartments, Privileges, Planes], *Krasnaya Zvezda*, January 26, 2006. The 2005 U.S. military budget of $522 billion (including funding for Iraq and Afghanistan) is from the Center for Arms Control and Nonproliferation, "U.S. Military Spending vs. the World," February 6, 2006, 1, www.armscontrolcenter.org/archives/002244.php (accessed August 11, 2006). The dollar equivalent Russian 2005 expenditures (651,362 million rubles, as projected by Cooper) is calculated on the basis of $1=R28.3, the average exchange rate for 2005, to yield $23 billion or $45.77 billion in a Purchasing Power Parity equivalent. The Russia/USA ruble/dollar PPP factor of 1.99 for 2005 has been calculated by comparing the dollar equivalent

of per-capita Russian GDP, $5,364, with the same statistic (projected to 2005) in PPP terms: $10,700. (The Russian per-capita number for 2005 is from *Vedomosti*, "VVP udvoilsya za tri goda" [The GDP Has Doubled in Three Years], February 3, 2006, www.vedomosti.ru/newspaper/article.shtml?2006/02/03/102420 (accessed August 11, 2006); the PPP equivalent is from "Rank Order-GDP-Per Capita (PPP)," *CIA World Factbook*, www.cia.gov/cia/publications/factbook/rankorder/2004rank.html (accessed May 17, 2006).

About the Author

Leon Aron is a resident scholar and director of Russian studies at the American Enterprise Institute in Washington, D.C. He was born in Moscow and came to the United States as a refugee from the Soviet Union in June 1978 at the age of twenty-four; two months later he enrolled at the Graduate School of Arts and Sciences at Columbia University, concentrating in media studies, public opinion, and political sociology. While researching and writing his doctoral dissertation, he worked in advertising and marketing research in Manhattan. He received a Ph.D. from Columbia University in 1985.

Dr. Aron has written about the Soviet Union and Russia since 1987: first as senior policy analyst at the Heritage Foundation and, since 1992, at the American Enterprise Institute. For the past eight years he has written a quarterly *Russian Outlook* essay on political, social, economic and cultural aspects of Russia's post-Communist transition. He was also a Peace Fellow at the U.S. Institute of Peace in 1992–93 and taught a graduate seminar at Georgetown University.

Dr. Aron has contributed numerous essays and articles to newspapers and magazines, including the *Washington Post*, the *New York Times*, the *Wall Street Journal*, the *Times* (London), *Newsday*, *The National Interest*, *Post-Soviet Affairs*, and the *Times Literary Supplement*. A frequent guest of television and radio talk shows, he has commented on Russian affairs for *60 Minutes*, *The Newshour with Jim Lehrer*, *Charlie Rose*, CNN International, C-Span, National Public Radio's "All Things Considered" and "Talk of the Nation." Between 1990 and 2004, he was a commentator at the Voice of America's weekly radio and satellite television talk show *Gliadia iz Ameriki* ("Looking from America").

Dr. Aron has co-edited and contributed a chapter to *The Emergence of Russian Foreign Policy* (U.S. Institute of Peace, 1994). In 2000, he published the first full-scale scholarly biography of Russia's first elected leader, *Yeltsin: A Revolutionary Life* (St. Martin's Press).

He lives in Virginia with his wife, Dr. Carol D. Schiavone, and daughters Andrea and Daniella.

Index

modeled on Chekhov, 150–53
Federal Assembly, changes under Putin,
237–39
Federal political structure changes
under Putin, 288–89
Federal Security Service (FSB), 98–100,
183, 242, 294
Federation Council, 237–38, 241
Federation for Internet Education, 225,
305
Financial-industrial groups, 52–53, 55
Fletcher, Giles, 231
Foreign policy
under Putin, 311–15
under Yeltsin, 58–61, 65, 67,
70–72, 184–85
Fradkov, Mikhail, 300
France, 48, 261, 314
and Algeria, 265
Frank, Semyon, 146
Freedom, see svoboda
Freedom of speech, 247–48
opposition press, 248–49
Fukuyama, Francis, 70

Gaidar, Yegor, 38, 54, 60, 198, 279
Gandhi, Rajin, 266
Ganina, Maya, 12
Gastronomic renaissance, 157,
161–62
Gazprom, 55, 233, 305, 317
G8 summit in St. Petersburg, 297, 306,
316
Georgia, 67, 245, 251, 260, 315, 317
Ger, Ergaly, 132–36
Germany, 7–8, 59
Ghana, 212
GKchP-2 scenario, 283–84
Glasnost, 3, 29, 31–32, 177, 193
Soviet myths shattered by, 4–13
Gogol, Nikolai Vasilievich, 137, 140,
158, 165

Golts, Alexander, 274, 282
Goncharov, Ivan, 140
Gorbachev, Mikhail, 30, 47, 59, 198,
202, 312
and beginning of perestroika, 33,
36, 38, 40
and glasnost, 3, 4, 10, 13
history's evaluation of, 31–32
and 1991 Lithuanian crisis, 18, 20,
23–24, 26, 28, 31–32
Gorky, Maxim, 10
Grachev, Pavel, 276
Grain, 53, 74, 178, 340n.3
Graves, Robert, 133, 201
Gref, German, 84–85
Griboedov, Alexander, 148
Grocery stores, 163–64
Grossman, Vasily, 8, 11
Grozny, 253, 254, 255
Gusinsky, Vladimir, 250

Hamas, 313, 316
Havel, Vaclav, 66, 195–96
Hayek, Friedrich, 54
Health care disaster, under Soviet state,
5–6
Herzen, Alexander, 190
History
of conscription, 271–73
of intelligentsia political culture,
143–46
of land ownership, 73–75
of Russia, end of 19th century,
141–43
Holmes, Richard, 196
Homo Soveticus, 190
Hungary, 59

Idushchie bez Putina, 246–47
Illarionov, Andrei, 284–85
India, 266
Indonesia, 183, 187, 211